MR. LINCOLN

IN THOUGHTFUL POSE
Photograph by Brady, attributed to the year 1862.

MR. LINCOLN

BY J. G. RANDALL

Edited by Richard N. Current

Illustrated

Dodd, Mead & Company New York 1957

PREFACE

PROFESSOR RANDALL'S FOUR-VOLUME STUDY *Lincoln the President* (1945–55) was, in his words, "conceived both as biography and as history." This book, *Mr. Lincoln,* is conceived as biography. It incorporates those parts of the larger work which deal primarily with Lincoln the man and with his personal relationships.

Here is the Illinois lawyer and politician as he viewed the world and as his neighbors viewed him. Here is the supposed lover of Ann Rutledge and the actual devoted husband of Mary Todd and indulgent father of Mary's children. Here is the ambitious rival of Stephen A. Douglas, besting Douglas and going to Washington as President-Elect, amid rumors of a plot on his life. Here, with his grief-crazed First Lady, is the President in his daily routine and in his continual crises, finding surcease in humor as he deals with troublesome generals, hostile congressmen, and politicians of his own party seeking his defeat. Here is the Lincoln of the Emancipation Proclamation and the Gettysburg Address, the real person behind the symbols of Freedom and Union. And here is the man in his relationship to God, at least as he saw it.

This book does not contain the whole of Lincoln. Indeed, as Professor Randall believed, the subject is far too big even for four volumes. Nor does the book give a narrative summary of Lincoln's life. These pages do provide, however, a succession of word pictures and verbal X-rays which come as close to revealing the "real Lincoln" as any biography has done. Professor Randall succeeded admirably in what he set out to do. His purpose was to revise a distorted Lincoln image or, rather, to restore the hidden reality underneath the popular image. Let him explain the task in his own words:

"If sources are diligently re-examined, then by the same token the product may become 'revisionist.' Even in a simple matter it is not easy after the passage of years to recover the true picture. If the past situation was complicated, if many factors went into its making, if observers at the time lacked full understanding or differed as to what it meant, and especially if it has become controversial, then an uncommon effort is needed to disengage reality from the accumulated deposit which the years have brought.

"What happens over and over is that a certain idea gets started in association with an event or figure. It is repeated by speakers and editors. It soon becomes a part of that superficial aggregation of concepts that goes under the heading 'what everybody knows.' It may take decades before a stock picture is even questioned as to its validity. Evidence is then unearthed, some of it being first discovered, or brought to light after having been forgotten or neglected. Discoloring is corrected, partisan misrepresentation—perhaps accepted unawares by the public—is exposed, predilections and presumptions stripped away. Historical insight cuts through with a new clarity. In this process the historian does not claim to arrive at perfection, but he does hope by fresh inquiry to come nearer to past reality.

"This is called 'revision,' but that suggests mere change or rewriting; a much better word for it would be historical restoration. Where a building belonging to a past age has disappeared or fallen into ruin, there is the process of studying available traces and records, examining the period, and gradually building up a 'restoration' to show the structure as it originally stood. With a like motive the historian seeks out original records, excavates, so to speak, clears away unhistorical debris, and endeavors, if he can, to restore events and essential situations of the past.

"Popular ideas of Lincoln are in large part traceable to that picturesque but provocative individual, William H. Herndon. One should give him credit for tireless searching, but the Lincoln he has given us needs reconsideration. To take Herndon at face value is no longer permissible; we can now see his actual material. A body of sources may not be all of a piece. Some of Herndon's statements have greater validity than others. He was Lincoln's partner for many years; he tried in his way to give the world both Lincoln's greatness and the everyday man. One can doubt his accumulated masses of reminiscence and still give a measure of credence to descriptions which arose from close daily association.

"How near we can come to a recovery of the real Lincoln is not easy to say; for these pages the effort at recovery has been a matter of primary record, contemporary portrayal, and direct evidence. Such portrayal is not easy for the inner man—perhaps that is why Mark Twain considered biography to be little more than 'clothes and buttons'—but for Lincoln there is more revelation of his deepest thought than is usually realized. It is desirable to seek historical appraisal in terms of large perspective, but that is not the whole task. There remains the close-up view—the mobile face, gesture, playful quip, laugh or sigh, small talk and off-duty jest. Both the broad picture and the complete limning of the immediate portrait may be unattainable in the full sense. Yet a new delineation may have value without aspiring to finality.

"The theme is not one for hasty conclusions. One could easily emphasize the many contradictions that pervade the inquiry, yet such is the nature of historical investigation. A distinction is not worthless because it breaks down at the border, and a showing of unlike factors does not invalidate essential truth.

"If, therefore, one discovers opposites in Lincoln research, if a generalization is worked up only to be followed by the finding of counteracting evidence, that should be taken as indicating that the subject itself is many-sided. A seeming inconsistency should not greatly disturb the mature student. Some would have said that Lincoln 'saw everybody'; yet often he was inaccessible. He had a dignity and appropriateness, yet an 'irresistibly ludicrous' informality. He dripped with sadness, yet exploded with laughter and anecdote. Among all our Presidents he was one of the most resourceful and eloquent in his use of the English language, yet he often slipped back into the cruder dialect of untutored folk. One could quote him for high eloquence but also for frivolity. He was denounced as a dictator; yet he was the very opposite of the militarist and the supposition that he trampled on civil rights needs to be reexamined. There were those who from lack of understanding assailed him as a war maker; yet in his inaugural of 1861 he spoke with pathetic eagerness for peace, and in the interview with Mrs. Gurney he said that if he had had his way the war would never have begun. Some writers picture Lincoln as a great strategist or a supreme military genius; others point to incompetence and lack of effective control in military administration as directed from Washington. Instead of being upset by such contradictory elements one learns to reserve judgment, to give the second look, to keep in mind that history is not always reducible to easy generalization."

In fairness to Professor Randall it should be explained that parts of the present book (sections eight through ten of chapter XI; four through eight of chapter XIV; six through nine of chapter XV; and virtually all of chapter XVI) were originally written by me, with the aid of Professor Randall's notes. It should also be explained that, in tailoring materials from the four volumes to fit them together in one, I have taken occasional liberties with the original text. The changes, however, are slight: they are not such as to detract from the distinctive flavor of Professor Randall's deliberate and ruminative style. Since the original four volumes are exhaustively documented, there seems to be no need for reproducing the footnotes in this book. Nor is a bibliography included here: the curious reader is referred to volumes two and four of *Lincoln the President*.

To provide a select list of suggested further readings would be invidious. If I were bold enough to recommend just two or three of the best recent approaches to Lincoln, I might mention Benjamin P. Thomas' *Abraham Lincoln* (1952), the ablest of all the one-volume biographies; Paul M. Angle and Earl Schenck Miers' *The Living Lincoln* (1955), a judicious compilation of Lincoln's own writings from the eight-volume *Collected Works;* and David Donald's *Lincoln Reconsidered* (1956), a group of sensible and delightful essays.

I am happy to acknowledge my continuing indebtedness to Ruth Painter Randall, who suggested the apt title *Mr. Lincoln,* and to Rose Bonar Current, who served faithfully as typist and critic.

R. N. C.

Contents

1. A Man's Outlook 1

2. Thus Stood Lincoln 26

3. The Ann Rutledge Story 52

4. The House on Eighth Street 73

5. Rise to Fame 100

6. Springfield to Washington 124

7. Presidential Days 143

8. Lonely White House Pair 165

9. Attention of the President 195

10. The Gift of Laughter 213

11. Commander in Chief 240

12. These Honored Dead 278

13. Public Relations 296

14. Vindictives and Vindication 317

15. The Great Emancipator 341

16. God's Man 373

Illustrations

In Thoughtful Pose . . . . Frontispiece

Facing page

Earliest Known Portrait 10

The Macomb Ambrotype 15

Lincoln at Fifty 46

Lincoln's Full Figure 79

"Here I Have Lived" 110

Belittling the Incoming President 143

Hoop-Skirt Splendor 174

A White House Reception 207

"A Marble . . . Would Roll Hipward" 238

The Gardner Full Figure—1863 247

Best Newspaper Report of Lincoln's Words at Gettysburg 262

Not Entirely a Failure 271

"President Lincoln Is a Joke . . ." 302

Lincoln and Tad 335

Lincoln in 1860 and 1865 366

MR. LINCOLN

Chapter One

A MAN'S OUTLOOK

IN THE YEAR OF OUR LORD 1860 THE UNITED STATES WAS AT peace. In all that was sound and fundamental, in every instinct that was normal and sane, the people of America, and their genuine friends abroad, wanted that peace to endure. It is true that vicious forces were at work which would sweep beyond the point where reason could check them. An incredible and devastating war was to come; that war would become an absorbing preoccupation, greedily claiming energies that might have gone into natural pursuits; then, during and after the fighting those who survived would look back and discover in the "pre-war" age only elements of strife and seeds of sectional hate.

Yet to refer to the period as "pre-war" is only retrospection, however much it may be supported by massive historical studies that eternally point toward the Civil War as either the terminus or the point of departure of all discussion. Must an age be only ante- or post-? While a country is at peace are not the facts of peace worthy of note for their own sake?

I

Abraham Lincoln of Illinois thought that they were. He deplored strife and sought to dissociate himself from sectional

1

hatred. Occupied with a considerable law practice, but recognized as an outstanding leader in Illinois and mentioned for the presidency, he made it his business in the period preceding his presidential nomination to emphasize the peacetime pursuits of his country and to recover for his own day some of the nation-building stimulus of the fathers. He was concerned with problems of slavery, and with such a handling of those problems as would allay strife, as he hoped; but this was not all. He turned his thoughts also to discoveries and inventions, to the "iron horse," to "hot-water power" harnessed to help mankind, to the "seventy or eighty thousand words" of the English language, to influences that tend to "bring us together" and "make us better acquainted," to the harvest-machine and the "steam plow," to the problem of fifty bushels of wheat to the acre.

He made observations on the size of farms, disliking mammoth ones. He gave thought to the farmer as a man, to the farmer's pride in his work, to the laborer's enjoyment of the fruit of his labor, to the relation of labor and capital. He disliked the "mud-sill" theory, "that whoever is once a hired laborer, is fatally fixed in that condition for life." He was concerned for the "prudent, penniless beginner," anxious that he should acquire a surplus and one day arrive at the point where he could own his own land and tools. It was not only untutored folk who must labor, he reflected; men with education must work. The country could not sustain them in idleness; the laborer should not be "a blind horse upon a tread-mill." These workings of the mind do not make sense in terms of sectional strife; nevertheless these were Lincoln's thoughts. He was like the majority of the people of the nation. He was thinking of peace.

He had been about considerably, this Lincoln, more than is usually supposed. He knew Illinois, and chiefly the picturesque life of the eighth judicial circuit which he had traveled for over twenty years. He had journeyed rather widely in other states, from the eastern seaboard to Kansas, from New Hampshire to New Orleans. Men of culture and training were his constant associates, but pioneers came closer to the springs of his origin. The areas of his birth (Kentucky), his boyhood (Indiana), and his rising career (Illinois) had been pioneer regions; he had moved west as pioneering itself moved west. He had pondered the history of his people. He knew the law, not from books only, but from life. He could draw a deed, collect a claim, argue an assumpsit; yet he could also advise a client to avoid litigation. He could put himself in his client's place. Law treatises and court reports, passing under the processes of his mind, had given him a respect for principles that must prevail because they are fundamental.

He would tug at a problem and wrestle until he could make sense of it. Complicated though it was, he would not rest until he had mastered it. It is interesting to read what editors of his works call "fragments." In these bits of writing his concern was not mental gymnastics; it was clarification of some issue of his day, whether or not he was thinking of a particular speech or statement for publication. He would pose a question, then try to answer it, using processes of thought and speech to solve a thing, turn it around, see it whole, apply it to his times. In this manner as a boy, in early backwoods days, he had laid his own foundations in study. Self-education was his way; it had made him familiar with a few serviceable classics; what is more, it carried over into adult life. This was his liberal education.

His methods of thought and study had never proceeded in bookish fashion nor in the academic style. It was not sufficient that he know what a thing meant; it was not his to use unless it sounded right as he himself spoke it. When he could make it click in his own language, he felt that he had it; then he could impart it to others. Latin phrases or classical allusions, not uncommon in his day even on the frontier, did not appeal to him. They were like a frilled shirt, the kind of thing someone else might wear—Orville Browning or Ninian Edwards perhaps—but not himself. He did not use language to display his own learning, but to clinch a point. He had become adept at stump speaking, having learned to meet people by small groups or by shouting and jostling thousands and to divert and instruct them with ready anecdote and frontier oratory. His speeches had not only content; they had flavor.

He knew the ways of politicians, the manner in which things are arranged among leaders, the give and take of party maneuver. For politics he had a natural gift. He took to it avidly. As for ambition, the desire to rise and be influential, he had it in marked degree; at times it had become an almost pathetic craving. Yet he had met disappointment, and meeting it, had reasoned and tried to believe that it did not matter. Some of the accessories of ambition, such as self-conceit or low intrigue, he had somehow avoided. He could retaliate sharply, at times too sharply; yet he was learning, though perhaps slowly, to take a rebuff or feel an affront, but give no sign. He referred to himself as having come of "second families," and spoke of his early life in terms of undistinguished poverty.

Mr. John L. Scripps of Chicago wrote to William H. Herndon of Lincoln's conscientiousness and sincerity in supplying data for what became the Scripps campaign biography of 1860. "The chief difficulty I had to encounter," wrote Scripps, "was to induce him to communicate the homely facts . . . of his early life. . . . 'Why Scripps' said he . . . 'it is a great piece of folly to attempt to make anything out of my early life. It can be all condensed into a simple sentence, and that sentence you will find in Gray's Elegy; "The short and simple annals of the poor." That's my life, and that's all you or any one else can make of it.' "

His humility, however, did not end with self-depreciation, for he did not lack confidence; it was a quality of deferring to others, of working with men. It became more marked with him as the years passed. His character had defects and inadequa-

cies; it had not reached its final phase. There were elements
in the man yet undeveloped, indeed unsuspected.

II

There is no room here for the details of Lincoln's early
life: his ancestral heritage, his birth, boyhood, young manhood,
lowly family, hardscrabble surroundings, limited schooling and
persistent self-education, his father's shifting from one unim-
proved farm to another. Much could be said of Lincoln in tiny
New Salem: his adventures and misadventures there as store-
keeper, postmaster, mill manager and surveyor; his prowess in
frontier sports; his rapid progress in making friends; his familiarity with debt and financial failure; his slowly widening opportunities; his early recognition among pioneer neighbors in
the drawing of legal papers; his service in the Black Hawk War
in which he was made captain by the men of his company.
These matters, vivid and important as they are, are not treated
here; it is too much to ask that one book contain everything
about Lincoln.

From England to Massachusetts, to Pennsylvania, to Virginia, to Kentucky, to Indiana, to Illinois—such was the course
of this branch of Lincolns over the generations. Contributions
of three states were of abiding significance: Kentucky and Indiana influences remained with Abraham Lincoln as Illinois
became his chosen home. He could not in later years identify
the precise place of his birth though he knew the approximate
location. It remained for later investigation to mark the site—
the farm of the sinking spring near Hodgen's mill not far from
Elizabethtown. The little that is known of the mother in that
log-cabin birth but emphasizes the utter obscurity and limitations of her brief life, which was one with that of the American
pioneer woman. Of that other Kentucky home to which the

Lincolns moved when Abraham was two years old, he had more vivid memories: a cabin "on Knob Creek, on the road from Bardstown, Kentucky, to Nashville, Tennessee, at a point three or three and a half miles south or southwest of Atherton's Ferry, on the Rolling Fork." That knobby region, richer in wild beauty than in fertility, took its place in Lincoln's enduring impressions of little things in these earliest years: of pumpkin seeds planted on a hillslope and washed down by a dashing rain, of boys' adventures in and about the creek, of catching a fish and giving it to a passing soldier, of attending ABC schools kept by Riney and Hazel, of an old stone house—the Kirkpatrick place—where young people gathered for dances, of laboriously carrying water to the cabin and grist to the mill. It was here that the pithy informality of Lincoln's familiar conversation, with its wealth of anecdotes, began, but this did not exhaust Kentucky's contribution. Cultured Lexington, heart of the Blue Grass, center of gentlemanly living, being the birthplace of Mrs. Lincoln, was the scene of family visits by her husband. Lincoln kept up with Kentucky newspapers while in Illinois; indeed early Illinois itself was in considerable part a projection of Kentucky people and ideas into the West. The pioneers of New Salem were largely from Kentucky. All three of Lincoln's Springfield law partners were born in that state. His friend Joshua F. Speed was of Kentucky and his visits to Speed's Louisville home in 1841 was of more than ordinary personal importance. His developing political concepts followed the Clay pattern. The state of his childhood never ceased to hold a special place in his thought and feeling. Ties to Kentucky held strong and sure; they would later give the key to much of his presidential policy. Still later he was even to be suggested as one of the commonwealth's two sons to be honored in Statuary Hall in the Capitol at Washington. Take it all in all, from his earliest breath to the public burdens of the fuller years, Kentucky was a part of Lincoln.

III

It was in the woods and brush of southern Indiana that Lincoln spent fourteen basic years from the age of seven to his majority at twenty-one. Indiana too was part of him. If he had an appreciation of natural beauty, he did little to show it, but no visual impression of the lusty youth in the setting in which he moved would be complete without the picturesque features of the Indiana country: its thick-grown hills, its abundant game and fish, its wild fruit, its sassafras, pawpaw and dogwood, its heavier beech, maple, poplar and walnut, its tanagers and jays, its serene sky and friendly scene. Outwardly his life, in these teen-age years of sturdy growth, was one with that of his undistinguished father, Thomas Lincoln, and of that rugged individual and unforgettable country cousin, Dennis Hanks. Inwardly there was something of Indiana that offered a stimulus to the poetic sense; there was a reaching out for the mastery of a few books, and there was trial of skill in tentative public speaking. Home ties, neighbors none too close, pioneering labors, early intellectual questing, were associated with the Indiana years. Much of all this was buoyant energy, though there was deep tragedy in the illness, death, and crude, remote burial of his pioneer mother. Much of it also was raw pioneer life—packing through from Kentucky, rigging up a half faced camp in the brush, rearing a log cabin, squatting on land that was but slowly acquired by legal right, going to school "by littles" to Crawford, Sweeney, and Dorsey, spending long hours in that noble institution, Jones's village store at Gentryville, hearing an occasional preacher, never ceasing to wield the ax. Keeping soul and body together—an expression found in Lincoln's works as well as in the works of Dennis Hanks—was the pioneer's main preoccupation, but it is not to be forgotten that there was culture within the range of Lincoln's long legs and that the reading of well chosen classics was a basic factor in the determined self-education of the growing youth.

In this Indiana period the spell of the river, beckoning to unexplored worlds beyond the bend, was upon him. Floating on broad western currents all the way down to New Orleans by flatboat and traveling back by steamer, he found new experiences and gained wider contacts. Earning a few dollars by carrying passengers from the Indiana shore to passing steamers, the gawky youth was haled before the majestic presence of Squire Pate in the log house that served for home and court, charged with violating the laws of Kentucky by infringing upon ferrying rights. There was the dark threat of a heavy fine, but the squire settled the case of "Kentucky versus Abraham Lincoln" by enlightened interpretation of the statute and dismissal of the charge. Enduring impressions of the mystery and practical value of the law were thus engraved upon the mind of the eager youth.

Thus passed these important Indiana years. When Lincoln left the Hoosier state his physical stature had been reached; his thought was opening to national problems; his political maturity was far in the future, but he knew his mind as to the party of his choice. He was a Clay man in a Jacksonian family and a Democratic state. His politics came by independent reasoning, not by inheritance or inertia. He had known in Indiana a definite, not-to-be-repeated phase of western life. It was Indiana before the railroads. It had no dependence on factories though it needed local handcraftsmen, one of whom was Thomas Lincoln; its long journeys were by foot or horseback; its traffic by river craft, ox cart, or pioneer wagon; its farming resembled that of many centuries before; each community was a self-sufficing world. "Local self-dependence was well-nigh perfect," George Cary Eggleston has written. "The town depended on the country and the country on the town, for nearly everything that was eaten or woven or otherwise consumed." Men growing up in this setting learned much that was not in books. "Better still, each unlearned the prejudices, the bigotries, and the narrownesses in which he had been bred, and life in the West took on a . . . breadth of tolerance and sympathy, a generous humanity such as had never been known in any of the . . . provincial regions that furnished the materials of this composite population." From now on Lincoln's character as a man and an American would include something of the Hoosier genius—a mixture having its own distinct and friendly human ingredients, a product of migration and intermingling, a down-to-earth quality, a sense of humor, a self-dependence, yet a blending of customs, a western flavor of ideas and folkways.

IV

In Lincoln's time Illinois was not all unbroken prairie, woods, wild life, and Indians. He lived in the state from 1830 to 1861 and during that time the population of Illinois increased from 157,445 to 1,711,951. In 1860 Illinois was the fourth state in population in the Union, exceeded only by New York, Pennsylvania, and Ohio. Most of the states of the Union at that time had less than half the population of Illinois. In no state in those three decades could one have better witnessed the stirrings of American growth from the breaking of virgin sod to the busy throb of great cities and modern industry. Nowhere else could one have had a better view of what all this meant in human migrations, surveyings, boom towns, fabulous increase of land values, speculative fever, and the multifarious types of improvements and readjustments that a rising community exhibits.

Lincoln saw the world of civilized society starting from scratch and developing around him. He not only saw it; he was part of it. The man who was moved to lecture on discoveries and inventions, who thought of Young America moving on to material and moral conquests, had seen the burgeoning of a great society with his own eyes. In 1840 few towns of Illinois had more than two thousand people. It is a curious fact that the largest Illinois settlement by far in the middle forties was the Mormon city of Nauvoo, beautifully situated on the broad Mississippi about a hundred miles northwest of Springfield. Here, in the 1840's, when Chicago was a stripling village of less than 5,000, and Springfield a muddy little town recently planted on the prairie, stood the largest city in Illinois, with a population of more than 20,000 and a great Temple costing a million dollars.

Dickens might find an Illinois town crude with its hitching racks, its mud and slime, its music of pigs and frogs; but Gustave Koerner, who lived in the region through which Dickens hastily passed, remembered an extraordinary social circle in historic Kaskaskia (the old capital) with its wealthy families, its "large and handsome Catholic seminary for ladies," and such gifted and forceful leaders as Nathaniel Pope, Pierre Menard, William Morrison, and Elias Kent Kane, "a descendant of a very well known family in New York, a relative of Chancellor Kent and of Judge Kane of Philadelphia and of the north-pole explorer, Elijah Kane." Vandalia, capital in the days of Lincoln's earlier legislative service, had only eight hundred people, but in the season of the legislature it was a center of fashion and society. When Springfield became the capital, it was no less gay with its "hops" and levees and its young ladies taking occasion to visit Springfield relatives during the legislative session, a custom by which Lincoln himself was not unaffected.

Adolescent Illinois had its quota of religious denominations, the Methodists, Baptists, and Presbyterians being specially active. It had its hopeful colleges. Shurtleff College (later located at Alton) was organized in 1827; McKendree College was founded at Lebanon in 1828; Illinois College, a kind of New Haven in Illinois, began at Jacksonville in 1829; Knox

Meserve Collection—"Meserve No. 1"

EARLIEST KNOWN PORTRAIT

Daguerreotype said to have been made in Springfield in 1846, the year of Lincoln's election to Congress. The clothes are more carefully correct and the hair much smoother than was usual with Lincoln. The vigorous face, athletic form, and rugged hands give an impression of force and early strength.

College at Galesburg was born in 1837 under the original name of Prairie College; Jubilee College was founded in a rural setting near Peoria two years later by the Right Reverend Philander Chase, pioneer bishop of the Episcopal Church. Rockford College began at Rockford in 1847. Other early colleges in the state were McDonough College at Macomb, Blackburn at Carlinville, Illinois Wesleyan at Bloomington, and Northwestern University at Evanston. The state had also its Bible societies, its theological seminaries, its public schools, inadequate to be sure, its state superintendent of public instruction (from 1854) its girls' seminaries, its laws for teachers' qualifications, its state medical society and medical colleges, and its ubiquitous press, for there was a surprising number of newspapers including not a few in the German language. The commonwealth was not lacking in its lyceums, theaters, library associations, dramatic reading societies, hippodromes, circuses, literary or musical festivals, and courses of public lectures. An example of its intellectual activity was a solemn discussion of "Comparative Capabilities of the Human Intellect in 'Different Sexes'" conducted at the "Owl Club" of Ottawa in 1850. Nor was the state backward in its agricultural fairs, shooting matches, and balloon ascensions (as early as 1859).

In the view of William H. Herndon, Lincoln's unique partner-biographer, there was human excellence in Illinois in its primitive pioneer aspects. The settlers in the great West, thought Herndon, "were men of culture—so were the women—God bless 'em if culture includes sharp observation—quick & broad experience and a manly reason of or about men—commerce—laws—institutions—human nature and the world & its affairs generally." Herndon had "never seen such a people"; "for good horse sense . . . the old settlers were . . . equals, if not . . . superiors" of people in Massachusetts.

Men with whom Lincoln grew up in Illinois were largely Southern by birth and antecedents. Among his Southern-born associates one may mention John Todd Stuart, Stephen T.

Logan, William H. Herndon, Orville H. Browning, David Davis, Ward H. Lamon, Stephen A. Hurlbut, Archibald Williams, Ninian W. Edwards, Usher F. Linder, Richard Yates, John J. Hardin, William Butler, Albert T. Bledsoe, W. L. D. Ewing, Josiah Lamborn, Jesse B. Thomas, and Orlando B. Ficklin. The first settlers of central and southern Illinois, said Herndon, "came from the limestone regions of Virginia—Kentucky—Tennessee &c and were men of giant strength— . . . mentally strong. They were . . . individualists. They had no education and no culture but good nature helped them. The strong *alone* . . . could get here and the strong *alone* could survive. . . ." Identifying himself with these men, Herndon wrote: ". . . the struggle for life in the wilderness—& the South gave us . . . mental force & forest life makes us sad—and thoughtful. I think that by nature we were a great people. We were rude and rough—had no polish nor culture. Each man and woman was himself or herself. . . . Lincoln was Lincoln—Grant Grant —Douglas was Douglas. Had Lincoln been a man of high culture—polish—of literary taste . . . he may have been a good country lawyer—that's all." Just what Herndon meant by this will be for the reader to judge: perhaps he had in mind a quality of understanding derived from experience of life, a practical wisdom, a distinct originality in contrast to the conventional or imitative conduct that comes from academic polish or bookish training. As to his emphasis upon crudeness, he had already spoken of the settlers as people of "culture," then a few sentences later had said they had "no . . . culture." It was a matter of finding words to express shades of meaning; the meaning itself was not obscure.

V

The politicians' world in Illinois in the day of Lincoln's earlier career has been drawn from life in the vivid pages of

Governor Thomas Ford. It was not an inspiring picture. Because of the want of true "issues" and the scramble for favor, as explained by Ford, an election became "one great fraud, in which honor, faith, and truth were . . . sacrificed, and politicians were debased below the . . . popular idea of that class of men." Government might mean one thing to the people; its purpose in the minds of politicians was another matter. They had a "destiny to accomplish, not for the people, but for themselves." With the people caring little for matters of government, said Ford, the "politicians took advantage of this lethargic state of indifference . . . to advance their own projects, to get offices and special favors from the legislature, which were all they busied their heads about." Politicians, he said, operated on the principle that "the people never blame any one for misleading them"; it was merely a matter of supporting or opposing measures because of their popularity or unpopularity at the time. A "public man," said the governor, "will scarcely ever be forgiven for being right when the people are wrong." That was why "so many" politicians were "ready to prostitute their better judgments to catch the popular breeze." Whatever may have been the basis of parties in their early origin, Ford observed that "little big men, on both sides . . . feel the most thorough hatred for each other; their malice often supplying the place of principle and patriotism. They think they are devoted to a cause, when they only hate an opponent; and the more thoroughly they hate, the more . . . are they partisans." Party newspapers, he thought, promoted and perpetuated this unhealthy state of things.

The convention system—i.e., the holding of conventions for party nominations—was an innovation in Illinois in the thirties which many defended because of its tendency to promote party concentration, but to Governor Ford it seemed "a most admirable contrivance to enable active leaders to govern without much responsibility to the people." Digesting the arguments of the time, the governor said: ". . . it was urged, that

the whole convention system was a fraud on the people; that
it was a mere fungus growth engrafted upon the constitution;
that conventions themselves were got up and packed by cunning, active, intriguing politicians, to suit the wishes of a few."
Referring to politicians' methods generally, Ford wrote: "The
State [party] leaders . . . give the word to the little cliques
. . . in each county; these . . . convey it to the little big
men in each neighborhood, and they do the talking to the
rank-and-file of the people. In this way principles and men
are put up and put down with amazing celerity. And gentle
reader . . . this is government! and if there is in point of fact
any other sort, its existence cannot be proved by me, and yet
I have been governor of the state for four years."

The unlovely situation thus reflected in Governor Ford's
pages is a necessary backdrop for a treatment of Lincoln as a
developing leader. Lincoln himself spoke bitterly of "the spirit
of party" taking "the lead in the councils of the State," of a
party going beyond all expectations to "assume to itself the
entire control of legislation," even invading the "sanctuary of
the Constitution," and entering "with its unhallowed and
hideous form into the . . . judiciary system." At the time
Lincoln the Whig, with other Whig colleagues, was denouncing
what the opposite party had done in the Illinois legislature by
enacting a measure through which they obtained control of
the state judiciary. With rising indignation not unlike that of
Governor Ford but from a different angle, Lincoln in a statement signed by himself and other Whigs continued:

. . . measures were adopted by the dominant party to take possession of the State, to fill all public offices with party men, and
make every measure . . . operate in furtherance of their party
views. The merits of men and measures . . . became the subject
of discussion in caucus, instead of the halls of legislation, and decisions there made by a minority . . . have been . . . carried into
effect by . . . party discipline, without any regard whatever to the
rights of the people or the interests of the State.

THE MACOMB AMBROTYPE

The better of two ambrotypes taken at Macomb, Illinois, August 26, 1858, the day before the debate with Douglas at Freeport. Remarkable for striking facial contours, depth of personality, and sadness combined with confidence.

Simultaneously with this Whig circular, Lincoln and his Whig colleagues in the legislature placed on the record of the lower house a signed protest on this same subject of party abuse apropos of the judiciary bill. They declared in part: "To the majority of a Legislature whose idol is party supremacy, we have addressed our reasons in vain. Announced as a party measure for party purposes, it has been strengthened by the startling admission [of such purpose], and it only remains for us to present to the people of the country, the causes of our opposition, ..." It is amusing to note that Nicolay and Hay, in their huge biography, refer solemnly to Lincoln's having "uttered the voice of the conscience of the party."

It was, of course, with parties and politicians that Lincoln had to work. That in so doing he kept his record clear is an achievement whose full value is not perceived until the Ford portrayal of the political merry-go-round in Illinois is read and appreciated. It cannot be denied that Lincoln was a party man; he had to be if he wanted a political career. He worked by and through party organization; he engaged in party maneuvers; it was as party candidate that he obtained elective office. But it is also worth noting that he saw the evils of party politics and that the worst party excesses never had his approval. In coming days of presidential leadership he was to speak of parties as existing on a low plane. "In . . . time of national peril" he "would have preferred to meet . . . upon a level one step higher than any party platform, because . . . from such more elevated position we could do better battle for the country we all love than . . . from those lower ones where . . . we . . . expend . . . our ingenuity and strength in finding fault with and aiming blows at each other."

VI

In the pioneer legislature of Illinois Lincoln had his earliest experience of public service on more than a local stage. Elected in 1834 at a time when earning the bare necessaries of life was a major problem, he served continuously through four terms till 1841. That he was the leading man of his party at Vandalia and later at Springfield, was signified by his service as Whig floor leader and by caucus support as speaker of the lower house; his party being in the minority, he was not elected to this office. Making his mark in a body controlled by opponents, he was a man of influence beyond the average of legislators. He phrased petitions for friends to present and drafted bills for others to introduce. This part of his service would have remained almost hidden but for the recent discovery in the Illinois archives of papers recognizable as of Lincoln's handwriting but not otherwise identifiable. Out of legislative sessions he used his time well in the study of law. "When the legislature met, the law-books were dropped, but were taken up again at the end of the session," he wrote in his autobiography.

Lincoln's one term in Congress (1847–49) fell in the period of the Mexican War and just before the 1850 crisis between North and South. His election as representative in 1846 showed strength especially in two respects: he became the only Whig in Congress from Illinois, and his victory at the polls was won over the redoubtable pioneer preacher, Peter Cartwright. Taking his seat after all the battles of the Mexican War had been fought, Lincoln voted and spoke to the effect that the war had been unnecessarily begun by President Polk, but he was always careful in later years to add that he had supported supply bills and measures favorable to officers, soldiers, and their families.

On the slavery question, while in Congress, Lincoln voted for the Wilmot proviso to prohibit slavery in national territory to be acquired from Mexico, and he worked out a formula of conservative legislation for the abolition of slavery in the District of Columbia. According to Lincoln's proposal children born of slave mothers after 1850 were to be "free," but during minority were to be dependent upon their mothers' owners for support and education, being meanwhile treated as apprentices to such owners. Slaves then held in the District were to remain slaves, but owners, if they wished, could emancipate them at any time, receiving "full value" from the treasurer of the United States. Lincoln was thus applying the process of gradual emancipation. The board for the fixing of compensation was to consist of none other than the President of the United States, the secretary of state, and the secretary of the treasury. Fugitive slaves from the outside, finding their way into the District, were to be arrested and returned to owners. Finally a vote of free white male citizens over twenty-one years of age was to be taken in the District, and the act was to go into force only if a majority favored it. Here Lincoln applied the principle of a popular referendum on a congressional statute.

Thus the man who was later to become the emancipator was making an early tentative effort toward liberation. In doing so his approach was vastly different from that of radical abolitionists. It is true that he was seeking to deal with the question only on a very limited scale and at a time when slavery was strongly entrenched in the United States. He could hardly have gone farther in the existing Congress, but the significant point is that he recognized the realities. The phrasing of the bill—which if passed would have made Lincoln somewhat famous for a legislative measure even if fame had given no greater rewards—revealed the character and point of view of Lincoln the statesman: his conservatism, his patience in letting a process work itself out over the years, his lack of antagonism toward the South, his regard for the rights of slaveholders, his attention to legal details, and his valuing of popular and democratic processes.

(Lincoln fulfilled his duty in Congress, did committee service, watched out for Illinois interests in such a matter as land grants, and on party affairs showed himself an ardent hardworking Whig and supporter of General Taylor, candidate for President in 1848.)His speech in the House on July 27, 1848, filling thirty pages of his *Works*, was an example of rollicking and badgering campaign oratory, more suitable for the western stump than for the halls of a legislative body. Pertaining to no legislative proposal, it was a purely party speech, viewing Cass with alarm and pointing with pride to Taylor; it was a rather unconvincing defense of the candidate against the accusation of having no declared principles. The speech represents an exuberant, likable, joke-cracking Lincoln; it gives a clue to what he must have been when he let himself go on the hustings; but it does not give us the man at his best. Lincoln did not rise to his full stature when speaking merely the party language. Much the same can be said as to what we know of his campaign speeches in 1848 in New England, at Worcester, New Bedford, Boston, Lowell, Dorchester, Taunton, Chelsea, Cambridge, and Boston again, these being mostly unrecorded except in briefest summary. One of his tasks in these speeches was to show why men of Free Soil tendencies ought not to vote for the Free Soil candidate, but for Taylor. In this same campaign he spoke also in Maryland and canvassed "quite fully," and successfully in his own district in Illinois.

Lincoln's congressional term had given him little distinction, and there may have been somewhat of a feeling of futility in his mind as he returned to Springfield to resume the practice of law "with greater earnestness than ever before," as if political leadership were no longer his main preoccupation.)This futility may have increased as the nation met and temporarily averted

a great crisis in 1850 without his help, and as General Winfield
Scott led a declining Whig party to defeat in the campaign of
1852. In that year, by Lincoln's own words, he "did less than
in previous presidential canvasses" owing to "the hopelessness
of the cause" in Illinois. Lincoln's political frustration can be
rather definitely dated. It belonged to the period 1849 to
1854. He saw his former partner Stephen T. Logan go down
to defeat as candidate for Congress to succeed him; this could
have been interpreted as an adverse verdict on Lincoln's record
in his own district, while the action of the national Whig party
in nominating Scott could have been deemed a repudiation of
President Fillmore. That a Whig administration was in power
(1849–1853) was small consolation to Lincoln; Illinois was of
the opposite persuasion.

The greatest humiliation came in 1849 when Lincoln, seeking a crumb of patronage in the office of commissioner of the
general land office, was passed over and Justin Butterfield, a
Whig who had opposed Taylor, was chosen. Having made a
real effort to obtain the appointment, and feeling that he had
a claim upon the Taylor administration, Lincoln was deeply
mortified.

VII

If in seeking Lincoln's view of things one opens a window,
that window may be the concept of Young America versus
Old Fogy, for Lincoln himself used that approach. By Young
America he did not mean militant expansionism nor war-
making "manifest destiny." Boastful patrioteering or flag-
waving was not his thought. To know what his thought was,
one may read his essay or lecture on "Discoveries, Inventions,
and Improvements," delivered in and around Springfield on
various occasions in 1858, 1859, and early 1860. In its flow

of sentences it marks Lincoln as something of a stylist, but that is secondary. The main point is that in lecturing on discoveries and inventions he was thinking of enlightenment, of progress down the centuries, of the emancipation of the mind, of men rising from the "dark ages." He stood in wonder of human achievement, in admiration of "articulate sounds rattled off from the tongue," of "phonetic writing," of "representing . . . sounds by marks," and of printing, which he considered the "better half" of writing. He thought the process was not ended. In considering inventions, he considered even more the factor of inventiveness, the "destined work of Adam's race to develop . . . hidden treasures." Some of the mines had been overlooked. "There are more mines above the earth's surface than below it," he said. "All nature—the whole world, material, moral, and intellectual—is a mine . . ." Thus viewing Lincoln on the threshold of the presidency, one notes how strife and sectionalism was not his main concern. Contemplating the aspiration of his people, his mind was reaching out in terms of normal progress and peaceable endeavor.

It had not been otherwise at the beginning of his political career. Having read Lincoln's statements in the late 1850's, one can go back to the thirties, when his thought was in its formative stage, its expression being already definitely Lincolnian in epigrammatic force. In those days when Lincoln as a youth was living close to the frontier, he had given some of his best pronouncements. He pointed to the greatness of his country, which in his view was a matter of free institutions in a setting of law, order, and community will. Reverently he referred to the edifice which the Fathers had bequeathed and of which men of his generation were "legal inheritors." He spoke of "that fair fabric which for the last half century has been the fondest hope of the lovers of freedom throughout the world." He thought of what the nineteenth century of the Christian era meant in "the great journal of things happening under the sun." He found its meaning in a political "system

. . . conducing more essentially to the ends of civil and religious liberty than any of which the history of former times tells us."

The Fathers had possessed the land. They had upreared the edifice. For his own generation the task, he thought, was to "transmit" the heritage "unprofaned . . . undecayed . . . and untorn by usurpation." It was a solemn duty, not a thing to prate about, and on this theme young Lincoln uttered a stinging warning of "danger" and "ill omen." If destruction was to come to the fair democracy of America, he believed that "we must ourselves be its author and finisher." He was thinking of the rough and ready vigilantism of his day, of men setting themselves up as bigger than the government, of mob law, of lynching, of those who regard government as a bane and "make a jubilee of the suspension of its operations." He was thinking of those arrogant, law-defying influences which a century later were to go by the ugly name of Fascism. His views on this point were unmistakably given. If one doubts it, let him read Lincoln's address before the Young Men's Lyceum of Springfield, January 27, 1838, as good a speech against Fascism, or elements characteristic of Fascism, as was ever delivered.

It would be by "suicide," he thought, if American destruction should come by "disregard of law," by "wild and furious passions," by "savage mobs." Any supposition that by mob savagery he meant free men asserting their rights or aggrieved citizens seeking redress is belied by the context. That was not the problem he was discussing; those were not the elements causing the violence that distressed him. The days of the Revolution were over, he said. He was thinking of "dead men . . . dangling from . . . trees . . . in numbers almost sufficient to rival the native Spanish moss . . . of the forest." It was an ugly spectacle and he was not mincing words. He spoke of vicious men being "permitted to gather in bands of hundreds and thousands, and burn churches, ravage and rob provision-stores, throw printing-presses into rivers, shoot editors, and hang and burn . . . at pleasure and with impunity. . . ."

It is obvious that Lincoln in 1838 was giving a comment on his own time; if one thinks of the alleged purity of that early age it is a shock to realize the turbulent conditions that were causing so much concern to one who believed in democracy. It was Herndon's recollection that the occasion of this lyceum speech, whose "essence" was "obedience to and respect for law," was the "burning of a negro by a mob in St. Louis." Lincoln, however, was dealing with a serious and widespread problem, not with one incident. Revolutionary agitation had degenerated into frontier vigilantism; this had further deteriorated into lawless violence. There had been bad men in Illinois—kidnappers, counterfeiters, horse thieves, desperadoes, and outlaws. Crime ranged widely; it was wholesale; law enforcement was local and ineffective. Courts being inadequate, a group known as "regulators," wishing to enforce order, had set up their extra-legal organization, with its irregular military force, conventions, trials, and executions in the name of the people. Development of this situation, however, had taken a downward trend till the result was a condition of private warfare—gang against gang—with the "regulators" pursuing a course little better than the thieves. Finally the legislature and governor had to step in to tone up the courts and put down the regulators.

Lincoln had his answer to this ill omen: ". . . let every man remember that to violate the law is to trample on the blood of his father, and to tear the charter of his own and his children's liberty." He continued: "Let reverence for the laws be breathed by every American mother to the lisping babe that prattles on her lap; let it be taught in schools, in seminaries, and in colleges; let it be written in primers, spelling-books, and in almanacs; let it be preached from the pulpit, proclaimed in legislative halls, and enforced in courts of justice. And in short, let it become the political religion of the

nation. . . ." Bad laws, he thought, should be repealed, but
while on the books they should be "religiously observed." If
there should be an unprovided case not covered by law, he
would have people bear with it till "proper legal provisions
be made . . . with the least possible delay."

The American experiment was successful, he proclaimed,
but some man of ambition might rise to smash the edifice,
some man to whom a seat in Congress or a presidential chair
would not be enough. If such a person should spring up, some
designing chief bigger than the law, someone of "the family
of the lion, or the tribe of the eagle," the temple must be
upheld by "pillars, hewn from the solid quarry of sober reason."
"Reason . . . unimpassioned reason—must furnish all the materials for our future support and defense." All this would have
to be met by solidarity, not division. It would "require the
people to be united with each other, attached to the government and laws, and generally intelligent. . . ."

For that broad intelligence he favored popular education,
and this in the earliest of his collected addresses. Education,
he said at the age of twenty-three, was "the most important
subject which we as a people can be engaged in." Its value
would be that "every man . . . may duly appreciate the value
of our free institutions." These were his sentiments far back
in the days when as an ungainly New Salem youth he was
stepping out for political office for the first time in his life.
He was addressing his neighbors in Sangamon County as a
candidate for the state legislature and in doing so he was
apologizing for having been "more presuming than becomes
me," but already he felt it "a privilege and a duty to take that
stand which . . . might tend most to the advancement of
justice."

VIII

Among the nation's founders it is clear that Jefferson offered more of a cue for interpreting Lincoln than Hamilton. In a halting way Lincoln favored a protective tariff. Somewhat more confidently he favored a national bank. He believed in those measures that emphasized the functions of the Federal government, especially in the matter of expenditures within the states for public works ("internal improvements"). These, it is true, were Hamiltonian, though it should not be overlooked that in 1843 Lincoln was careful to quote Jefferson in support of a Federal tariff for the promotion of domestic manufactures. When, however, one has enumerated a few matters of this nature, the similarity to Hamilton ends. On fundamental issues Lincoln's unlikeness to Hamilton and his resemblance to Jefferson are evident. Even in the matter of federalism Lincoln was closer to Jefferson than to Hamilton. Hamilton would have reduced the states to subordinate divisions and would have set up a life president and life senators, with state governors appointed by the national government. Lincoln could not support any such extreme program. He could, however, agree largely with Jefferson without surrendering his national policies, for Jefferson, though a prophet of state rights, actually did important things—e.g., in the Northwest Ordinance, the Louisiana Purchase, the Lewis and Clark Expedition, and the giving of advice looking to the Monroe Doctrine—which mightily promoted the success and prestige of the Federal government. It was in the bedrock of his beliefs that Lincoln was like Jefferson. The Declaration of Independence was his platform, his confession of faith. In those deeply sincere passages in which he expressed worshipful reverence for the Fathers, there was a Jeffersonian accent that was unmistakable. He favored human rights above property interests, repudiated (as noted above) the mudsill theory, spoke up for the farmer and the laborer, and withal showed trust in the people, which Hamilton assuredly did not. He favored the extension of popular education, a policy as prominent in Jefferson's urging and achievement as it was noticeably absent in Hamilton's.

Lincoln frequently mentioned Jefferson, turning to him as to a basic authority. In the index to his writings, letters, and speeches, as edited by Nicolay and Hay, there are nineteen references to Jefferson while there are only two to Hamilton. References to Jefferson were on fundamental and far reaching matters; of the two meager citations of Hamilton, one was the briefest allusion to his support of the United States Bank, while the other was a passing mention of the New York leader as anti-slavery, which could have been said equally, indeed more emphatically, of Jefferson. Lincoln was shocked to note the repudiation by a Virginia clergyman of Jefferson's doctrine of human equality. The repudiation, he thought, sounded "strangely in republican America." "The like was not heard," he said, "in the fresher days of the republic." He found it painful in later troubled days to note that adversaries had "adopted . . . declarations of independence in which, unlike the good old one, penned by Jefferson, they omit the words 'all men are created equal.'" In 1854, the year of his stepping out for larger leadership in public affairs, he referred with admiration to Jefferson as "the author of the Declaration of Independence . . . a chief actor in the Revolution; . . . who was, is, and perhaps will continue to be, the most distinguished politician of our history. . . ."

Chapter Two

THUS STOOD LINCOLN

I

Lincoln once (in 1859) penned a description of himself. With a characteristic quirk and amusing brevity the lines of that self portrait were as follows: "If any personal description of me is thought desirable, it may be said I am, in height, six feet four inches, nearly; lean in flesh, weighing on an average one hundred and eighty pounds; dark complexion, with coarse black hair and gray eyes. No other marks or brands recollected." His friend H. C. Whitney, of the law circuit, wrote: "He was six feet and four inches in height, his arms and legs were disproportionately long, his feet and hands were abnormally large, he was awkward in his gait and actions. His skin was a dark, sallow color, his features were coarse:—his expression kind and amiable:—his eyes were indicative of deep reflection, and, in times of repose, of deep sorrow as well. His head was high, but not large: his forehead was broad at the base, but retreated, indicating marked perceptive qualities, but not great reflective ones: and in this phrenology is sadly at fault. He wore a hat measuring seven and one-eighth. His ears were large; his hair, coarse, black and bushy, which stood out all over his head, with no appearance of ever having been combed."

It was common to speak disparagingly of Lincoln's appearance, whether one was referring to his face, his figure, or his clothes. One observer wrote: ". . . his phiz *is* truly awful." To another it seemed: ". . . he is the *homeliest* . . . and the *awkwardest* man in the Sucker State." Edwin M. Stanton's description in 1858 was: "A long, lank creature from Illinois, wearing a dirty linen duster for a coat, on the back of which the perspiration had splotched wide stains that resembled a map of the continent." The adjective "raw-boned" came to mind in characterizing him; Whitney said he "might have passed for an ordinary farmer, so far as appearances were concerned." His habiliments were country styled and careless, his tall hat innocent of nap, his carpet-bag dilapidated, his outer garment "a short circular blue cloak, which he got in Washington in 1849, and kept for ten years."

It is not easy to make up a composite of differing descriptions, and one should not give sole attention to comments by such an unfriendly and supercilious person as Stanton. In attire the quality that seemed to stand out was negligence of fashion rather than slovenliness. Whitney records that, though his clothes and shoes needed brushing, Lincoln was "scrupulously clean and close shaven." In years of growing prominence his dress improved. "When he first ran for the legislature he . . . wore a blue jeans coat, claw hammer style, short in . . . sleeves, and . . . tail . . . homespun linen trousers, a straw hat and 'stogy' boots." "He commenced to dress better in the spring of 1858, and when he was absent from home on political tours usually did so: after he became President he had a servant who kept him considerably 'slicked up': but he frequently had to reason Lincoln into fashionable attire, by telling him his appearance was 'official.'"

In passages which only William H. Herndon could write (and which are buried in manuscript collections) one gets flashes of Lincoln as pictorial as those of the camera, portraits which convey a setting and a sense of motion and sound as well as visual impressions of the man's face. Herndon's words are repetitious; he piles them high; yet there is a photographic quality in his record; he describes something he has seen. He seldom speaks of Lincoln's face or form alone; physical descriptions in the Herndonian manner usually blend with recordings of the man's mind, moods, and character. Often he goes into long paragraphs of psychoanalysis: the reader is spared these disquisitions, which are less significant than the pictorial passages. One of these, despite the repetition, is presented here as a kind of sample:

"Thus stood, walked—felt—thought, willed—acted and looked Abraham Lincoln: he was not a pretty man . . . , nor was he an ugly one: he was a homely man, careless of his looks, plain looking and plain acting: he had no aristocratic pomp—display or dignity so called. . . . Lincoln had . . . that inner quality which distinguishes one person from another, as much as to say 'I am myself and not you.' . . . Lincoln was easy of approach up to a certain limit and very democratic: he appeared simple in his carriage general behavior and bearing: . . . his sadness—gloom and melancholy dripped from him as he walked along. . . . Mr. Lincoln was sad and . . . humorous by turns. . . .

"Mr. Lincoln sometimes walked our streets cheerily, . . . perhaps joyously and then it was, on meeting a friend, he cried—How'dy, clasping one of his friends in both of his wide long big bony hands, giving his friend a good hearty soul welcome. On a winters morning he might be seen stalking and stilting it toward the market house, basket on his arm, his old grey shawl wrapped around his neck, his little Willie or Tad running along at his heels, asking a thousand little quick questions, which his father heard not. . . . When he thus met a friend on the road he said that something . . . put him in mind of a story which he heard in Indiana or Egypt or elsewhere and tell it he would and there was no alternative in his friend but to patiently stand and hear it."

Herndon reached out for rugged adjectives as he described his partner. He "was a great big—angular—strong man—limbs large and bony: he was tall and of a peculiar type." He "grew up like the forest oak, tough—solid—knotty—gnarly, standing out . . . against the storm, . . . defying the lightning." Herndon added: ". . . his mind was tough—solid—knotty—gnarly, more or less like his body: he was . . . a tall and big boned man and his speech was tall—strong . . . & enduring. The convolutions of his brain were long: they did not snap off quickly like a short thick mans brain: . . . when those convolution[s] . . . threw off an idea it *was* an *idea, ...*" In attempting to explain this to one of his numerous correspondents, Herndon wrote: "Please see Lincoln's strong—terse—knotty—gnarly and compact words—driven together as by a sledge hammer. . . ." "No other man on the continent," declared Herndon, "could have stood what Lincoln did in Washington: he had a frame of *iron*."

One returns by a kind of irresistible fascination to Herndon's voluminous descriptions, too long to be fully quoted. In a prodigality of adjectives and phrases, the verbose partner-biographer produced something of a *tour de force*. With his matter-of-fact literalness combined with originality of depiction he had the makings of Lincoln all measured, weighed, taken apart, tagged, and put together again. "Abraham Lincoln [wrote Herndon] was about six feet four inches high, . . . having good health and no gray hairs. . . . He was [a] thin—tall—wirey—sinewy, grisly—raw boned man, . . . standing he leaned forward—was what may be called stoop shouldered, ... His usual weight was about 160 pounds. [Lincoln himself gave his average weight as 180.] . . . His blood had to run a long distance from the heart to the tips of his frame, and his nerve force . . . had to travel through dry ground a long distance before the muscles & nerves were obedient to his will. His . . . build was loose and leathery. . . . The whole man . . . worked slowly—creakingly, as if it wanted oiling. Physically he was a very—very powerful man, lifting with ease 400—or 600 pounds. . . . When Mr. Lincoln walked he moved cautiously, but firmly, his long arms—his hands on them hanging like giants hands, swung down by his side. He walked with even tread . . . the inner sides of his feet were parallel, if not a little pigeontoed. He did not walk cunningly —Indian like, but cautiously & firmly. In walking Mr. Lincoln put the whole foot flat down on the ground at once, not landing on the heel. He lifted his foot all at once—not lifting himself from the toes, and hence had no spring or snap or get get get [sic] up to his walk. He had the economy of fall and lift of foot, though he had spring or apparent ease of motion in his tread. Mr. Lincoln walked undulating up & down, catching and pocketing tire—weariness & pain all up and down his person, ... In sitting down on common chairs he was no taller than ordinary men from the chair to the crown of his head. A marble placed on his knee thus sitting would roll hipward, down an inclined plane. His legs & arms were abnormally—unnaturally long, & hence in undue proportion to the balance of his body. It was only when he stood up that he loomed above other men."

Herndon's inventory or bill of particulars, goes on unceasingly from Lincoln's head and brain to the size of his hat, (7⅛) the measure from ear to ear and from front to back, forehead, hair ("almost black and lay floating where the fingers or the winds left it"), cheek bones, jutting brows, heavy jaws, nose ("having the tip glowing in red, and a little awry toward the right eye"), chin, and eye brows ("like a huge rock on the brow of a hill"). "His face was . . . shriveled—wrinkled and dry, having here and there a hair on the surface. . . . His lower lip was thick—material and hanging undercurved while his chin reached for the lip up curved. . . . There was a lone mole on the right cheek and Adam's apple on his throat."

One would not forget that face—the face of the Macomb ambrotype, the Volk life mask, the beardless Hesler profile.

The bony structure, with strong planes and angles, gave the head a sculptural quality; hollows and creases showed ruggedness of character; the look of the eyes added a haunting sadness. The mouth, while heavy lipped and full of strength, was sensitive and expressive. If one takes a paper and conceals one side of the Macomb face at a time, there is an impression not easy to describe—not only the obvious fact of asymmetry which artists have noted, but different facets of the man's nature which that asymmetry suggests. No first glance would take in every aspect of this countenance. The Americanism of the man is revealed with an effect that is almost startling if one looks at the full standing form and then tries to imagine that figure in court costume, with knee-breeches, close fitting stockings, and buckles. There was little of Europe here, as Lowell noted. The man's appearance was both unique and related to a well known American type, the type that might have been found among people close to the woods or mountains.

One factor of his appearance was not seen in photographs: the sparkle of the face in animation noted by those who described him from life, but too much a part of the face in action to be captured by the camera. "The moment Lincoln took his seat at the pho machine [wrote Herndon] & looked down the barrel of it he became sad—rather serious, as all business with him was serious, life included." To Whitney it seemed: "His mobile face ranged . . . through a long gamut: it was rare that an artist could catch the expression, and Lincoln's face was of that kind that the expression was of greater consequence than the contour of the features." When Lincoln was "moved by some great & good feeling—by some idea of Liberty or Justice or Right then [wrote Herndon] he seemed an inspired man." "It was just then that Lincoln's nature was beautiful and in complete harmony with the laws of the great Eternal. I have seen him in this inspired condition and thought that he was molded in the Spirits best mold." Again Herndon wrote: ". . . he was odd—angular—homely but when those little gray eyes . . . were lighted up by the inward soul on fires of emotion, defending the liberty of man or proclaiming the truths of the Declaration of Independence . . . , then . . . all those apparently ugly or homely features sprang with organs of beuty [*sic*]—or sank . . . into the sea of . . . inspiration that on such occasions flooded up his manly face." In somewhat the same sense Herndon wrote: "You will find the plains, mountains & outlines of Lincoln's head & face hard to catch: they are so subtle." This aspect of singular attractiveness in Lincoln's countenance in moments of animation, something of the inner man shining through the weather-beaten countenance, was so clearly noted by various observers that it comes down to us with as much authenticity as the photographs themselves.

II

On the matter of Lincoln's popularity in Illinois the evidence is not all of a piece. "Lincoln was the favorite of everybody," wrote Herndon, and the manner in which people crowded round to hear his droll stories was proverbial. In the New Salem area in his earlier years he was popular for local reasons: he had been a wrestling champion, and had favored improvements desired by the people of the region. On the other hand, speaking of the attitude of Springfield, Herndon wrote: "Mr. Lincoln was not appreciated in this city, nor was he at all times the most popular man among us. The cause of his unpopularity, or rather want of popularity here, arose out of two grounds—1st He did his own thinking and 2nd he had the courage of his convictions, and boldly and fearlessly expressed them."

This comment by Herndon is seemingly corroborated by cold figures. Though for four terms (1834–1841) he was of the Sangamon County delegation in the state legislature, and despite his influence in procuring the removal of the capital to Springfield, the people of that county had a habit, on larger matters, of voting either against Lincoln when he was a candidate or against men of Lincoln's choice. The strength of the Democratic party in the Springfield area was of course a factor in producing this result, which is not conclusive as to Lincoln's popularity. That in the troubled years of agitation and war he obtained as high a vote as he did in a section where the Republican party was unpopular, is significant, as also the fact that he sometimes carried his city of Springfield though not carrying the county of Sangamon.

That Lincoln should have referred to his own popularity is a matter of interest. In his autobiography (1860), after mentioning his service in the Black Hawk War, he wrote: "Returning from the campaign, and encouraged by his great popularity among his immediate neighbors, he . . . ran for the legislature, and was beaten [1832],—his own precinct, however, casting its votes 277 for and 7 against him—and that, too, while he was an avowed Clay man, . . . the precinct the autumn afterward giving a majority of 115 to General Jackson over Mr. Clay. This was the only time Abraham was ever beaten on a direct vote of the people." When one recalls Lincoln's knack of exact statement together with his habit of understating his own achievements, this autobiographical comment gives us the best indication that his local popularity was both real and of importance to himself.

III

A sobriquet commonly has less value as biographical record than as an influence in shaping a man's superficial reputation. The idea that Lincoln was a kind of backwoods character is a misconception suggested in part by his sobriquet of "rail-splitter." It is true that Lincoln's origin was in a back-woods environment, and it is interesting to note that his father's long life of over seventy years was lived almost entirely in remote backwoods settings, but Lincoln's early life had many windows into the larger world, and his rail splitting, for which he neither apologized nor bragged, was of much less significance than his cultural associations. Because of such factors as his marriage into an aristocratic Kentucky family and his first partnership (beginning in 1837) with the courtly and socially favored John Todd Stuart, his opponents as early as 1843 actually put him down as the candidate of pride, wealth, and family distinction.

Nor is it adequate to refer to Lincoln as a country lawyer. In the forties and fifties he was one of the outstanding lawyers of Illinois at a time when Illinois was a populous and flourishing state, well suppled with able attorneys. Lincoln handled important cases and many of them, often practicing before the Illinois supreme court and in the Federal courts. He was admitted to practice before the Supreme Court of the United States and was counsel in Lewis v. Lewis decided in 1849. This implied a considerable standing at the bar. Lincoln could even be referred to as a corporation lawyer, though far indeed from the type suggested by that term in its modern connotation; he successfully handled a highly important case for the Illinois Central Railroad, from which he collected a fee of five thousand dollars, and was one of a group of lawyers retained by a combination of manufacturers who resisted the McCormick Harvester Company.

Yet the homespun quality pertaining to the country lawyer was not foreign to Lincoln. Most of his cases were prosaic enough and even boresome to review, but some were redolent of the country or picturesquely associated with common people, as his famous defense of Duff Armstrong or his recovery, on behalf of a widow of a Revolutionary soldier, of an excessive fee charged by a greedy pension agent. The Duff Armstrong case, memorable for the calendar incident and its association with the redoubtable Clary's Grove boys, gives no more concept of Lincoln the lawyer than many other cases which are unknown in the popular mind. Incidentally, the setting of this case has been distorted: though it occurred in 1858 it is usually thought of as belonging to a period more than twenty years earlier, a moving picture, "Young Mr. Lincoln," having dramatized it in the younger setting.

Lincoln's prowess in the law has probably been overstated, yet there is ample evidence that his name as counsel carried prestige in a suit. Local attorneys would work up cases for Lincoln to argue when court days came round. In the case of Ward H. Lamon this extended to the forming of a partnership, the Danville attorney being proud to advertise under the title "Lincoln & Lamon." Little of Lincoln's practice was in criminal cases; the main substance of it was in civil suits. His proportionate share of criminal business was much less than the ratio which such cases bore to the total on the dockets of a typical court in his circuit. If it be asked how far he "won" his cases—though winning in the law is not such a clear-cut matter as is often supposed—it is Paul M. Angle's conclusion that he was much more successful in the higher courts than on the circuit; especially "in the Supreme Court of Illinois, both as to the extent of his business and the degree of success he enjoyed, Lincoln's record was outstanding."

Though much of Lincoln's most important work was outside and apart from the famous eighth judicial circuit, it was inevitable that he should become bracketed with that circuit in popular memory. The practice of lawyers riding from one county seat to another was a picturesque feature of the times which Lincoln evidently enjoyed, for he "was the only lawyer who traveled over the entire circuit; he . . . made it a practice to attend every court, and to remain till the end."

This circuit, which sprawled widely over central Illinois, is remembered for its combination of pioneer flavor with legal talent, but above all for the fact that Lincoln was a part of it. One passes over its agenda—crime, slander, riot, damages, promissory notes, divorce, the value of a saw mill, responsibility for loss of sheep by foot rot, or ownership of a litter of pigs. One remembers rather the off-duty aspects, the migratory life of the ponderous judge, David Davis, and his coterie of attorneys jogging over dirt roads, sometimes stopping at farm houses, holding protracted night discussions of politics or philosophy, sleeping "two in a bed, and eight in a room," enlivening the taverns with hilarious excitement, conducting "office" consultations, according to the weather, under a tree or "on the sunny side of a court house," holding "orgmathorial court" with mock solemnity, and, not the least of it, meeting the people of country and town, to whom the semi-annual "court week" was a shining period of shopping, entertainment, and political agitation.

It was natural and inevitable that the traveling lawyers should correlate their court practice with speech making. At Bloomington in September 1856, for example, finding himself on a case before the McLean circuit court (Bishop *v.* Illinois Central Railroad Co.), Lincoln addressed a Republican gathering in Major's Hall. It was reported that he spoke with "great eloquence and power. He showed up the position of the Fillmore party in fine style. . . ." Another example was when Lincoln, while in Urbana on court duty, addressed a meeting at the court house on October 20 of the same year. Lincoln's travel arrangements were known in advance and in July 1856, when his arrival in Chicago on legal business was anticipated, it was hoped that his arrangements would "permit him to meet the universal wish of the people of Chicago" by addressing them on political issues. A few days later Lincoln was reported having addressed an open-air Republican meeting at Dearborn Park. Color and excitement were thus added to circuit duties. The lawyers were there—sometimes a choice assemblage of them. So were the crowds. The people demanded speeches and the lawyers needed no coaxing to satisfy them.

IV

The law was Lincoln's livelihood; it was the absorbing object of his self-directed efforts as a young man arduously preparing for a career; it was his avenue of acquaintance; it was for long years his main interest. His practice embodied all phases of a lawyer's work, from jury eloquence to business documents, from office consultation to elaborate briefs and pleadings. One could write a considerable book to show the kaleidoscope of human problems, large and small, which passed before his eyes in his capacity as lawyer, and another book to exhibit, in Lincoln the lawyer, the essential qualities of Lincoln himself, his habits of thought and his character as a man. It was largely through the law that he acquired his knowledge of American institutions, of democratic traditions, of civil rights and duties.

It was also in the law that Lincoln exhibited one of his most characteristic traits, his knack of taking a complicated subject, going to the core of it, and coming through with a lucid statement of essentials. It was Herndon's observation that he was deficient in the knowledge of legal technicalities. He "knew nothing of the laws of evidence—of pleading or of practice, and did not care about them: he had a keen sense of justice and struck for that, throwing aside forms—methods and rules of all law. Lincoln looked for justice through forms, pure as a ray of light flashes through a fog bank."

Herndon thought he knew in what respects Lincoln excelled as a lawyer and in what respects he felt short: ". . . if Mr. Lincoln had his time and thought that he was right, and could get the case swung to the jury, freed from technicalities he was a good lawyer, but if he did not have his time—did not think that he was right, and could not get his case swung to the jury, . . . then he was a very weak brother. In the Circuit Courts of the United States he was a good lawyer, because the practice of the Courts was liberal—moved slowly—freed from technicalities and gave Lincoln his own time to arrange his ideas and his plans for attack or defence. . . . But it was in the Supreme Court of the State of Illinois that he was truly a great lawyer, & no where else." Herndon believed this to be true because in the state supreme court Lincoln had time to prepare; everything that went before the court, the record of the case and briefs of counsel, was put in writing in advance. Sureness of slow reasoning rather than nimbleness or resourcefulness in inventing legal pitfalls, seems to have been Lincoln's forte. In this respect Lincoln compared himself to an old jack-knife that opens more clumsily and cuts more slowly than a "woman's little knife," but could "do more execution."

There is both autobiographical detail and keen human wisdom in a Lincoln fragment, dated 1850, in which he set down his advice to lawyers. First of all he stressed diligence, attention to correspondence, leaving nothing for tomorrow which could be done today. He pointed out the importance of examining the books, noting authorities, giving close attention to the examination of titles and the drafting of decrees. Emphasizing extemporaneous speaking as "the lawyer's avenue to the public," he nevertheless warned against the "fatal error" of too much speech making, especially if relied upon as a substitute for "the drudgery of the law." He continued:

Discourage litigation. Persuade your neighbors to compromise whenever you can. Point out to them how the nominal winner is often a real loser—in fees, expenses, and waste of time. As a peacemaker the lawyer has a superior opportunity of being a good man. There will still be business enough.

Never stir up litigation. A worse man can scarcely be found than one who does this. Who can be more nearly a fiend than he who habitually overhauls the register of deeds in search of defects in titles, whereon to stir up strife, and put money in his pocket? A moral tone ought to be infused into the profession which should drive such men out of it.

. . . .

There is a vague popular belief that lawyers are necessarily dishonest. I say vague, because when we consider to what extent confidence and honors are reposed in and conferred upon lawyers by the people, it appears improbable that their impression of dishonesty is very distinct. . . . Yet the impression is common, almost universal. Let no young man choosing the law . . . for a moment yield to the popular belief—resolve to be honest at all events; and if in your own judgment you cannot be an honest lawyer, resolve to be honest without being a lawyer. Choose some other occupation, rather than one in the choosing of which you do, in advance, consent to be a knave.

Toward those traits in a lawyer that smacked of chicanery, sharp practice, or anti-social attitudes Lincoln was indignant. In this he had both a high conviction of the ethics of his profession and a deep sense of personal integrity. Though not setting himself up as a "knight-errant of the law," as Beveridge has pointed out, he had been known to withdraw from a case during trial after being convinced that justice was not on the side of his client. It was not in him, said his friend Gillespie, to "attempt to bolster up a false position." "He would abandon his case first."

That Lincoln could be slighted by fellow counsel in a case to the point of stinging humiliation and chagrin, and yet take the snub in generous good spirit was shown in the McCormick reaper trial. The McCormick Harvester Company was suing an Illinois manufacturer named Manny, together with eastern firms, for infringement of patent rights. It was a Federal case, first set for trial in Chicago, then shifted to Cincinnati. Lincoln was retained as counsel for the defendants (McCormick's rivals); others employed on the same side were George Harding of Philadelphia, Edwin M. Stanton of Pittsburgh, and (for assistance in preparation) Peter H. Watson of Washington, later assistant secretary of war and president of the Erie Railroad. Lincoln was impressed with the importance of the case, and made elaborate preparation, only to find himself excluded from active participation in the trial. Evidence was not put in his hands in advance, and it was Harding and Stanton who presented the argument. There are various versions of what passed between defense counsel. Lincoln's associates may simply have been watching their client's interests in a trial where a member of the Illinois bar proved not so indispensable as was expected, and where only two attorneys were needed in argument. Others have seen in the incident, not without cause, evidence of the disdain which smart eastern lawyers felt toward the gawky, unpolished, ill-dressed, and unprepossessing Lincoln—"that d——d long armed Ape" as Stanton is said to have called him. Lincoln was deeply hurt and disappointed; yet he took the incident in good part. He yielded to superior talent, sat with rapt attention while the arguments were given, and accepted a lesson in the need for heavy study if he were to measure up to eastern lawyerly standards. In appointing Stanton secretary of war in 1862 he rose magnanimously above personal resentment; as for Stanton, his manner toward his Chief was never to lose its overbearing tone.

Though careful to charge and collect what was due him, Lincoln wanted no more. Not only would he not "consent to be a knave"; he would decline to accept unjustifiably high fees; if a case were questionable, he would refuse it. There was no unctuousness about such conduct; it was a matter of practicing what he preached. It is this that makes the more interesting those passages in which he extended advice. He had been through it himself; he warned that there was no royal road to success. In the midst of his campaign for the presidency he took the time to answer an inquirer who wanted to know "the best mode of obtaining a thorough knowledge of the law." He wrote:

. . . The mode is very simple, though laborious and tedious. It is only to get the books and read and study them carefully. Begin with Blackstone's "Commentaries," and after reading it carefully through, say twice, take up Chitty's "Pleadings," Greenleaf's "Evidence," and Story's "Equity," etc., in succession. Work, work, work, is the main thing.

On the basis of many years of partnership William H. Herndon made the following statement in which Lincoln the lawyer was blended with Lincoln the man:

. . . In 1843–4 [actually late in 1844] Mr. Lincoln and I became partners in the law business in Springfield, but did business in all the surrounding counties. Our partnership was never legally dissolved till the night of his assassination. The good man the noble man, would take none of my fees made in the law business after his election to the Presidency. Mr. Lincoln was a safe councilor, a good lawyer and an honest man in all the walks of life.

. . . Mr. Lincoln was a cool, cautious, conservative, and long headed man. Mr. Lincoln could be trusted by the people. They did trust him and they were never deceived. He was a pure man, a great man, and a patriot. In the practice of law he was simple honest, fair and broad minded. He was courteous to the bar, and to the court. He was open candid and square in his profession, never practicing on the sharp or low. Mr. Lincoln met all questions fairly, squarely, . . . , making no concealments of his . . . intentions in any case. He took no snap judgments, nor used any tricks in his business. . . .

Mr. Lincoln never deceived his brother in a law case. What he told you was the exact truth. . . .

V

It is incorrect to regard Lincoln as versatile, or brilliantly accomplished in many fields. He was no Leonardo da Vinci, no universal genius; nor was he so variously gifted or widely read as, for instance, Thomas Jefferson. His main interest was in politics, using that word both in its original and derived sense. His studies focused on problems of government and of peaceful American development. It should of course be added that, over and above his main occupation as lawyer and political leader, Lincoln was an inventor, a surveyor, fond of geometry, something of a specialist in western river transportation (no mean subject), an athlete, a soldier (for a brief period, including re-enlistments, in the Black Hawk War, 1832), a lecturer (briefly), a newspaper owner (again briefly), and an orator. In the period before his career took shape he had been ferry boy, flatboatman, mill manager, small town clerk and merchant, day laborer at odd jobs, and postmaster. By his own statement he had "thought of learning the blacksmith trade." He had been a part of his growing community wherever fortune had landed him, helping in community tasks while earning his livelihood. Later, in days of prominence, he referred to himself as a working man; it was a satisfaction to him to identify himself with the ranks of labor. His range of activities, however, had not been so wide as to be remarkable. Farming was not his occupation at any time after he struck out for himself in 1831. Only on a limited scale, in New Salem days, was he ever a business man. He had neither a native nor a developed taste in art; country merry-making was more to his liking than classical music; and, while growing up in picturesque regions, he showed little conscious appreciation of the beauties of nature. Yet there was latent poetry in the man, there was fondness for Shakespeare, and there were times when he expressed himself in verse.

VI

As a speaker Lincoln ran the gamut from stumps in the woods through village platforms to juries, outdoor crowds, and cultured audiences. In the speaking to which he was accustomed there were no tables "to hit, beat and . . . bang"; the speaker's whole form was visible; he stood out "fully to public view." Lincoln did not like his speeches to smell of the study. In going over his debate with Douglas for publication he did not embellish, elaborate, or revise; he "only corrected his speeches—made them talk as he had talked on the stump."

. . . When he rose [wrote Herndon] to speak to the jury or to crowds of people he stood inclined forward—was awkward—angular—ungainly—odd . . . ; he was a diffident man, somewhat, and a sensative one, and both of these added to his oddity—awkwardness . . . as it seemed to me. Lincoln had confidence, full and complete confidence in himself, ... Lincoln's voice was, when he first began speaking, shrill—squeaking—piping—unpleasant: his general look—his form—his pose—the color of his flesh wrinkled and dry, his sensativeness & his momentary diffidence, everything seemed to be against him, but he soon recovered. I can see him now—in my mind distinct. On rising to address the jury or the crowd he . . . generally placed his hands behind him, the back part of his left hand resting in the palm of his right hand. As he proceeded and grew warmer he moved his hand to the front of his person, generally interlocking his fingers and running one thumb around the other. Sometimes his hands, for a short while, would hang by his side. In still growing warmer as he proceeded in his address he used his hands—especially and generally his right hand in his gestures: He used his head a great deal in speaking, throwing or jerking or moving it now here and now there—now in this position and now in that, in order to be more emphatic—to drive the idea home. Mr. Lincoln never beat the air—never sawed space with his hands—never acted for stage effect—was cool—calm, earnest—sincere—truthful—fair—self

possessed—not insulting—not dictatorial—was pleasing—good natured, had great strong naturalness of look, pose, and act—was clear
in his ideas—simple in his words—strong, terse and demonstrative:
he spoke and acted to convince individuals and masses: he used . . .
his right hand, sometimes shooting out that long bony forefinger of
his to dot an idea or to enforce a thought, resting his thumb on his
middle finger. Bear in mind that he did not gesticulate much and *yet*
. . . every organ of his body was in motion and acted with ease—
elegance and grace—so it all looked *to me*

As Mr. Lincoln proceeded further . . . , if time—place—subject and occasion admitted of it, he . . . gradually warmed up—
his shrill—squeaking—piping voice became harmonious, melodious
—musical, . . . with face . . . aglow: his form dilated—swelled
out and he rose up a splendid form, erect straight and dignified: he
stood square on his feet with both legs up and down, toe even with
toe— . . . he did not put one foot before an other: he kept his feet
parallel and close to and not far from each other. When Mr. Lincoln
rose up to speak, he rose slowly—steadily—firmly: he never moved
much about on the stand or platform when speaking, touching no
desk—table—railing: he ran his eyes slowly over the crowd, giving
them time to be at ease and to completely recover himself, ...
He frequently took hold with his left hand, his left thumb erect, of
the left lapel of his coat, keeping his right hand free to gesture in
order to . . . clinch an idea. In his greatest inspiration he held both
of his hand [*sic*] out above his head at an angle of about fifty degrees—hands open or clinched according to his feelings and his
ideas. If he was moved in some indignant and half mad moment
against slavery or wrong . . . and seemed to want to tear it down—
trample it beneath his feet and to eternally crush it, then he would
extend his arms out, at about the above . . . angle with clinched
big, bony, strong hands on them—. If he was defending the right—
if he was defending liberty—eulogizing the Declaration of Independence, then he extended out his arms—palms of his hands up-
ward somewhat at about the above degree—angle, as if appealing
to some superior power for assistance and support; or that he might
embrace the spirit of that which he so dearly loved. It was at such
moments that he seemed inspired, fresh from the hands of his crea-
tor. Lincoln's gray eyes would flash fire when speaking against slav-

ery or spoke volumes of hope and love when speaking of Liberty—
justice and the progress of mankind—

VII

In days when lyceums were a prominent feature of intellectual life Lincoln took briefly to the lecture platform, but
most of the contemporary comments on this phase are disparaging or even devastatingly unfavorable. The lecture that
Lincoln fixed up for the purpose was the one on "Discoveries,
Inventions, and Improvements" which has already been noted;
he delivered it in Springfield and other Illinois towns in 1858,
1859, and 1860. One of his hearers at Pontiac, Illinois, in
January 1860 observed that Lincoln was a "Big Gun" in the
political world, but that the "people . . . were disappointed"
in the performance. In Bloomington, about a year before his
nomination for the presidency, Lincoln actually refused to give
a scheduled lecture because on arriving to do so he found
too scant a crowd.

Herndon's explanation of Lincoln's venturing into the
lecture field was that he felt hurt by his "failure" as inventor
and eulogist and by his frustrated attempt to pick up the
German and Latin languages "by some short cut," but, thought
Herndon, he "had none of the elements of a lecturer." These
efforts, said Herndon, before "the elite and cultured" were
"utter failure and very disappointing: they went the way of
his Clay eulogy." Though the lecturer "thought so much of
one of these efforts" that he presented a copy as a friendly
remembrance, Herndon reported that "Lincoln's friends were
deeply and thoroughly mortified at all of these efforts." Yet in
its main content and in the pithy phrasing of some of its
passages, the lecture when read today carries real significance.

VIII

Lincoln's character was treated at great length by Joseph Gillespie of Edwardsville, Illinois, whose association with the Illinois leader went back to the time (1840–1841) when they were fellow members of the state legislature. From this portrait we gather that he was "genial but not very sociable," "ambitious but not very aspiring," skillful in story telling yet thinking his debate with Douglas "too grave & serious" for such levity. "He did not seek company but when he was in it he was the most entertaining person I ever knew." In "the discussion of great questions," said Gillespie, Lincoln thought "nothing adventious [sic] should be lugged in as a make weight. That was contrary to his notions of *fairness*." He was a man of comfortable means, but did not reach out for easy gains in land speculation as did Judge Davis. His children "ran over him"; he was "powerless to resist their importunities." Gillespie had "seen him on several occasions display great heroism." He was sensitive where he thought he had fallen short, as when he "was pitted by the Whigs in 1840 to debate with Mr. Douglas." Conscious of his failure and deeply distressed, he "begged to be permitted to try it again" and Gillespie had "never heard . . . such a triumphant vin[di]cation. . . ."

The importance of his homely origin in the molding of his outlook and in the shaping of his conversation is borne out by Gillespie's description. He was "never ashamed of the poverty and obscurity of his early life," was "master of . . . frontier life and woods craft," full of anecdote of "boyish days amongst his country playfellows," and had "the happiest faculty of turning . . . reminiscences to good account." "He never missed the nib of an anecdote. He always maintained . . . that the best stories originated with Country boys & in the rural dis-

LINCOLN AT FIFTY

Claimed to have been taken by S. M. Fassett of Chicago in 1859; also attributed to Alexander Hesler of Chicago. It was in 1859 that Lincoln was beginning to be spoken of for the Presidency.

tricts. He had great faith in the strong sense of Country People and he gave them credit for greater inteligence [*sic*] than most men do. . . . Mr. Lincoln had more respect for & confidence in the masses than any statesman this Country has ever produced He told me in the spring of 1864 that the People were greatly ahead of the poloticians. . . . He prized the suggestions of . . . unsophistocated People more than what was called statecraft. . . ." Mr. Gillespie continued:

. . . Mr. Lincoln could hardly be considered a genius, a poet, or an inventor but he had the qualities of a reformer He endeavored to bring back things to the old landmarks but he never would have attempted to invent and compose new systems He had boldness enough when he found the building rocked and going to decay to restore it to its original design but not to contrive a new & distinct edifice He believed that the framers of our government expected slavery to die out and adapted the system to that end but that their views were being frustrated by adventitious circumstances by which we were surrounded. . . . He contended that we were more indebted to our government than it was to us and that we were not entitled to greater credit for our liberality of sentiment on political questions than others equally liberal who were born and raised under less favorable auspices. . . .

Tracing further the Gillespie Lincoln, if we may so call it (for Gillespie's accounts were full and circumstantial), we find a man "contemplative rather than speculative," "fond of astronomy . . . and mechanical science," anxious "to trace out the source and development of language," touched with "a slight tinge of fatalism," "a believer in destiny," one who put trust "more in Divine power than in human instrumentality." He "had a remarkably inquiring mind . . . [which] roamed over the whole field of knowledge . . . with special interest [in] those which were of a practical character . . . [with] a solid and indisputable basis." Being "undemonstrative," his salient traits were not perceived at first acquaintance; hence he was "sometimes misunderstood." He "would rather disoblige

a friend than do an act of injustice to a political opponent."
His never failing anecdotes were both humorous and illustrative; the application was perfect, yet entertainment was also
the motive. Clearness and simplicity of statement he "cultivated with . . . assiduity." Logic appealed to him more than
ornament; his forte was "an immense stock of common sense."
"Mr. Lincoln was a great common man," "the representative of
the unsophisticated People."

Perhaps a man is never great to his valet. Herndon had at
times served almost as Lincoln's caddie (though such a statement conveys no idea of Lincoln's generous and partnerlike
attitude towards him); yet in the close-up view, if we can trust
his later accounts, the younger man saw always the soul and
spirit of the older. Lincoln was Herndon's great enthusiasm.
That he idolized and worshiped the man of "mystery" whom
he "knew well," is beyond doubt. When writing on Lincoln
he would burst into a tribute as if a spring of deep feeling
were released. Emphasizing Lincoln's plainness and admitting
his faults, he also repeatedly stressed what he thought his
greatness. Whatever might have been Lincoln's changing aspects, Herndon saw him "through all situations, positions &
conditions . . . one and the same—ever honest, & simple, &
sincere . . . a primitive type of character. . . ." He found him
"incapable of falsehood—of base deception or of fraud"; "humble—tender—forbearing—liberal— . . . tolerant. . . ." "Lincoln," he said, "rose over so many disadvantages that he seems
to me a hero. . . ." "Mr. L's life is a sweet—clear—clean—
manly noble life." Lincoln was "a great man," "truly a noble
man." Herndon considered him "Christ like" in his charity
and liberality.

IX

It would require deep understanding to depict Lincoln, thought Herndon. It could not be done with superficial strokes: "he was Lincoln and Lincoln alone, and none exactly like him." "Mr. Lincoln," he said, "thought too much and did too much for America and the world to be crammed into an epigram or shot off with a single rocket: he was too close to the touch of the divine everywhere and too near to the suggestions and whisperings of nature for such quick work, done with a flash." He did not want Lincoln retouched by overfriendly art or too-refined portraiture. "Mr. Lincoln can stand unstaggeringly up beneath all *necessary* or other truths."

Such were his moods that he would sometimes pass by his friends unnoticed on the streets; to Herndon this did not matter, except that he "felt for him" in moments of suffering. He was "sad and cheerful by turns—he was good natured generally, but it was terrible to see him mad"; ". . . a gloomy man at one moment and a joyous man the next." Herndon often repeated that he was unknown, "a big mysterious man," a puzzle to friends and neighbors, a "hidden man" who kept his secrets, a man of "deep prudences," a man to admire but "hard to get at." Yet Lincoln's moods did not overwhelm or engulf him; they are rather to be regarded as among the elements blended in that composite which became his character. If he achieved serenity, he did not come by it easily. His philosophy, which gave steadiness to a sensitive, troubled nature, was chiefly a reliance on the working of elemental and eternal laws; his "patience sprang from his philosophy—his calm quiet waiting on the events of the times—his coolness . . . —his charity . . . and . . . want of malice."

Viewed in retrospect the rise of Abraham Lincoln to influence and leadership was no inscrutable mystery. Given the conditions, the result was natural and logical. Politically, as will appear in later pages, the man was "available." He had distinctiveness—oddness perhaps, but without unfortunate eccentricities. He had no antagonisms, no attachment to special interests; yet he had character. He came from a large and "doubtful" state, from a broad section whose votes in 1860 were to be decisive of the outcome. He had a log-cabin origin, though this was less of an asset than has been usually supposed; he had also a peculiar reputation for honesty and a flair for appealing to what was fundamentally and basically American. If one takes a cue from Frederick Jackson Turner, Lincoln embodied the West when the West was the most characteristically American of the sections. From the great prairie environment he had drawn his strength. In western campaigning he had developed aptness in assimilating the subject matter of politics and skill in the art of public appeal. His apprenticeship had been served, not chiefly in office (save as state legislator and briefly as congressman), but on the law circuit, the hustings, the political forum.

He was no stranger to the arts of rhetoric. No one could rightly call his speeches crude; on the contrary they sometimes rose to the height of literary mastery, though in familiar conversation and informal utterance he lapsed into colloquialisms. Not offending the scholar, his addresses seized the understanding of the man in the street. He had his own style, his special tang. In all his careful expression there was simplicity combined with distinction, an economy of competently chosen words, an easy flow of sentences, and a readiness in epigram which served well in the place of brilliant scintillation. Some of his statements have that unerring quality of hitting the target that stamps them as proverbs or aphorisms.

The tricks of the agitator or demagogue were foreign to Lincoln's nature. He avoided emotional harangues. This avoidance was total; his manner was not that of the rabble rouser,

the passionate orator, the professional patrioteer. There was in
Lincoln more of Euclid than of Demosthenes. He kept on a
conservative keel, yet managed to infuse into his leadership
enough stirring enthusiasm to rally the reformer and to make
a campaign seem a crusade for a cause. Few leaders were less
given to sentimentalism; few were more concerned with reason
and mental testing. Though it cramped his soul to operate
within the limitations of a party, and though as candidate he
was to be everyone's game, he appreciated the meaning of
statesmanship. He was made of better stuff than that of politicians reaching out for the spoils of office. No understanding of
Lincoln in the days of his coming ordeal will be complete
without envisaging the man he was and viewing his qualities
against the quiet background of peace within which he had
developed for fifty years.

Chapter Three

THE ANN RUTLEDGE STORY

F ROM UNCERTAIN AND CONFLICTING MEMORIES OF A COURTSHIP in picturesque New Salem the story has amazingly grown until the romantic linking of Abraham and Ann has become universal. In drama it has usurped the spotlight. Perhaps the majority of those who think of Lincoln not only believe that Ann Rutledge was the only woman he ever loved; they go on from there to the fictional assumption that an unambitious and lazy lad became a student of law and a man of note only because of Ann, that her death left him crushed in spirit, that her memory remained his inspiration through life, that his tenderest emotions were always thereafter in retrospect, and that real love for the woman he married was non-existent.

I

For the historian the problem is that of tracing the account to its sources, finding the evidence, noting how far the testimony holds together, and rejecting those elements that are but the froth and chaff of unchecked imagination. One may trace the popularizing—indeed the exaggerated exploitation— of the tradition to Herndon; it was he who gave it wide publicity, filled in the gaps, added his irrepressible contribution of psychoanalysis, and set the pattern which has become familiar to millions. Back of Herndon, to be sure, there were vague memories reaching to far-off New Salem days which in some manner tended to connect the name of Lincoln with that of Ann Rutledge.

An early mention of the story in print—a very obscure mention—was in an article written by John Hill and published in the *Menard Axis* of Petersburg, Illinois, February 15, 1862. Under the title "A Romance of Reality" the author, son of Sam Hill of New Salem, strung out an unflattering account of an awkward youth, a store clerk, a soldier who reached the field of action after the war was over, keeper of a stallion, day laborer, infidel writer, surveyor, hog drover, and love-sick swain. The reader was then informed that this was none other than Abraham Lincoln, President of the United States. On the theme of the love-sick swain there was a passage telling how this youth had met an angelic lady, could think of naught but her, found his feeling reciprocated, and awaited the day when the twain would be one flesh. The lovely beauty died; melancholy fell upon the lad; friends noted his strange conduct; they kept him under guard to prevent suicide. That, in summary, was the story. Ann's name was not mentioned, but the identity was plain enough. This obscure mention of the matter was long buried, though contained in the Herndon collection; only recently has it been brought to light.

Hill was not the best witness of New Salem days, he was addressing an anti-Lincoln audience, he was riding a theme, his memories were indirect (through his father), his account was published long after the supposed event, and there were flaws in his narrative. His passage has been summarized above because in the literature of the subject it has a certain priority in that it is pre-Herndonian.

From November 16, 1866, however, the subject was peculiarly Herndon's. On that date he delivered in Springfield a lengthy, lush, and sentimental lecture under the title "Abraham

Lincoln. Miss Ann Rutledge. New Salem. Pioneering and *the*
Poem." With fruity periods and lavishly bestowed adjectives
he told the world that "Abraham Lincoln loved Miss Ann
Rutledge with all his soul, mind and strength," that she "loved
him as dearly," that they "seemed made in heaven for each
other," that Ann was "honestly engaged" to two men at the
same time, that she sickened under the conflict of emotion
and duty and died, that Lincoln's heart was buried with her,
that reason left him, that he was racked in heart and body, that
he lost his logical faculty, speaking incoherently and wildly
(Herndon supplied Lincoln's imagined words at great length),
that he rose up a man once more after visiting "Bolin" Green,
that from then he was radically changed (for the better), but
that he committed the poem "Immortality" to memory and
was ever thereafter influenced by the solemn contemplation of
these deep thoughts.

Paul M. Angle published an excellent study of this subject
in 1927, but did not use the Herndon manuscripts, which were
not then available to the historical profession. Concerning the
familiar romance Angle concluded that "it is entirely traditional." He added: "No reliable contemporary record has ever
been discovered. Instead, there are numerous reminiscences,
put in writing at the request of Herndon, who, once given the
lead, followed it tirelessly."

This fits the case. Herndon did have something of a "lead"
in none too reliable recollections. A careful study of the Herndon manuscripts reveals what those recollections were and
confirms Angle's conclusion that all the material was non-
contemporary—i.e., none of it belonged in or near the eighteen-
thirties. In his lecture, Herndon invites all who doubt his story
to come to his office and look over his records; now after nearly
eight decades the author is happy to accept the invitation for
this inspection.

As Herndon's papers reveal, old settlers, or in some cases
their children, told of a friend of Lincoln's, a beautiful girl

named Ann Rutledge, who had been engaged to one John McNamar and had died. Her lover was using the name McNeil; while building his fortunes in the West he did not want to be traced by his family. He had left New Salem, spending some years with his people in New York (sometimes misstated as Ohio); he had returned shortly after Ann's death. There was the tradition that Lincoln was greatly saddened by the girl's death; this, and the engagement to McNamar, are the factors that stand out most clearly in the mosaic of New Salem reminiscence.

The subject appealed to all the sentimentalizing and psychoanalyzing impulses of Herndon's nature. He talked to survivors of those days or if he could not reach them he had them interviewed by proxy or got their statements by correspondence. He labored with an assiduity that gave importance to his very questions. The resulting mass of confused and contradictory evidence, found in his voluminous manuscripts, serves as the chief basis for the famous tradition so far as it had basis; the lecture and Herndon biography added the glowing details.

The vagueness of reminiscence given after many years is familiar to all careful historical students. The historian must use reminiscence, but he must do so critically. Even close-up evidence is fallible. When it comes through the mists of many years some of it may be true, but a careful writer will check it with known facts. Contradictory reminiscences leave doubt as to what is to be believed; unsupported memories are in themselves insufficient as proof; statements induced under suggestion, or psychological stimulus, as were some of the stories about Lincoln and Ann, call especially for careful appraisal. If reminiscences are gathered, but only part of them used, that again is a problem. When faulty memories are admitted the resulting product becomes something other than history; it is no longer to be presented as a genuine record.

II

Looking into what Herndon collected, we find varying responses to his inquiries; the whole constituted a product he could not well digest. A Miss Berry and a Miss Short were mentioned mistakenly and a Miss Owens quite definitely as objects of Lincoln's attentions during Ann's lifetime. Samuel Hill and William Berry were added to the list of Ann's suitors. As above noted, it was generally agreed that the girl was betrothed to McNamar, and that Lincoln was plunged into gloom after her death. Mentor Graham, New Salem schoolmaster, briefly supported the tradition of the Lincoln-Rutledge engagement. In an interview with Herndon he is reported to have said: "Lincoln and she was engaged—Lincoln told me so—she intimated to me the same: He Lincoln told me that he felt like committing suicide often, but I told him God higher purpose . . . [etc]." These words were scribbled by Herndon; over his own signature Graham referred even more briefly to a "momentary derangement" in Lincoln caused in part by "the death of one whom he dearly and sincerely love[d]."

Mrs. Lizzie Bell, daughter of Mentor Graham, furnished none too reliable glimpses of a quilting party where Ann kept her eye on Mr. Hill, while Lincoln flirted with another girl, with the result that "Lincoln & Ann had a fly up, but on her death bed she sent for Lincoln & all things were reconciled." Incidentally, Herndon's note on the page containing this reminiscence described both Mentor Graham and his daughter as "cranky—flighty—at times nearly non copus mentis—but good & honest." In evaluating their contributions one should remember this comment. One should also remember that, by Mrs. Bell's own statement, she was a child at the time and did not know these things of her own knowledge.

Though one does not wish to bear down too severely upon the schoolmaster, whose educational influence on Lincoln has probably been exaggerated, one should note the following statement written by Graham to Herndon in 1865: ". . . I saw him [Lincoln] frequently when a lad about 12 years of age though was not personally acquainted with him this was at his residence at the place of birth in the winter of 1819 & 20 I went to school in the County of Hardin Ky . . . , during my attendance . . . I often past by old Mr. Lincoln's house & often saw his son Abraham out about the premises. . . ." In this, of course, Graham was badly mistaken as to what he claimed to have remembered. The Lincolns moved from the birthplace location when Abraham was two years old (1811); they left Kentucky for Indiana when he was seven (1816). That the schoolmaster was at fault or confused (at least as to dates) in this case does not necessarily overthrow his New Salem recollections; but, taken in connection with Herndon's comment made in the period when he was interviewing Graham and his daughter, they do suggest the need for wholesome doubt. At any rate Graham's contributions on the Lincoln-Rutledge romance were meager, especially so in what he himself wrote. His account was more concerned with Lincoln's life in the New Salem period and with his own function in teaching the future President.

One of Herndon's principal witnesses—a lengthier one than Graham—was R. B. Rutledge, Ann's younger brother who was seventeen the year she died. After recounting Ann's engagement to John McNamar and the latter's long absence, Rutledge (in a statement attested by John Jones) declared:

In the mean time Mr Lincoln paid his addresses to Ann, . . . and those resulted in an engagement to marry, conditional to an honorable release from the contract with McNamar. There is no kind of doubt as to the existence of this engagement. David Rutledge [a brother long since dead] urged Ann to consummate it, but she refused until such time as she could see McNamar—inform him of the change in her feelings, and seek an honorable release. Mr Lincoln lived in the village, McNamar did not return and in August 1835 Ann sickened and died. The effect upon Mr Lincoln's mind was terrible; he became plunged in despair, and many of his friends feared that reason would desert her throne. His extraordinary emotions were regarded as strong evidence of the existence of the tenderest relations between himself and the deceased.

At another time Rutledge wrote:

. . . the facts are Wm Berry first courted Ann and was rejected, afterwards Saml Hill, then John McNamar, which resulted in an engagement to marry at some future time, he McNamar left the Country on business, was gaun some years, in the meantime and during McNamars absence, Mr Lincoln Courted Ann and engaged to marry her, on the completion of the sudy of law. In this I am caroborated by James Mc [McGrady] Rutledge a cousin about her age & who was in her confidence, he say in a letter to me just received, "Ann told me once in coming from a Camp Meeting on Rock creek, that engagements made too far a hed sometimes failed, that one had failed, (meaning her engagement with McNamar) and gave me to understand, that as soon as certain studies were completed she and Lincoln would be married. . . ."

Here is one person reporting what another person had written him concerning what that person recollected he had inferred from something that Ann had casually said to him more than thirty-one years before! Anxious though he was to please, Rutledge could not accept Herndon's emphasis upon Ann's pining away because of conflicting emotions in her maiden heart. He courteously but firmly disagreed and reminded Herndon that Ann died of brain fever.

There are inconsistencies and contradictions in Rutledge's assertions, and in reading his labored statements one can sympathetically understand his difficulty in reconstructing a picture of what happened. A writer of today ought not to put a higher value on his recollections than he himself did. He confessed uncertainty on points of Herndon's questioning and spoke of comparing notes with others. In part this consultation may have been intended to supplement his own knowledge, which he did not claim to be complete in itself. In the law of evidence, however, it is insisted that testimony ought to come straight. If witnesses arrange their recollections so as to make them agree, or if they seek to build them up where they admit uncertainty, the result lacks the validity of statements obtained from witnesses separately and unretouched. One must give full credit to the sincerity of R. B.'s effort to deliver the truth and some investigators might not consider that his product was rendered less valuable by this consultation. It is not an easy problem. Rutledge was not always able to make his words convey his idea as to the engagement between Lincoln and Ann. At one point he said it was "conditional"—i.e., dependent upon release from McNamar; elsewhere he stated that it was "not conditional . . . but absolute." On Lincoln's mental suffering Rutledge wrote: "I cannot answer this question from personal knowledge, but from what I have learned from others at the time, you [Herndon] are substantially correct." In contrast to this the attested statement had said: "The effect upon Mr Lincoln's mind was terrible; . . . [etc.]" In R. B. Rutledge's letters there were cases in which he told his questioner that he (Herndon) was in error; yet he confessed liking Herndon's lecture, which, incidentally, had not been confined to Ann Rutledge, but had included a glowing description of the timber, bottoms, bluffs, meadows, hills, flowers, lichen, moss, rolling brook, wild fruit, birds, animals, fish, and more especially the early settlers of New Salem and the surrounding region.

The nature of Rutledge's recollections, however, is best indicated by a qualifying statement at the outset of his attested account:

I trust largely to your courtesy as a gentleman, to your honesty and integrity as a historian, and to your skill in writing for the public, to enlarge wherever my statements seems obscure, and to condense and remove whatever seems superfluous. . . . Many of my statements are made from memory with the aid of association of events; and should you discover that the date, location and circumstances, of the events here named should be contradictory to those named from other sources, I beg of you to consider well the testimony in each case, and make up your history from those statements, which may appear to you best fitted to remove all doubt as to their correctness.

Rutledge did his sincere best, but what we have in his testimony is dim and misty with the years; he became double indirect where he quoted James McGrady Rutledge and others; and his record is qualified by his prefatory caution to Herndon as to how to use it. Yet if one adopts the familiar Ann Rutledge tale, this is a sample of the type of material he must accept.

III

The testimony of James Short, a close and true friend of Lincoln and of the Rutledges, deserves consideration if one has to deal with far-off rememberings. He lived in the Sand Ridge area near the farm where Ann spent the last few years of her life. (This farm was about seven miles north of New Salem.) There is a matter-of-fact quality untinged by sentiment in his statement. He said:

Mr L. boarded with the parents of Miss Ann Rutledge, from the time he went to New Salem up to 1833. In 1833 her mother moved to the Sandridge & kept house for me, until I got married. Miss R. staid at N. S. for a few months after mother left, keeping house for her father & brothers, & boarding Mr L. She then came over to her mother. After my marriage, the Rutledges lived about half a mile from me. Mr L. came over to see me & them every day or two. I did not know of any engagement or tender passages between Mr L and Miss R at the time. But after her death, which happened in 34 or 35, he seemed to be so much affected and grieved so hardly that I then supposed there must have been . . . something of the kind.

That Lincoln was deeply saddened by Ann's death was generally reported by these witnesses, several of whom retrospectively inferred, as did James Short, that if he grieved so much, he "must have been" in love with her.

John McNamar, Ann's fiancé who was in the East at the time of the alleged Lincoln-Rutledge courtship, wrote in 1866: "I never heard and [i.e., any] person say that Mr Lincon addressed Miss Ann Rutledge in terms of courtship neither her own family nor my acquaintances otherwise." McNamar knew the Rutledges well not only because of his engagement to Ann but because he had bought half of the Rutledge farm, this being referred to as a "family arrangement." If Lincoln did court Ann to the point of bethrothal, and McNamar who was known to be engaged to her was not told of this fact when he returned to New Salem, human nature in country towns has radically changed! McNamar was respected by his neighbors and his word was trusted. He said that two prominent men, personal friends of his, told him Lincoln "was Grieved very much" at Ann's death. Bowling Green was said to have feared that the young man's grief might impair his mind; he took him to the Green home for a week or two and "succeeded in cheering him Lincoln up. . . ." But Mrs. Green thought Ann loved McNamar as much as Lincoln, though the former had been absent so long, and one of Ann's aunts said she thought Ann would have married McNamar if she had lived. Again Mrs. Green, sometimes called Mrs. "Bolen" Green, was quoted as saying that Miss Owens visited the New Salem region "for about a year next preceding the death of Miss Rutledge" and that "Lincoln went to see her frequently during that time She living handy to Salem." James Short denied that Lincoln refused to eat after Ann's death and John Hill said that he bore up very well until, some days afterwards, a heavy rain fell which unnerved him.

Various other witnesses contributed fragments of reminiscence. W. G. Greene, an intimate friend of Lincoln in New Salem days, agreed that Lincoln and Ann were engaged, and that his friends feared he would commit suicide after her death. Caleb Carman stated that Lincoln loved Ann but said he did not know "mutch" about it, as he was not in New Salem at the time. A cousin of W. H. Herndon, J. R. Herndon, referred to Miss Rutledge and said he had "know dout he [Lincoln] would have married iff she had of lived." L. M. Greene asserted they were engaged; William McNeeley presented hearsay evidence that Lincoln was "insane" after Ann's death; Henry McHenry described Lincoln's depression and desire for solitude, but added that some thought it was due to an increased application to his law studies. George Spears approved of Herndon's lecture, but remarked with refreshing candor that while he had lived through the time and events mentioned, he could not remember about them. Jasper Rutledge, relative of Ann born after her death and brother of James McGrady Rutledge, gave the traditional family version. He added the detail that McNamar's real name was revealed by his signing of some deeds (he had been using the name McNeil) and that Ann was suspicious of a man with two names. According to his account, correspondence between Ann and McNamar gradually ceased and Ann and Lincoln became engaged. Mrs. Sam Hill endorsed the main points of the Rutledge tradition, but gave it as her "honest opinion" that Ann would have married McNamar if he had returned before her death. Henry Hohhiner (?) expressed his "opinion" that Lincoln and Ann were engaged, while Jason Duncan thought Lincoln refrained from courting Ann because of her engagement to McNamar.

So the testimony runs—some *pro*, some *con*, some inconclusive, all of it long delayed reminiscence, much of it second- or third-hand, part of it consisting of inference or supposition as to what "must have been" true. The old settlers were contradictory among themselves. One of them wrote concerning an alleged bit of early Lincoln reminiscence: "If that old Lady . . . who says, Lincoln made a crop for her husband some time in 1831–32 or 33, was not a *woman,* I would say she *lied* like *hell. . . .*"

One must now consider the statement of Isaac Cogdal regarding an interview he said he had with President Elect Lincoln in Springfield some time between November 1860 and February 1861. Cogdal was a farmer and former brick mason who studied law late in life, being admitted to the bar in 1860. He lived in the Rock Creek precinct and had known Lincoln when they were both young men, being some three years younger than Lincoln. According to Cogdal's story as it comes to us, Lincoln asked him to come to his office in the State House and talk over old times and acquaintances of New Salem days. The manuscript record runs as follows:

Abe is it true that you fell in love with & courted Ann Rutledge said Cogdall. Lincoln said, "it is true—true indeed I did. I have loved the name of Rutlege to this day. I have kept my mind on their movements ever since & love them dearly"— said L [Just before this is the statement that Lincoln had asked Cogdal where the Rutledges were, an inconsistency not explained.] Ab—Is it true—said Cogdall, that you ran a little wild about the matter: I did really—I ran off the track: it was my first. I loved the woman dearly & sacredly: she was a handsome girl—would have made a good loving wife—was natural & quite intellectual, though not highly Educated—I did honestly—& truly love the girl & think often—often of her now.

The most obvious thing about this effusive statement is its unLincolnian quality. The record is Herndon's memorandum of an interview with Cogdal, who was presumably reconstructing from memory what Lincoln had said to him some years before. Words ascribed to Lincoln have been refracted by passing through two minds, and have been exposed to the possible embellishment of both Cogdal and Herndon. It has been suggested that Lincoln's friends did not usually address him as "Abe" but in this record of jottings "Abe" and especially "Ab" may have been abbreviations, for Herndon troubled himself very little about periods. "Jas" without a period is used for James in the same manuscript. On the other hand, Lincoln is quoted as having addressed Cogdal as "Ike," and Cogdal may have called him "Abe" when they were young men. Lincoln was a man of deep reserve about personal matters. As President Elect he guarded his speech with the utmost care. His lack of reticence here seems as unnatural as the language attributed to him.

B. F. Irwin mentioned hearing the story of the Cogdal interview. Irwin, who stated in an August letter that Ann died and Lincoln took it very hard, wrote in September that his informants differed as to Miss Rutledge's death. He followed this with a statement which illustrates how twisted some of these recollections could become: "Cogdal says she [Ann] was living in Iowa in 1860 as Lincoln told him and Lincoln did say in 1860 that he . . . loved her still. . . ." The same letter mentioned that Ann was unfavorably impressed with Lincoln, who was poor and awkward, while McNamar and other suitors had much more to offer.

Cogdal's story comes to us with such indirectness in the telling as to becloud with doubt what was actually said. Lincoln was not a man to express himself so effusively to friends. "Lincoln never told Speed nor Gallespie nor Judge Matheny— nor myself of this courtship—death and unsanity" wrote Herndon. He added: ". . . he was the most reticent & mostly secretive man that ever existed: he never opened his whole soul to any man: he never touched the history or quality of his own nature in the presence of his friends." That Herndon's lecture with its tale of Lincoln and Ann was news to Speed is known by his own statement. In the face of such reticence the Cogdal record seems artificial and made to order. It was given out after Lincoln's death; it presents him in an unlikely role; it puts in his mouth uncharacteristic sayings.

There is, to the writer's knowledge, no thoroughly verified utterance by Lincoln, written or oral, in which Ann Rutledge is even mentioned, though one does find Lincoln's own statements concerning women whom he knew in this period— namely, Sarah Rickard and Mary Owens.

IV

The effect of Ann's death on Lincoln seems to have been exaggerated by local gossip. Mrs. E. Abell, at whose cabin Lincoln was staying at the time of Ann's death, wrote in detail about his deep grief over the event, but added "the community said he was crazy he was not crazy but he was very disponding a long time." It is worthy of note that while she had first-hand knowledge of Lincoln's grief, she said she could tell little about the courtship. Less than a month after Ann's death a close friend of Lincoln, Mathew S. Marsh, wrote his brother a letter containing a newsy paragraph devoted to Lincoln, which fails to mention any sorrow or abnormal condition of his at this time. The letter establishes the fact that Lincoln was attending to his postmaster duties as usual, and there is a record of a survey which Lincoln made, dated September 24, 1835, in his usual handwriting which shows that he was carrying on his surveying work. This was at a time when, according to Herndon's embroidered account, Lincoln was a mental wreck. "He slept not," said Herndon, "he ate not, joyed not . . . until his body became emaciated and weak, and gave way. His mind wandered from its throne. In his imagination he muttered words to her he loved. His mind, his reason . . . walked out of itself along the uncolumned air, and kissed and embraced the shadows and illusions of the heated brain." (A choice example, this, of Herndon's combination of soaring psycho-analysis with glowing language.)

By the statement of her brother, Ann Rutledge died on August 25, 1835. The fall of 1836 found Lincoln absorbed in a prolonged courtship of Mary Owens. She had visited New Salem three years before—when Ann was living—and even then (i.e., in 1833), by his own statement, Lincoln considered her a desirable matrimonial partner.

How did Herndon regard the known fact of Lincoln's courting of Mary Owens? He did not believe that Lincoln's profession of love for the lady could be taken otherwise than seriously. He thought "the letters expressed his honest feelings and his deepest convictions and that they were written sin-cerely—truthfully and honestly." Lincoln, he said, "was in love [with Miss Owens]—deeply in love." Herndon had written effusively of the Ann Rutledge romance; now he spoke of Lincoln being thoroughly in love with Miss Owens; again he had it that Lincoln, in the period of his courtship of Miss Todd, "saw & loved an other woman—Miss Edwards and . . . de-sired to break away from Miss Todd & to join Miss Edwards." In telling of Lincoln's affections being given to Miss Edwards (this without adequate foundation), he mentioned the incident as "Miss Edwards flitting a cross the path"—this flitting made

Lincoln "crazy *the second time.*" Taking all that Herndon said, one gets the impression that he almost considered his hero weak-minded in the matter of women. As for Herndon's collaborator, he states specifically that Lincoln proposed marriage to at least four women: Ann Rutledge, Mary Owens, Sarah Richard, and (of course) Mary Todd.

In striking contrast to the Rutledge romance, there is ample documentation for the Owens courtship. We have several letters which Lincoln wrote her in which he discussed the question of her marrying him, and a complete account of the whole affair, including Miss Owens's refusal of his marriage proposal, which Lincoln wrote to his friend Mrs. O. H. Browning. In 1866 Mary Owens herself (Mrs. Vineyard) wrote: "From his own showing . . . his heart and hand were at my disposal, ..." This statement, indeed the full record on this point, fails to harmonize with the popular concept that Lincoln's whole life was influenced by his love for Ann.

Herndon treasured the Ann Rutledge story. Referring to Nicolay and Hay's articles in the *Century* he wondered if they were going to "suppress" the tale. He called it "the finest story in Lincoln's life." It is the stuff of which poetry and song are bodied forth—young love, the picturesque life of a vanished pioneer town, the tragic death of a beautiful young woman, the beating of rain and storm upon a new made grave, the age-long questioning concerning human mortality.

But there is repeated mention in the manuscripts of Herndon's worried doubts on the subject. The fact of Ann's engagement to McNamar seems greatly to have bothered him. Writing to Weik when the biography was in proof, he said: "Again the more I think of the Ann Rutledge story the more do I think that the girl had two engagements—i.e. that she was engaged to two men at one and the same. . . . I shall change my opinion of events & things on the coming of new facts and on more mature reflection in all cases—and so excuse me for 'sorter' wabbling around." Herndon's account, which was to establish the story indelibly in the public mind, was already in printer's proof; yet here he is confessing that he is " 'sorter' wabbling around" in regard to the engagement of Lincoln and Ann.

In the collection of Oliver R. Barrett in Chicago there is a stone (turtle shaped, about ten inches long) whose inscription records that A. Lincoln and Ann Rutledge "were betrothed here July 4, 1833." (The carving is clear enough. The "J" in July is ignorantly reversed.) The pedigree of the stone, as often in such cases, is incomplete. One can get statements as to its having been found in New Salem, also as to its carving resembling that of an ax handle bearing Lincoln's name; back of that, information is lacking. There are various counts against this stone if considered as a genuine record cut by Lincoln. Herndon, prominent advocate of the romance, said definitely that Ann stood firm in her feeling toward McNamar "up to 1834" and that Lincoln proposed to her in 1835. He said that "Soon after this . . . engagement Ann was taken sick . . . ," this being her final illness. It has already been noted that she died in 1835. Without presuming to give a date to a matter that is alleged but not verified, it may be noted that those who would build up a case for the Lincoln-Rutledge engagement will rely upon various recollections and upon the analysis of Herndon who believed such an engagement to have existed; they will therefore have great difficulty in arguing for the betrothal on so early a date as July 4, 1833. They will be confronted with Lincoln's own written statement that in 1833 he did not object to "plodding life through hand in hand" with Mary Owens. They will also have to remember that, where the Lincoln-Rutledge engagement was spoken of, it was related to a considerably prolonged absence of McNamar; in July 1833 Ann's lover had not been absent that long. (In a letter to George U. Miles, May 5, 1866, McNamar wrote that he left New Salem "in 32 or 33." The words "or 33" were then crossed out.) Another point to remember is that in 1833 (well on in his twenty-fifth year) Lincoln certainly knew how to form his letters; he would not have carved a reversed "J". To put the criticism of the stone in the very mildest form, too little is known of it to establish its authenticity. It is not known by whom or when it was made.

Space is lacking in which to show how other biographers have dealt with the Ann Rutledge theme. Many of them do little more than repeat Herndon. Beveridge bases his full account on Herndon's material and presents Lincoln's engagement to Ann largely along the line suggested by R. B. Rutledge, as above quoted. Yet he admits that Lincoln's courting of Ann was "misty" and states that "No positive [i.e., unconditional] and definite engagement resulted." W. E. Barton accepts the tradition. "Abraham Lincoln and Ann truly loved each other," he writes. Yet Barton adds on a later page: "We know very little about the Ann Rutledge incident. If Lincoln wrote any letters to Ann they were not preserved. If there is any other documentary proof of their love-affair, it is unknown. We know that much that has been told about it is unreliable."

V

To recapitulate: In its origin the Ann Rutledge story rests on wavering memories recorded many years after the event. No proved contemporary evidence is known to exist. Herndon did not invent the romance. He loved the truth and sought it eagerly. Whether he always found it is another matter, but if he did we know that it had to undergo his inevitable phychoanalysis before it emerged. He did elaborate the story, publicize it, and cast it into the mold which it has retained in popular thought. From the doubtful beginning of distant memory there has evolved a full-grown tradition; in the now classic form which the tradition has taken the main handiwork is that of Herndon. Few indeed were familiar with the episode prior to

Herndon's sensational lecture of 1866, which came a considerable time after Lincoln's death. Other biographers, in presenting the story, have followed the Herndon line; but the reader will recognize that the quoting of many repetitions of Herndon and Weik adds nothing in terms of historical contribution. Reminiscences gathered long after the event were not all in favor of the romance; they were contradictory and vague. The two elements on which there is agreement are Ann's engagement to McNamar and Lincoln's grief at her death. Concerning the first of these elements it may be noted that in the popular conception of the Rutledge story, John McNamar is the forgotten man; yet it is worth while to note a passage that brings poignantly to light the feeling of the one who, after all, was Ann's acknowledged and accepted lover. ". . . I cut the Initials of Miss Ann Rutledge on a b[o]ard at the head of her grave 30 years ago," wrote McNamar to Herndon in 1866. It was McNamar, not Lincoln, who marked Ann's grave. As to Lincoln's grief it has been seen that his alleged derangement of mind is without adequate substantiation; in the "uncolumned air" of Herndon's lecture it is nothing more than fiction.

Whether Lincoln was in love with Ann, or grieved over the untimely death of one who was both a lovable young woman and a dear friend; whether his grief was due to a romantic attachment or to a temperament subject to gloom and deeply sensitive to the tragedy of death; whether Ann loved him or was friendly to but unimpressed by one who called himself a "friendless, uneducated, penniless boy"; whether there was an engagement between them or it was Ann's intention to marry McNamar when he returned, are matters open to question. Ann's feeling and intent are left in considerable doubt by contradictions in regard to an engagement between them, by the opinion of some that she was unimpressed with him and would have married McNamar if she had lived, and by the unanimous testimony that she was engaged to McNamar.

Whatever may have been the true situation as to Lincoln and Ann, that situation seems now well nigh unrecoverable. As to a romantic attachment, it has not been *dis*proved. It is more correct to characterize it as *un*proved; as such it has been a famous subject of conjecture. It is a memory which lacks support in any statement recorded in Ann's lifetime. Since it is thus traditional and not reliably established as to its nature and significance, it does not belong in a recital of those Lincoln episodes which one presents as unquestioned reality.

As a historical puzzle or an exercise in the evaluation of reminiscence the Lincoln-Rutledge story is a choice subject; but its substance is far from clear while its fringe is to be discarded from the record of established history. By that fringe we mean the elaboration, the trimmings and embroidery, the fictional sentimentalizing, the invented poeticisms, and the amazing aura of apocryphal material that have surrounded the whole overgrown tale.

The present treatment has been concerned only with essential results in the telling, though masses of documents have gone into the investigation. To spin out the analysis into an extended account would, in the writer's view, not change the conclusion, though a full exhibiting of the subject would require a reproduction of numerous letters and jottings, an amassing of details about each witness with a studious examination of each bit of testimony, and withal a portrayal of the vanished background of New Salem.

Assuredly the effect of the episode upon Lincoln's later life has been greatly exaggerated—or rather, fabricated. Nor should one lightly overlook the shabby manner in which the image of Ann has tended to obscure the years of Lincoln's love and devotion for Mary, his wife, and to belittle her love and devotion for him. There is no need to comment on the expansive popular embellishment of the story—in novels, dramas, radio scripts and the like—nor to remind the reader of the voluminous flow of literary invention which has out-Herndoned Herndon in our own day. Evaluation of the evidence, which one seldom finds anywhere but which has been attempted in the preceding pages, is the only answer to the inquiry as to where the pedestrian course of history ends and the limitless soaring of fiction begins.

Chapter Four

THE HOUSE ON EIGHTH STREET

THE TANGLED STORY OF LINCOLN'S COURTING OF MARY TODD AND the years of their married life are themes that call for more than common historical caution. In much of the writing concerning these matters regard for Lincoln often coexists with gross unfairness toward his wife. To do simple justice to that wife, and by honest inquiry to restore a kind of balance in the use of what evidence we have concerning this American home, is the plainest duty of a biographer.

I

Mary's story began amid genteel and well favored surroundings. Aristocratic background, ambition, conversational skill, and a vivid interest in politics were attractively combined in the person of this Springfield belle. Coming of a socially prominent and distinguished family of Lexington, Kentucky, she lived in the fine mansion of her brother-in-law, Ninian Wirt Edwards, son of Governor Ninian Edwards. That she and Lincoln should become acquainted was inevitable; it belonged to the natural course of events that she should know men of

73

political prominence at the capital. Douglas also was of her circle, though emphasis on his seeking her hand has probably been overdone.

Study of the Lincoln-Todd courtship is rendered difficult by inadequacy of contemporary evidence and by the unreliable nature of the account by Herndon. Herndon's amazing recital reads as follows:

The time fixed for the marriage was the first day in January, 1841. Careful preparations for the happy occasion were made at the Edwards mansion. The house underwent the customary renovation; the furniture was properly arranged, the rooms neatly decorated, the supper prepared, and the guests invited. The latter assembled on the evening in question, and awaited in expectant pleasure the interesting ceremony of marriage. The bride, bedecked in veil and silken gown, and nervously toying with the flowers in her hair, sat in the adjoining room. Nothing was lacking but the groom. For some strange reason he had been delayed. An hour passed, and the guests as well as the bride were becoming restless. But they were all doomed to disappointment. Another hour passed; messengers were sent out over town, and each returning with the same report, it became apparent that Lincoln, the principal in this little drama, had purposely failed to appear! The bride, in grief, disappeared to her room; the wedding supper was left untouched; the guests quietly and wonderingly withdrew; the lights in the Edwards mansion were blown out, and darkness settled over all for the night. What the feelings of a lady as sensitive, passionate, and proud as Miss Todd were we can only imagine—no one can ever describe them. By daybreak, after persistent search, Lincoln's friends found him. Restless, gloomy, miserable, desperate, he seemed an object of pity. His friends, Speed among the number, fearing a tragic termination, watched him closely in their rooms day and night. "Knives and razors, and every instrument that could be used for self-destruction were removed from his reach."

The necessary point of departure is to go to Herndon's source. In 1840–41 he was not yet associated with Lincoln in the practice of law, and was not of the Edwards circle. He makes no claim to have been present on the alleged occasion he glibly described, but got his material, or rather an inadequate cue, many years later from Mrs. Ninian W. Edwards, Mary Todd's sister, who seems to have made three statements on the subject in two interviews with Herndon and one with Weik. In her first statement her words as recorded in Herndon's handwriting were: "Lincoln & Mary were engaged—Every thing was ready & prepared for the marriage—even to the supper &c—. Mr. L. failed to meet his engagement—Cause insanity."

A number of years later, Mrs. Edwards made a second statement to Herndon, which also is available only in his handwriting. This time she referred to "the match" being "broken off," but said nothing of a non-appearing bridegroom on a wedding occasion. Her statement to Weik appears as follows in Weik's diary of December 20, 1883: "Called on N. W. Edwards and wife. Asked about marriage Mary Todd to Lincoln—Mrs. E. said arrangements for wedding made—even cakes baked but Lincoln failed to appear. At this point Mr. Edwards interrupted —cautioned wife she was talking to newspaper man—she declined to say more—had said Mary greatly mortified by Mr. Lincoln's strange conduct. Later were reunited—finally married."

There is also a vague record by Weik of recollections in later life by James H. Matheny, who, as Weik said, was one of Lincoln's "two best men." In this passage, which is poorly constructed as a historical treatment, it may be Weik rather than Matheny who states that the "marriage was originally set for a day in the winter of 1840–41, probably New Year's Day," but that Lincoln "failed to materialize at the appointed time."

Such is Herndon's statement and such his evidence. All of it comes through indirectly; none was even approximately contemporary. Many who must have known whether such an event had occurred seem not to have been sought out or questioned. Mrs. Edwards's account came no nearer to the picturing of an actual wedding party than the statement that "Every thing was ready & prepared for the marriage—even to the supper &c—," and the later statement (attributed to her by Weik) that "arrangements for wedding [were] made—even cakes baked but Lincoln failed to appear." Her story stops short of Herndon's narrative in that she makes no mention of invitations issued, of guests assembled, of the bride "bedecked," of her grief, of the untouched wedding supper, of messengers sent out over town, of the guests' wondering departure after hours of waiting. These details are made up; they are fictional embellishments supplied for the Herndon-Weik biography.

It is obvious that Herndon did not assemble all the material he might easily have found, nor did he rightly use the material he had. In his papers there is a record of a statement by Ninian W. Edwards commenting on Lincoln's courtship with Mary Todd and telling how Lincoln loved Matilda Edwards (of which, however, the alleged lover gave no hint directly or indirectly!), how the engagement with Miss Todd was broken in consequence, and how Mary released Lincoln, who "went crazy as a *loon*." In this statement, however, there was a significant omission; there was no mention, not even the faintest suggestion, of a wedding occasion and an absent groom. Herndon also had a statement by Lincoln's friend James H. Matheny representing Lincoln as being greatly distressed at being "driven into the marriage" with Miss Todd, but giving no hint of his absence at the time of a planned wedding, this in spite of the fact that Matheny was the man described by Weik as one of Lincoln's "two best men."

II

With so much pen swinging on so thin a basis, no competent historian will accept as authentic the Herndon-Weik story of the wedding party and the defaulting groom. Weik's passage on his conversation with Matheny is vague as to what Matheny actually said. Mrs. Edward's testimony, aside from the fact that it only partially upholds Herndon's narrative, is insufficient; it exists in a kind of vacuum; it stands unsupported in the complete absence of contemporary proof. Mr. Angle has pointed out that recollections of the matter involve flat contradictions of Herndon's statements, and that no marriage license was issued, "which would hardly have been the case had he [Lincoln] changed his mind at the last moment."

Some might make light of the failure to take out a marriage license, or construe it as consistent with Lincoln's default. Yet the tale of that default, in conjunction with the known lack of a license, suggests a most excessive degree either of deception or of mental derangement. To suppose that a wedding was planned with Lincoln not fully intending to go through with it, to assume that that is why he took out no license, and to believe that he nevertheless permitted wedding plans to go forward to the assembling of guests on the appointed night as Herndon asserts, is to put a severe strain on the reader's credulity, a strain which becomes disbelief in the lack of substantiating evidence.

The fact that no license was issued, as shown by the records of Sangamon County, does not in itself refute the wedding-default story, but it harmonizes with the complete absence of any known facts whatever as of 1840–41 tending to suggest that a wedding was arranged. This, however, is not all; the matter has importance in another sense, for it happens that in one of

Herndon's effusive literary flourishes—a kind of rough draft for this portion of his biography—we have the following: "The time came on for Mr Lincoln & Miss Todd to be married. The license for their marriage was issued by the Clerk of the County Court. . . . The hour was set—the room where the ceremony of marriage was to be performed was . . . richly and gorgeously draped. . . . The cultured—the wealthy—the brilliant were there, merry and happy. . . . Parson Dresser had, as supposed the license in his hands— The brides maid and the groomsman were dressed and anxious to perform their part. . . . [etc.]" The chief point of this whole business is that Herndon was drawing on his imagination, depending on no source for his details, yet supplying those details with fabricated minuteness. This particular mention of the issuing of the license was not given in his book; we are dealing here with an earlier draft; but so far as the wedding default is concerned the passage was of a piece with his published biography; this detail was dropped, but others, equally the product of invention, were kept. Herndon, lawyer that he was, made this statement concerning a non-existent license "issued by the Clerk of the County Court," in precisely the same sense in which he invented other aspects of the alleged scene. The falsity of his statement as to the license is of significance in judging his credibility.

Persons close to the Edwardses and to Lincoln had no recollection to support Herndon's narrative. Mrs. Elizabeth J. Grimsley, cousin of Mary Lincoln, remembered only an interruption in the courtship due to Lincoln's depression; Mrs. John Todd Stuart had "never heard" of the alleged absent groom till Herndon brought out his book; Mrs. Joshua F. Speed likewise had "never heard" of it; Mrs. B. S. Edwards, sister-in-law of Ninian W. Edwards, declared it a "fabrication." Mary's surviving sisters emphatically denied it. One of these sisters, Mrs. William Wallace of Springfield, née Frances Todd, said: ". . . he did not break off one wedding," adding that she "would have known of it" if such an incident had occurred. One should note also the

L. C. Handy Studios

LINCOLN'S FULL FIGURE

L. C. Handy studios state that this is a copy of an old original print discovered about 1931 in the effects of the sculptor, Henry Kirke Brown, who made a statue of Lincoln in Union Square, New York. Photographer not identified. Made probably in 1860.

statement by Mary Todd's niece, Katherine Helm: ". . . Emilie Todd (Mrs. Ben Hardin Helm), Mary Todd's sister, who at this writing [1928] is living and possessed of all her faculties, declares Herndon's story to be absolutely false. . . ."

Then there is the question of Lincoln's presence in the Illinois legislature in this unhappy period. Though his attendance during January 1841 has been referred to as showing "negligence," he was present at least for a time on nineteen of the twenty-six days when sessions were held that month. Such presence, including a number of votes, does not bear out the theory of "insanity." His record in these weeks falls short of his habitual punctuality, but his illness in this month would account for nearly all his absence, which has been greatly exaggerated and misrepresented. On the day known as "the fatal first of January, 1841," he was recorded present. On this point again, we have an instance of the unreliability of Herndon; he stated that "Lincoln did not attend it [the legislature] for some weeks"; this is a flat misstatement.

An excellent basis for doubting that a wedding had been planned as Herndon states is that Mary Todd made no mention of it in a letter she wrote in mid-December of 1840 to her close friend Mercy Levering, later Mrs. James C. Conkling. In this letter Mary gave details of what went on in her own affairs and in the Edwards circle, mentioned Lincoln and Speed, chatted of matrimony in general, and gave reports of newly married friends in particular. She had not written to "Merce" for a considerable time and was giving news from "the hill," by which she meant the Edwards home. Her letter is nicely phrased. It is spicy and refreshingly natural. Miss Todd had an air in such things.

III

From the man who has been called Lincoln's most intimate friend, Joshua Fry Speed, we have another account of the troubled courtship which Herndon misused. Since history is a matter of evidence, and evidence a matter of statements by those who knew, the quality of Herndon's history at this point is best revealed by first giving the Speed statement and then noting how Herndon twisted it. We have Speed's statement in the Herndon-Weik manuscripts. It is undated; it is in Herndon's handwriting, not Speed's; it obviously belongs to the period after 1865 in which Herndon was collecting his material; it has all the appearance of being Herndon's record of an interview with Lincoln's friend; it is a hasty job, less legible than Herndon's usual hand; it is disjointed and hard to make out. It reads as follows:

In 1840 Lincoln went into the southern part [?] of the state as election canvasser debater speaker—Here first wrote his *Mary*—she darted after him—wrote him—Lincoln—seeing an other girl—& finding he did not love his wife [*sic*] wrote a letter saying he did not love her—.

[Here the manuscript has the following insertion:] Speed saw the letter to "Mary" written by Mr Lincoln. Speed tried to persuade Lincoln to burn it up. Lincoln said—"Speed I always knew you were an obstinate man. If you won't deliver it I will get some one to do it. I shall not deliver it nor give it to you to be delivered: Words are forgotten—misunderstood— . . . but once put your words in writing and they stand as a living & eternal monument against you. If you think you have *will* & manhood enough to go and see her and speak to her what you say in that letter, you may do that. Lincoln did go and see her—did tell her &c—Speed said—Lincoln tell me what you said and did"—Lincoln told him—Speed said—The last thing is a bad lick, but it cannot now be helped—Lincoln kept his promises and did not go to see her for months—they got together somehow.

[Here the insertion ends; the statement continues:]—tell the conversation—between Lincoln & Speed—Went to see "Mary"—told her that he did not love her—she rose and said "the deceiver shall be deceived wo is me"; alluding to a young man she fooled—Lincoln drew he[r] down on his knee—kissed her—& parted—he going one way & she an other—Lincoln did love Miss Edwards—"Mary" saw it—told Lincoln the reason of his change of mind—heart & soul—released him—[At this point there is a marginal insertion which reads as follows:] Lincoln went crazy—had to remove razors from his room—take away all knives and other such dangerous things—&c—it was terrible —was during the special session of the Ills Legislature in 1840 [End of marginal insertion.] Lincoln married her for honor— feeling his honor bound to her—

Turning now from Herndon's basis (his own account of the Speed interview) to the Herndon-Weik biography, we find a result both subtly and palpably different from the record. The biography has it as follows:

. . . One evening Lincoln came into our store and called for his warm friend Speed. . . . Lincoln, drawing from his pocket a letter, asked Speed to read it. "The letter," relates Speed, "was addressed to Mary Todd, and in it he made a plain statement of his feelings, telling her that he had thought the matter over calmly and with great deliberation, and now felt that he did not love her sufficiently to warrant her in marrying him. This letter he desired me to deliver. Upon my declining to do so he threatened to intrust it to some other person's hand. I reminded him that the moment he placed the letter in Miss

Todd's hand, she would have the advantage over him. 'Words are forgotten,' I said, 'misunderstood, unnoticed in a private conversation, but once put your words in writing and they stand a living and eternal monument against you.' Thereupon I threw the unfortunate letter in the fire. 'Now,' I continued, 'if you have the courage of manhood, go see Mary yourself; tell her, if you do not love her, the facts, and that you will not marry her. Be careful not to say too much, and then leave at your earliest opportunity.' Thus admonished, he buttoned his coat, and with a rather determined look started out to perform the serious duty for which I had just given him explicit directions."

. . . Speed was satisfied, from the length of Lincoln's stay, that his directions had not been followed.

"Well, old fellow, did you do as I told you and as you promised?" were Speed's first words.

"Yes, I did," responded Lincoln, thoughtfully, "and when I told Mary I did not love her, she burst into tears and almost springing from her chair and wringing her hands as if in agony, said something about the deceiver being himself deceived." Then he stopped.

"What else did you say?" inquired Speed, drawing the facts from him.

"To tell you the truth Speed, it was too much for me. I found the tears trickling down my own cheeks. I caught her in my arms and kissed her."

"And that's how you broke the engagement," sneered Speed. "You not only acted the fool, but your conduct was tantamount to a renewal of the engagement, and in decency you cannot back down now."

"Well," drawled Lincoln, "if I am in again, so be it. It's done, and I shall abide by it."

Immediately following this, Herndon gives the famous above-quoted narrative of the wedding party and the absent

Lincoln. The reader may compare the Speed statement with the account given in the Herndon biography. The Speed account presents a severed engagement, a painful scene in which Lincoln tried to break the troth only to find himself drawing Mary to him and kissing her, after which Mary, seeing his perplexity, "released" him. The biography, on the contrary, treats the incident not as a release but as a ratification of the engagement; only so could it have been used as setting for the story of the wedding default. The biography's comment that things "went on smoothly as before" is not justified by Speed's statement. Above all, Speed made no mention of Lincoln's wedding default. This is very significant; if such default had occurred Speed would certainly have known of it. He had a long correspondence with Lincoln on matters of the heart in this period, he was of the Edwards circle, and Lincoln made an extended visit to his home (Louisville, Kentucky) in 1841.

Mrs. Edwards also referred to Mary's release of Lincoln. Her words come to us thus: "The world had it that Mr L backed out and this placed Mary in a peculiar situation & to set herself right and to free Mr Lincoln's mind she wrote a letter to Mr L stating that she would release him from his engagements. . . . Mrs L told Mr L that though she had released him . . . yet she . . . would hold the question an open one—that is that she had not changed her mind, but felt as always." The date and sequence of this release as mentioned by Mrs. Edwards are a bit vague, so that a Herndonian might ask: Could not the release have been given after Lincoln had failed to appear at the wedding? This would sound better if there were any proof that such default ever occurred. In the absence of proof such a query suggests a debater begging the question; it implies assent to the thing which remains to be proved. Among other factors, Mary's lack of resentment, for which there is supporting evidence, is difficult to reconcile with the absent-groom story. The fancy touches which Herndon gratuitously added must be borne in mind in any discussion of the subject.

What, then, did happen in this troubled courtship? Taking all the evidence we have and sifting it carefully, one is led to the picture of a severed engagement—not a troth rudely broken, but an episode in which Lincoln's painful struggle with doubt and Mary's reluctant yet unresentful release were the main factors. The incomplete history of the case does not hold together without that release. Lincoln's deep and shattering depression, which may have approached the stage of collapse and prostration, is evident in his own letters of the period. Writing to John Todd Stuart, January 23, 1841, he referred to himself as "the most miserable man living," and in his letter to Speed on March 27, 1842, he used the expression "that fatal first of Jany. '41," which evidently referred to an acute crisis in the disturbed courtship.

A letter which Lincoln wrote on January 20, 1841, to John Todd Stuart concerning Dr. Anson G. Henry, his physician, also bears upon the matter. Lincoln said: "I have, within the last few days, been making a most discreditable exhibition of myself in the way of hypochondriaism[?]. . . ." He considered Henry "necessary" to his "existence," and sought Stuart's influence to have the physician appointed postmaster at Springfield; otherwise he would leave the city. Stuart was at that time congressman and Lincoln's law partner. Lincoln added that his heart was "verry much set" upon this appointment; he concluded as follows: "Pardon me for not writing more; I have not sufficient composure to write a long letter." All the evidence is that Lincoln's condition was that of severe mental distress with accompanying effects upon his health, that the interrupted courtship was the cause of it, and that he was making a conscious and deliberate effort toward restoration of normal life.

IV

The renewal of the engagement in 1842 was assisted by Mary's friend, Mrs. Simeon Francis, wife of a prominent Springfield editor, the reconciliation being related to Lincoln's generously taking the blame for a partisan newspaper skit which Mary and her friend Julia Jayne had perpetrated at the expense of a prominent Democratic politician, James Shields. Writing to Mrs. Gideon Welles in the year of Lincoln's death, Mary Todd Lincoln recalled the Lincoln-Shields incident, in which a duel was arranged and its consummation narrowly averted, and gave interesting details concerning her relation to Lincoln prior to their marriage. ". . . I committed his [Shields's] *follies*, to rhyme," she wrote, "and very silly verses they were, . . . offensive to the Genl." With her customary surplus of commas Mary proceeded: "A gentleman friend, carried them off, and . . . one day, I saw them, strangely enough, in the daily papers. Genl Shields called upon the Editor, and demanded the author. The Editor, requested *a day*, to reflect upon it. The latter called upon Mr Lincoln, to whom he knew I was engaged & explained to him, that he was certain, that I was the Author. Mr. L. then replied, Say to Shields, that 'I am responsible.['] Mr. L. thought no more of it, when about two weeks afterwards, . . . Shields . . . demanded satisfaction. . . ." There is here a reference to the planned duel and the reconciliation of the men. Mary added: "The occasion, was so silly, that my husband, was always so ashamed of it, that . . . we . . . agreed—never to speak of it. . . . This occurred, six months, before we were married. . . . We were engaged & greatly attached to each other—Two years before we were married." When the wedding came it was a quiet affair in the Edwards home. The date was November 4, 1842. It was a ring-and-book ceremony conducted by the Epis-

copal minister, Charles Dresser. On the ring which Lincoln gave
to Mary were inscribed the words: "Love is eternal."

V

Mr. and Mrs. Abraham Lincoln started their married life
at the Globe Tavern in Springfield where room and board could
be had for four dollars a week. Later they lived for a time in a
modest cottage; in 1844 they acquired their residence on Eighth
Street. It was a comfortable and dignified house, unpretentious
but not lacking in architectural taste. In 1856 it was enlarged
by the addition of an upper story.

The humble setting at the outset of their wedded life contrasted strongly with the spacious living to which Mary Todd
had been accustomed. The contrast was similar to that between
their early environments. Where she had memories of being
driven to Madame Mentelle's fashionable school by a liveried
coachman in the Todd carriage, his recollections were of lonely
trips through a pioneer's woods to fetch water to the cabin.
Beauty of clothes and furnishings, parties and entertainments,
pride of family and social prominence, were the things that
mattered to her; to the young man of backwoods origin these
things were never to matter much or penetrate deeply into his
consciousness.

"She is the very creature of excitement . . . and never
enjoys herself more than when in society and surrounded by a
company of merry friends" wrote a member of the social group
of Springfield in which Mary Todd had had a lively part. Her
early letters bear out this description; they are full of vivid
interest in people and affairs, with frequent italics to show her
intensity of feeling. They are lightened with playful humor as
when she refers to the two children of a widowed suitor of hers
as "his two *sweet little objections.*" The slow-tongued young

lawyer, by Mrs. Edwards's statement, hung upon her sparkling conversation as if fascinated.

Mary Lincoln had the virtues of her defects. Along with outbursts of temper and emotion there was enthusiasm for undertaking and achievement, interest in dress and fashion, contagious zest for the color of life. Her qualities were complementary to those of her husband. She was to be a stimulus to him, even if at times that stimulus was somewhat of an irritant. His friends unanimously testify to his sadness, his periods of absent thought when he saw nothing around him. To his reflective mind she added vivacity; to his indifferent abstraction she brought a wholesome preoccupation with the affairs of daily living. Dependence on each other was reciprocal; she needed his reasoned statements, his seeing both sides of a question where she saw only one—her own, his tolerance and patience; these needs were to grow as her congenital lack of self-control increased.

They had their congenialities. Both loved politics with absorbing interest; both were politically ambitious. His advancement was their mutual aim in life. Each had a sense of literary style. Emilie Todd Helm tells of Mary reading and reviewing books for her husband and of his great respect for her judgment. Both loved theatrical entertainment and never missed anything of the kind if they could help it. Both idolized their children. These things became welding influences.

In its Springfield phase the life of these contrasting personalities lasted more than eighteen years. In ten years Mary Lincoln bore four sons: Robert Todd Lincoln on August 1, 1843; Edward Baker Lincoln on March 10, 1846; William Wallace Lincoln on December 21, 1850; Thomas ("Tad") Lincoln on April 4, 1853. When elected to the presidency Lincoln had three sons, Edward having died in 1850.

Lincoln's doings have become more a matter of record than Mary's. For her, life was a strenuous round of childbearing, tending babies, feeding and clothing a household, sewing, struggling with servants, watching constantly to keep a suitable establishment, carrying on alone when her husband was away on the circuit—in short enduring the strains of any wife and mother. Lincoln, too, when in town, was busy with home tasks; a neighbor recalled that "he kept his own horse—fed & curried it—fed and milked his own cow: he sawed his own wood generally when at home."

These years saw some triumphs for Lincoln, some disappointments. Major episodes were his election to Congress in 1846, his defeat for the senate in 1855 and 1858, and the supreme climax of his nomination for the presidency and election to that office. The house on Eighth Street mirrored these events. It witnessed family reunions on the occasions of the master's return from circuit travel. The furniture—ornate iron stove, cut-glass prisms of the candlesticks on the mantel, lady's chair designed with due allowance for hoop skirts, heavy lace curtains, whatnot, hassocks, sofa, mirror, oval-framed pictures— each of these objects, satisfyingly Victorian and suitable, as *Leslie's* said, to "a gentleman in comfortable circumstances," had for the Lincolns its personal history and its family association.

VI

The question of the happiness or unhappiness of the Lincolns has been as controversial as the matter of the defaulting bridegroom. Herndon fixed the popular conception of this marriage as a tragically unhappy one, and of Mary Lincoln as an intolerable shrew. His descriptions of her stormy tongue and temper, her lack of self control, and her violence when in a rage are familiar not only in his own pages, but in countless authors who have followed him. The story which he tells of Lincoln's asking a man, who had been abused by Mrs. Lincoln, if he could not endure for a few minutes what he, Lincoln, had endured for fifteen years, alone would fix the whole concept of a miserable marriage in the reader's mind. In the uninhibited language of the Herndon manuscripts this story has much more detail and vividness than in the biography, and one can better judge the nature of the evidence. According to this account, Lincoln was reclining on the counter in "Edwards' store" telling one of his best stories, when the man—his name was Tiger—called him outside, told him of Mrs. Lincoln's abuse punctuated with blows of her broom, and demanded that her husband do something about it; Lincoln then sadly asked the above question. There is no evidence that Herndon was present on the occasion, but such a tale would quickly go the rounds among men who lingered in the store, then went home and told their wives.

Other incidents from the manuscripts may be mentioned briefly. A passerby and a neighbor witnessed Lincoln one day being pursued in his own backyard by "a little low squatty woman with a butcher knife in her hand." Noticing that other people were approaching, Lincoln unceremoniously carried his infuriated wife back into the house, rising to the occasion in action and language! Such is the story. Herndon claims not to have witnessed this incident of home life; he had it secondhand from a neighbor of the Lincolns named Whitehurst, whose account is given only through Herndon's memory; though he dated the occurrence about 1857, same period as the Tiger story, he wrote his version in 1886.

Again in 1857 (this must have been a bad year) Mary is alleged to have asked her abstracted husband three times to mend the fire; then, wrote Herndon, she "blazed away at Lincoln with a stick of stove wood"; when he appeared next day his nose was "fixed up with court plaster." This tale came from a servant girl; Herndon added: ". . . it is more probable that it is true than untrue. I believe it: it went around among the members of the bar as true."

There is no doubt that Mary Lincoln had an ungovernable temper. That she suffered in later life from temporary insanity is a matter of court record, but that was after life had dealt crushing and devastating blows. Dr. W. A. Evans, whose account is based on historical material medically interpreted, finds in her no breakdown of intellect, but rather a kind of excess, amounting at times to abnormality, in emotional reactions. Dr. Evans's account is by no means entirely unfavorable; he gives her "first suspiciously false note" as of January 1861 in the matter of purchases in New York. Mrs. Lincoln's physician, Thomas W. Dresser, son of the minister who married the Lincolns, also referred to her abnormality as belonging chiefly to the tragically clouded period of her later life. He wrote: "She was bright and sparkling in conversation. . . . Her face was animated and pleasing; and to me she was always an interesting woman; and while the whole world was finding fault with her . . . , it was clear to me that the trouble was a cerebral disease."

Mrs. Lincoln's personality must be reconstructed from incomplete sources, with constant allowance for unfriendly testimony. Even so, much of that record, to say the least, is creditable. Scattered incidents of bad temper, indirectly transmitted and interpreted by a roughhewn mind disposed toward an unfavorable judgment, do not constitute the whole story of the Lincoln marriage. Things that made for content and affectionate adjustment rarely found their way into the record, especially as gathered by Herndon. Friends did not set pen to paper in order to report the normal, everyday incidents of this home. It is remembered that she was quick tempered, caustic, and tactless of speech; touchy, proud, and willful. It is too often forgotten that she was endowed with natural kindness, that she bore herself with gaiety and grace, that there was sparkle in her face and speech, that she rose to the standards of a gentlewoman, that rearing and education fitted her for cultured society, and that she brought a full measure of affection and devotion to the countless unrecorded duties of wife and mother.

In a lengthy account of Mrs. Lincoln angrily dismissing her servant Sarah, Herndon said, after telling of the hiring of Sarah, "Everything went on well for sometime, Mrs L bragging on her Sarah all the while to her neighbors & visitors." Evidently there were intervals of tranquillity in the household. To Weik, his literary collaborator, he wrote: "Lincoln, you know, was not a social man, and hence those little *incidents* in his office and around his hearth which you want so much are hard to gather and to get, for they are few and far between." It is well to observe that "few and far between," to note that these stories were usually second hand, and to question how much Herndon knew at first hand about that hearth. He said, "This woman was to me a terror," "She was a tigress," and again "She hates me yet *I can* and *will do* her justice." Writing freely to Weik he filled pages with comments of which the following is an example: "This domestic *hell* of Lincoln's life is not all on one side"; ". . . sometimes he would rise and Cut up the very devil for a while—make thing[s] more lively and 'get.' "

To "do . . . justice" is not always the same as being just; to love the truth, which Herndon did in his way, is not synonymous with knowing and understanding it. Herndon's testimony is refracted by his own emotions and mentality. He disliked and feared Mary Lincoln, perhaps the more because of his love for her husband, whom he represented as the victim of her temper. With his frontier, earthy type of mind, he "was firmly convinced that truth could be got at by intuition, and he never doubted his own clairvoyant capacity."

To go further and explain in full the mutual dislike between Herndon and Mrs. Lincoln, and to give the documents, would require too much space. Her background was aristocratic, his quite the opposite. In attitudes, tastes, and standards they were miles apart. As a radical abolitionist and as a man whose drinking habits led to occasional sprees, he was not likely to be regarded by her as the most suitable partner for her husband. One can point to at least one friendly incident. When Herndon, in the earlier stages of assembling material for his biography, sought Mrs. Lincoln's help, she took the trouble in the period of her crushing bereavement to write him a gracious and cordial letter, promising an interview, referring to her husband's "truly affectionate regard" for his partner, and adding that those who idolized him were "very precious" to her and hers. By January of 1874, however, there had been a definite break between them, brought on by Herndon's lecture on Lincoln's religion, in December of 1873, in which he quoted her in a manner which she resented. She indignantly and flatly denied statements which Herndon attributed to her; Herndon published a spirited refutation of her denial; from then on their relation was that of open warfare. In interpreting Herndon's above quoted statements—calling her a "tigress" and noting how she hated him—it is not easy for the historian to know how much of this feeling harked back to the days when the Lincolns lived in Springfield and how much stemmed from the open break of 1873–74, but since this complete break occurred many years prior to the publication of Herndon's famous book, one must remember that when as a biographer he dealt with Lincoln's wife, Herndon was writing of a woman toward whom he had been for a number of years definitely unfriendly.

The statement of James Gourley, Lincoln's back-door neighbor for many years, as preserved in manuscript by Herndon, sums up the situation in the Lincoln household: "Lincoln & his wife got along tolerably well, unless Mrs L got the devil in her: Lincoln . . . would pick up one of his children & walked off—would laugh at her—pay no earthly attention to her when in that wild furious condition." His further comment is a bit of testimony that any human being might be content to hear: "Mrs & Mr Lincoln were good neighbors."

Mary's sisters, Mrs. Frances Wallace, who lived in Springfield, and Mrs. Emilie Todd Helm, who had ample association with the Lincolns on family visits, both made statements after the Herndon life had been published. Their reaction to Herndon's use of backdoor gossip can easily be understood. Mrs. Wallace said: "I don't see why people should say Mr. Lincoln's home life was not happy, for I certainly never saw a thing there that would make me think either of them was unhappy. He was devoted to his home, and Mrs. Lincoln thought everything of him. She almost worshiped him. . . . Why, she was devoted to him and to her children. And he was certainly all to her that any husband could have been."

"They understood each other thoroughly," wrote Mrs. Helm, "and Mr. Lincoln looked beyond the impulsive words and manner, and knew that his wife was devoted to him and to his interests. They lived in a quiet, unostentatious manner. She was very fond of reading, and interested herself greatly in her husband's political views and aspirations. She was fond of home, and made nearly all her own and her children's clothes. She was a cheerful woman, a delightful conversationalist, and well-informed on all the subjects of the day. The present writer saw Mr. and Mrs. Lincoln together for some part of every day for six months at one time, but saw nothing of the unhappiness which is so often referred to."

This testimony has been simmered over the gentle fire of family affection and loyalty, and the historian would prefer it raw, so to speak, but it is logical to use the evidence of those who were closest to the Lincoln family life.

In *Mary, Wife of Lincoln,* by Katherine Helm, Mrs. Helm's daughter, Mrs. Lincoln appears as a devoted wife who was proud of her husband, watched carefully over his health, saw that he was warmly or suitably dressed, had faith in him, and opposed her gay moods to his dark ones.

Life-like pictures flash out from Mrs. Helm's account as quoted by her daughter: Mary calling Mr. Lincoln back to wrap his throat in a muffler, patting his arm with a little air of coquetry, wearing her new dress of "white silk with blue brocaded flowers scattered over it." In the latter incident, Mr.

Lincoln had come home from his office to find her dressed in this creation of her own fashioning, and had been reminded he also must change his clothes to go to the Edwards's supper party. With a smile, he said, "Fine feathers enough on you to make fine birds of both of us," and added, "Those posies on your dress are the color of your eyes." Mary said to her sister "You see, Emilie, I am training my husband to see color. I do not think he knew pink from blue when I married him."

VII

Both Herndon and Mrs. Helm agree that the Lincolns idolized their children and spoiled them. Herndon gives several accounts of Lincoln's bringing one or more of the boys to the office on a Sunday morning while Mrs. Lincoln was at church. They pulled the books out of the shelves, scattered legal papers, spilled ink, smashed pens, and generally tore up the office. Herndon wrote: "I have felt many & many a time that I wanted to wring their little necks and yet out of respect for Lincoln I kept my mouth shut. Lincoln did not notice what his children was doing or had done."

The junior partner returns to the subject in another letter; again he "wanted to wring the necks of these brats and pitch them out of the windows." One wonders if Herndon went to the office on Sunday mornings to salvage what he could from the wreckage. Perhaps his silent endurance can be explained by this statement: "He [Lincoln] worshipped his children and *what* they worshipped[;] he loved what they loved and hated what they hated. . . ."

It was Herndon who preserved the familiar picture of Lincoln hauling his babies in a little wagon up and down the pavement in front of his house. A child would fall out, and lie squalling while the abstracted father pulled the wagon on, unaware of what was happening.

"It was the habit—custom of Mrs. Lincoln [wrote Herndon] when any big man or woman visited her house to dress up and trot out Bob—Willie or Tad and get them to monkey around—talk—dance—speek—quote poetry &c &c. Then she would become enthusiastic & eloquent over the children much to the annoyance of the visitor. . . ." Herndon adds that Lincoln would make some remark about the children being "rareripes" but quickly states that he was proud of his children and blind to their faults.

All the basic fulfillment of parenthood was in this marriage. Looking back, Mrs. Lincoln could write in later years, in one of her tender and loving letters to her daughter-in-law, that most mothers "consider that in the outset in life—a nice home —loving husband and precious child are the happiest stages of life." In another letter of affectionate reminiscence she expressed indignation at the suggestion that she had ever whipped a child. "In the first place," she wrote, "*they* never required it. A gentle, loving word, was all sufficient with them. . . ."

Old accounts of stores in Springfield bring the house on Eighth Street into near focus. They show Mrs. Lincoln busy with her needle; they suggest old-fashioned thoroughness in home dosing; they bring to mind in dry record the things that were worn, eaten, and used in this residence. Among the Lincoln purchases one reads of "5 yds. Drilling," "13½ yds. Muslin," "16 lbs. Batting," "10½ yds. French Chintz per Lady," "16 yds. Plaid Silk," "36 yds. Buff Linen," "Castor Oil," "Calomel," "Box Pills," "Bottle Vermifuge," "Syrup Ipecac," "1 pair Boys Boots by A. Lincoln," "1 pair Boys Boots per Lady," "2 doz. Whalebones," large purchases of wall paper, "1 pair White Gloves per Robert," "2 pair Heavy Drawers," "6 doz. Pearl Buttons," "1 paper Horse Powder," "8 lb. Turkey @ .10," "6 Doz. Eggs @ 8⅓," "1 Hooped Skirt per Lady," "2 Barlow Knives," "10 cords of Wood," and numerous entries of such items as candles, thread, sugar, coffee, blacking, buttons, and matches.

Hospitality in the Lincoln home was somewhat limited by circumstances, but O. H. Browning records on February 5, 1857, that he had attended a "large & pleasant party at Lincolns" that night. Writing to her sister Emilie on the sixteenth of the same month, Mrs. Lincoln tells of giving a party, presumably the one Browning mentions, to which five hundred people had been invited, though, owing to a rain and the counter attraction of a bridal party in Jacksonville, only three hundred came. Mrs. Lincoln's pride and satisfaction in this party are evident in her letter. Isaac N. Arnold spoke in nostalgic reminiscence of the dinners and evening parties at the Lincoln home, the excellence of Mrs. Lincoln's table, the "cordial and hearty Western welcome" of "both host and hostess," "her genial manners," and his "wit and humor, anecdote, and unrivalled conversation."

VIII

A direct source for the relationship between Abraham and Mary Lincoln is found in a series of four letters which they wrote each other in the spring and summer of 1848 while he was in Washington in Congress and she was visiting the Todd family in Lexington. Not written for publication, they are the unstudied messages between a husband and wife who had been married for more than five years; to examine them is to let the couple themselves come back and testify as to their marriage.

In the first of these missives he tells her that when she was with him he thought she hindered him somewhat from attending to business, but since she left and he had nothing but business it had grown "exceedingly tasteless" to him. He adds "I hate to stay in this old room by myself." He shares her delight over Eddie's treasured baby words, and tells of shopping for little plaid stockings for his young son. Mrs. Lincoln's inability to get along with people is hinted when he says "All the house—or rather, all with whom you were on decided good terms—send their love to you— The others say nothing—" The following paragraph was written by an affectionate and considerate husband: "And you are entirely free from head-ache? That is good—good—considering it is the first spring you have been free from it since we were acquainted— I am afraid you will get so well, and fat, and young, as to be wanting to marry again— Tell Louisa I want her to watch you a little for me— Get weighed and write me how much you weigh—" Daily happenings that she would be interested in complete the letter. He asks what Bobby and Eddie thought of "the little letters father sent them," and adds "Don't let the blessed fellows forget father—" He signs it "Most affectionately."

Her letter written two or more weeks later deals with family news and events with much tender detail about the children. There are hints of coquetry in her lines as there is indulgent fondness in his. She expresses her longing for him: "How much, I wish instead of writing, we were together this evening, I feel very sad away from you." She reassures him: "Do not fear the children, have forgotten you, I was only jesting. Even E— eyes brighten at the mention of your name."

His next letter hints at Mrs. Lincoln's shortcomings and reveals his own wish for their reunion: "The leading matter in your letter is your wish to return to this side of the Mountains. Will you be a *good girl* in all things, if I consent? Then come along, and that as *soon* as possible. Having got the idea in my head, I shall be impatient till I see you."

These are the normal letters of a husband and wife who were adjusted, loved each other, and had common aims and interests. He does not hesitate to remind her of the results of her lack of self-control—that was nothing new to either one— but in his light way of touching on such things he suggests his adjustment to them.

All in all, the house on Eighth Street sheltered a typical American family where father and mother were united by love of their children, common interests, ties of affection, and the pattern of daily family life. To the extent that her tempestuousness was abnormal, the marriage was rendered difficult, but the husband had accustomed himself to this imperfection as husbands—and wives—have been adjusting themselves to imperfections from the beginning. In the larger picture each gave to the other full fidelity and devotion. Mrs. Lincoln, writing to a friend in later life, could say, "It was always, music in my ears, both before & after our marriage, when my husband, told me that I was the only one, he had ever thought of, or cared for."

In the first year of her bitter widowhood, referring to the last three weeks of Lincoln's life, she wrote: "Down the Potomac, he was almost boyish in his mirth & reminded me, of his original nature, what I had always remembered of him, in our own home—free from care, surrounded by those he loved so well & by *whom*, he was so idolized."

It was the destiny of the Lincolns to live the latest years of their married life in the pitiless ordeal of war, personal sorrow, and fiercely ungenerous publicity. In an unfriendly White House these cruel forces were to beat upon an ailing woman in her forties whose lack of emotional balance unfitted her for the strain; in different manner they bore upon a harried President whose deepening sadness was a matter of general comment. It was well for them that their earlier years had not been without their meed of daily happiness.

Something of all that those years of married life had meant and a consciousness that a certain phase of life had closed, might well have been in Lincoln's mind when he came to speak the moving words of his farewell to Springfield on February 11, 1861. He referred to events of deep personal meaning, the birth of his children and the loss of little Eddie. His words suggest that other domestic joys and griefs were in the unexpressed mental picture of those years. His utterance seemed tinged with premonitory homesickness for something past which, in retrospect, he found good.

Chapter Five

RISE TO FAME

I

(THE YEAR 1854 IN LINCOLN'S LIFE HAD MARKED A RENEWAL OF political activity. After the close of his uneventful term in Congress in 1849 there had been a period of recession and passivity) in which it appeared that Abraham Lincoln's story was to be that of a fameless Illinois lawyer, but in 1854 the Kansas-Nebraska question was changing the face of parties and offering a challenge to new leadership. It was plain that (Lincoln's great opponent would be Stephen A. Douglas, with whom he had debated as long ago as the 1830's,) unless, as some feared and others hoped, Douglas would go over to the Republicans and become their leader.

(In October 1854 the State Fair was in progress at Springfield, and the "gathering, devoted primarily to the interests of the farmer, became a rendezvous for state politicians," causing resentment as members of the Agricultural Society saw political leaders distracting the people's attention from their "Annual Jubilee and School of Life." This tendency of politicians to invade other than political domains was both a sign of the times and an American trait. It was a field day for political agitation, and both Lincoln and Douglas spoke at length before audiences in the hall of the House of Representatives. Two weeks later at Peoria they met again, each making an extended address. Repeating the Springfield speech of October 4, Lincoln was in his best campaigning form as he urged his countrymen to purify the republican robe, to wash it white, to readopt the Declaration of Independence, to turn slavery "back upon its existing legal rights," to save the Union, and in doing so to "make and to keep it forever worthy of the saving.")This he urged in terms of "Fellow-countrymen, Americans, South as well as North," joining in "the great and good work."

Between those October debates of 1854 and the great debate of 1858 Lincoln had continued his political activity, though busy with law practice, had been drawn somewhat tardily into the Republican party, had received 110 votes as vice-presidential nominee in 1856, and in that year had spoken many times for Frémont, whom he disliked. Then on June 16, 1858, the Republican state convention at Springfield gave him its highest honor next to endorsement for the presidency by nominating him for United States senator. Having been the leading Whig of Illinois while yet in his thirties, he was now its leading Republican.

On the occasion of this nomination Lincoln delivered a carefully prepared speech which was not only to become one of his most famous; it was also to require frequent explanation and interpretation. "If we could first know *where* we are," he said, "and *whither* we are tending, we could then . . . better judge *what* to do, and *how* to do it." Then he proceeded:

We are now far into the *fifth* year, since a policy was initiated, with the *avowed* object . . . of putting an end to slavery agitation.

Under . . . that policy, that agitation has not only, *not ceased*, but has *constantly augmented*.

In *my* opinion, it *will* not cease, until a *crisis* shall have been reached, and passed—

"A house divided against itself cannot stand."

I believe this government cannot endure; permanently half *slave* and half *free*.

I do not expect the Union to be *dissolved*—I dot [sic] expect the house to *fall*—but I *do* expect it will cease to be divided.

It will become *all* one thing, or *all* the other.

Either the opponents of slavery, will arrest the further spread of it, and place it where the public mind shall rest in the belief that it is in course of ultimate extinction; or its *advocates* will puch [sic] it forward, till it shall become alike lawful in *all* the States, *old* as well as *new*—*North* as well as *South*.

Warming to his argument, Lincoln denounced what he called Douglas's "care not" policy regarding slavery, declared that slavery was being extended by putting "this and that together," observed that "another nice little niche" remained to be filled by a decision of the Supreme Court denying a state the power to exclude slavery, thus making slavery "alike lawful in all the States," and predicted the day when the people would "awake to the reality . . . that the Supreme Court has made Illinois a slave State," unless what he called the "present political dynasty" should be overthrown. Then he took care to destroy the argument that Republicans should turn to Douglas as their leader, conceding that Douglas was "a great man," but adding, in a rather ill chosen phrase, that " 'a living dog is better than a dead lion.' " He ended with the plea that if the Republicans should stand firm when their enemy was faltering, they would surely have the victory.

From the standpoint of correct representation of what was happening at the time, the speech was susceptible of criticism in at least two respects: (1) It implied a conspiracy or understanding between Douglas, Taney, Pierce, and Buchanan which (in the sense of a deliberate plot or agreement among these men) was quite fanciful and nonexistent. (2) It assailed Douglas and his popular sovereignty as if in Douglas's mind the policy had never been intended otherwise than as promoting the proslavery cause in the territories. The battle royal that Douglas was waging with the Buchanan administration on that very point, ought to have been sufficient refutation of such a charge.

There were yet other points open to question in this house-divided speech. Just what did Lincoln mean when he said that the Union would become all one or all the other? What Lincoln was in fact trying to do in this whole period was to put the damper on sectional conflict. Over and again that position was clearly stated. Yet people who knew nothing of that, or chose to ignore it, would quote this phrase and picture Lincoln as a man who would either insist on uniformity as to slavery or else divide the country—a man who would perhaps assent to disunion as many abolitionists were quite willing to do. Lincoln did not mean it that way. He thought of a peacefully continuing Union, as his very words in the whole passage implied; in this continuing Union he seemed to envisage a future day when uniformity as to slavery would exist, but he was not demanding disunion while it should not exist. Yet it was not the whole speech, nor even the connected passage, that was quoted; rather, it was only those few challenging words that kept recurring when Lincoln was mentioned. The fact that Lincoln was no firebrand and that he did not intend disunion nor any attack upon legitimate Southern rights, would be overlooked, especially by his opponents who would make it appear that he would oppose any type of Union-saving compromise.

At the time the speech went well. It added to Lincoln's fame, caused him to be in wide demand, and served as an opening salvo in the coming party contest in Illinois. It gave Lincoln's party an issue not only against Democrats generally but against Douglas at a time when otherwise men were thinking of the close similarity of Douglas to those Democrats who, like Trumbull, were now shifting to the new Republican party and being received with ready endorsement. One thing Lincoln could not endure was to have it thought that Douglas was Republican timber. Lincoln was concerned not only with promoting his party but with exerting large leadership within the party.

II

The coming legislature of Illinois would have the constitutional function of choosing a senator of the United States, and the extralegal obligation (or practical necessity) of restricting its choice to the two recognized party candidates. It looked like a close matter, and Lincoln was pushing hard. He was determined to follow on Douglas's trail, address audiences in the same places, and give a resounding reply to every one of his opponent's pronouncements. He was preparing carefully, assembling material, keeping a political notebook, writing letters, courting his friends in and out of the state, and watching the matter of alignment with the right groups. He would have pursued Douglas in any case had there been no special series of seven formal "joint debates." When Douglas's speaking engagements were announced, and when the Democratic senator was shifting emphasis away from Lincoln by assailing Trumbull, Lincoln seized the initiative, using Norman B. Judd of Chicago as intermediary, and formally challenged Douglas "to divide time, and address the same audiences the present canvass." In a personal interview at Bement, Illinois, the agreement between the two senatorial candidates was duly sealed, and from then on the joint debates were the subject of main interest in the prairie state.

Considering that there were only seven such joint debates,

the sizable state of Illinois was pretty well canvassed. The selection of places went by congressional districts, the Chicago area having already been the scene of a lively encounter between the candidates (July 9–10, 1858, at the Tremont House). The first two debates were in northern Illinois, at Ottawa on August 21 and Freeport August 27. Far down in "Egypt" the third debate was held at the picturesque Southern-like town of Jonesboro on September 15. The midway point was reached at Charleston in eastern Illinois on September 18. This was near the Thomas Lincoln home, in a region "prolific in Republicans." Then in October the contest would draw to its close with debates at Galesburg on the seventh, at Quincy on the thirteenth, and lastly at Alton on the fifteenth. Election day, a time of excitement and some disorder, was to come on Tuesday, November 2.

People of the time thought of it as a "momentous" encounter. Writing of the canvass while it proceeded, men noted that it was something new, that both men were material from which Presidents might be made, and that Illinois was "the battleground of the year." A vigorous, some said "desperate," fight was expected.

Stump speaking was a powerful magnet in the Middle West, and huge crowds poured out. It is amusing to read the estimates of these crowds, varying according to partisan claims of the papers in which they appeared. A Chicago crowd amounted to thirty thousand by one account, twelve thousand by another. An open-air crowd at Charleston, drawn from adjacent counties in a strictly rural district, was estimated at from "twelve to fifteen thousand." The canvass was more than a contest; it was a spectacle and a show, replete with all the devices and claptrap of rough-and-ready campaigning. It was clamorous and colorful, with bands, bells, artillery salvos, fluttering banners, fireworks, torchlight processions, placards, rockets, floats, decorations, shouts and cheers, boys hired for the congenial task of making a racket, and at Charleston a gayly bedecked wagon carrying thirty-two "pretty and intelligent ladies" representing the thirty-two states in the Union. It was noted with pride that a Lincoln procession from Mattoon to Charleston was headed by the "Bowling Green Band" from Terre Haute.

Speeches were long, but attention was good despite the difficulties of open-air acoustics and the discomfort of crowding masses. Rivalry was keen. Each side was eager to have the largest flag, the longest parade, the best and loudest music. The debates were stenographically—or, as they said, "phonographically"—reported, but each journalist colored his descriptions by his obvious preference for Douglas or for Lincoln. The wordy discourses were not all reason and light. There was twitting and banter, maneuvering for party advantage, and the shaping of appeals for local effect. Emphasis was upon the position that each party and each champion took on the "vexed question" of slavery in the territories. Lincoln made more effort to confine the discussion there than Douglas, who sought to broaden the controversy to cover the disruptive issue of social and political equality between the races and to associate Lincoln and the Republicans with all the stigmas that attached to abolitionists, whose popularity in large parts of Illinois was at zero level. Douglas was effective in ridiculing Lincoln's party, scoring its lack of a consistent name: up north they were Republicans or Abolitionists; at Springfield they avoided the name Republican, but referred to their meeting as "a Convention of all men opposed to the Democratic part"; in lower Egypt they advertised a "meeting of the Free Democracy" whereat Trumbull would speak. "Did you ever hear," said Douglas, "of this new party, called the 'Free Democracy'?" "What object have these Black Republicans in changing their name in every county? . . . They have one name in the north, another in the center, and another in the south."

On the practical question as to how slavery could be excluded from a territory if the people so desired, being pinned down on this point by Lincoln's famous question at Freeport, Douglas "emphatically" answered that it could be done by "local police regulations." Sensing at once that his assertion conflicted with the Dred Scott decision, he added that the people of a territory would have "the right . . . to make a Slave Territory or a Free Territory . . . under the Nebraska bill" despite the attitude of the Supreme Court on the "abstract question." If it be said that this involved a certain disregard of the Olympian finality and sanctity of the Court, an equal objection to the Court's infallibility was evident on Lincoln's side, such objection being counted a virtue. Douglas rode hard on Lincoln's house-divided declaration, declared that the "Black Republican" party had been abolitionized, and sought to make it appear that Lincoln and his partisans favored Negro equality.

On two points Douglas spoke with particular scorn and bitterness. (1) He resented the use of the ax against him by the Buchanan administration because he refused to allow his popular sovereignty to be distorted into a proslavery maneuver as at Lecompton. (2) He was equally indignant at the alliance of Illinois Republicans with Buchanan Democrats, both groups assailing him for agreeing with Lincoln in the Lecompton matter.

For each state its own laws, for each territory its own popular decision, was Douglas's principle. For the country, union and tolerance, defeat of the one party he deemed purely sectional, return to early principles. He would have each state allow or disallow slavery as it should choose; he also thought that each state should choose whether to give or deny the vote to Negroes. In the peroration of his first speech opening the joint debates, he grew eloquent on the theme of a nation that had grown great, had crossed the Alleghenies, and had turned "the prairie into a garden" on the principles of the "fathers" who "intended that our institutions should differ," knowing "that the North and the South . . . [had] different climates, productions, and interests." What he opposed was "trying to array all the Northern States in one body against the South, to excite a sectional war between the Free States and the Slave States, in order that the one or the other may be driven to the wall."

III

The amenities of debate were honored. There was some horseplay, but for the most part the etiquette though perhaps not altogether the purest ethics of forensic discussion was preserved. Verbal assaults were sharp and crushing, but unseemly personalities were usually avoided, and one witnessed the spectacle, as Douglas said, of a "large mass of people" made up of "various . . . parties" giving "kind and respectful attention" not only to friends, but to those with whom they disagreed. At Springfield in July 1858, according to the New York *Herald*, whenever either Lincoln or Douglas referred to the other, it was "in the kindest, most courteous and dignified manner." There was taunting, chaffing, and derision; yet it stopped short of offensive insult. Douglas held Lincoln up as a man who kept a "grocery"—i.e., who sold liquor—which Lincoln denied, who had made a kind of bargain to dissolve both the Democratic and Whig parties in order to erect an abolitionist party under the name Republican, who proclaimed abolition doctrines, and who "had to be carried from the platform" at Ottawa because of embarrassment at Douglas's questions. When Lincoln stated that he would be sorry to have to vote on the admission of another slave state, Douglas said: "I trust the people of Illinois will not put him in a position [as senator] which he would be so sorry to occupy."

Lincoln's manner toward Douglas was usually respectful and free from personal ill-feeling. Sometimes his banter took the form of ironic compliment, as when he blandly commended his opponent for "gradually improving"—i.e., becoming more severe against the Buchanan administration. For this Lincoln claimed credit, flattering himself that Douglas had taken his advice. Lincoln, as he himself said, had used no "vulgarity or blackguardism." Some months after the debates he was careful to point out that he felt "no unkindness . . . toward Judge Douglas." As for Douglas, his attitude was indicated by a Cincinnati newspaper in which it was noted that while he was "able and bold," his relations with Lincoln were "friendly."

In argument Lincoln drove in his strokes wherever he sensed a weakness in Douglas's position or an embarrassment because of matters for which, if all the truth were told, Douglas was not to blame. He severely scored Douglas's indifference as to slavery and riddled his popular sovereignty creed as either proslavery or unjustifiably noncommittal on a moral issue. He twitted Douglas for his inconsistency in once favoring the Missouri compromise and later opposing it. On the Dred Scott decision Lincoln's position in debate was a bit like having it both ways: the decision was riddled, yet Douglas was rapped for taking a position not in accord with it. Asserting that in former years there had never been a man who said that the Declaration of Independence did not include Negroes in the term "all men," Lincoln said that Taney was the first man who said it and next to him was Douglas.

Not allowing Douglas an interpretation that would preserve his favorite doctrine, Lincoln showed popular sovereignty to be inconsistent with the Supreme Court's decision. Here he was on firmer ground. Douglas, of course, could not be blamed for the inconsistency. He believed in a doctrine which the Court had pretty well demolished. He was in a dilemma; it was not of his making, but it gave him no end of embarrassment. Lincoln was not the man to let him off or avoid making him squirm; this particular inconsistency was one of Lincoln's most telling points. The great difference was that it cost Lincoln nothing, and gained him much, to denounce the Court, since

the winning of Southern support was not a prime object of the
Republican party. Douglas had to consider all parts of the
country. It would be fatal for him to offend the South. Rights
all around, thought Douglas, were protected by what he called
popular sovereignty. It injured no one.

Lincoln too had his embarrassment which Douglas did not
hesitate to exploit. It was the stigma of abolitionism. He repudiated it with spirit, asserting at Alton that Douglas was
trying to place him "in an extremely Abolition attitude" before
an audience which had "strong sympathies southward." On
various occasions Lincoln explained his house-divided declaration. He went so far as to say (in the month before the first
joint debate) that in his half-slave-half-free speech he did not
say he "was in favor of anything"; he was making "a prediction
only—it may have been a foolish one, perhaps."

Was Lincoln regretting his famous slogan? Only to the
extent that it was being used to make him appear as an abolitionist or a promoter of strife and war. In explaining it he
brought out what he insisted was the "real issue" of the whole
contest: that slavery was wrong, that peace and harmony in
the country prior to 1854 had been based on the belief that it
was "in course of ultimate extinction," that these were the
sentiments of the fathers, and that he intended only to resist
the "farther spread" of the institution, and to "place it where
the founders . . . originally placed it." This sentiment he repeated, with renewed declarations against slavery as a wrong,
many times. He did not hedge on his house-divided declaration
in the sense in which he said it should be interpreted, but he
did resent Douglas's effort to make it appear that he was
stirring up sectional strife. He agreed that diversity of institutions according to state choice was desirable; "instead of being a
thing to 'divide the house' . . . [he said] they tend to sustain
it." But he insisted that the territories—future homes of free
men—be kept free, not only for the native born but for "Hans,
and Baptiste, and Patrick, and all other men from all the world."

In the upper view (during the campaign of 1860) Lincoln stands inside
he fence with Willie and Tad. Lower view shows Lincoln front parlor
ketched by special artist and published in *Leslie's Illustrated Newspaper,*
March 9, 1861.

Reducing the matter to the simplest terms, he said: "The real issue in this controversy . . . is the sentiment . . . of one class that looks upon the institution of slavery as a wrong, and of another class that does not look upon it as a wrong." His party, he said, looked upon it "as being a moral, social, and political wrong."

IV

Lincoln's electioneering in 1858 was not confined to the formal joint debates. Indeed, if one thinks of what was doing in Illinois in the summer and fall of 1858 rather than of particular things singled out for historical emphasis, the famous seven debates were a minor fraction of the whole story. The period of July to October 1858 was a time of intense activity. He traveled almost constantly. Cheering crowds met him, escorted him through the streets, greeted him with banners and brass bands, and everywhere insisted on hearing him speak. He did not disappoint them. Besides the seven formal debates he spoke in this period at Clinton, Beardstown, Havana, Bath, Peoria, Henry, Augusta, Amboy, Carlinville, Bloomington, Edwardsville, Greenville, Danville, Urbana, Pekin, Oquawka, Monmouth, Lincoln, Mount Sterling, Carthage, La Harpe, Macomb, Petersburg, and many other places. At the last-named town, so close to the familiar New Salem haunts, Lincoln's address before "a large and enthusiastic assembly" was referred to as his sixty-second speech of the 1858 campaign. During all this time, in addition to the joint debates and numerous minor speeches, he conferred with party workers, struggled with his correspondence, took a hand in the party affairs of this or that district, arranged to have thousands of his speeches printed (not omitting German-language copies), and managed to attend several local Republican conventions as at Tremont on August 30.

The adventures of Lincoln in this senatorial campaign included dining with Douglas, riding a river packet to be met at
the wharf by cheering adherents, witnessing a balloon ascen-
sion, attending barbecues, celebrating with German Turners
and parading firemen, sitting at Macomb for the famous ambrotype, being carried on the shoulders of admirers, meeting
men of his company in the Black Hawk War who greeted him
on the platform of one of the towns, and recalling at the same
town (Bath) that as a surveyor he had staked it out of a
"wooden wilderness." At one place he rode in a Conestoga
wagon drawn by six white horses. A "constant stream of old
friends" met him at Hillsboro. At Sullivan his supporters interrupted Douglas and a "brawl" was "narrowly averted." The
weather was cruelly hot, and at Winchester it was remarked
that "His horses were white with sweat and he and his friends
were black with dust." Crowds were huge; much of the speaking was in the open air; and a typical speech would last for
two hours. Add these labors to the weary journeyings and one
can believe that there was truth in the opposition report that
he looked "jaded."

This vigorous popular campaigning meant a strenuous
effort for Lincoln, but it was an American show, an exciting
recreation for many thousands, a series of reunions with friends,
and a genuine demonstration of Lincoln's popularity in Illinois.
His arduous trips, his readiness to meet everyone, the homely
incidents of his wide ranging itinerary—all the informal and
spontaneous aspects of his electioneering—meant as much as
his many long hours of speaking. People expected all this. They
seldom thought of sparing him. To Lincoln it all came naturally; this was one of the sources of his strength. Few political
leaders have known the people by way of wide travel and close
personal association as did Lincoln. Some would make it appear that in 1858 Lincoln was after bigger stakes, that he was
in reality campaigning for the presidency. For this supposition

there seems to be no adequate basis so far as Lincoln's 1858 intentions were concerned. Nevertheless, the many popular incidents and associations of the canvass against Douglas, as well as the content of his speeches in that campaign with the publicity they received in the nation, were a significant part of his road to larger leadership.

On election day (November 2, 1858) Douglas was "triumphantly sustained" by the "invincible Democracy of Illinois." Yet the *Illinois State Journal* pointed out that a fair apportionment of legislative seats according to population would have given Lincoln's friends forty-one members in the lower house and fourteen in the upper (majorities), as compared with the actual result, by which in the lower house the membership was forty to thirty-five in Douglas's favor, while in the upper house Lincoln had only eleven senators, the Douglas and Buchanan elements having fourteen.

Lincoln felt his defeat keenly, but looked to the future, promised to "fight in the ranks," urged that the "fight must go on," and declared that the "cause of civil liberty must not be surrendered at the end of one or even one hundred defeats." He took comfort in the thought that the "popular vote of the state" was with him. The "plain old Democracy" was on his side; the "silk-stocking Whiggery," the "nice exclusive sort," was against him. He was glad he had made the race. It gave him "a hearing on the great and durable question of the age." Even though he should "now sink out of view, and . . . be forgotten," he had "made some marks . . . for the cause of civil liberty."

V

After the debates with Douglas it was remarked that Lincoln, like Byron, awoke and found himself famous. His office holding had been slight, his public career meager, yet he was now a political personage. Numerous invitations to speak had to be declined. He had reached a point where every word he said had to be carefully weighed for its effect both upon his own fortunes and upon those of his party. His correspondence with well known leaders of the Republican party showed how his counsel was being sought in other states than his own. Typical examples were his exchanges of letters in 1859 with Schuyler Colfax and Henry J. Raymond. To each of these it was as if he had said: do nothing that will rock the Republican boat. The prospects of the party were now an important concern, and for this reason he warned Colfax that local Republican groups ought to make no declaration that could not safely be generalized as the position of the whole party. We should "look beyond our noses," said Lincoln, and "say nothing on points where it is probable we shall disagree." Colfax's reply recognized the expediency, if also the difficulty, of this advice for a party made up of "men of all shades . . . of opinion."

In these matters Lincoln was definitely conservative. He still looked back to Jefferson as the source of right principles, the more so as he accused Jefferson's party of defection from the standard of their founder, but for his own party and his own time he wanted no radicalism, no abolitionist excess, no striking of the wrong note. "The chief and real purpose of the Republican party," he said in one of his 1859 speeches, "is eminently conservative." His was not, however, the reactionary type of conservatism. His praise of Jefferson, written in declining an invitation to attend a Jefferson's birthday celebration in Boston, was a reaffirmation of liberal faith in matters of fundamental right, and on one subject concerning which many politicians were timid, he spoke out boldly—the matter of prejudice against foreigners. It may be counted as one of the main evidences of Lincoln's liberal mind that in an era of what was called "Americanism"—an age rife with laws, movements, propaganda, and pressure politics directed against Catholics and immigrants from Europe—Lincoln stood out as one of the none-too-numerous leaders of his party who labored for tolerance among peoples.

Asked whether he favored the constitutional amendment recently adopted by Massachusetts to curb aliens and delay their acquisition of political rights, he answered clearly that he was opposed to it. To Theodore Canisius, German-American publisher at Springfield, he wrote: "Understanding the spirit of our institutions to aim at the elevation of men, I am opposed to whatever tends to degrade them. I have some little notoriety for commiserating the oppressed negro; and I should be strangely inconsistent if I could favor . . . curtailing the . . . rights of white men, even though born in different lands, and speaking different languages from myself." In May 1859 Lincoln purchased control of the German newspaper which Canisius was publishing, the *Illinois Staats-Anzeiger*. By the contract the types, etc., were to "belong to Abraham Lincoln"; Canisius was to have full use of them, and if he conducted the paper according to agreement "until after the Presidential election of 1860" the "said press, types &c" were to become Canisius's property. It was stipulated in the bond, however, that "said paper, in political sentiment, [was] not to depart from the . . . Republican platforms," nor "to print . . . anything . . . designed to injure the Republican party." It is clear that Lincoln was courting the German vote. This, however, was a matter of principle; he was not courting the nativist or intolerantly nationalist vote. He had the courage to repudiate those with whom he could not work because of principle. His policy was not that of the trimmer-politician who accepts all kinds of support, however diverse, and endeavors to repel no one.

In prominent speeches in 1859 at Columbus, Ohio, and Cincinnati, Lincoln carried forward the same type of political campaign as in the 1858 debate with Douglas. Indeed, these Ohio speeches were also a debate with Douglas who had previously spoken in the same cities. The emphasis of these speeches was that in yielding to Douglas's popular sovereignty one yielded everything to the slave interests. Considering the savage fight waged against Douglas by Southern ultras, this might seem like strange doctrine.

VI

When all was said it was realized that Lincoln did not have much of a record in public life and that few men had any concept of his life story. Jesse W. Fell of Bloomington, Illinois, thinking at an early date of Lincoln as presidential timber, was not troubled by the lack of a record. "What the Republican party wants [he thought], to insure success in 1860, is a man of popular origin, of acknowledged ability, committed against slavery aggressions, who has no record to defend and no radicalism . . . to repel votes. . . ." Fell did think, however, that more should be known of Lincoln's personal history, so at his request Lincoln prepared a very brief autobiography, submitting it to Fell on December 20, 1859, with the comment: "There is not much of it, for the reason, I suppose, that there is not much of me." Fell took Lincoln's tiny self-sketch, made some additions, and sent them to Joseph J. Lewis of Westchester, Pennsylvania. Thus there appeared in the *Chester County Times,* Westchester, Pennsylvania, February 11, 1860, what W. E. Barton has called the first published life of Abraham Lincoln. Lincoln's modest account covered less than six hundred words; the Westchester enlargement was more than six times as long. Some of the statements were definitely pointed toward a Pennsylvania constituency, as for example the passage recommending Lincoln as "a consistent and earnest tariff man." In his sketch Lincoln had not mentioned the tariff. Lewis stated, contrary to fact, that "Mr. Lincoln was among the first to join in the formation of the Republican party." In referring to the Lincoln-Douglas debates the Lewis article showed marked prejudice against Douglas, even berating him for supporting majority rule. The article had all the earmarks of a campaign biography, though belonging to the period of the prenomination canvass. It had a wide circulation "not only in Pennsylvania but in Illinois and throughout the country." The Chicago press reproduced it "almost entire, in response to the inquiry, then become general, 'Who is Abraham Lincoln?'"

VII

As a continuance of his campaign of political speech making, but in a larger arena, Lincoln traveled to New York in February 1860 where, at the Cooper Institute, on the evening of the 27th he delivered one of his most significant speeches. There had been an earlier effort to have him speak in lyceum fashion at Plymouth Church, Brooklyn; after further consultation the place was shifted to New York, the purpose was changed to that of politics, and sponsorship of the address was assumed by the "Young Men's Central Republican Union of New York City," an organization which included such youths as William Cullen Bryant, aged sixty-five, and Horace Greeley, aged forty-nine. At the Cooper Institute Lincoln spoke as the contender against Douglas (the rising Democratic presidential possibility), and, in the immediate scene, as challenger against Seward. With Bryant presiding and Greeley present it was clearly an anti-Seward sponsorship under which he appeared. Greeley's *Tribune* gave special emphasis to the speech. It was almost as if it were the *Tribune's* party.

Lincoln's theme was a formulation of the principles on which the Republican party should face the electorate in 1860; but instead of attempting a full coverage of issues he spoke only of the slavery question. Federal slavery restriction, he urged, was consistent with the doctrines of the fathers. All that Republicans asked was to leave slavery where the fathers left it, as an evil to be tolerated but not extended.

His party, he urged, was not sectional. It would do no wrong to the South; it would deny the South no essential right. It was conservative, not revolutionary. It would stick to ways that were old and tried. It was the South, he said, that wanted a change, wishing to reject the old policy, though disagreeing among themselves as to any substitute. The John Brown raid, he insisted, was not of Republican instigation, nor was it traceable to Republican activity. Accusations to that effect were a slander. "Republican doctrines and declarations," he said, "are accompanied with a continual protest against any interference whatever with your slaves, or with you about your slaves. Surely, this does not encourage them to revolt." The power of emancipation, Lincoln clearly recognized, was not in the Federal government. As for the "judgment and . . . feeling against slavery in this nation," that was a thing that could not be destroyed; it was therefore better to keep it in the peaceful channel of the ballot box; to do otherwise would hardly lessen the number of John Browns. The threat that Southerners would not abide the election of a Republican President, that they would break up the Union in that event, blaming the crime upon the Republicans, he compared to the case of a highwayman terrorizing his victim.

In such passages there was indignation and biting sarcasm in Lincoln's speech. In its main emphasis, however, it was conciliatory toward the South. He advised his party associates to yield to Southerners wherever possible, to "do nothing through passion and ill temper," to try to determine what their demands involved, and make every effort to "satisfy them." "Wrong as we think slavery is," he urged, "we can yet afford to let it alone where it is. . . ." He concluded: "Neither let us be slandered from our duty by false accusations against us, nor frightened from it by menaces of destruction to the government, nor of dungeons to ourselves. Let us have faith that right makes might, and in that faith let us to the end dare to do our duty as we understand it."

Other speeches by Lincoln in this general period were in the same vein. Though not mere repetition, they struck the same note, emphasizing that slavery was wrong, but hoping for a cure, together with an abatement of factional strife and controversy. Besides the speeches mentioned in Ohio in 1859 he had spoken in that year at various places in Illinois, Wisconsin, Iowa, and Kansas. Now in February-March 1860 he made a New England tour, speaking in Providence, Concord, Manchester, Dover, Exeter (where his son Robert was a student), Hartford, New Haven, Meriden, Woonsocket, Norwich, and Bridgeport. He arrived home in Springfield on March 14.

He was not merely a passive candidate, but was concerning himself actively with matters preliminary to the Republican national convention. Viewing his own chances for the presidential nomination at this stage, he reasoned that he was not the first choice of a great many, and that wise strategy was to give no offense, looking for second-choice support (for the presidency) if and when first choices should fail. That he was now eager for the prize, which he considered not hopeless, is shown by his offering to furnish one hundred dollars to a Kansas supporter, expecting him to serve as delegate.

VIII

Lincoln was fond of playing "fives" (handball) and it was the recollection of one of his neighbors—James Gourley—that he played the game on the day before his nomination, and "probably he played some on the morning—early." That he was playing "a game of ball" when the dispatch was handed

to him announcing his nomination has been emphatically denied by T. W. S. Kidd, court crier in Springfield. The detail is
unimportant except that in the personal feeling toward Lincoln
one looks always for the close-up view and the personal touch.
According to Kidd, he had been at the telegraph office awaiting
dispatches, enduring the suspense until the balloting began at
Chicago. Then he stepped into a store and was standing there
when yell after yell was heard and a messenger ran to him with
the news. People gathered quickly around him in great numbers, but, wanting to get out of the crowd, he remarked: "Well,
there is a little woman who will be interested in this
news . . . ," and started for home. Herndon, however, pictures him in a large arm chair in the office of the *Illinois State
Journal* when the news came; he records also the remark about
telling the little woman the news.

In attempting to study Lincoln at close range, especially
at climactic points in his life, one is impressed both with the
importance given to small details by neighbors and the frequency with which recollections are fragmentary or contradictory. In addition to Gourley and Kidd there were various
others who told of this exciting day in Springfield. We have
the narrative of Clinton L. Conkling who explained that while
the convention was in progress Lincoln remained in Springfield, going to his law office as usual, watching telegrams, and
joining "in a game of hand ball, . . . favorite pastime of the
professional men of the town." According to this account, Lincoln came into James C. Conkling's law office on the morning
of May 18 (the day of the nomination), stretched himself on a
settee, and chatted with James C., who had been in Chicago
and had returned to Springfield. After Lincoln had left the
office, according to this version, Clinton L. Conkling, having
learned the big news, met him "on the west side of the Square"
and was the first to tell him of his nomination, after which
the nominee was surrounded by excited crowds.

Gourley's reminiscence suggests the opposite of elation:

"he was agitated—turned pale—troubled." Directly after the nomination, said Gourley, he went home from the *Journal* office. If he hoped to retire to his own thoughts he was unsuccessful; at his house he was soon joined by friends in considerable number.

Next day, while the town of Springfield thrilled with demonstrations, music, fireworks, and festivity, the parlor in the house on Eighth Street became the scene of a restrained and solemn ceremony as the committee from the Chicago convention formally notified Lincoln of his nomination as President. Gustave Koerner, in describing the scene, mentioned that Lincoln "looked much moved, and rather sad, . . . feeling the heavy responsibility thrown upon him." Carl Schurz, member of the committee, wrote:

Mr. Lincoln received us in the parlor of his modest frame house. . . . There the Republican candidate for the Presidency stood, tall and ungainly in his black suit of . . . new but ill-fitting clothes, his long tawny neck emerging gauntly from his turn-down collar, his melancholy eyes sunken deep in his haggard face. Most of the . . . committee had never seen him before, and gazed at him with surprised curiosity. He . . . did not present the appearance of a statesman. . . . Standing up with folded hands, he quietly . . . listened to the dignified . . . speech . . . by Mr. Ashmun, the president of the Convention, and then he responded with a few appropriate . . . and well-shaped sentences. . . . Then followed some informal talk . . . in which the hearty simplicity of Lincoln's nature shone out, and . . . the committee took its leave.

Lincoln's response had been modest and brief, yet not colorless: he almost wished the "high honor" had fallen to another; he tendered "profoundest thanks"; he expressed himself as "painfully sensible of the great responsibility." By a literal reading it could almost be inferred that Lincoln was leaving open the question of his acceptance. He promised to read the platform and later to respond in writing "without . . . unnecessary . . . delay."

This he did formally, again very briefly, on May 23, accepting the nomination, endorsing the platform, imploring Divine assistance, hailing the Constitution, and striking the note of "perpetual union, harmony, and prosperity."

From among the millions of American citizens, delegates of a leading party had chosen one man. Upon him was now focused the hopes of party success, and beyond that the dread responsibility of chief magistracy. No longer for him the bustling county seat, the long rides on the circuit, the stir and challenge of western law practice. Abraham Lincoln was now candidate for President. He sat for his portrait to the photographer Alexander Hesler of Chicago. The camera caught him in perfect pose and expression; the Hesler profile is the finest of the Lincoln pictures. Without the beard, it has the sculptural ruggedness of the remarkable life mask by Leonard Volk. Lincoln now wrote out the basis for his campaign biography, producing an autobiography which was all fact and no flourish; yet for its priceless glimpses of early life, its accuracy, and its unstudied revelations of character, it remains, now as in 1860, an indispensable source for any Lincoln biographer.

Soon the campaign "lives" appeared—the first trickles of a vast torrent of Lincolniana. With almost incredible promptness these books fell from the press. Though priority in this field has been disputed, the "Wigwam Edition," published by Rudd and Carleton of New York, has been judged by a careful writer, Ernest J. Wessen, as the "first campaign life of Lincoln." Published on June 2, 1860, it was offered in paper wrappers at the price of twenty-five cents. The candidate's first name was spelled "Abram." No author's name appeared. The book was at once popular; 12,000 copies were sold within a week. Two days later came another paper-bound work by a journalist and popular writer, David V. G. Bartlett—price, twenty-five cents. Third place has been assigned to an anonymously written book brought out by Thayer and Eldridge of Boston and known to collectors by the publisher's name. It seems to have appeared about June 7, though "registered for copyright" on May 28, ten days after Lincoln's unforeseeable nomination. On June 11 there appeared a tiny 32mo volume edited and published by Reuben Vose of New York. Only a few pages were devoted to Lincoln's life; the rest consisted of Republican platforms (1856 and 1860), Lincoln's Cooper Union speech, and miscellaneous campaign material. The public was invited to apply to the publisher for other political publications, including, curiously enough, "5000 copies of the *Conservative*," which "contains the names of five hundred of the richest men in New York." Other biographies followed in quick succession.

Among the more substantial campaign biographies of 1860 was that by John L. Scripps, for whom Lincoln wrote the autobiography above mentioned. The Scripps book was closer to Lincoln and more truly a biography than any other of the campaign books. Yet none of the 1860 lives were particularly notable: they relied on "shears and pastebrush," they bore the quality of padding, hasty writing, and party propaganda. It would have been better if the people had been given the superb Hesler profile along with Lincoln's autobiography undiluted and unadorned.

Chapter Six

SPRINGFIELD TO
WASHINGTON

I

IN THE FRENZIED PERIOD BETWEEN HIS ELECTION AND HIS DEPAR-
ture for Washington Lincoln remained continuously at Springfield except for brief visits to Chicago and to Coles County. The
governor's office in the Illinois state house had been turned
over to him and he kept regular hours there through November
and December. As visitors poured in—statesmen, politicians,
old friends, newspaper correspondents, office seekers, and casual callers—Lincoln met them with cordial informality. Those
who saw him were favorably impressed by his witty conversation and unaffected friendliness, albeit they learned little to
allay their concern as to the new leader's position and policy.
Lincoln would appear quite early at the governor's office; beginning at ten he would hold a reception till noon, meeting
all callers. "Altogether, probably no other President-elect was
as approachable for everybody," was the comment of Henry
Villard. In the afternoon he was again at his office attending to
correspondence with the help of secretaries and meeting men
of importance by appointment. "In the evening old friends
called at his home for the exchange of news and political views.

At times . . . he would go to the telegraph or newspaper offices after supper, and stay there till late."

His mail was "immense." Letters poured in from autograph collectors, place seekers (including some Southerners), anxious citizens, and politicians of many grades. Republican politicians who had labored to defeat him now sought his confidence on the supposition that Lincoln had "forgotten their treachery" and would "accept them as his advisers."

On the most devastating question of the day, the disintegration of the nation by the progress of secession, Lincoln maintained an attitude of such calmness that he was thought by some to be either unaware of the true situation or lacking in policy. Readers of the Chicago *Tribune* were told that Mr. Lincoln "does not . . . believe that any of the States will . . . go off and organize a Confederacy" and further that "Abraham Lincoln and the Republican party will not interfere with the rights of the South." He was reported to have expressed "doubts as to the practicability of holding the Slave States in the Union by main force, if they were all determined to break it up." Up to the time of his departure for Washington, according to Villard, he "did not dream that his principal duty would be to raise great armies and fleets . . . for the suppression of . . . rebellion. . . ." He found abolitionists a constant embarrassment, both because of their importunity and on account of the deliberate misrepresentation of himself as a *"confrere* of Garrison, Phillips, and Company." When these abolitionists called on him it was with a sense of proprietorship and usually with the zeal of an exhorter.

Both Thurlow Weed and William H. Seward saw Lincoln in this prepresidential period at Springfield, but their visits were in marked contrast. Seward's was not even a stop-over. Returning from Kansas, he passed through Springfield (October 1) and exchanged a few trivial words with Lincoln who turned up at the station to greet him. He was in Springfield only as long as his train stood there. Concerning this incident a caustic journalist remarked that "the meeting . . . was conventional and formal, as if each was afraid of his own virtue in the presence of the other." Weed paid two visits to Springfield in 1860. The first was on May 24 directly after the Chicago nomination which left the New York manager so disappointed "as to be unable to . . . talk on the subject." This conversation lasted five hours. According to Weed's later account dressed up for public display, its main significance was that Weed admired Lincoln's good sense and left the interview prepared to work "with a will" for his election. It was Gideon Welles's belief, however, that the full story did not appear in these reminiscences and that Weed was "intrusive to impertinence in presenting and pressing his claims." Welles goes on to relate that Lincoln's Illinois friends were at special pains to make friends with the gentleman from New York, that they invited him to visit Springfield after the nomination, and that Weed "greedily availed himself of the courtesy" while postponing his visit until after the first rush from Chicago was over, reaching Springfield by a roundabout course involving a boat trip on the Mississippi. Lincoln made no commitments in the interview, and, contrary to the roseate picture in Weed's memoirs, Welles was of the opinion that the New York politician returned to Albany in "not a very complacent state of mind." All the evidence leads to the supposition that in this period Weed expected, if nothing else, at least to be a kind of patronage dispenser and political manager for the new administration, as he had certainly expected to be in the event of Seward's nomination and election.

Weed's second visit to Lincoln, which was the object of a special trip from Albany, coincided with the secession of South Carolina (December 20, 1860). According to his memoirs, which again have the quality of public rationalization, Weed found Lincoln amusing, quaint, agreeable, and full of anecdotes. He stated specifically that Lincoln did not tell indelicate stories to his knowledge, but Villard, who saw much of him, asserts precisely the contrary. The substantive matters on which Weed and Lincoln conferred were chiefly two: compromise proposals to deal with the sectional crisis, and cabinet-making.

The President Elect's visitors included many other notables: Giddings, Trumbull, Cameron (December 30), Chase (January 4), Bates, Amos Tuck, Francis P. Blair, Jr., Browning, Judd, William Kellogg, David Wilmot, George Opdyke, Hiram Barney, Judge Hogeboom, M. Romero (Mexican minister), and Horace Greeley. Sometimes Lincoln would call on such men at their hotels; at other times they would meet him in his home or state-house office. While the new leader was secretive as to his plans the identity of his visitors could not be concealed, and journalists, as at present, spun out their stories accordingly. Rumors and guesses clustered round these interviews, and special emphasis was placed upon those visitors who came upon Lincoln's invitation, such as Chase and Bates. Some of the visitors wore homespun as in the case of an old man from Mississippi who was given an interview and expressed the wish that every Southerner could talk face to face with the President Elect. "Offensively democratic exhibitions of free manners occur every once in a while," wrote the *Herald* reporter. "Churlish fellows will obtrude themselves with their hats on, lighted segars and . . . pantaloons tucked into their boots. Dropping into chairs, they will sit puffing away and trying to gorgonize the President with their silent stares, until their boorish curiosity is . . . satisfied."

In the harassment and strain of a cruelly difficult position these visitors found a man who displayed little showmanship and lacked dramatic exuberance but who kept an even keel and exhibited outward calm, often illuminated by flashes of prairie humor. Gloom and sadness characterized his features as he "perceived . . . the danger of the situation," but in spite of this, when in company, he was "as jovial and . . . droll as usual." "Of Mr. Lincoln the politician," wrote an interviewer,

"I say nothing; but Lincoln, the man, I was delighted with."
Lincoln's reticence in this period was counted a virtue. "The
singularly small amount of self-revelation that he has given
since his nomination" was mentioned as "one of the best . . .
indications." This democracy of manner stayed with Lincoln
after he left Springfield and there was comment on the "perfect
identity, in all his broad, shrewd, western rusticity of style
between President Lincoln and good Neighbor Lincoln of
Springfield aforetime." It was felt that his new importance
made "not the slightest impression on his nerves, proving that
the great office [was] not too much for him." From *The Times*
in London came the comment that "Mr. Lincoln can do anything he sets his mind to, partly from natural pliability, partly
by an immense power of fixing his attention on whatever is
before him."

Young Henry Villard, perhaps because he was employed
by the New York *Herald,* found the Illinois leader in many
ways unsatisfactory. He disliked what he called his coarse
"license" in telling stories and confessed a feeling of "disgust"
and "humiliation" toward a man whom he was far from wor-
shiping as hero. "I could not have persuaded myself [he wrote]
that the man might possibly possess true greatness." Earlier
he had been "no great admirer of the Republican standard-
bearer" though he had desired his election. This same observer wrote of Mrs. Lincoln as imprudently taking presents
from office seekers. "She does not appear to realize [said the
Herald writer] that she has been elected to preside at the
White House the next four years."

II

Of the two trips which Lincoln made outside Springfield
in the pre-presidential interval the first was political and the

other intimately personal. On November 21, 1860, he took train at Springfield in the presence of a large crowd and proceeded to Chicago for a conference with Hannibal Hamlin. Mrs. Lincoln accompanied him and Senator Trumbull was also in the party. Lincoln was dodging ovations and avoiding speechmaking, and just before his departure he had disappointed Republican jollifiers by refusing to speak at their grand celebration. The train stopped at Lincoln and Bloomington; at each place Lincoln made a brief platform appearance, giving a sentence or two of greeting. Dealing only in generalities, these remarks were those of a leader who had decided to make no speeches but who could not refuse the courtesy of greeting friends and expressing appreciation. At Bloomington he stepped out on the platform of his car and thanked the people of "Old McLean" (County) for their part in placing him in his present position, declaring that the people will do well when they are well done by and that it was his intention to "do well by the people." Retiring into the car amid cheers he shook hands with acquaintances, while Trumbull added a few remarks, commending the people for supporting the "whole Republican ticket."

At Chicago Lincoln discussed cabinet matters with Vice President Elect Hamlin, visited the Republican wigwam and other buildings, and held a reception which occupied the morning of November 23. He attended church in company with Isaac N. Arnold, spoke briefly at a mission Sabbath school, and spent an uneventful rainy day on the return to Springfield. Real business had been transacted, for shortly after this Hamlin confidentially quoted Lincoln as saying that Gideon Welles's appointment to the cabinet was more probable than that of any other New Englander. In this consultation Lincoln conferred upon Hamlin a unique distinction. In the case of no other statesman did he make a trip for the purpose of an interview while President Elect.

At the end of January Lincoln made an arduous two-day

trip via Charleston, Illinois, to a remote spot in Coles County to see his aged stepmother, Sarah Bush Johnston Lincoln, widow of Thomas Lincoln. Besides the rail trip to Charleston there was a ten-mile rural drive which even then stopped short of the Thomas Lincoln cabin, for the more accessible frame house of a neighbor, with a convenient location on the highway, had been placed at Lincoln's disposal. Among the reminiscences pertaining to this occasion is that of James A. Connolly, a Charleston lawyer, who stated that Lincoln missed the regular passenger train at Mattoon where a change of cars was necessary and arrived a number of hours later on a freight caboose. Those who met Lincoln at Charleston had a long wait. "Presently," said Connolly, "we saw a tall man . . . make his way through the long expanse of slush and ice beside the track. . . . [Q]uite a crowd of natives were gathered on the platform to see him. I confess I was not favorably impressed." In this bit of reminiscence we have glimpses of Lincoln dropping formality and addressing his old friend A. P. Dunbar as "Aleck," spinning out backwoods stories, delighting those who chatted with him, but disappointing some who merely glimpsed his "awkward, if not ungainly figure." Herndon records that on this visit, besides seeing his stepmother, Lincoln met members of the Johnston and Hanks families, visited his father's grave, gave directions for a suitable stone marker, and made a brief public address at Charleston. If fully recorded the episode would offer a picturesquely quaint and pathetic incident in Lincoln's personal life. There was drama in the homespun rusticity of the surroundings, the informality of the President Elect, the painful lowliness of relatives contrasted with the distinction of the illustrious son, and the genuine affection of Sarah Lincoln for the boy of whom she had seen little in thirty years. It was characteristic of Lincoln and of the time that the deep human interest of the visit was not played up in public print.

III

As the time for Lincoln's departure from Springfield on the long way to Washington approached, his last hours at home were occupied with official cares, social obligations, and homely incidents of a peculiarly western or Lincolnian flavor. A public reception was given at his home on the night of February 6, 1861; it was described as a large affair, made brilliant by beauty, fashion, and the political elite, with hundreds in attendance. Vacating their home, "breaking up housekeeping," the Lincolns stayed a few days at the Chenery House. The chores of packing were partly performed by Lincoln himself; the personal trunks, tied with his own hands, bore his label: "Lincoln, Executive Mansion, Washington." On Sunday, February the tenth, his last day in Springfield, he turned up at the Lincoln-Herndon office for a talk with his partner and chatted easily of incidents in his early practice. On departing he asked that the old sign be permitted to hang so that clients might understand "that the election of a President makes no change in the firm of Lincoln and Herndon." Next day there was enacted one of the most touching scenes of his life as he took his departure from Springfield, bound for untold anxieties in Washington. Friends had gathered despite the stormy weather and the early hour, and Lincoln, rising to a level that was rare among rear platform appearances, spoke his few words of parting; they were as perfectly fitted to the occasion as any of his more formal speeches:

My Friends [he said]: No one, not in my situation, can appreciate my feeling of sadness at this parting. To this place, and the kindness of these people, I owe everything. Here I have lived a quarter of a century, and have passed from a young to an old man. Here my children have been born, and one is buried. I now leave, not knowing when or whether ever I may return, with a task before me greater than that which rested upon Washington. Without the assistance of that Divine Being who ever attended him, I cannot succeed. With that assistance, I cannot fail. Trusting in Him who can go with me, and remain with you, and be everywhere for good, let us confidently hope that all will yet be well. To His care commending you, as I hope in your prayers you will commend me, I bid you an affectionate farewell.

Synchronous with the beginnings of the Confederacy, the presidential journey came at a time of widespread apprehension for the new chief and for the government itself. Extra precautions were taken in dispatching the presidential train. The time card of the Great Western (Wabash) Railroad Company, printed under date of February 11, 1861, for the use of its employees, contained the following injunction: "It is very important that this train should pass over the road in safety. . . . Red is the signal for danger, but any signal apparently intended to indicate alarm . . . must be regarded, the train stopped, and the meaning of its ascertained. Carefulness is particularly enjoined."

Of the President's traveling party some went all the way, some made only the trip from Springfield to Indianapolis, others joined the train en route for rides of varying length. Robert Lincoln was on the train as it left Springfield. Mrs. Lincoln, with the other two boys—William and Thomas— boarded it at Indianapolis. The party also included the private secretaries, John G. Nicolay and John Hay; Elmer E. Ellsworth, Lincoln's young friend who would soon fall at Alexandria; army officers (Col. E. V. Sumner, Major David Hunter, Capt. George W. Hazard, Capt. John Pope); relatives of the Lincolns (Dr. W. S. Wallace, Lockwood Todd); men of political prominence in Illinois (David Davis, Norman B. Judd,

Orville H. Browning, Governor Richard Yates, Ward H. Lamon); and others so slightly known that their presence seems
wholly incidental. W. S. Wood, an eastern railway official, was
present in a managerial capacity. The army officers, who took
very seriously their duty of guarding the President without
satisfying others on this point, were there by action of the war
department.

IV

The last three days of Lincoln's journey, with their plots,
rumors, and detective foils, would make a "thriller" if fully
told; at least some attention must be given to this episode.
Without an understanding of what went on, one might fail
to appreciate the excitement of these pre-inauguration days
and wrongly interpret a change of schedule which caused un-
deserved public censure.

Thursday, February 21.—The presidential party traveled
from New York to Philadelphia with a scheduled stop at
Trenton where Lincoln spent some hours, visiting the legislature of New Jersey and making speeches to the senate and
house of representatives. He recalled his childhood reading of
Washington's crossing of the Delaware, recognized again that
he was addressing party opponents, and suggested amid prolonged cheers that for the preservation of "peace" it might be
necessary "to put the foot down firmly."

The party traveled on to Philadelphia and put up at the
Continental Hotel. In the evening Lincoln spoke at the mayor's
reception. Meanwhile behind the scenes there had been close
and anxious consultation between S. M. Felton, president of
the Philadelphia, Wilmington and Baltimore Railway, Allan
Pinkerton, head of a Chicago detective agency, and N. B. Judd,

Lincoln's Chicago friend. The gist of it all was that Pinkerton's agents and spies reported a conspiracy to murder the President Elect as he passed through hostile Baltimore on February 23. Meeting secretly with Lincoln at the Continental, Pinkerton, Judd, and Felton explained the danger and urged him to cut remaining engagements and travel to Washington that night. At this point Judd alone of the presidential party knew of these consultations and suggestions as to change of plan. Lincoln cross-examined his interviewers and listened to their warning. Then, though facing possible assassination, he refused to abandon his Friday engagements at Philadelphia and Harrisburg.

About noon of this Thursday a page touched the arm of Frederick Seward as he sat in the Senate gallery at Washington. Soon he was informed by his father, Senator Seward, that General Scott had independent reports of the Baltimore plot and that Lincoln must be found and his arrangements changed. Colonel Charles P. Stone, a man of high reputation (which radicals were later to smear), had reported the plot to Scott, who had conveyed the information to Seward for transmittal to Lincoln. Traveling to Philadelphia, Frederick Seward managed with the help of Ward Lamon to see the President Elect alone, and Lincoln was given to know that "different persons . . . pursuing separate clues" had concluded that the plot against his life was real. Judd states that he and Pinkerton devoted nearly the whole of that night, with railway and telegraph officials, to the task of arranging the difficult details of what was to follow.

Friday, February 22.—Lincoln's day began and ended at Philadelphia with a side trip to Harrisburg. In the early morning of this Washington's Birthday the new executive officiated in a scheduled flag-raising at Independence Hall, speaking to a group in the building and to a crowd outside. In this setting, where thought inevitably reverted to the Declaration of Independence, he offered the hope "that in due time the weights would be lifted from the shoulders of all men, and that all should have an equal chance." If the country could not be saved without giving up that principle, he added, "I was about to say I would rather be assassinated on this spot than surrender it." Speaking with "deep emotion" and giving rein to sentiment, he recalled the dangers and toils of Revolutionary soldiers, and stressed his belief that the Declaration was vital in 1861. There would be no giving up, he said; yet he particularly explained that his policy did not involve "bloodshed and war."

Lincoln kept all his Friday engagements, traveling laboriously to Harrisburg, making two solid public speeches there, greeting a large crowd in a reception at the state house, and attending a hotel banquet given by Governor Curtin. At Harrisburg the men of the presidential party were informed by Judd of the suspected plot, and Lincoln was confronted with the problem of a night ride that would avoid the Baltimore danger. Unlike other cities and states Maryland and Baltimore had extended no official invitation to Lincoln and had arranged no speeches or receptions. The authorities had even failed to supply adequate police protection. Marshal George P. Kane described the plot rumors as "political *canard*, receiving a . . . coloring of reality from the . . . expressions of a class of people who . . . are mostly to be found . . . in public barrooms."

It had been publicly announced that about mid-day of Saturday the 23rd Lincoln would pass through Baltimore and that he would arrive at Washington that evening. To omit passing through the streets of an inhospitable city was a less serious matter than cutting the speaking engagements of Friday, and the President Elect, despite danger of ridicule and misunderstanding, reluctantly yielded to his advisers and consented to a secret night ride. With one companion, Ward Lamon, he took a special train at Harrisburg with precautions to evade notice, entered the sleeper of a regular train at Philadelphia about eleven at night, and passed unnoticed through Baltimore in the early hours before daylight.

Saturday, February 23. Lincoln pulled into Washington at six a.m., and was met at the station by Congressman E. B. Washburne of Illinois. Though one finds conflicting claims as to this detail, Washburne stated that it was he who met Lincoln as he stepped off the train in company with Pinkerton and Lamon, that the four men entered a carriage and drove rapidly to the Willard Hotel, that they were shown into a receiving room, and that Seward then entered, "out of breath and . . . chagrined to think he had not been up in season to be at the depot on the arrival of the train." The previous night ride had involved elaborate arrangements for cutting wires, intercepting messages, holding the night train at Philadelphia until a "package" was delivered (a Pinkertonian touch), preventing fire, putting guards at bridges and at a railway ferry, and creating the illusion that Lincoln had spent the night as planned at Harrisburg.

The activities hinted at in this curtailed chronology must not be set down as mere nervousness. Events were soon to show that Maryland and Baltimore were capable of violence. Though some of the wildest rumors were canards (especially regarding a suspected *coup d'état* by which the "rebel" government would seize the capital), yet there was official information which could not be known to be so false as to be ignored. Secret service men of the Federal government were not then in the President Elect's party; had they been, Lincoln would have had even a poorer chance of resisting the demands for a change of schedule. The American method did not involve a pervasive national police, nor even an embryonic one; local police systems were unco-ordinated, and it was, governmentally speaking, nobody's business in particular to see the President through in safety. Neither Lamon, Judd, Felton, nor Pinkerton had any governmental authority to act. Had President Buchanan de-

tailed a military force to escort the President Elect, it would
have added to the trouble besides being out of line with
precedent. Had Lincoln been assassinated anywhere but in the
District of Columbia, the national government would have
been without authority even to punish the guilty party. Assurances of safety in Baltimore were unconvincing. George P.
Kane, marshal of Baltimore, emphatically denied that there
existed in his city any danger of mob action or of violence toward any public functionary, but his statement was dated
January 16, while Lincoln was to pass through on February 23.
Kane himself was anti-Lincoln and feeling was at high pitch.
The papers for many days had been full of serious talk of
suspected violence. It was not as if Lincoln had evaded danger
in the line of duty. He did not even have any ceremonial appointments in Baltimore; the passing through the streets was
intended only as a necessary link in the itinerary. After he left
Harrisburg his next duties were in Washington. He changed
his plan not merely on the basis of Pinkerton's reports (Pinkerton having been brought into the picture on private arrangement by Felton and Judd) but on independent advice from the
capital. In such matters a public chief is neither a free agent
nor at liberty to take the public into his confidence.

What leaders have to suffer from, however, is not so much
the essential situation as the manner in which it is publicly
viewed. There were sorry consequences of Lincoln's night ride.
He was reported going through Baltimore in a fictitious "Scotch
plaid cap and . . . long military cloak," a fabricated description that has been traced to a journalist later imprisoned for
forgery. Cartoonists were particularly devilish in their carica-
tures of this imagined disguise. Opposition papers spread themselves on the subject and even Lincoln's friends were humili-
ated at the manner of his arrival in Washington.

V

The nine days between Lincoln's entry into the capital city and his inauguration were wearisome and difficult. On the day of his arrival he called upon President Buchanan and was introduced to members of the outgoing cabinet. With severe stress behind the scenes he had to make many public appearances. Congress, the mayor of Washington, hotel throngs, serenaders, members of the Supreme Court, and delegates to the Peace Conference had to be greeted, smiled upon, and in some cases addressed with an appropriate speech. Of more than common significance were the polite calls of his three 1860 rivals: John Bell, Stephen A. Douglas, and John C. Breckinridge. At Willard's the pressure was terrific, allowing "hardly . . . a chance to eat or sleep." Springfield, the harassed leader is reported to have said, was "bad enough . . . , but it was child's play compared with this tussle here." "I am fair game for everybody of that hungry lot." The horde of office seekers and the round of greetings and appearances allowed little time for public problems, yet his cabinet was not yet formally announced nor his inaugural address finally revised.

That form of studiously favorable publicity which modern journalists turn on or off at will had been denied to Lincoln. In general it cannot be said that he had a "good press" at the threshold of office. Showmanship failed to make capital of his rugged origin, and there faced the country a strange man from Illinois who was dubbed a "Simple Susan," a "baboon," or a "gorilla." Writers of this period labeled Lincoln an "ape" (this being a favorite term in the South), a "demon," or an "Illinois beast." On one occasion it seemed to a Washington correspondent that his "attempt" at speaking was "crude, ignorant twaddle, without point or meaning." There was the pre-

posterous rumor that he had avoided a train because he feared
a wreck and had then counseled his wife and sons to take it.
Publicity was unfortunately given to a trivial act of the traveling President Elect in kissing a little girl, described by Charn-
wood as the "dreadful young person" who claimed credit for
those ill-designed whiskers which now disfigured Lincoln's
face. To Charles Francis Adams the younger it seemed that
while Sumner "talked like a crazy man" and Seward "was
laboring under a total misconception," the "absolutely unknown" Lincoln was "perambulating the country, kissing little
girls and growing whiskers!" An impertinent journalist linked
the whiskers theme with the choice of a New York hotel: "Mr.
Lincoln, having . . . brought his brilliant intellectual powers
to bear upon the cultivation of luxuriant whiskers . . . , has
now . . . concentrated his mental energies upon the question
—what hotel he shall stop at in New York." Though Lincoln's
social *faux pas* have been exaggerated, there were men in the
East who thought him lacking in polite ways and innocent of
savoir faire. From this it was an easy step to consider him deficient in sagacity and qualities of statesmanship. This was one
aspect of the matter that gave point to the criticisms apropos
of the night ride to Washington. It was a lowering of a prestige
that at best was none to high. " 'What brought him here so
suddenly?' was on everybody's tongue." Yet some of the comments on the secret ride were favorable, recognizing that a
calamity or at least an insult had been averted, that Lincoln
had taken the advice of good counsellors, and that, even from
the standpoint of Baltimore, the change was fortunate.

VI

President Buchanan, Secretary of War Holt, and General
Scott had paid heed to the possible danger of violence, and

March 4, 1861, found Washington under unusual military protection, with guns commanding Pennsylvania Avenue, cross streets under guard, riflemen on housetops, new-drilled volunteers on parade, and "brawny young Republicans" on hand, "determined to see . . . [Lincoln] installed in office." The militaristic touch had aroused the suspicions of the House of Representatives which had formally asked the reason for "so large a number of troops in this city." In answer Secretary Holt referred to disorders in the South and to the belief of "multitudes" in a conspiracy to strike at the government, which belief he "fully shared." The general apprehension of a "raid upon the capital," and the open threat that Lincoln would never be inaugurated, he thought, could not be ignored. Buchanan explained that, on March 1, there were only 653 "troops" in Washington exclusive of marines stationed at the navy yard, that these troops were there "to act as a *posse comitatus,* in strict subordination to civil authority," and that the existing condition of "high excitement," with rumors filling the air and threats freely expressed, was such that he "could not hesitate to adopt precautionary defensive measures." Of course the protection of the government was not a mere matter of these 653 men. Contemporary accounts speak of a city full of troops, of "[t]housands of young men . . . well armed," and especially of District of Columbia volunteers. These latter were organized by Colonel Charles P. Stone, charged with the defense of the capital, but they were not yet mustered into the Federal service and would not be Federal "troops" in the sense of Buchanan's message. When thanked in Lincoln's behalf by Leonard Swett for his precautions, Stone replied that Lincoln should not be grateful to him, that he had opposed his election, and that his efforts were for "saving the Government." Very much the same attitude toward Lincoln characterized the great majority of those who then held national office.

Amid these military and quasi-military activities Lincoln performed the exacting duties of inauguration day. He entered

President Buchanan's carriage at Willard's, and these diverse individuals rode side by side, in company with other "distinguished citizens," along the historic avenue. Buchanan was described as grave and silent, Lincoln "calm and but little affected by the excitement around him." For hours the human stream poured on toward the Capitol, the majority being Northerners according to the quaint remark of a reporter who noted the "lack of long haired [i.e., Southern] men in the crowd." Part of the pageantry was a car decorated to symbolize the Union, the states and territories being represented by girls in white, the float being drawn by six white horses whose housing bore the word "Union." The parade was a Republican affair; marching delegations were politically sympathetic toward the incoming President. It was reported that Lincoln had to kiss the thirty-four states of the Union. Arm in arm Lincoln and Buchanan entered the senate chamber where they faced crowded and brilliant galleries, while surging and heaving masses struggled in vain to view them. Here they attended a brief ceremony, Buchanan sighing "audibly, and frequently," Lincoln "impassive as an Indian martyr."

On a temporary platform at the east front of the unfinished Capitol Lincoln faced an immense outdoor throng as he swore to "execute the office of President of the United States, and . . . defend the Constitution . . . ," the oath being administered by Chief Justice Taney, whose court and whose opinion Lincoln had criticized. Near Lincoln on the platform were Buchanan, Breckinridge, and Douglas. In later accounts one finds the dramatic story of how Senator Douglas held Lincoln's hat as he spoke his inaugural message, a fascinating and beautifully symbolic bit of Lincoln-Douglas biography for which a strictly contemporary source—i.e., an account written by a witness in March 1861—is difficult to find. None of the newspaper reports or other accounts written *at the time,* within the knowledge of the author, mentions the hat incident. A writer in the *Atlantic Monthly* in August 1861 described

Douglas's sympathetic behavior at the inauguration without mentioning the hat. The reference commonly given for the incident is "The Diary of a Public Man," published in 1879, but this diary, while rich in picturesque detail concerning Lincoln, has become a *cause célèbre* among historians and must be used with reservations. It purports to have been written in 1860–61 (December to early March), but as research on the subject now stands it is untraceable. Its authenticity is unproved, not to say doubtful. (Those who accept the diary as authentic need look no further.) J. G. Holland referred to the hat incident, and his account has value, but his book did not appear until 1866. Nicolay and Hay give only a passing reference to the holding of the hat, relegating it to a minor position in a footnote and offering it not as their own statement, but merely as part of a quotation from the post-war Holland account. If they knew of the incident from direct observation or from contemporary statements, they give no sign of it. This is not to assert that the hat incident did not occur. The point is rather that a careful biographer looks for contemporary evidence, and where such evidence is lacking, or has not yet been found, it is his duty to say so. Henry Watterson reminiscently repeated the hat-holding story, reporting it as a witness, but his account has by no means the value of a strictly contemporary record.

Much more could be said of the vast crowds, of the incidents of inauguration day, of the hand-shaking, of the relief that came when no violence occurred, and of the President's ball that night. Lincoln's voice was described as "strong and clear," the cheers "loud and long." "The opening sentence, 'Fellow-citizens of the United States,' was the signal for prolonged applause. . . . Again, when, after defining certain actions to be his duty, he said, 'And I shall perform it,' there was a spontaneous, and uproarious manifestation of approval, which continued for some moments."

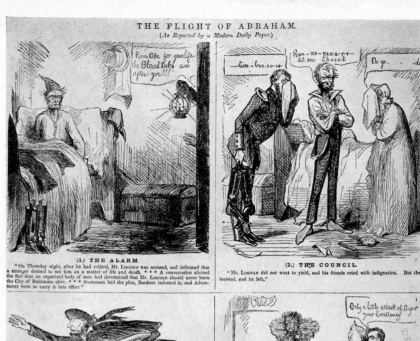

THE FLIGHT OF ABRAHAM.

(As Reported by a Modern Daily Paper.)

(1.) THE ALARM.

"On Thursday night, after he had retired, Mr. LINCOLN was aroused, and informed that a stranger desired to see him on a matter of life and death. * * * A conversation elicited the fact that an organized body of men had determined that Mr. LINCOLN should never leave the City of Baltimore alive. * * * Statesmen laid the plan, Bankers indorsed it, and Adventurers were to carry it into effect."

(2.) THE COUNCIL.

"Mr. LINCOLN did not want to yield, and his friends cried with indignation. But they insisted, and he left."

(3.) THE SPECIAL TRAIN.

"He wore a Scotch plaid Cap and a very long Military Cloak, so that he was entirely unrecognizable."

(4.) THE OLD COMPLAINT.

"Mr. LINCOLN, accompanied by Mr. SEWARD, paid his respects to President BUCHANAN, spending a few minutes in general conversation."

BELITTLING THE INCOMING PRESIDENT

These cartoons, about the time of Lincoln's inauguration, are typical of the widespread ridicule resulting from his secret night ride into Washington. *Upper Left:* Lincoln is aroused from bed. Organized enemies, he is informed, have determined that he shall never leave Baltimore alive. *Upper Right:* As his friends weep, Lincoln reluctantly yields to the demand that his itinerary be changed. *Lower Left:* Lincoln is unrecognizable in a Scotch plaid cap and a long military cloak. (This disguise was entirely imaginary, but was presented as news of the day.) *Lower Right:* Lincoln shivers with "a little attack of Ager" as he and Seward greet President Buchanan. An amusing trick of the artists of that day was always to exaggerate Buchanan's topknot. The four cartoons appeared in *Harper's Weekly*, Mar. 9, 1861, five days after Lincoln's inauguration.

Chapter Seven

PRESIDENTIAL DAYS.

AMONG THE STORIES THAT HAVE COME DOWN TO US IS THAT OF
Lincoln's remark when a friend from back home asked him
"How does it feel to be President of the United States?" In
reply, so the story goes, he referred to a man who was tarred
and feathered and ridden out of town on a rail. When someone
in the crowd asked how he enjoyed it, the tarred-and-feathered
one answered: "If it were not for the honor of the thing, I'd
much rather walk."

I

Since, when he entered upon the presidency, Lincoln was
hardly known at all outside the United States, descriptions by
foreign observers sounded often like the report of some notable,
or curious, discovery. The wholly unusual quality of the man
appealed to English journalists, who have forever delighted in
detailing to their readers the unusual and unbelievable things
in America, and where these journalists had the knack of pictorial reporting the result was striking and memorable. An early
account published in England was that of the famous British
correspondent, William Howard Russell, of the *Times*. For
March 27, 1861, Russell made a more than usually interesting

143

entry in his *Diary*. He turned up at the department of state where Secretary ("Governor") Seward arranged to take him over a few steps and introduce him to the President in the White House. The minister from the new kingdom of Italy, the Chevalier Bertinatti, entered the mansion at the same time. They were received in "a handsome spacious room, richly and rather gorgeously furnished, and rejoicing in a kind of '*demi-jour*,' which gave increased effect to the gilt chairs and ormolu ornaments." Since this was a set occasion—a formal audience of the President to receive the new diplomat—Seward's son said to Russell: "You are not . . . supposed to be here."

The diary continued: "Soon afterwards there entered, with a shambling, loose, irregular, almost unsteady gait, a tall, lank, lean man, considerably over six feet in height, with stooping shoulders, long pendulous arms, terminating in hands of extraordinary dimensions, which, however, were far exceeded in proportion by his feet. He was dressed in an ill-fitting, wrinkled suit of black, which put one in mind of an undertaker's uniform at a funeral; round his neck a rope of black silk was knotted in a large bulb, with flying ends projecting beyond the collar of his coat; his . . . shirt-collar disclosed a sinewy muscular yellow neck, and above that, nestling in a great black mass of hair, bristling and compact like a ruff of mourning pins, rose the strange quaint face and head, covered with its thatch of wild republican hair, of President Lincoln."

The whole effect was by no means unfavorable upon this urbane Englishman. He continued: "The impression produced by the size of his extremities, and by his flapping . . . ears, may be removed by the appearance of kindliness, sagacity, and the awkward bonhommie of his face; the mouth is absolutely prodigious; the lips, straggling and extending almost from one line of black beard to the other, are only kept in order by two deep furrows from the nostril to the chin; the nose itself—a prominent organ—stands out from the face, with an inquiring, anxious air, as though it were sniffing for some good thing in the wind; the eyes dark, full, and deeply set, are penetrating, but full of an expression which almost amounts to tenderness; and above them projects the shaggy brow, running into the small hard frontal space, the development of which can scarcely be estimated accurately, owing to the irregular flocks of thick hair carelessly brushed across it. One would say that, although the mouth was made to enjoy a joke, it could also utter the severest sentences which the head could dictate, but that Mr. Lincoln would be ever more willing to temper justice with mercy, and to enjoy what he considers the amenities of life, than to take a harsh view of men's nature and of the world, and to estimate things in an ascetic or puritan spirit."

Since coming to the United States Mr. Russell had been supplied with doubting remarks as to whether Lincoln was a "gentleman." "I have heard," he wrote, "more disparaging allusions made by Americans to him on that account than I could have expected among simple republicans, where all should be equals; but . . . it would not be possible for the most indifferent observer to pass him in the street without notice."

The President's western cordiality was brought up short by the stiffness of Seward and the "profound diplomatic bows of the Chevalier Bertinatti." Then Lincoln "suddenly jerked himself back, and stood in front of the two ministers, with his body slightly drooped forward, and his hands behind his back, his knees touching, and his feet apart." When Seward presented the Italian diplomat, "the President made a prodigiously violent demonstration of his body in a bow which had almost the effect of a smack in its rapidity and abruptness." (We have here an impression quite different from Herndon's slow-motion picture.) After the ceremony of diplomacy the President was presented to Russell. "Conversation ensued for some minutes, which the President enlivened by two or three peculiar little sallies, and I left agreeably impressed with his shrewdness, humor, and natural sagacity."

Starting to tell how Lincoln looked, men would glide into

comment on his nature or temperament. Those who met him
were aware that the man had more than was revealed at first
glance, something of depth and at times of mystery. He was
described as a man of "deep prudences," a man of contrasts,
"retired, contemplative," yet highly sociable, often in gay mood,
yet given to a sadness that was impenetrable. The humorist,
David R. Locke (Petroleum V. Nasby) wrote: "I never saw so
sad a face." Perhaps the briefest vignette combining the inner
and the outer personality is Donn Piatt's: "This strange, quaint,
great man."

The contrast between Lincoln's rugged and unfashionable
appearance and the sometimes unexpected quality of his inner
poise and dignity is well indicated in the following description
by an English observer:

"Fancy a man six foot high, and thin *out* of proportion;
with long bony arms and legs, which somehow seem to be always in the way; with great rugged furrowed hands, which
grasp you like a vise . . . ; with a long, scraggy neck, and a
chest too narrow for the arms at its side.

"Add . . . a head . . . covered with rough, uncombed
and uncombable hair that stands out in every direction . . . ;
a face furrowed, wrinkled and indented, as though it had been
scarred by vitriol; a high, narrow forehead, and, sunk deep
beneath bushy eyebrows; two bright, somewhat dreamy eyes,
that seem to gaze through you without looking at you; a few
irregular blotches of black bristly hair, in the place where beard
and whiskers ought to grow; a close-set . . . mouth, . . . and
a nose and ears which have been taken by mistake from a head
of twice the size.

"Clothe this figure, . . . in a . . . badly-fitting suit . . .
puckered up at every salient point . . . ; put on large, ill-fitting
boots, gloves too long for the long bony fingers, and a fluffy
hat, . . . ; and then add to all this an air of strength, physical
as well as moral, and a strange look of dignity coupled with
all this grotesqueness, and you will have the impression left

upon me by Abraham Lincoln."

Still another British description of unusual quality is that of the journalist, George Augustus Sala, who met the Emancipator early in 1864 at a reception in the White House. Steered through the crowd by Senator Sumner, he found himself face to face with the "Tallest Man of All." Next moment his hand was in the "cast-iron grip" of Abraham Lincoln, which made the handshaking painfully memorable. On this occasion the President wore gloves, "a pair of white kids, which the tallest of Barnum's four giants might have envied." Referring to the cartoon sketches in *Punch*, Sala noted that the artist, John Tenniel, had "seized upon that lengthy face, those bushy locks, that shovel beard, that ungainly form, those long, muscular, attenuated limbs, those bony and wide-spread extremities." Lincoln was so tall, according to this observer, "that, looking up in his face, you might, did not respect forbid you, ask, 'How cold the weather was up there.' He is so tall, that a friend who had an interview with him . . . [said] that when he rose there did not seem the slightest likelihood of his getting up ever coming to an end. He seems to be drawing himself out like a telescope." These touches might be second-hand, for we have the same remarks elsewhere.

The Englishman then commented on the President's "dark face, strongly marked, tanned and crows-footed, and fringed with coarse and tangled hair, . . . so uncouth . . . that it narrowly escapes being either terrible or grotesque." He hastened, however, to add that this impression was obviated "by a peculiarly soft, almost feminine, expression of melancholy, which . . . seemed to pervade the countenance of this remarkable man." This was the more striking because our British friend remembered that he was in the presence of "the great joker of jokes—the Sancho Panza made governor of this Transatlantic Barataria; but there the look was—the regard of a thoughtful, weary, saddened, overworked being; of one who was desperately striving to do his best, but who woke up every morning to find the wheat that he had sown growing up as tares; of one who was continually regretting that he did not know more—that he had begun his work too late, and must lay down his sceptre too early."

In a very brief interview Lincoln remarked upon the unfavorable impression which foreigners were apt to carry away from a country when they only saw it in a state of war; he hoped that the Englishman's sojourn would be pleasant. To this visitor the President told no stories, and talked no politics.

One more impression gained on this occasion is worth recording. "Mr. Lincoln," wrote Sala, "does not stand straight on his feet, but sways about with an odd sidelong motion, as though he were continually pumping something from the ground—say Truth from the bottom of her well—or hauling up some invisible kedge anchor. It gave me the notion of a mariner who had found his sea-legs, and could toe a line well, but who had to admit that there was a rough sea running."

A valuable first-hand record was that of Mrs. Cornelia Perrine Harvey, who wrote an account of an undated wartime interview with Lincoln in which they discussed the establishing of military hospitals in the North. "I had never seen Mr Lincoln before," she wrote. "He was alone in a medium sized office-like room, no elegance about him, no elegance in him. He was plainly clad in a suit of black, that illy fitted him. No fault of his tailor however, such a figure could not be fitted. He was tall and lean, and as he sat in a folded up sort of a way in a deep arm chair, one would almost have thought him deformed. . . . When I first saw him his head was bent forward, his chin resting on his breast, & in his hand a letter, which I had just sent into him. He raised his eyes, saying, Mrs. Harvey? I hastened forward. . . . The President took my hand, hoped I was well, but there was no smile of welcome on his face. It was rather the stern look of the judge who had decided against me."

Mrs. Harvey was promoting a plan for Northern hospitalization of wounded and sick soldiers, urging that Southern swamps were unhealthy and that the government was responsible for thousands of soldiers graves in the South. Lincoln knew that the military authorities opposed the plan, and he feared that if the men were sent North they would never come back. As he spoke, wrote Mrs. Harvey, "a quizzical smile played over his face at my slight embarrassment." She filled in with further touches: "He threw himself around in his chair, one leg over the arm and spoke slowly." "His face was peculiar, bone, nerve, vein, and muscle were all so plainly seen, deep lines of thought, and care, were around his mouth, and eyes."

A description of Lincoln by Seward has come down to us in a record written by Henry Bellows, head of the Sanitary Commission. In April 1863 Bellows dined with the secretary of state and on the next day he wrote his wife a full account of the conversation. "Mr. Seward," wrote Bellows, "had a great deal to say about the President. He always describes him as the most single-hearted, sincere, affectionate candid of men— patient to a fault—easy to get along with—doing ample & generous justice to each & all his ministers. He says his judgment & comprehension are admirable; his right-mindedness infallible. That he has an admirable intellect not invigorated by personal wilfulness, or ambition or intense earnestness—but a little weakened by gentle, mild & candid qualities & affections. That he is afraid of doing injustice, or hurting peoples' feelings. . . . He was most irregular as to his meals & took them *cold* usually & in a hurry—after breakfast, he was shaved, probably at the time when, & as often as *it was convenient to the barber* —for his sense of justice & kindness made him consult his own comfort & convenience last—then, he rec'd, any & every body, as long as time held out—selecting from the hundreds applying those he thot best entitled to come—and except on Cabinet days Tuesday & Friday, he spent his day morning & evening till 11. in this way. The actual work thrown on him by his ministers was small. He had a notion he was a servant of the people & that he was there to hear their complaints & he spent his time at it."

II

It will be well to keep in mind two contrasts: Lincoln's rough-hewn exterior contrasted with a dignity that came from some inner source, and the seemingly casual informality of his demeanor as opposed to his exquisite handling of delicate or difficult situations.

The rail-splitter aspect has been overstressed. Lincoln was no stranger to cultured society. He was not ignorant or naïve. There was method in his simplicity, *savoir faire* in his bland unconventionality. This does not mean that his manner was artful in the sense of being affected or assumed. It means rather that he knew his way about. Seemingly artless, his behavior nevertheless amounted to skilled craftsmanship.

People were distressed at his lack of "style." He did not look like a President. He slouched in his chair. He hated gloves and wore them awkwardly. An acquaintance wrote that he had "a habit . . . of passing his right hand slowly around his head and through his unkept hair, when actively engaged in thought. His clothing was in hopeless disorder, and I thought him then, and think him now, the most ungainly man that I have ever seen." Gamaliel Bradford, in his delightful but outdated essay on Mrs. Abraham Lincoln, wrote: ". . . it must always be remembered that she had the . . . most undomestic and unparlorable figure of Lincoln to carry with her, which would have been a terrible handicap to any woman." To be *unparlorable* in the Victorian age was indeed a handicap. It was a day of fuss and feathers, of zouaves at home and monarchical trappings abroad.

What must the homespun leader have felt as Siam offered

him several pairs of elephants? The offer came in a masterpiece of Siamese-English: "Somdetch Phra Paramendr Maha Monghut, by the blessing of the highest superagency of the whole universe, the King of Siam, the sovereign of all interior tributary countries adjacent and around in every direction, . . . to his most respected excellent presidency, the President of the United States of America . . . [etc.]."

The King wrote that he was sending a sword and a photographic likeness of himself, holding his daughter in his lap, to the President. He then offered to send several pairs of young elephants to the United States to propagate their kind and to serve as beasts of burden, "since elephants, being animals of great size and strength, can bear burdens and travel through uncleared woods and matted jungles where no carriage and cart roads have yet been made." He would have the United States send ships for the elephants, then added: "At this time we have much pleasure in sending a pair of large elephant's tusks, one of the tusks weighing 52 cents of a picul, the other weighing 48 cents of a picul, and both tusks from the same animal . . . that thereby the glory and renown of Siam may be promoted."

In reply Lincoln assured the King of his appreciation and accepted the gifts to be placed in the government archives as a token of Siam's friendship. As to the elephants, the monarch was informed: "Our political jurisdiction . . . does not reach a latitude so low as to favor the multiplication of the elephant." He also explained that "steam on land, as well as on water, has been our best and most efficient agent of transportation in internal commerce." After contemplating all this oriental magnificence it must have come as a relief to Lincoln to read a letter in which a group of French liberals praised him in earnest and scholarly fashion, addressing him simply as "Citizen Abraham Lincoln."

One may perhaps think of the President's job as legal or official, having to do with executing the laws, sending messages to Congress, serving as Commander in Chief of the army and navy, preserving, protecting, and defending the Constitution. It is all this, but it is much more. Beyond the duty that was official, Lincoln had to remember the adjustment that was personal. In addition to laws, orders, and constitutional matters, he had the constant challenge of human situations.

In his practice of the art of human relations Lincoln regularly and consciously applied that quality known as "tact." That is a way of conveying the idea, but tact is not one thing only. It is a number of qualities working together: insight into the nature of men, sympathy, self control, a knack of inducing self control in others, avoidance of human blundering, readiness to give the immediate situation an understanding mind and a second thought. Tact is not only kindness, but kindness skillfully extended. Charity does not always please, while even a reproof may be tactfully given. Human tact involves *savoir faire,* restraint, patience, ability to reach a person indirectly rather than by frontal attack, approaching a situation in terms of adjustment rather than by way of deadlock or "showdown." Tact requires poise, a potent factor in self control; it constitutes the opposite of brusqueness, clumsiness, or impulsive blurting out of one's feelings.

The finest tact is in terms of the greatest need, or the most intense provocation to be untactful. Lincoln was not only considerate. He was considerate toward Seward, who calmly planned to conduct his administration for him; toward Weed, whose grasping for Warwick-like power in 1861 was a serious embarrassment; toward Chase, who became the center of a radical drive to displace the President; toward Stanton, who was described by men of that day as "mercurial," "discourteous," "unreliable," "brusque," "uncivil," "dictatorial," "disrespectful to the President," and almost impossible to deal with. Lincoln kept the most diverse and troublesome men in his cabinet; at least he kept them there so long as that was where they could do the least harm.

III

Any day's run at the White House was crowded, tiring, and strenuous. According to Ben: Perley Poore, the President was an early riser. In the morning he would devote two or three hours to correspondence, with a glance at the newspapers. He would have breakfast about nine, then walk over to the war department building, a few steps from the White House. Returning to the White House, he would go through the morning's mail with his private secretaries. The preliminary screening of the mail, and the discarding of crank missives, was the function of W. O. Stoddard. Some of the letters would be endorsed and sent to the appropriate department. Others were entrusted to a secretary who would make a note of Lincoln's suggestions for a reply. Still others would be retained by the President to be answered by himself. Nicolay and Hay were important and efficient helpers, but it is no disparagement of their valuable assistance to say, what is not fully realized, that Lincoln gave close and careful attention to his correspondence. He often wrote a letter twice (the first draft and the final copy) in his own hand, and was even known to draft entirely in his handwriting a letter to be issued over Hay's name. "Every letter," wrote Poore, "receives attention"; he added that all that were "entitled to a reply" received one, "no matter . . . how inelegant the chirography might be."

Letter writing over, the rest of the day would be taken up with manifold activities—social, official, ceremonial, often trivial, and always time consuming. About four o'clock the President would decline seeing any more callers. He and Mrs. Lincoln would then go for a drive, or sometimes he would ride horseback. Dining at six, he was usually joined by personal friends. His visits to the war office were for a variety of purposes: chatting with a general (often Halleck), reading the military telegrams as they came over the wires (though of course these messages could have been brought to him), hearing what was new so that he could tell it, exchanging funny stories, enjoying the peculiar argot of the telegraph office, holding informal conferences, escaping White House crowds, and seeking a retreat to avoid interruption when composing an important state paper. The vivid account by David Homer Bates indicates that Lincoln found enjoyment in these war department intervals. "His tall, homely form," wrote Bates, "could be seen crossing the well-shaded lawn between the White House and the War Department day after day with unvaried regularity. . . . He seldom failed to come over late in the evening before retiring, and sometimes would stay all night in the War Department." "Three or four times daily," wrote Gideon Welles, "the President goes to the War Department and into the telegraph office to look over communications." It was natural for Welles to feel that he had less of a share in the President's daily attention than was due to a member of the cabinet and the head of the navy department.

The war-department retreat was even referred to by Lincoln as his "office." In a telegram on an October day in 1864 he wired former Secretary of War Cameron: "Am leaving office to go home." The telegram was dated: "War Department, October 11, 1864." It implied a distinction between the "office" in the war and navy building and "home," which meant the White House.

Lincoln's self-forgetfulness and his informal intimacy with private secretaries sometimes made an amusing picture. In his diary of April 30, 1864, Hay noted: "A little after midnight . . . the President came into the office laughing, with a volume of Hood's works in his hand, to show Nico[lay] and me the little caricature 'An unfortunate Bee-ing,' seemingly utterly unconscious that he with his short shirt hanging above his long legs & setting out behind like the tail feathers of an enormous ostrich was infinitely funnier than anything in the book he was laughing at. What a man it is! Occupied all day with matters of vast moment, deeply anxious about the fate of the greatest army in the world, with his own fame & future hanging on the events of the passing hour, he has such a wealth of simple bonhommie & good fellowship that he gets out of bed & perambulates the house in his shirt to find us that we may share with him the fun of one of poor Hood's queer little conceits."

A glimpse of a harassed Executive unable to escape interruption even after going to bed appears in the following diary entry by Hay (November 2, 1863): "Tonight Schenck sent for copies of the correspondence between the President and Bradford. The Tycoon came into his room with the despatch in his hands, clad in an overcoat pure & simple reaching to his knees, & sleepily fumbled for the papers in his desk till he found them & travelled back to bed. I took the letters to the telegraph office & sent them off about midnight."

IV

In what would now be called "off the cuff" speaking Lincoln showed restraint and reluctance. He disliked commonplace utterance in public; if he spoke at all, he wanted his words to be effective and not too repetitious. On one occasion, being taken by surprise at a serenade, he asked Fenton of New York to precede him and give him "a peg to hang on." Achieving a "peculiarly quaint" remark which "raised a good laugh," he considered it a happy exit line and withdrew.

When in May 1862 he spoke to the soldiers of the Twelfth Indiana Regiment, he began by saying, "It has not been customary heretofore, nor will it be hereafter, for me to say something to every regiment passing in review. It occurs too frequently for me to have speeches ready on all occasions."

After thanking the men for their satisfaction as to his own performance "in the difficulties which have surrounded the nation," he added that it was the soldiers who were more to be thanked. The nation, he said, "is more indebted to you, and such as you, than to me. It is upon the brave hearts and strong arms of the people of the country that our reliance has been placed in support of free government and free institutions."

The speech just mentioned included all fighting men while showing special recognition to those who faced him; for the boys who thus heard and saw their President it was an incident to remember, a high spot in their war experience. Again in late October 1864 Lincoln favored a regiment with a speech. Addressing the 189th New York, and not forgetting that he was speaking just prior to a presidential election, he praised the soldiers for sustaining his administration, recognizing that they had "not only fought right," but "voted right."

There could be no neglecting, or dodging, of serenades. They could happen when least expected, but they could certainly be expected because of an outstanding or notable event. When told that a serenade "was coming" just after the emancipation proclamation of September 1862, and asked if he "would make any remarks," Lincoln said "No"; yet he did say a few words. Referring to himself as "environed with difficulties," and avoiding any comment in support of his proclamation, he shifted the emphasis, and the glory, from himself and his administration to "those who, upon the battle field, are endeavoring to purchase with their blood and their lives the future happiness and prosperity of this country." Speaking at a time of military deliverance (just after South Mountain and Antietam), he mentioned "battles bravely, skillfully and successfully fought" and called for three cheers for the "brave officers and men who fought those successful battles."

This call for cheers, seemingly a little thing, gave the President a graceful cue to bow out. It fitted perfectly the mood of the crowd, which was in "glorious humor" that night, serenading and demanding speeches not only from Lincoln, but also from Secretary Chase, Cassius M. Clay, and Attorney General Bates.

On the whole Lincoln did not perform badly in response to serenades. "The speeches of the President at the last two serenades," wrote Hay in November 1864, "are very highly spoken of." There were times when some of his most quotable and epigrammatic phrases were delivered in such offhand speeches, though they presented unusual difficulties, not only as to preparation and delivery, but also as to reporting in the papers. A serenade response by Seward was "horribly butchered" in the *Chronicle*, and in order to avert a similar fate Hay wrote out one of Lincoln's night speeches "after the fact" (it was Lincoln's; Hay watched the reporting of it), while for the next serenade the President carefully wrote his words in advance and read them from manuscript.

V

How did the lanky President look on horseback? Very well, according to Nicolay; awkward and careless, according to others. When a "grand review" of the army was held near Washington on November 20, 1861, with fifty thousand men in line, the President rode out in his carriage, then mounted his horse. "Seward I think," wrote Nicolay, "remained in his carriage." The occasion was something of an endurance test, Cameron giving out and dismounting midway in the performance, "while the President went through the whole without the least symptom of fatigue." He rode up and down before the standing troops; then he and the officers took their stand on an acclivity while the soldiers marched past. "Hay and I," wrote Nicolay, "started home near sundown and the columns had not yet finished passing." "The President," he noted, "rode erect and firm in his saddle as a practised trooper—he is more graceful in his saddle than anywhere else I have seen him."

In contradiction of this—a minor example of the contradictions that run all through the Lincoln subject—we have a critical and ludicrous (indirect) account of Lincoln's technique when reviewing troops. A gentleman wrote from Wall Street, New York, to admonish the President as to "the receiving of military citizens (as all the volunteers are)." He thought it was a serious matter whether the Chief Executive pleased them or not; "soldiers write home to their friends in this town with reference to their disappointment in your bearing and manners when reviewing them—"

They say [he continued] when you are on horseback, and platoons of men marching by you, that you lean about and turn your head to talk with people behind you, when they claim that you should sit erect & talk to nobody and look straight at the saluting soldiers—that you ought to assume some dignity for the occasion even though your breeding has not been military— It makes but little difference whether the demand is reasonable or not—it dont require half so much sacrifice on your part, to rectify it as it does of the men to go from their homes for the hardship they undertake—

And when you are passing lines of soldiers, reviewing them, afoot, they say you take your boys along, and straddle off as if you were cutting across lots, to get somewhere in the quickest time you can, and pay a good deal more attention to your own getting along, than to the soldiers whom you start out to review—

These things dont sound well at all— The influence is bad here— The complaint may be frivolous and based on a mistake: but such things are written home here and fortify Raymond in his position of advertising for a "Leader"— He has got over that, rather, but there is no need of your being so infernally awkward, if these things are true— For God's sake consult somebody, some military man, as to what you ought to do on these occasions in military presence— Nobody will volunteer advice, probably, and if you are arbitrary and conceited on these little things, as Webster used to be, you will alienate your friends and go where he went and John Tyler too, towit where a man has no party—I dont mean a political party, but a great and universal body guard of men who speak well of you and will do anything to bear aloft and above reproach your administration—

The gentleman informed the President that the people cared "a mighty sight" about their soldiers. Even an autocrat would have to give attention to army evolutions and to let the soldiers know that, in reviewing them, he appreciated the business in hand. He would have the President know that his manner was as important as his talk. A lawyer in his office could rest his feet on a table, but not the Commander in Chief of the Armies of the United States. He must "pretend" to be a soldier even if his knowledge was deficient. The letter continued:

You had better let some officer put you through a few dress parades in your leisure moments, if you can get any, and get some military habit on you so you shall feel natural among military men— Dont let people call you a goose on these *very, very* important relations to the Army—

Mrs Lincoln is growing popular all the while, because people say she is mistress of her situation— She aptly fits herself to the times— The dinner service she bought at Houghout's makes people think she is "in town"—they like to talk about her and say she has a good deal of sense and womanly wit about her—she is coming into excellent reputation in this naturally prejudiced city against you and her both—

My impression is that you will do well by paying more attention to your manners and make less effort at wit and story telling— All well enough in private but publicly it is a nuisance— Your talent is conceded—be a gentleman and courtly in your manners when you ought to be— Now I dont care whether you take this well or ill— I voted for you and have a desire to be proud of your administration and I dont wish to see you over slaughed by these damaging stories when you could prevent it so easily—

Walt Whitman, who saw Lincoln frequently in Washington days, thought that the President and his cavalry guard, with sabres drawn, made "no great show in uniforms or horses." Whitman lived on the route the President took to and from the Soldiers' Home. "Mr. Lincoln," he wrote, "on the saddle, generally rides a good-sized, easy-going gray horse, is dressed in plain black, somewhat rusty and dusty; wears a black stiff hat, and looks about as ordinary . . . as the commonest man. . . . Sometimes one of his sons, a boy of ten or twelve [Tad was ten in 1863], accompanies him, riding at his right on a pony."

VI

Combining his function as ceremonial head of state with that of responsibly active Chief Executive, Lincoln found increasingly heavy demands on his time. Visiting the Navy Yard, he "personally and minutely inspected" its foundries and workshops where six hundred men were employed. One night at the observatory he "took a look at the moon & Arcturus." Pausing at the Capitol on one of his rides, he viewed the newly placed statuary of the east pediment. This evoked a bit of presidential art criticism; he "objected to Powers's statue of the Woodchopper, as he did not make a sufficiently clean cut." Fairs sought him out for a speech, a personal visit, a gift, or a written statement. The president of the Sanitary Commission, returning from California, brought and personally handed him "a present of great beauty and value from a few citizens of that state"—a gold box bearing the letters "A L" and containing "a number of singularly beautiful golden crystals . . . embedded in fine velvet."

Another "interesting ceremony . . . at the White House" was the "presentation to President Lincoln of a truly beautiful and superb vase of skeleton leaves, gathered from the battlefield of Gettysburg." They had been gathered by the ladies of the Philadelphia Sanitary Fair, at which over a million dollars had been raised for soldier welfare. Gettysburg was an exalted theme; tribute to the nation's defenders at Bloody Angle had already been paid. The speaker of the Gettysburg address was now called upon to sound the same note; and that, shortly after the death of Edward Everett. It was one more among countless demands upon the President's time and energy, but the occasion could not be passed off lightly. Though the event was reported as "wholly unexpected," Lincoln responded with a speech. It was like being asked to paint the lily. "So much," wrote Lincoln, "has been said about Gettysburg, and so well said, that for me to attempt to say more may, perhaps, only serve to weaken the force of that which has already been said." Lincoln did not paint the lily. He acknowledged the gift "with emotions of profoundest gratitude," referred handsomely to the departed Everett, paid appropriate tribute to the women of America, and gave assurance that the "kind wishes" extended to him were sincerely reciprocated.

Personal tragedies of the war were repeatedly brought home to the President in the funerals at which his attendance was required. A service for Col. Elmer E. Ellsworth, shot down in Alexandria early in the war, was held in the White House, May 26, 1861. Known to the nation as the dashing commander of a volunteer regiment of zouaves, and as the first striking example of a martyr to the Union cause, he was further known to Lincoln as a youth of zest and gusto who had studied law in the Springfield office, had participated in the 1860 presidential campaign, and had accompanied the President Elect on his trip to Washington. Lincoln was present at the rites for General Amiel W. Whipple who fell in battle at Chancellorsville, in May 1863, and at the ceremony for fifteen victims of an accident at the arsenal grounds in June 1864. On the latter occasion it was estimated that 25,000 people attended, coming by boat and every type of conveyance. When it was found in January 1864 that Lincoln could not attend the funeral of John Hughes, Catholic archbishop of New York, a letter was sent in the President's behalf by Secretary Seward in which the distinguished prelate's national service was acknowledged and tribute was paid to his loyalty, fidelity, and practical wisdom.

X   At times the President would honor an occasion by being part of an audience. He attended the lecture on the battle of Gettysburg delivered by Dr. J. R. Warner in May 1864 in the hall of the House of Representatives, and was present in the same hall when Anna E. Dickinson, abolitionist girl orator, spoke for the benefit of the Freedmen's Aid Association. His attendance was duly announced to stimulate the sale of tickets. He also attended when Bayard Taylor, in December 1863, delivered his lecture on "the geographical, social, political and economic history of Russia." On the numerous occasions when the President's attendance was requested but had to be declined, the declination required a letter from himself or a secretary; at times such a communication took on the nature of a state paper.

✗ Despite constant demands in Washington Lincoln was to a considerable extent a traveling President. Besides the well known speaking occasions at Gettysburg and Baltimore, the record of his presidential travels, if compiled, would include an expedition to Norfolk and Fort Monroe (May 1862), where he actually took a hand in directing operations, various trips through Hampton Roads and up the James, the famous conference at Hampton Roads, a hurried visit to West Point to consult General Winfield Scott, a visit by boat to Mount Vernon, excursions on the Potomac, a trip to Point Lookout, many visits to soldier camps and to the headquarters of McDowell, McClellan, Hooker, Meade, and Grant, and notable visits late in the war to City Point and Richmond. Sometimes he would take Tad with him, sometimes Mrs. Lincoln, or one of his private secretaries, or Ward Lamon, or Noah Brooks. Where a cabinet secretary accompanied the President, it would usually be Seward or Stanton, or less frequently Bates or Chase.

Of his visits to the army one of the most extended and noteworthy was that of April 4–10, 1863, when he combined recreation and duty by spending six whole days at Hooker's headquarters for the Army of the Potomac at Falmouth, Virginia. In the party were the President, Mrs. Lincoln, their beloved Tad, Dr. A. G. Henry, Noah Brooks, a Mr. Crawford, and Attorney General Bates. There were several reviews, in grand style, of what was considered the finest and biggest army in the world. Henry was very sure that the nation had the right man (Hooker) and that he would promptly "take his army into Richmond" and "to New Orleans if necessary." It was reported that 15,000 well mounted cavalry, 300 pieces of field artillery, and "about 150,000 of the finest looking, & best disciplined Infantry . . . ever seen in one Army" passed before the reviewing President whose visit would "add intensity to their zeal and confidence."

Noah Brooks's pen added color to the spectacle. The President wore a high hat and rode "like a veteran." Tad rode with the cavalry in charge of a mounted orderly, "his gray cloak flying in the gusty wind like the plume of Henry of Navarre." "It was a grand sight to look upon, this immense body of cavalry, with banners waving, music crashing, horses prancing, as the vast column came winding like a huge serpent over the hills past the reviewing party, and then stretching far away out of sight." After the review the President insisted on going through the hospital tents, "Stopping and speaking to nearly every man . . . and leaving a kind word as he moved from cot to cot." When the party rode from camp to headquarters, "tremendous cheers rent the air from the soldiers, who stood in groups, eager to see the good President."

Welles thought the President traveled too much. In his "intense anxiety" concerning the military situation in June 1864 the President visited Grant at his headquarters. Welles disapproved of "these Presidential excursions" and tried to discourage them, though Stanton and Chase, he said, favored them. "He can do no good," thought Welles. "It can hardly be otherwise than harmful, even if no accident befalls him. Better for him and the country that he should remain at his post here. It would be advantageous if he remained away from the War Department and required his Cabinet to come to him."

Travel was arduous and a good deal of time was thus consumed, but business was attended to on some of these trips, and they may have afforded variety, diversion, and much needed recreation to a cruelly burdened President. They gave him direct contacts outside Washington (contacts inside the capital being rather uninspiring); at times they would enable him to skip a cabinet meeting. At an early stage in the war the New York *Times* informed its readers that the President was "given to unannounced journeying." "His trip from Harrisburg about fifteen months since took the nation by surprise [the secret night ride through Baltimore to Washington in February 1861]; his recent visit to the army and navy yard at Fortress Monroe and Norfolk was as unexpected as it was significant; and the last excursion, taking the whole North by storm, is but one of a similar series."

Chapter Eight

LONELY WHITE HOUSE PAIR

λ Throughout his life as president, though this has not been sufficiently understood, one should think not alone of Lincoln, but always of the Lincolns. They were a close-knit couple—not that all their tastes were similar; it was rather that they were united; their concerns were mutual. Their children meant everything to them. The welfare of each was inseparable from that of the other. Mrs. Lincoln wrote: ". . . my husband told me that I was the only one he had ever thought of, or cared for." (Referring as a young man to his feeling for Mary Owens, whom he knew before he met Mary Todd, Lincoln had written that he was "a little in love with her.") As to the Lincolns being a loving and thoroughly devoted couple there can be no doubt on the part of those who know their story.

I

Mrs. Lincoln, not being of a blasé temperament, was elated by her high position, enjoyed it (at first), and plunged into the dazzling new life with buoyancy and enthusiasm. One of her sisters even referred to her "court." Her first duty as she saw it was to make a suitable and properly furnished abode out of the sadly unpresentable White House. No informed person could deny the need for such a transformation. There was a congressional appropriation of $20,000 for fitting out the President's mansion and when she undertook the expenditure of this seemingly large amount she had her first lesson in the intricate economics of officialdom.

✗ In her love of beautiful things and her honest wish to perform her task suitably, she was flattered by merchants, carried away by her own quick approval of the purchases she wanted, and victimized by the rather general tendency to gouge that impersonal entity known as "the Government." Mrs. Lincoln did not perform badly in what she bought, but in the lack of a proper check on her ordering she did exceed the appropriation. At the moment of purchase the problem of budgeting was not her main thought. (There was more to it than that; it seemed beyond Mary Lincoln's power to think straight about money matters.) She was in tears when she realized what she had done: tears of penitence and also of distress when she saw that she was creating a difficulty for her overworked husband.

To Lincoln the need for all this refurbishing did not register as with her, and when the matter was brought up by the commissioner of public buildings—B. B. French—the President was indignantly disgusted. He stood ready to pay the excess—about $7,000 over the appropriated amount—but the matter was adjusted by Congress with deficiency appropriations. Of course this business of exceeding an appropriation and appealing to Congress to make it up, while undesirable in terms of finance, was a familiar procedure. It is a procedure which has not yet been outmoded.

This episode of the expenditures was but one of many which brought heartaches for Mary Lincoln. The White House, with humanity crowding its doors, was becoming a lonely and a hostile place. As the months passed the bitter extent and depth of that hostility became a sore trial to this lady of unstable health. Her physical strength was never adequate to

these demands of public life. She was shaken by chills and
fever, had devastating migraine headaches, and suffered a
severe head injury in a carriage accident. Emotional instability
and (beginning with the presidency) a species of irrationality,
were parts, though minor parts, of her constitution, along with
an unsteadiness of nerves. Was she to blame for this? A fully
explanatory answer to this question cannot be easily given.
All the conditions involved, and all the balancing factors including fine attributes, would have to be considered. To give
the answer has not been within the reach of superficial writers
—certainly not of Herndon. It would take a physician and a
well informed and understanding one at that. A sudden noise—
the slamming of a door—would send her nerves quivering.
Calmness had not been her forte. She had always had a
timidity, a tendency toward panic in a storm, and a sense of
insecurity. These qualities did not make for the fullest self
control in an emergency. Yet speaking generally as to her
public conduct she did show poise, mastery, and control; her
social deportment was excellent.*

II

Social occasions in the President's mansion were elaborate
and stately, though often overcrowded. Shortly after the 1861
inauguration the Lincolns held their first "levee or reception."
Among those attending was William H. L. Wallace, an attorney
of Ottawa, Illinois, on an office-seeking visit to Washington.
He wrote to his wife: "The throng was immense. Ladies
crinoline suffered mercilessly. The crowded [White House]

* There was one sad exception which would be greatly misunderstood if
taken as typical. It came near the end of Lincoln's life and involved an unfortunate scene created by Mrs. Lincoln (at City Point in March 1865) who
was angered by a general's wife (Mrs. Ord) riding horseback beside the President,

was thickly sprinkled with the gay uniforms of the army &
navy & the diplomatic corps. Mr. Lincoln wore white kid
gloves & worked away at shaking hands with the multitude,
with much the same air & movement as if he were mauling rails.
Mrs. Lincoln seemed from the happy glance I had of her, to
be doing her part of the honors with becoming grace."

For her at least since she was not well during the White
House years, something was done to ease the strain on these
exacting occasions. William O. Stoddard, whose post of duty
was by Mrs. Lincoln's side, relates that she stood some steps
to the right of the President and farther back; much of the
procession would sweep past without shaking the hand of the
First Lady. "Her hand," wrote Stoddard, "is not so hard as his,
and could not endure so much grasping and shaking. Even his
iron fingers weary sometimes."

The general party in March 1863, at the close of the winter
social season, was typical. People formed in line awaiting
entrance. Long before 8:30, the hour set for the opening, it
was reported that "crowds of ladies and gentlemen" filled the
approaches to the entrance of the mansion. In an effort to keep
the crowd under some control a file of soldiers was stationed
at the doors. "Mr. Lincoln stood in the reception room, with
Mrs. Lincoln on his right, and after the ladies and gentlemen
were presented to the President and his lady they passed on
and entered the East room, where the promenading took place."
So wrote the reporter, first person plural, for the Washington
Chronicle. He continued: "In the latter room we noticed several
distinguished officers, both of the civil and military departments of the Government, accompanied by their wives, daughters, and friends. . . . The ladies endeavored to rival each
other in the brilliancy of dress, and it would take a *Jenkins*
to decide which was the belle of the evening. . . ."

Next year another of the huge levees was described as
surpassing all its predecessors. "The reception last evening,
being the last of the season, attracted an overflowing at-

tendance; indeed, the 'oldest inhabitant' would be at a loss to name one in the history of Washington so densely crowded. It is within bounds to state that thousands, on account of the immense throng, were unable to pay their respects to the President and Mrs. Lincoln, the latter of whom was exquisitely attired, and excited general admiration."

"The President," wrote the reporter, "was, as usual, affable and urbane to every one who approached him, bestowing upon all a friendly smile and cordial grasp of the hand, and to his official and social intimates a warm salutation and a pleasant word." The "distinguished personages" who were present in "large number" included members of the cabinet, senators, representatives, officers of army and navy, and foreign ministers.

✗ New Year's Day was regularly the occasion of a general public reception. For this event in 1862 the newspaper accounts glittered with journalistic superlatives. The affair was "very brilliant." The people who attended in large numbers were "of the first order of Society." "The President never appeared in finer spirits, and Mrs. Lincoln, supported by a bevy of the fairest of the metropolis, received with grace and elegance." Then came a mention of the man with whom Lincoln almost fought a duel in 1842. "General Shields [James Shields of Illinois, former senator, brigadier general of volunteers] made his appearance at the levee, and being originally from Illinois, and an acquaintance of the President and his family, was the special object of attention by Mr. and Mrs. Lincoln." After this levee was over, "a choice party was invited to listen to several patriotic songs from the Hutchinson Family in the red room."

✗ The first day of 1863 is remembered in history for the definitive proclamation of emancipation, but for Lincoln the hours and moments as they passed were harassing and exhausting. In addition to the public handshaking (or jerking) the President had a distressing interview with Burnside (who was getting nowhere in Virginia) and was confronted with the resignations of the highest ranking army leaders: Halleck, general in chief, and Burnside, commander of the Army of the Potomac. The trouble was temporarily patched up and the two resignations withdrawn (which did not solve the Burnside problem, or the Halleck one either), but on the historic day when they were proffered, those resignations were ugly facts. One of the features of the New Year's Day reception of 1864 was the attendance of the diplomatic body with "felicitations . . . as cordial as they were demonstrative." The entire corps were present with the exception of the minister from Nicaragua; detained by illness, he sent his "most friendly apology."

After officers, diplomats, and special groups had been received in the morning, a kind of free-for-all party followed. About noon, "The doors were thrown open, and the crowd surged in, trampling on one another's heels and toes, and doing some considerable damage to hats, bonnets and fine dresses." Entering at the front (the north door) of the White House, and moving first to the right, the sweeping mass of humanity pushed "through the Green, Blue and Reception rooms; and near the west door of the latter stood President Lincoln, and with a smile for all, [he] shook hands with his visitors of high and low degree." Ward Hill Lamon, marshal of the District of Columbia, made the presentations to the President; B. B. French, commissioner of public buildings, the introductions to Mrs. Lincoln. In the meantime the Marine Band "discoursed excellent music." Visitors passed into the great East Room, and "thence out by a substantial platform through one of the windows onto the pavement." "Coverings were placed over the elegant carpets in all the rooms, in order to prevent them being soiled by the mud." The throng of army officers, estimated at "between five and seven hundred," had assembled in the lower hall of the war department building, "completely jamming its entire space." In orderly formation "they proceeded at 11¼ A.M. to the Executive Mansion on their errand of courtesy, headed by the distinguished General-in-Chief [Halleck]."

For Gideon Welles, ever ready to see that his diary was informed on such matters, the undignified wedging and squeezing at these functions reflected no credit on the Chief's household organization. Describing one of the large parties, he wrote: "It was a jam, not creditable in its arrangements to the authorities." Observing that the "multitude were not misbehaved, farther than crowding together in disorder and confusion," he added: "Had there been a small guard, or even a few police officers, present, there might have been regulations which would have been readily acquiesced in and observed. There has always been a want of order and proper management at these levees or receptions, which I hope may soon be corrected." The big reception to open the year 1865, however, showed the same lack of order. It was held on Monday, January 2, and the people enjoyed it, but Welles thought a "little more system at the President's would improve matters."

So it went: dinners, receptions, matinees, concerts, perhaps a picnic for Negroes on the White House lawn, serenades, introductions, parades, reviews, generals to greet, foreign dignitaries to receive, crowds shaking the President's hand, studio pictures to be posed for, delegations or committees to be heard and answered, Sanitary Fairs to be attended or addressed by letter, speeches to be made, soldiers to be visited in camp or hospital, presentations, openings, dedications, inspections—no end to the continual round, while through it all the nation's existence and fate depended on the manner in which the gravest and most serious problems were faced and handled by the President.

A casual or random glance would find Lincoln speaking to a regiment, reading a prepared address of welcome to a diplomat, attending a funeral, visiting an observatory, testing a new gun, attending a lecture, or visiting the Capitol to observe progress on the construction of the unfinished dome.

Unusual interest in Washington society attached to the

wedding of the famous belle, Kate Chase, daughter of the secretary of the treasury, to Senator (former Governor) William Sprague of Rhode Island. On this occasion "a large and brilliant concourse of guests thronged the hospitable mansion of Secretary Chase. . . . The President of the United States, members of the Cabinet, the diplomatic corps, eminent officers of the army and navy, with citizens of Washington and friends invited from a distance, lent distinction to the scene, as their wives and daughters shed grace and beauty on the gay assemblage."

These incidental and miscellaneous duties collected their toll of energy, time, and thought. To be constantly called upon to say and do the appropriate thing on innumerable occasions, giving attention to each small duty without revealing boredom, is one of the exacting trials of a public man. Yet the people wanted to see their President. They pressed their attentions upon him. It was out of the question, nor was it desired by Lincoln, to deny them access. For thousands it was precisely these small occasions for which Lincoln in person was remembered.

An impressive lady reformer has left a unique first-hand account of President and Mrs. Lincoln. Mrs. Jane Grey Swisshelm was a journalist, an aggressive abolitionist, vigorous newspaper editor, and lecturer. For a time she conducted at Pittsburgh the antislavery paper, the *Saturday Visiter;* at times she contributed to Greeley's *Tribune;* later at St. Cloud, Minnesota, she published the St. Cloud *Democrat.* Coming to Washington in January 1863, and in spite of being a Republican, she did not wish to meet President and Mrs. Lincoln, regarding Lincoln as an "obstructionist" to the cause of abolition. She resisted various opportunities to meet the Lincolns, but at last she was persuaded to attend a levee at the White House (April 2, 1863). The notable alteration of her impressions of the Lincolns when she met them face to face was recorded in her words as follows:

"I watched the President and Mrs. Lincoln receive. His sad, earnest, honest face was irresistible in its plea for confidence, and Mrs. Lincoln's manner was so simple and motherly, so unlike that of all Southern women I had seen, that I doubted the tales I had heard. Her head was not that of a conspirator. She would be incapable of a successful deceit, and whatever her purposes were, they must be known to all who knew her.

"Mr. Lincoln stood going through one of those dreadful ordeals of hand-shaking, working like a man pumping for life on a sinking vessel, and I was filled with indignation for the selfish people who made this useless drain on his nervous force. I wanted to stand between him, and them, and say, 'stand back, and let him live and do his work.' But I could not resist going to him with the rest of the crowd. . . ."

Later Mrs. Swisshelm attended a Union meeting (March 31, 1863) attended by the President and his cabinet. She gave her record of the scene as follows: "He is very tall, and very pale. He walked quickly forward, bowed and took his seat. He was dressed in a plain suit of black which had a worn look; and I could see no sign of watch chain, white bosom or color. But all men have some vanity, and during the evening I noticed he wore on his breast, an immense jewel, the value of which I can form no estimate. This was the head of a little fellow ["Tad" Lincoln], about seven years old, who came with him and for a while sat quietly beside him in one of the great chairs, but who soon grew restless and weary under the long drawn out speeches . . . , and who would wonder [wander] from one Member of the Cabinet to another, leaning on him and whispering to him, no doubt asking when that man was going to quit and let them go home; and then would come back to father, come around, whisper in his ear, then climb on his knee and nestle his head down on his bosom."

Mrs. Swisshelm was impressed by the simplicity of the President forming one of the audience and by the picture of the father with his boy. She wrote: "As the long, bony hand

spread out over the dark hair, and the thin face above rested
the sharp chin upon it, it was a pleasant sight. The head of a
great and powerful nation, without a badge of distinction,
sitting quietly in the audience getting bored or applauding
like the rest of us; soothing with loving care the little restless
creature so much dearer than all the power he wields—a power
greater than that exercised by any other human being on earth."

III

When a dinner was given, or some other party which was
invitational, the Lincolns, like all presidential couples, were
sure to encounter grief on the question as to whom to invite. In
this respect one of the White House functions was described in
the New York *Herald* as a "blunder." To the one who used this
phrase it meant that the "wrong people" had been invited, the
"right" ones neglected. Later, however, S. P. Hanscom of the
Herald was able to inform his illustrious editor, James Gordon
Bennett, that "corrections" had since been made. "Some of the
first families in the country have been invited who were before
neglected, while it is a fact that parties were invited who would
not be admitted to the first circles in New York, Boston, or
Philadelphia. The whole programme has changed in regard to
the lines drawn with reference to the Diplomatic *Corps*, Brigadier Generals, and some Colonels, such as Mr. Astor &c., who
were ruled out."

As topics of general discussion, White House affairs were
comparable to crises in foreign relations. "Next to the British
question," wrote one of the journalists, "the forthcoming party
at the White House is the principal subject of comment. The
limitation of the number of invitations to only five hundred
and fifty occasions many disappointments and heart burnings."
The "general expression of disapprobation," he added, "makes

Brady photograph, National Archives

HOOP-SKIRT SPLENDOR

Mrs. Lincoln during the presidency, photographed by the famous Civil War photographer, Mathew B. Brady. The tilt of the nose suggests the vivacity so often spoken of by her friends.

it very questionable whether the gratification afforded to the five hundred and fifty favored guests will compensate for the sore disappointment and chagrin occasioned to five thousand five hundred who believe themselves equally entitled to the distinction of an invitation. The whole affair is regarded as a social blunder much to be regretted."

This dispatch was written on February 2, 1862, but soon the correspondent had come to see things in a different light. Next day he wrote:

"The wise course which is being pursued by Mrs. Lincoln, in returning to the customs of the early days of the republic, in her manner of receiving visitors, is applauded by all excepting some few envious individuals who are unable to procure invitations. It is fully time that festivities at the residence of the President of the United States should cease to be infested by crowds of individuals, neither whose manners, habits, nor antecedents entitle them to a place in respectable society. It cannot be expected, crowded as Washington is, that every candidate for office, every petty placemonger, every contract seeker, every quidnunc, whose time hangs heavily on his hands of an evening, should feel entitled as one of the 'great unterrified,' to while away his hours in companionship with the ladies who compose the refined circle of the accomplished lady of our excellent President. It was not so in the days of Washington and Adams. . . . The party [here he referred to the large reception to be held on February 5, 1862] . . . is the uppermost topic of conversation. Over eight hundred invitations have already been issued. The preparations are upon a scale of the greatest magnificence."

It is unimportant to speculate on the reason for the change of tone in the *Herald* correspondent's dispatches of the second and third of February. Perhaps by the latter date he had received his invitation. When he presented his lavish report of the party as held, he marshaled his best adjectives to describe "a truly brilliant array of fashion, beauty and manliness." He went on: "Such a display of elegance and taste and loveliness has perhaps never before been witnessed within the walls of the White House. . . . The President . . . greeted the guests with courteous warmth, and chatted familiarly with many whom he recognized as old friends. He was attired in a plain suit of black." Mrs. Lincoln, the reporter added, was "in half mourning for Prince Albert." To take this newspaper account of this fifth-of-February party in 1862 would be most inadequate. As will be seen later, the occasion was to become a ghastly memory for the Lincolns.

William O. Stoddard of the President's secretarial staff had a *bon mot* for that type of formidable occasion that was called a "ball." When, because of the crowding masses of people, there was no dancing, he thought the affairs could have been so called only by those who were "thinking of cannon balls." After considering all the cabinet members, judges, diplomats, admirals, generals, and governors, with their wives, he measured the floors with a tape line to estimate "standing-room." Custom, he said, required for each President a "routine of official dinners, dull, stately, costly affairs, . . . in a wearisome string through the season." In addition to the usual worries attending such affairs there was, in the case of the Lincolns, "the perpetual peril of having some official jollification set down beforehand for the evening after the arrival of stunning news from the army."

It was not a matter of Washington people only. Over the country, "great society people," together with "the would-be great," wrote in for invitations. Many "applications" had to be rejected, which swelled "the storm of absurd disapprobation . . . aroused by this unfortunate 'reception with refreshments.'"

Not merely admission, but recognition of personal importance, was demanded. The desire was not merely to be accommodated but received as specially favored gentlemen, with cards of invitation second to none. This business of inviting people "as gentlemen," or in such manner as to recognize degrees of personal prestige, could not fail to be serious in a democracy where human worth and equality was emphasized in principle. It was evident that in social invitations equality was not wanted in practice. Men could be invited as officials; that was not always easy, but at least it was a recognized principle. Where, however, cards of invitation were given to officials, other—e.g., reporters—might "be admitted," though without cards. The trouble was that this would not satisfy certain "proudly indignant" individuals. If they could not attend "as gentlemen" they would not attend at all. They had to be told that everyone who had a card of invitation received it by reason of official character, not because of "social position." The reporter of a leading paper would, of course, not be excluded, but he was to understand that he "had no more right to an invitation [by official card] than . . . any hod-carrier on Pennsylvania Avenue." As a precedent (not precisely an analogous one), Stoddard mentioned the prideful conduct of Charles Dickens, who "refused to perform his theatricals before the Queen, at her command, because he was not a gentleman of England, and could not be received at court." Such situations bring to mind the fact that to the exclusive minded the word "gentleman" connotes superiority, and that many who theoretically praise democratic "equality" do not at all object to exclusiveness so long as they are within the chosen circle.

The presence or absence, also the manner and facial expression, of diplomats was a matter of special observation. In a period of strained relations between the United States and Britain it was noted that no difficulty could have been guessed from the deportment of Lord Lyons, British minister. "No American," it was noted, "has shaken hands more heartily than he with the President. . . ." On the same occasion Stoddard observed: "France is not here, and it is understood that he will not come to-night; but if his absence has any ominous diplomatic meaning the hint is utterly lost upon Mr. Lincoln." The White House was "not a good workroom for intrigue."

IV

Of the three living Lincoln sons—Robert, Willie, and Tad —only two were part of the daily White House scene; for Robert, who came of age in the summer of 1864, was attending college at Harvard. It was Willie and Tad, with their exuberance and pranks, who gladdened, while they also complicated, home life in the presidential household, if home life it could be called. Abraham and Mary Lincoln loved their little sons with a love that was ardently reciprocated. Yet with official business conducted in the mansion—endless conferences, visitings, and interviews—there was little chance to enjoy family life.

Willie, their third son, was ten years old when his father became President. Well endowed, good looking, and lovable, he was the center of animated boy life, which included parties in which his mother took a special interest. "Willie Lincoln," wrote his playmate Julia Taft Bayne, "was the most lovable boy I ever knew, bright, sensible, sweet-tempered and gentlemannered." Willie and Tad, she wrote, "were two healthy, rollicking Western boys, never accustomed to restraint, and the notice which their father's station drew upon them was very distasteful. Willie would complain, 'I wish they wouldn't stare at us so. Wasn't there ever a President who had children?' "

In the wretched unhealthiness of Washington, with its shocking lack of adequate sanitation, Willie caught a serious illness, and it was announced on February 8, 1862, that "the usual Saturday reception at the White House and the levee on Tuesday would be omitted, on account of the illness of the second son [he was really the third son] of the President, an interesting lad of about eight years of age [another error], who has been lying dangerously ill of bilious fever [at another time reported as typhoid] for the last three days. Mrs. Lincoln has not left his bedside since Wednesday night [February 5], and fears are entertained for her health."

Days passed while the Lincoln household was plunged in anxious gloom. It was reported on February 11 that the lad had been "very ill," but was "much improved." Next day it was stated that the "little son" was "reported out of danger." In the altered tempo of life at the White House not only the levee, but the "usual Cabinet meeting" was dispensed with, while the President was often at the bedside. On February 18 Attorney General Bates noted in his diary: "The Prest.'s 2d. son, Willie, has lingered on for a week or 10 day[s], and is now thought to be *in extremis*[.] The Prest. is nearly worn out, with grief and watching."

As the grieving President and his wife continued their agonized vigil it was announced that the boy was "pronounced past all hope of recovery." Next came the report: "The White House is still overspread with the gloom of the expected death of the President's second son, who is reported more easy to-day, but no hope of his recovery is entertained. The President and Mrs. Lincoln are overwhelmed with grief." In the midst of all this it was noted that Tad was "now threatened with a similar sickness." In his unceasing solicitude for his sons Lincoln "gave them their medicines and spent as much time as possible in the sickroom."

V

In a letter written at the time it was reported of Mrs. Lincoln: "She is . . . just now sadly affected both of her little boys

are down with fever, and one is very dangerously sick. She &
the president have been watching for ten days, & she looks haggard enough."

On February 20 there was the "same routine," with the
President "very much worn and exhausted." As Nicolay wrote:
"At about five o'clock this afternoon [February 20] I was lying
half asleep on the sofa in my office when his entrance roused
me. 'Well, Nicolay,' said he, choking with emotion, 'my boy is
gone—he is actually gone!' and, bursting into tears, turned and
went into his own office."

"Me and father" had been pals or companions in frolic,
travel, and adventure, as well as at home. When he was but
eight years old, in June 1859, Willie had written to a friend from
Chicago: "This town is a very beautiful place. . . . Me and
father have a nice little room to ourselves. We have two little
pitcher[s] on a washstand. The smallest one for me the largest
one for father. We have two little towels on a top of both
pitchers. . . . [etc.]"

To those who have a feeling for the Lincolns as a family
there has come the thought—if Willie had lived. He was thus
described by Mrs. Elizabeth Todd Grimsley: "Willie, a noble,
beautiful boy of nine years, of great mental activity, unusual
intelligence, wonderful memory, methodical, frank and loving,
a counterpart of his father, save that he was handsome. He was
entirely devoted to Taddie who was a gay, gladsome, merry,
spontaneous fellow, bubbling over with innocent fun, whose
laugh rang through the house, when not moved to tears. Quick
in mind, and impulse, like his mother, with her naturally sunny
temperament, he was the life, as also the worry of the household. There could be no greater contrast between children."

Mrs. Grimsley continued: "Our first Sunday in the White
House, we all went to the New York Avenue Presbyterian
Church, Dr. Phineas D. Gurley's, which had been decided upon
as the church home, and ever after, the boys attended the Sabbath School, Willie conscientiously, and because he loved it,

Tad as a recreation, and to be with Willie."

Tad recovered, though his illness was no slight matter. He was now the one boy living in the White House. It is impossible to put on paper the depth and intensity of Lincoln's grief, of Mary Lincoln's, and of Tad's. On March 2 Mrs. Ninian W. Edwards, Mary's sister, visiting the White House, wrote in a letter to her daughter: "It is enough to feel . . . that my presence here, has tended very much to soothe, the excessive grief, that natures such as your Aunt's experience. And moreover to aid in nursing the little sick Tad, who is very prostrated with his illness and subdued with the loss he evidently suffers from, yet permits no allusion to. His mother has been but little with him, being utterly unable to control her feelings." On March 12 Mrs. Edwards wrote again: "Your Aunt Mary still confines herself to her room . . . and at times, gives way to violent grief. . . . Tad is still feeble, can barely walk a few steps at a time. He deeply feels the loss of his loving brother."

Another touching record of Tad's grief remains. In the series of home letters just mentioned, Mrs. Edwards referred to a trunk she was sending home to Springfield. In it Tad was sending two toy railroad cars to a little cousin. Mrs. Edwards wrote "It[the trunk] contained *two cars* that belonged to Willie. Tad insisted upon sending them to Lewis [Edward Lewis Baker, grandson of Mrs. Edwards], saying he could not play with them again."

VI

It was in this month of February 1862 that a favorable turning point was reached in the bitter war, with the important western victories at Fort Henry and Fort Donelson. It was stated in the papers that the "rebellion . . . [was] receiving fatal blows" under Lincoln's administration. Much was to be made of Washington's Birthday that year. Meetings for public celebration all over the country had been planned. "As a patriot and as President of the United States," wrote one of the journalists, "Mr. Lincoln has occasion to feel the proudest satisfaction in the success of our arms on land and sea; while, as a father, he is called to endure the severest domestic calamity. There is an indescribable gloom in the White House. The muffled bell, and the profound silence in those noble rooms . . . produce a strange effect upon the visitor who goes there to look upon the lifeless form of the pretty boy, . . . the sprightly, sweet tempered and mild mannered child, ... To-day the obsequies of little Willie took place. . . . Mrs. Lincoln . . . was too ill . . . to be present at the funeral ceremonies. . . . Here [in the East Room] were seated in a circle President Lincoln and his oldest son Robert, and the members of his Cabinet. . . . Mr. Lincoln was bowed down with grief and anxiety, and looked as if nearly worn out with watching."

In New Hampshire a former President, who would not ordinarily have been moved to write to Lincoln, broke silence to send a touching letter of sympathy and condolence. On the eve of taking office in 1853, Franklin Pierce had suffered a devastating bereavement when his eleven-year-old son, Benny, had been killed before his eyes in a railway accident. On matters concerned with the spiritual life he had been reticent. Now came the following letter in Pierce's hand:

Concord N.H.
March 4, 1862

My dear Sir,

The impulse to write you, the moment I heard of your great domestic affliction was very strong, but it brought back the crushing sorrow which befel me just before I went to Washington in 1853, with such power that I felt your grief to be too sacred for intrusion.

Even in this hour, so full of danger to our Country, and of

trial and anxiety to all good men, your thoughts will be, of your cherished boy, who will nestle at your heart, until you meet him in that new life, when tears and toils and conflict will be unknown.

I realize fully how vain it would be, to suggest sources of consolation.

There can be but one refuge in such an hour,—but one remedy for smitten hearts, which, is to trust in Him "who doeth all things well", and leave the rest to—

"Time comforter & only healer
When the heart hath bled"

With Mrs Pierce's and my own best wishes—and truest sympathy for Mrs Lincoln and yourself

I am, very truly
yr. friend
Franklin Pierce

His Excy—
    A. Lincoln
        Presdt &c
      &c &c

VII

For Mary Lincoln the death of Willie came as a crushing and shattering blow. Social functions were sharply curtailed. Never again would the life of the First Lady have the glamor of its first brief phase. When a lady nurse, quickly summoned to attend the broken woman, arrived, she found the President where one could have expected to find him, by the bedside of his sick wife.

It was his habit to be constantly solicitous of her, sending daily telegrams when she or he was away, keeping her informed of military movements (knowing her deep interest in the

progress of national events), and constantly striving to have
some sister or cousin on hand to assist and keep her company.
For her part she found numerous ways of helping him: con-
triving to overcome his moods of depression, suppressing her
own complaints to avoid worrying him with them, offering
relaxation, watching out for his meals (which he neglected),
and instituting the practice of a daily carriage ride. Thought
for his safety amid the lurking dangers and cruel burdens of his
position was with her a constant anxiety.

Deprived of any element of joy by the death of her beloved son, the White House became for Mrs. Lincoln a storm
center and a kind of dismal trap. Whatever she did or omitted
to do, she was sure to be criticized. An example was the expensive and elaborate party (on February 5th) at the White
House within the period when Willie lay ill. It had been
planned well in advance and when Mrs. Lincoln considered
canceling it, which would have been her wish, she was assured
of her son's recovery while of course she could not forget her
function as hostess. She was in an agony of suspense while the
party was on as she realized that the boy was not improving;
afterward she had to endure the stabbing injustice of a devastating set of verses, misnamed a poem, on the "Lady President's Ball," a savage piece of misplaced sarcasm put in the
supposed mouth of a dying soldier and scoring her thoughtless
extravagance and gaiety while men of the army were writhing
and dying in neglect. The false implication that she did not
care as to the welfare of soldiers—anyone who knew her
realized that she cared very deeply—was of a piece with the
incredible campaign of abuse of which she was the victim. Yet
if she omitted social functions, she was equally denounced for
that. Parties and dinners were not in general omitted in Washington in war time, and when she cut down on them in those
months of '62 following Willie's death, she had to bear the
accusation that she was denying her people that to which they
were entitled. She was even accused of being a "rebel" at heart

and a Confederate spy in the White House. No one in the nation was a more firm and earnest Unionist than she. It should be added that she showed notable friendliness and understanding toward the colored people. The enduring tradition among those people of worshipful friendliness to her has vastly more validity than the fabrication of some—alas, too many—among the whites.

There were two things that somewhat sustained her in her prostrating grief: first, her realization that Lincoln suffered too and that it was her duty to hearten him; and in addition her service in soldier hospitals. It was an impressive sight to see her ministrations as she visited the sickbeds of the wounded, brought them delicacies from the White House kitchen, and by her presence and conversation reanimated the spirits of the men who on their part—so different from the alleged soldier in the poem—gave her a sincere and grateful response. In her sensitiveness to suffering she was deeply affected by the painful scenes she encountered, but this, together with the constant danger of contagion to herself, she heeded not. It was W. O. Stoddard's view that she missed a chance in public relations by not deliberately publicizing this hospital service. That was not her nature. In her own person she did not seek the limelight. Her feeling about the matter, in addition to the impulse to help, was that without these humane employments her heart would have been broken by the loss of her child.

Unscrupulous men wormed their way into the mansion, gained access to the lady of the house, and made her an unsuspecting victim of their low intrigues. Such a man was one John Watt, the White House gardener whose extracurricular activities and juggling as to payrolls revealed him to be a disloyal cheat. Another imposter was the fabulous Henry Wikoff, an unprincipled adventurer who had been dismissed from Yale and had seen the inside of prison. He was a traveler extraordinary, wealthy idler, courtier, amateur diplomat, frequenter of foreign courts, supposed authority on Napoleon III, and

purveyor-in-chief of various kinds of fancy gossip. The name
"Chevalier Wikoff" became attached to him because of an unimportant decoration he had received in Spain. This disreputa-
ble but socially attractive man ingratiated himself in Mrs.
Lincoln's favor for the furthering of his own intrigues, one of
which had to do with the smuggling of unauthorized information to James Gordon Bennett's *Herald*. (That Bennett denied
the connection with Wikoff was to have been expected both of
Bennett and his type of journalism.) The story of Wikoff's
machinations need not be given in detail here; the time came,
none too soon, when he was told by the President to leave the
White House and never return.

VIII

One finds a brief and optimistic comment on Chickamauga
in a telegram (September 24, 1863) which the President sent
from Washington to Mrs. Lincoln who was then in New York:
"We now have a tolerably accurate summing up of the late
battle between Rosecrans and Bragg. The result is that we are
worsted, if at all, only in the fact that we, after the main fighting
was over, yielded the ground, thus leaving considerable of our
artillery and wounded to fall into the enemie's [*sic*] hands, for
which we got nothing in turn. We lost, in general officers, one
killed and three or four wounded, all Brigadiers, while . . .
they lost six killed and eight wounded. Of the killed one Major
Genl. and five Brigadiers, including your brother-in-law, Helm;
and of the the wounded three Major Generals, and five Brigadiers."

It was thus, almost parenthetically, that Lincoln broke the
news to Mary of the death of the Confederate brigadier general
Ben Hardin Helm, husband of Emilie Todd Helm. (The announcement of the fact, in the necessary brevity of this message,

was enough; Lincoln was not a man to put his emotions into a
telegram.) None of Mary's sisters was closer to her or more
beloved than Emilie. Both she and Helm had visited the Lincolns in Springfield and Lincoln had affectionately called her
"Little Sister."

Toward this brother-in-law Lincoln at the outset of his
presidency had shown a marked friendship. According to the
account by Helm's daughter, Katherine, the President sent the
young man a cordial invitation to Washington and handed him
"a commission as paymaster in the United States Army with
rank of major." This was a great opportunity. "The rank of
major at his age, thirty, was very exceptional in the army.
Nothing had ever touched Helm like this." Here was a fine
career opening up for him if he would accept. It seems to have
been assumed that, at least for a time, the position would have
involved residence in Washington. To Helm the advantage
appeared in terms of the rank and the chance to be transferred
at an early date to one of the cavalry regiments. To Mary Lincoln, however, in need of having a member of her own family
close to her, the great appeal was that her sister could be with
her in Washington—a belle on social occasions in the White
House, a source of pride, her husband a dignified officer. In this
respect Helm had a decision to make that was not unlike that of
Robert E. Lee—except, of course, that the great Virginian
"went with his State" and the Kentuckian did not. Though
grateful to his brother-in-law for the generous offer, Helm
declined it. It was a painful choice, and in that choice one may
read the difficult problem of those men of the Blue Grass who,
though regretting the breaking of the Union, cast their lot with
the Confederacy.

Commanding a brigade of the division led by his friend and
neighbor J. C. Breckinridge (of the Confederate right wing
under Lt. Gen. Leonidas Polk), Helm's men had been brought
under terrific cross fire from Union breastworks in a "portion
of the line [which] proved to be one of the most hotly contested

positions of the entire battlefield." Struck while riding toward the enemy's works on the morning of September 20, Helm fell mortally wounded from his horse. He died that night. It was a fearful tragedy in the Todd family and a source of personal sorrow to the Lincolns. We are not speaking here of demonstrations of White House grief. Times were grim and feelings could not always be expressed. One could, of course, weep sincerely for Helm—as one could admire the character of Lee—without favoring the Confederacy. The general had done his Confederate duty. To prominent fellow-Lexingtonians his conduct was as "Kentuckian" as that of Breckinridge and Morgan. The fact that, to the Lincolns, Helm was an enemy had significance not as a matter of hatred between them, but as an added grief, a cause of Emilie's deep resentment, and a bitter, inscrutable token of the unnatural brothers' war. It made it no easier that the Lincolns were in such a position that their genuine grief could find no adequate expression.

The personal agony of war came now to the very White House, but without the sympathy and understanding of friends by which tragedy is customarily softened. Of the genuineness of the President's feeling there can be no doubt. David Davis had never seen him more moved "than when he heard of the death of his young brother-in-law." And what of Mary's feelings? There were thousands of war-bereaved Americans, but the barriers to the expression of feeling made Mary's grief the harder; it was as if she was shut off from the right to feel as a human being and a sister. Devotedly loyal to the Union, she rejoiced in Federal victory, but with a poignant sense of what warfare meant in human terms on both sides. Having brothers in what she herself called the "rebel" army, she utterly disapproved of the cause which they served; yet the rightness of that Union disapproval, which she felt as sincerely as any, was denied her. She became the target of Northern suspicion; "a single tear shed for a dead enemy would bring torrents of scorn and bitter abuse on both her husband and herself." That she was a Southerner was true, but that a Southern origin made it necessary to war against the United States she, and many thousands of Kentuckians, denied. Yet Southerners judged her harshly as an enemy and thought of her as having a stony indifference to "the sufferings of her own people." In all, she had four brothers in the Confederate army—George, Samuel, David, and Alexander. Of these only George survived the war. Sam was killed at Shiloh, David at Vicksburg, and Alec in 1862 in the fighting at Baton Rouge. If she wept for these of her kin on the other side, it had to be in secret. One cannot read her story as told by her niece, Katherine Helm, without realizing that there was no one in the land upon whom the unnatural hatreds and distortions of that day bore more relentlessly than upon her.

IX

Mrs. Helm had attended the last rites for her husband at Atlanta and then stayed for a time in the home of E. M. Bruce in Madison, Georgia. At her request Mr. Bruce wrote to Lincoln reporting the manner of the general's death: "although opposed . . . to your forces, it will . . . be a satisfaction to you to know that he fell at the head of his Brigade—honorably battling for the cause he thought just and righteous—he was *leading* his 'Kentucky Brigade' to a charge which was successful . . . and I know you can but admire him for his deeds, and will regret that he could not have survived the conflict, and shared in the glories of the victory." (The reference here was evidently to the temporary Confederate victory in the battle of Chickamauga.) Mr. Bruce added: "Mrs Helm is crushed by the blow—almost broken hearted—and desires to return to her Mother and friends in Kentucky. . . ." He therefore asked the President to have a pass sent to her to enter the Federal truce boat at City Point: the pass to be sent in triplicate to Mrs. Helm, to William Preston Johnston at Richmond, and to Bruce himself at Madison, Georgia. The letter ended with a personal message from Emilie: "Mrs Helm desires to be affectionately remembered to her sister."

Bound for Kentucky, Emilie made her way by sea to Fort Monroe, but was informed that she could not proceed further unless she took the loyalty oath to the United States. Though faced with what seemed a helpless situation—in Union hands and "almost penniless"—she refused the oath. The officer in charge, not unfriendly but at a loss what to do, wired the President for instructions. Back came the answering telegram: "Send her to me."

Thus it was that Emilie found herself spending a week at the White House under the affectionate care of her sister Mary and "Brother Lincoln." Yet in her diary she wrote: "Sister and I cannot open our hearts to each other as freely as we would like. This frightful war comes between us like a barrier of granite. . . ." Not by words but by clasped hands of sympathy their griefs were joined—Mary grieving for her lost Willie, Emilie for her husband. Knowing they would hurt each other, they avoided the topic of the war. Emilie wrote of Mary: "Her fine tact and delicacy fill me with admiration."

Emilie's arrival in Washington came shortly after the announcement of the President's broad plan of amnesty, in which an oath of allegiance was prescribed. Lincoln presented her with this oath, which he had prepared for her to sign, but she refused, not with any air of bravado but simply because her loyalty was elsewhere; the Federal oath would have seemed to her and her friends a repudiation of the cause for which her husband had died.

At every stage Lincoln had done what he could. Where it was a matter of sending a pass, facilitating the recovery of property in the South, or extending amnesty, he had given Emilie's situation his personal and considerate care, though always within correct conduct as Union President. He urged her to prolong her stay at the White House, despite the embarrassment that arose from outspoken people who could not understand, and hoped she would spend the summer of 1864 with the presidential family. In a statement in his own hand, "Whom it may concern," he expressed the wish that she might "have protection of person and property, except as to slaves." Back in Kentucky Emilie was again in the Todd fold and the Lexington scene but under poignantly hard times. A tone of bitterness now crept into her letters. On October 30, 1864, she wrote that her half-brother (Mary's brother) Levi Todd was dead "from utter want and destitution." "I would remind you," she wrote the President, "that your *minnie* [*sic*] *bullets* have made us what we are." It is needless to comment on Lincoln's hurt feelings, and Mary's, on reading those stinging and accusing words.

X

It did not help matters in Mary Lincoln's "furnace of affliction" (to use her own phrase) that Lincoln's secretaries, Nicolay and Hay, could exchange letters belittling her—Hay going so far with his overclever pen as to call her a "Hell-cat." To say the least, a greater respect should have been shown by the secretaries for the President's own wishes and attitudes; he was not ignorant of her imperfections, but he dealt with her in kindness and understanding. A private secretary, to serve adequately, should be an aide to the President. Mrs. Lincoln had her difficulties with these secretarial youths on matters of the household payroll and of social invitations.

To know this side of the story from the standpoint of the Lincolns will enable one better to realize why it was that the President planned differently for 1865. These young men were slated to be provided for by appointments abroad and it was

arranged that Noah Brooks should be private secretary for the
second presidential term. One of the ablest men in Washington,
Brooks was the correspondent of the Sacramento *Union*. He
has importance in the Lincoln story for his reportorial records
and for his specially intimate relation with the President; he
was one of the few spirits of whom Lincoln was genuinely fond
and with whom he felt comfortably at ease. It is Brooks who
has given us one of the most striking comments on the vicious
weapons aimed against Mrs. Lincoln. He knew and indignantly
resented the abusive slanders of the Washington rumor-factory;
he knew better, for he knew Mrs. Lincoln as she was. Brooks
wrote:

"The wife of the President has been so frequently and
cruelly misrepresented and slandered that, though hesitating
to approach so delicate a subject, your correspondent cannot
refrain from saying a word in strict justice to this distinguished
and accomplished woman. When the present administration
came into power, the National Capital was infested as well as
besieged by rebels, and every conceivable means was adopted
to render the members of the new Administration unpopular.
To this end slanders innumerable were circulated concerning
the habits of the President and his family; and it is not many
months since when candid and loyal men were to be found
believing that our temperate President drank to excess, and that
Mrs. Lincoln was a vulgar, ill-bred woman. Such stories are
scandalous, and though time has done justice to the President,
who is seen and read of all men, Mrs. Lincoln is denied the
privilege of defense, and in the privacy of a household clad in
mourning has not yet had justice done her by the public."

To Brook's mind the inexcusable outrage was that "loyal
people, more shame to them, without knowing the truth of what
they repeat, still allow themselves to become the media for the
dispersion of scandals as base as they are baseless." Feeling
most keenly that a correction was long overdue, he continued:

"It is not a gracious task to refute these things, but the

tales that are told of Mrs. Lincoln's vanity, pride, vulgarity and meanness ought to put any decent man or woman to the blush, when they remember they do not *know* one particle of that which they repeat, and that they would resent as an insult to their wives, sisters or mothers that which they so glibly repeat concerning the first lady in the land. Shame upon these he-gossips and envious retailers of small slanders. Mrs. Lincoln, I am glad to be able to say from personal knowledge, is a true American woman, and when we have said that we have said enough in praise of the best and truest lady in our beloved land."

This comment was part of a long article giving at some length a first-hand description of life as it was lived in the White House, a subject on which Brooks could speak with assurance. He was letting his far-off Pacific coast readers share with him the inside view of the mansion: its ante-room for those seeking the President, its parlors, upholstery and fittings, stain and damask, "profusion of ormulu work," vases and the like bought or presented during the administrations of Madison and Monroe, its grand piano, its full length portrait of Washington, its richly colored hangings. Most people, he said, admired the blue room, "formed in the graceful curves of a perfect ellipse," its windows commanding "a lovely view of the grounds in the rear of the house and of the Potomac."

No part of the mansion seems to have escaped him. He wrote of the family apartments, dining room, conservatory, servants' rooms, kitchen, and basement. There was no "Kitchen Cabinet," he noted, "but the present presiding lady of the White House has caused a terrible scattering of ancient abuses . . . below stairs." There had been "suckers" who stole from kitchen and conservatory, "spies in every room in the house." When they were dispersed, they "circulated innumerable revengeful yarns . . . and there were . . . credulous people who believed them." He noted how vandals had snipped off bits of lace, drapery and carpet as relics; he wondered how they could have the "cheek" to exhibit these objects to friends at home with accounts as to how they were stolen.

After all this elaborate description and this indignant refutation of fabricated yarns, the observant Brooks concluded: "Republican simplicity and Republican virtues [upper case in the newspaper] reign at the home of the American President; thousands of private citizens in our prosperous country are more luxuriously lodged, and more daintily fed; but, search the wide nation over and you will not find a more united household or a more noble and loving family than that which to-day dwells in all of the anxious cares of the White House."

What was said by Noah Brooks was made evident by another close and competent observer, Ben Perley Poore, who wrote: "The President's wife . . . ought not to be left unmentioned, although there is little of interest to chronicle in her daily round of serving, reading and visiting hospitals, which occupies the time of Mrs. Lincoln. She may have made mistakes—who does not? in her invitations, and thereby have provoked envious criticisms. Neither do those of the Democratic [party] era admit there can be any courtesy displayed here now-a-days. But I am sure that since the time that Mrs. Madison presided at the White House, it has not been graced by a lady so well fitted by nature and by education to dispense its hospitalities as is Mrs. Lincoln. Her hospitality is only equaled by her charity, and her graceful deportment by her goodness of heart." Not all the mud slinging and shameful abuse can rob Mrs. Lincoln of that which was admitted by contemporary writers not governed by prejudice: her performance as hostess and First Lady. She served with dignity in all the exacting social world of the presidency.

Chapter Nine

ATTENTION OF THE PRESIDENT

I

FEW MEN OF HIS TIME UNDERSTOOD THE EXTENT OF LINCOLN'S presidential burden. Patronage, dealings with Congress, public relations, civil and military duties, and an appalling amount of detailed business pertaining to the army, crowded upon his waking hours and robbed him of sleep. The unceasing demands upon him as the court of high appeal in numerous personal cases took heavy toll of his time and energy, of his patience and emotional endurance.

On hundreds of private requests the President had to give or refuse permission. What about the case of "Sue and Charlie" —Mr. and Mrs. Charles Craig, cousins of John Todd Stuart? Dislodged from their home by war's desolation, they wanted to go back and cultivate their farm near Helena, Arkansas. They needed a pass through the lines and assurance of non-molestation by the military authorities. Accompanied by Henry T. Blow of St. Louis ("old friend" of Lincoln, successful business man, and leading Republican), Sue called at night at the White House, saw Lincoln, and presented her request. Writing on a Sunday, Stuart informed his wife that "Mr. Lincoln . . .

granted all Sue's wishes and promised to have the papers made
out for her by tomorrow." This bit of personal business involved
"influence" of prominent men, use of the President as errand
boy, the writing of an official "ADS" (autograph document
signed) by the President, the making out of various papers, and
due attention to the details by the proper authorities. The matter was mentioned along with the problem of "a permit for
Cousin Ann [Mrs. Ann Todd Campbell of Boonville, Missouri,
cousin of Mrs. Lincoln] to trade in Cotton down the Mississippi." Stuart thought the affairs of sundry cousins were going
well. "How *we apples swim!*" he remarked.

An "old lady of genteel appearance" called with a "piteous
appeal." Having fitted up portions of the old Duff Green building in order to take in boarders, and having engaged members
of Congress to board there, she was given an eviction notice
with a quick deadline; aside from the "ruin" occasioned by the
loss of her financial outlay, she could find no other shelter for
her head. Her appeal was given personal consideration by the
President, resulting in his "ALS" (autograph letter signed) to
Secretary Stanton in the lady's behalf.

Were these trivial matters? Of course they were matters
that should never have been brought up to the President, but if
one is studying Lincoln's presidential days and how they were
spent, the accumulated weight of such things cannot be ignored; Lincoln's time was continually devoted to precisely such
appeals. A loyal Mississippi lady had taken the Federal oath
of allegiance and had leased her plantation "to parties of unquestioned loyalty." By military sanction it had been leased to
other parties. So Lincoln had to write to Adjutant General
Thomas to have the matter, about which he knew nothing,
straightened out. Could something be done about the request
of Dr. William Fithian, friend of Lincoln and substantial citizen
of Danville, Illinois, who wished to recover the remains of a
stepson in Missouri? Lincoln did what he could, wiring to General Samuel R. Curtis, asking that the necessary facilities be

extended. Was there a Confederate prisoner named Joseph J. Williams confined at Camp Chase, Ohio? Or was he at Camp Douglas near Chicago? Would the officer in charge "tell him his wife is here, and allow him to Telegraph her?"

Sometimes the request was for a recommendation. Though he had "but slight personal acquaintance" with Mrs. Lotty Hough, Lincoln knew of her by reputation and had "never heard ought against her." She was struggling to support herself and little boy. The President hoped that opportunities to succeed would be afforded her.

In unnumbered personal cases the President sought to relieve distressed human beings of the harassments of war. In a generalized letter of instruction to commanding officers in West Tennessee he wrote: "It is my wish for you to relieve the people from all burdens, harassments, and oppressions, so far as is possible, consistently with your military necessities; . . . the object of the war being to restore and maintain the blessings of peace and good government, I desire you to help, and not hinder, every advance in that direction."

It is remarkable that so many hardship cases and personal appeals came up to Lincoln himself. A Unionist-minded lady was reported to be seeking separation from her husband who was in the Confederate army. The President would not offer her, or any wife, "a temptation to a permanent separation from her husband," but if her mind was "independently and fully made up to such separation," he wished certain "property . . . to be delivered to her, upon her taking the oath" of loyalty. A lady with her six daughters wished to go to her father in Richmond, Kentucky; Lincoln directed the officer in command at Knoxville, Tennessee, to allow the trip. A poor widow had a son in the army, who for some offense had been sentenced "to serve a long time without pay, or at most, with very little pay." Lincoln wrote to his secretary of war: "I do not like this punishment of withholding pay—it falls so very hard upon poor families."

Sometimes an individual appeal would involve a broad public policy. Frequently the problem would be an excessive use of military authority in matters appropriate for the courts. A provost marshal, for example, seized a building, with premises and furniture, belonging to a lady whose husband "went off in the rebellion," though she was the owner of the property, independently of her husband. The basis of the seizure was vague, and the property was not taken for any military object. "The true rule for the Military," wrote the President, "is to seize such property as is needed for Military uses and reasons and let the rest alone." The case involved complicated and serious legal questions—whether either husband or wife was a traitor, which one owned the property, and whether the wife's property was confiscable for the treason of her husband—"all which," wrote Lincoln, "it is ridiculous for a provost-marshal to assume to decide." He directed that the case be adjusted and revised on these principles.

II

Often the thing desired of Lincoln was his signature. One jovial visitor stated that he would prefer it "at the foot of a commission." A lady wrote a "complimentary poem" to the President and asked for his autograph. Lincoln wrote: "I thank you for it, and cheerfully comply with your request." A bride-to-be, signing her name as Polly Peachblossom, asked the busy President for an autograph on an enclosed piece of silk, to be placed in her wedding quilt. "All the other Peachblossoms," she wrote, "had a silk quilt ready for their wedding and why should not I?" These little requests were satisfied with a sense of form suited to the occasion. When a wish for his autograph was expressed by Lady Villiers, Lincoln wrote: "I beg that her Ladyship will accept the assurance of my sincere gratification at this opportunity of subscribing myself Very truly Her Ladyship's obedient servant A. Lincoln."

There were numerous pleas for notes of introduction. And there was the case of "a fair, plump lady" of Dubuque. Just before a cabinet meeting she pressed forward, saying she "was passing East and came from Baltimore expressly to have a look" at the President. Among other questions he was asked to approve a benefit raffle. So a presidential telegram went to Mother Mary Gonyeag of Keokuk: "The President has no authority as to whether you may raffle for the benevolent object you mention. If there is no objection in the Iowa laws, there is none here." Sometimes in this endless round there would be a flash of homely kindness and human sympathy. Toward laboring people especially the President showed particular consideration. He held an interview with a committee of Philadelphia working women to hear their complaints. In the sewing that these women did they had a poor pittance which was "reduced one-half to gratify and enrich a class of grasping contractors." In the Forney press of Washington and Philadelphia we find the comment: "It is rather a unique spectacle to find the chief of a great Republic . . . quietly and patiently hearing the complaints of a committee of plain and humble women. . . . This, however, is one of the most beautiful examples of a republican Government. The voice of the poor is not often heard by the politician, and particularly the voice of poor women, who have no votes and no influence in primary conventions. . . . These persecuted women go to the President with their grievances, and tell him their story with the simple, homely way of the housewife. And the result is precisely what was anticipated by all who know Abraham Lincoln and his great, good heart. . . . The sewing women will hereafter receive justice. . . . The poor men and women will find that their greatest friend is the President, and that when their errand is justice, no one will be more patient, and sincere, and prompt than the laboring man of Illinois who sits in the Executive chair at Washington."

It might be a new invention that the President would be asked to pass upon. Often it was a personal request for employment. Perhaps it was the disunionists of Maryland or the Unionists of Eastern Tennessee who required attention. A congressman would offer his services. A governor would demand an explanation. Serious Indian troubles in Minnesota in the summer of 1862, "involving official frauds on the one hand and Indian depredations on the other," required an arduous trip by John G. Nicolay to the scene of turmoil, so that Lincoln might have at that distant point "an unprejudiced observer" who could be, if not an *alter ego,* at least a kind of domestic presidential envoy. In performing this duty—meeting with United States officials and conferring with Chippewa chief Hole-in-the-Day—Nicolay was absent for an extended period during which he wondered whether his scalp was safe. Next summer there was a flare-up of Indian trouble in Colorado, and again Lincoln sent Nicolay, this time "to accompany the Governor of Colorado Territory down to Connejos in the San Juan Valley and to conclude a treaty with the Utes." The secretary "looked upon that visit to Colorado as one of the rare experiences of his life." "A little black notebook that he carried in his pocket fairly explodes with adjectives praising the beauty of the scenery, the fantastic grades at which alleged roads climbed steeple-like peaks, only to drop again into valleys in a way to make a traveler's head swim."

Such things can be voluminously listed—it is like going over a file of government papers—but when that is done it is still difficult to recover an adequate picture of the executive job as it existed under Lincoln. To enumerate his diverse "problems" is not enough. One problem alone might be supercharged with vexation and annoyance; yet to analyze the intricacies of his tasks, or explore their limits and boundaries, is impracticable. In his routine of duties Lincoln had to have eyes and ears for all parts of the country and for matters within every department. Decisions had to be made as to the Almedan mine in California. Attention had to be directed to the breaking of ground for the Union Pacific Railroad, the restoration of Virginia, espionage in the Confederate capital, American participation in the London "exhibition of the products of industry of all nations" (1862), the bringing of produce through the military lines, "the subject of a Reciprocity Treaty with the Sandwich [Hawaiian] Islands," and to the request that Brigham Young be authorized to raise a force to protect the property of the telegraph and overland mail companies in Utah Territory.

The President's time, as he himself wrote, was subject to "constant and unexpected requisitions." At another time he referred to "the multitude of cares" claiming his "constant attention" because of which he had been "unable to examine and determine the exact treaty relations between the United States and the Cherokee Nation." One becomes accustomed to the unusual, and inmates of the White House, as Stoddard called them, became familiar with "this strange, unnatural, wartime atmosphere." "Mr. Lincoln," he wrote, "bears it better than could another man in his place, perhaps, but it is telling upon him perceptibly. . . . All kinds of people come on all kinds of errands, and most of them, nowadays, besiege the Capitol and the Departments, but there is a long list of persistent visitors who hang around the White House and wait for chances to see the President, even after they are assured that he cannot and will not see them."

III

In the face of all these demands the accessibility of the President and his willingness to meet people was a source of wonder, even though by many it was taken for granted. If, however, some found him "hard to see," that was but another evidence of the extent of his burdens. The White House staff sought as far as possible to protect him. There were "guards or footmen" whose duty it was to divert the many who called from curiosity or without sufficient business. Sometimes, because of this, those who had serious business could not see him. Charles D. Drake, chairman of a delegation from Missouri, having submitted documents "of great length," waited for three days seeking a conference in order to get the President's answer to some very serious and vexing questions pertaining to the muddled situation in Missouri. He remained in Washington for that purpose alone. Failing to see Lincoln, he left; then it turned out that this was a matter requiring such detailed and extended study that Lincoln wrote a long and involved answer, over two thousand words, in the nature of a substantial state paper. So much concentration was required by Lincoln when he got round to this task that others who sought audience with him had to be disappointed. "The President," it was reported, "excluded all visitors to-day. The Missouri delegation think he is at work on a reply to them."

Another caller wrote: "I called for a personal interview, & have done so many times since, but found you engaged with some Major General, cabinet officer, member of the Senate or House: or the throngs pressing upon you, their varied claims or propositions; & so . . . retired for a more favorable opportunity."

Often it required a good deal of endurance to succeed in meeting the nation's Chief, but the main point is that Lincoln wanted to see people, disapproved of anything that kept them away from him, submitted to constant annoyance, and actually did see an amazing number. Of course he had assistance and time-saving devices. Secretaries were at hand, ready for the immediate sending of telegraphic messages, a bell at his touch for summoning needed help, a clerk to sign land warrants [W. O. Stoddard], and authorities on many subjects ready to respond with specialized advice, as when George Bancroft was asked for historical information, or the storehouse of official lore was tapped for points as to procedures of earlier Presidents reaching back to Jefferson and even to Washington. The march of data into and out of Lincoln's mind would make an impressive procession. He was not as unmethodical as is sometimes supposed, was aware of the importance of files, and in tricky or serious matters was prudently careful to keep records of what he said and of the precise extent of his commitments.

None of his manifold problems came singly. They were tossed into the President's lap in heaps, with nagging persistence and exhausting repetition, bursting at times, or threatening to burst, into acute crises. Easier things—those for which a ready answer could be found—could be handled as department matters, or dealt with by subordinates. It was the bothersome, baffling, or painfully difficult aspects of a case, or questions involving larger trends of governmental action, that would reach the President. Broad trends, however, or what was called general policy, could never suffice for all the decisions Lincoln had to make. The very concept of "general policy" was somewhat illusory. The particular case, the human aspects of a situation brought before his eyes, had always to be considered.

To "see" Lincoln and shake hands with him was not the same as knowing him or having contact with his mind. The outward Lincoln, when people met him socially, might be playful, friendly, or seemingly relaxed. Finding him so, people would, in the fuller sense, not meet Lincoln at all. Leaving his presence they could have said something of his face and figure, his clothes, his smile, his manner of bowing and greeting; but they would not have known the burdens and perplexities of the Chief Executive within those clothes, nor would they have glimpsed the feelings and emotional stresses of the inner man.

It was fortunate that strength and patience were given to Lincoln beyond the usual measure. His rugged features were furrowed with anxiety. When Grant's army was hacking its way through the Wilderness there was a week when it was said that "he scarcely slept at all." Carpenter the artist met him in the "main hall of the domestic apartment on one of these days, . . . clad in a long morning wrapper, pacing back and forth a narrow passage leading to one of the windows, his hands behind him, great black rings under his eyes, his head bent forward upon his breast,—altogether such a picture of . . . sorrow, care, and anxiety as would have melted the hearts of . . . adversaries, who so mistakenly applied to him the epithets of tyrant and usurper." There was an irregularity about his eating habits; trays would be carried upstairs, but left untouched for long intervals. The "weary air . . . became habitual during his last years . . . and no rest and recreation . . . could relieve it." As he expressed it, the remedy "seemed never to reach the *tired* spot." The significant thing about all this strain and anxiety is that Lincoln endured it. It did not break him. His was not one of those "high-wrought nervous organizations" as has been said of Jefferson Davis. His nerves were under balance and control, and unlike Davis he had a great American sense of humor.

The whole nation, with constant attention to its great future, occupied his thought. Problems were not timed to suit his convenience; matters of peaceful development crowded in with the wretched tasks of war. Lincoln had to be mindful, not only of preserving the nation, but of the kind of nation he was preserving. A war was on, but affairs could not be static for that reason. Industrial growth, foreign relations, and westward advance required as much thought certainly as they had under Buchanan. Even the non-war activities under Lincoln were not "ordinary." Things that were formative, and would be effective for decades to come, aside from the battles and campaigns, took shape in Lincoln's four years.

IV

It is known of Arthur Hugh Clough that he wrote distinguished poetry. It is also known that he spent many hours wrapping and mailing brown paper parcels for Florence Nightingale. If biography is a story of how a man's life was spent, everyday things cannot well be omitted. In August 1862 Abraham Lincoln was watching for his chance—i.e., a victory—so that he might issue the emancipation proclamation. In that month, on August 9, he also gave his attention to a snuff-box presented by the son of Henry Clay. Perhaps the snuff-box, a memento of him who spoke "for the Union, the Constitution, and the freedom of mankind," was not such a small object to Lincoln, nor the service for Florence Nightingale a trivial thing for Clough. If an incident *seemed* small, it may have had real meaning. It could not be considered altogether insignificant that on May 30, 1864, Lincoln handed a little boy a note: "This little gentleman has seen me, and now carries my respects back to his good father, Gov. Hicks."

That was Lincoln's side of the correspondence on this small matter. The incident is of sufficient interest to justify us in noticing the circumstances on the Hicks side. The governor of Maryland had well served the Union cause in the severe crisis of secession, for which Lincoln had a lasting gratitude; after that he served usefully in the United States Senate. There is a quality of respect and dignity in the letters he wrote to Lincoln which one finds, in legible handwriting, in the Lincoln papers. In 1863 his ankle was so severely injured that the foot had to be amputated. He therefore paid his personal respects to the President through the assistance of his son. On the day of Lincoln's note just quoted, Hicks wrote to the President, concluding with the words: "I sit at yr door in carriage until I hear your determination. Wish I could climb the stair way as formerly, and see yr Honor myself. yr obt. Servant, Tho. H. Hicks."

Nor was it an unimportant detail when President Lincoln wrote to John H. Bryant of Princeton, Illinois (brother of William Cullen Bryant), concerning a monument to the memory of Owen Lovejoy, whose brother (Elijah P.) had fallen a martyr to the antislavery cause. In the late fifties the managers of the Republican party (notably David Davis) had worked hard, largely behind the scenes, to counteract the influence of such as Owen Lovejoy, who was an upstanding and fearless leader against slavery. Now, in May 1864, Lincoln wrote beautifully of his "increasing respect and esteem" for the man who "bravely endured the obscurity which the unpopularity of his principles imposed." It would indeed have taken a man of the highest principles and character to have earned the carefully phrased tribute which Lincoln paid. The President continued: "Throughout my heavy, and perplexing responsibilities here, to the day of his death, it would scarcely wrong any other to say, he was my most generous friend. Let him have the Marble Monument, along with the well-assured and more enduring one in the hearts of those who love liberty, unselfishly, for all men."

When the ladies in charge of the Northwestern Fair for the Sanitary Commission asked the President to donate the original draft of the emancipation proclamation, Lincoln sent it, thus parting with a manuscript which he valued highly. He wrote: "I had some desire to retain the paper; but if it shall contribute to the relief or comfort of the soldiers, that will be better." The paper was "offered for sale [as stated by Isaac Arnold] at the Sanitary Fair held at Chicago, in the autumn of 1863. It was purchased by Thomas B. Bryan, Esq., and by him presented to the Chicago Historical Society. . . ." In the great Chicago fire of 1871 this valuable Lincoln original was burned; had Lincoln kept the document, it would presumably have remained with his papers, which are now safely kept in the Library of Congress.

A WHITE HOUSE RECEPTION

This lithograph, entitled "Grand Reception of the Notabilities of the Natio[n] at the White House, 1865," and copyrighted by Frank Leslie in 1865, should [be] viewed as a generalized conception rather than a depiction of a specific event. Th[e] artist apparently confused a reception of March 1864, honoring General Gra[nt,] with the inaugural reception of March 4, 1865. Andrew Johnson was absent fro[m] the first of these occasions and Grant from the second, yet both men are picture[d] here. The drawing is interesting for its accurate representation of the East Roo[m] and its faithful likenesses of many "notabilities" who at one time or another we[re] there. Among them, in the right foreground, the President and the First Lady a[re] greeting Mrs. Grant. Near by are General Grant, Vice President Johnson, Chi[ef] Justice Chase, Secretary Stanton, Chase's daughter Kate, and Secretary Seward.

The personal attention of the President was also required in connection with the children's petition that he "would free all slave children," sponsored by Mrs. Horace Mann and handed to Lincoln by Senator Sumner. The thought that went into the writing of this letter to one of the notable Peabody sisters was Lincoln's own; the petition was preserved in his papers.

In addition to broad national causes—soldier relief, emancipation, and the like—requests kept piling up for merely local or personal favors. One such was mentioned by Secretary Welles: "The President sends me a strange letter from [Vice President] Hamlin, asking as a *personal* favor that prizes may be sent to Portland [Maine] for adjudication." The Secretary of the Navy did not like this. Such a matter "was not to be disposed of on personal grounds or local favoritism"; other New England ports would have equal claims; additional prize courts would be expensive; Portland had no navy yard or station, nor did it have facilities for examining captured vessels, or for confining prisoners. But, said Welles, Hamlin was not moved by such considerations; he wanted all this extra paraphernalia to be set up at Portland "and solicited them of the President, as special to himself personally."

Perhaps this language was a bit strong, though Welles was correct in principle. Nor can it be forgotten that Lincoln himself had played the politician, promoting merely local interests by way of log rolling, while in the legislature of Illinois. Where great advantage was attainable in wartime expenditures, facilities, and appointments, it was natural for many localities to seek their shares of that advantage, but it was essential that the nation's effort be not dissipated by such demands. Here was a case where Lincoln, under constant pressure from such appeals, was careful to refer the matter to the appropriate minister even in a request that was hard to deny because of the personal influence of the Vice President.

V

After one considers the seemingly small matters that had real significance, there remain hundreds that were small only, having no other meaning than to show how Lincoln was harassed, badgered, and importuned in innumerable requests that, to say the least, fell short of the national or patriotic motive. People continually tried to exploit him. He was asked to recommend cotton traders to the military authorities—i.e., to advise that particular men seeking profit in cotton trading be given military facilities. The answer came that the President could not write "that class of letters." Yet in some cases where trading in enemy territory was represented to him in the best light, he did give permission. Lobbyists for special interests crowded the hotel bars and could by no means be kept out of the White House. One of these is portrayed by W. O. Stoddard as coming out of Lincoln's room, propelled by a large foot. Some of those who sought to use Lincoln, wrote Stoddard, were "thieves, counterfeiters, blacklegs—the scum and curse of the earth." Toward such men Lincoln was not kindly. He was decidedly blunt.

As to the vast unceasing flow of these miscellaneous requests the reader must be spared, though Lincoln was not. A few instances will indicate the type. There came a request for the use of blockade vessels to bring out a "lady-relative" of a Chicago friend; for permission to a Mrs. Keenan for "her and her little nephew to pass our lines and go to her father in Rockingham, Virginia"; for cadets by the hundred to be appointed to West Point. So tormented was Lincoln "by visitors seeking interviews for every sort of frivolous and impertinent matter [wrote Francis F. Browne], that he resorted sometimes, in desperation, to curious . . . inventions to rid himself of the

intolerable nuisance." One of "these bores" was scared off by
the pointed statement, when the President was ill with the
varioloid (a light case of smallpox), that his disease was "very
contagious." "'Some people,' said the President, 'said they
could not take very well my proclamation; but now, I am happy
to say, I have *something that everybody can take.*'" When an
editor of a small weekly called at the White House claiming to
have been the first to suggest Lincoln's nomination for the
office of President, the busy Chief sought to escape him by
saying he was going over to the war department to see Stanton.
The editor then offered to walk over with him and Lincoln
said, "Come along." "When they reached the door of the Secretary's office, Mr. Lincoln turned to his visitor and said, 'I shall
have to see Mr. Stanton alone, and you must excuse me,' and
taking him by the hand he continued, 'Good-bye. I hope you
will feel perfectly easy about having nominated me; don't be
troubled about it; *I forgive you.*'"

VI

That the presidency under Lincoln was not limited to
legally official acts was shown by his leadership in the observance of Thanksgiving. It was through him that the day became
for the first time a matter of regular annual proclamation by
the President. By so using his position he was widening the
reach of the presidency itself, making it an institution touching the hearts and expressing the emotions of the American
people.

The religious ceremony of giving thanks for the harvest
and for other blessings was, of course, an old American custom,
as old as the early days of the Plymouth colony. Down the
years the custom had become established with special importance in New England, yet before Lincoln's administration

there was no regularly recurring annual proclamation by the President. Washington, John Adams, and Madison had called upon the people for specified days of public thanks or prayer, but these earlier presidential calls were not annual and were not associated with the harvest festival, nor with any particular time of the year. The days set aside ranged through January, February, April, May, August, September, and November. The occasions had to do with such matters as the establishment of the Constitution in 1789, the suppression of the whiskey insurrection in 1795, and the making of peace with Britain in 1815.

While the Thanksgiving custom was becoming more firmly established and was spreading to the South, it was the governors who issued the proclamations and indicated the days to be observed in their states. This was not fully satisfactory and in the 1840's a prominent and tireless editress, Sarah Josepha Hale ("Madonna in Bustles") began a campaign of persistent appeals year by year in *Godey's Lady's Book* urging that the governors concur in proclaiming a uniform date, the last Thursday in November. This idea took hold, though not completely; then in 1863 she had another plan. Would not a proclamation by the President, unvarying as to date from year to year, be the best device to establish Thanksgiving Day along with Washington's Birthday and the Fourth of July in the calendar of holidays? The President, she proposed, would proclaim a day of national thanksgiving for the District of Columbia, the territories, the army and navy, and American citizens abroad. Also she hoped he would "appeal" to the state governors to unite with him in proclaiming the same date so that the nationwide festival would become not only a common event for all, but also a great force for the Union. She continued this agitation through the fifties, though in the unenlightened politics of that decade the Union emphasis became inaudible in the noise and clamor of sectional agitation.

Mrs. Hale's letter to Lincoln, embodying her idea that the President should proclaim Thanksgiving, was written on September 28, 1863. Five days later Lincoln issued his eloquent proclamation. In the midst of "a civil war of unequaled magnitude" he noted that peace with other nations had prevailed and that the year had been "filled with the blessings of fruitful fields and healthful skies." Noting the continuance of peaceful industry amid war, he declared: "No human counsel hath devised, nor hath any mortal hand worked out these great things. They are the gifts of the . . . most high God. . . . I do, therefore, invite my fellow-citizens in every part of the United States, and also those who are at sea and those who are sojourning in foreign lands, to set apart and observe the last Thursday of November next as a day of thanksgiving and praise." The editress's appeal was repeated in 1864, and on October 20 of that year Lincoln issued the second regular annual presidential proclamation of Thanksgiving. He recommended "fervent prayers" to God for "inestimable blessings." (On July 15, 1863, Lincoln had issued a proclamation for national thanksgiving, setting August 6 as the date, but this was for notable recent victories; it was a special proclamation, not to be confused with the annual autumn custom.)

Lincoln had done it in his own way. Mrs. Hale's idea had been that the President should proclaim the event for those under national (as distinct from state) jurisdiction and should appeal to the governors for concurrence as to date. Instead of that procedure—which seemed confined to a pattern of jurisdiction, legal authority, and official right—Lincoln simply invited all his "fellow-citizens" to join in the common observance. So far as the President's proclamation was concerned the governors were not brought into the picture. The state executives, of course, also issued their own proclamations and it is of interest to note in the Lincoln Papers the handsome crop of gubernatorial proclamations of Thanksgiving in 1863 and 1864. The newer and more sparse the state or territory, the more elaborate was the printed proclamation. It was a matter in which the governors took pride.

It was fitting that the nationalizing of Thanksgiving should be associated with the man who led the country through what Allan Nevins has called the "Ordeal of the Union." The custom has been continuously followed by all subsequent Presidents, but in the case of its originator it had special significance. In making the proclamation Lincoln was acting not in terms of legal duty or appointed function, but rather as a focus of national thought, as the man to whom the people turned, the spokesman of the nation. The President does various things which cannot be encompassed if one has in mind only his official duties assigned by law. There is an irreducible core of presidential tasks, but beyond that there is a wider field of presidential spokesmanship, and it is worth while to remember how Lincoln performed, how he initiated certain manifestations of leadership, in this broader dimension. We are dealing here with a matter of public relations, with emotional and intangible elements of the national Union, with the virtue and merits of unity itself, and with the President as the embodiment of that unity.

Chapter Ten

THE GIFT OF LAUGHTER

I

A MAN MIGHT RECALL LINCOLN ONLY PARTIALLY, YET REMEMBER his laugh. An old-timer in Springfield wrote to Robert Todd Lincoln: "I remember only the general form of your father as I saw him in the office of Bledsoe and Baker, his height, his length of limb, the cheery laugh in response to a salutation seems to sound in my ears yet." His laugh has also been described as "boisterous," "ringing," "happy," "joyous," and "the President's life preserver." Henry Villard wrote: "A high-pitched laughter lighted up his otherwise melancholy countenance with thorough merriment. His body shook all over . . . and when he felt particularly good over his performance, he followed his habit of drawing his knees, with his arms around them, up to his very face. . . ." Though a laugh is curative and wholesome, there is an even warmer quality in a smile. A newspaper comment in 1860 was: "when he smiles heartily it is something good to see."

Without smile and laughter it would not have been Lincoln. He was born to a sense of humor. As a lad in the Pigeon Creek neighborhood of southern Indiana he had amused his friends, on the sly, with those salty verses, the "Chronicles of Reuben." Forney recalled that he "liked the short farce." He

was conversant with the humorists of his day. He could anticipate a joke in the making and see how it would be played by
such a man as Orpheus C. Kerr. (This pseudonym, a play on
"office seeker," was the trade mark of Robert H. Newell.) When
General Meigs once inquired who this individual was, Lincoln
remarked that his papers were in two volumes and that any one
who had not read them "must be a heathen." He enjoyed them
best when they poked fun at Welles or Chase. Some of those
aimed at himself "rather disgusted him." A sufficient reason for
this would have been the dull or misfit quality of some of the
anti-Lincoln thrusts.

Lincoln knew also the works of Petroleum V. Nasby (David
R. Locke). The humorist himself wrote: "The 'Nasby Letters'
. . . attracted his attention. . . . He read them regularly. He
kept a series in a drawer in his table, and it was his wont to
read them on all occasions to his visitors, no matter who they
might be, or what their business was. He seriously offended
many of the Republican Party in this way."

He particularly enjoyed a piece in which Nasby ridiculed
the opposition of men in the border states to the use of Negro
soldiers, and the quick change of opinion on this subject when
they realized the advantage of having colored men serve as
substitutes for unwilling whites. (It would not have been necessary to associate this attitude with the border region. The
same sentiment appeared in New England and elsewhere.) On
one occasion, when Noah Brooks spent a night at the Soldiers'
Home, the "President, standing before the fireplace, recited
the whole of Nasby's letter" which most people had forgotten.

Part of it ran: "Arowse to wunst! . . . Rally agin the
porter at the Reed House! Rally agin the cook at the Crook
House! . . . Rally agin Missis Umstid! Rally agin Missis Umstid's childern by her first husband! Rally agin Missis Umstid's
childern by her sekkund husband! . . . Rally agin the saddle-
kulurd gal that yoost 2 be hear! Ameriky fer white men!" If
such a passage does not seem very funny now, it may be be-

cause one cannot recapture its flavor when written. Satire must
have a target, and in this passage the target, now largely forgotten, was the inconsistency of contemporary anti-Negro
attitudes.

A great favorite with Lincoln, of course, was Artemus
Ward (Charles Farrar Browne), the foremost professional humorist of his day. It was Ward's "High Handed Outrage in
Utica" that Lincoln chose for reading to his impatient cabinet
on the day when he presented his emancipation proclamation
to them. Ward's humor, like Nasby's, was thoroughly dated.
Much of its flavor has evaporated. The droll spectacle of Ward
in action could be enjoyed only by the immediate audience as
they watched him exhibit his wax works or hold forth with
bland irrelevance on "The Babes in the Wood."

Lincoln never met Ward, whose highly advertised contacts
with the President were fictitious, but he did meet Jeems Pipes
of Pipesville, who instructed his hearers on "Eating Roast Pig
with the King of the Cannibal Islands." Pipes was the guest of
Lincoln in the White House, and an account has come down to
us of the President suggesting a bit of stage business for an act
imitating a stammering man. Suiting the action to the stammer,
Lincoln showed how "irresistibly ludicrous" it would be if Pipes
would punctuate his limping speech with an occasional whistle.
There is complete lack of dignity in the sound-picture that
comes before us: the President turned comedian, the humorist
catching on and rehearsing a trick of his trade, their hilarious
laughter at this bit of burlesque ringing through the corridors
of the Executive Mansion.

II

There is no need to box the compass as to Lincoln's stories.
Some of them were reminiscent of boyhood days in Indiana, a

state famous for fun and humor. Others, told with equal nostalgic relish, brought back the Illinois prairie days. Amusing incidents that he knew of personally would be stored in his retentive memory and brought to the front of conversation when needed. When some senators demanded a wholesale shakeup of the cabinet because one change had been made, the President was reminded of the farmer who went after seven skunks with a shotgun. "I took aim," said the farmer (as Lincoln retold it), "blazed away, killed one, and he raised such a fearful smell that I concluded it was best to let the other six go."

Of course Lincoln did not invent all, or most, of the stories he told. Some of them were old acquaintances, and many of the tales or quips attributed to him were not his at all, but were merely pinned on him. The story about Grant's whiskey drinking (Lincoln wanted some of the "same brand" for his other generals) is one of the most familiar, but it was disclaimed by Lincoln, who probably wished he had told some of the good ones for which he was credited. It has been suggested that one should thank a New York *Herald* writer, not the President, for this Lincoln story, and David Homer Bates mentions the Grant-and-whiskey remark as belonging to the category of stories that were current in former times, saying: "Lincoln disclaimed the story in my hearing. . . ." A similar remark in a slightly different form has been attributed to King George II. When some one mentioned that General Wolfe was mad, the King's reported comment was: "Mad, is he? Then I wish he would bite some of my other generals."

It was the view of W. O. Stoddard that Lincoln had "never so much as heard" the vast number of "so-called jokes" attributed to him. When a bit of foul humor was accredited (or debited) to him, the President's face would "flush and darken." In that sense there was hazard in the President's fame as a "funny man." Altogether unjustly, his humor was associated with thoughtless indifference or even with vulgarity. Not all the yarns gratuitously given him were harmless and the general reputation of being a joker was used against him. There were stories which he indignantly denied because they were forgeries made up by his enemies, and others which he disowned simply because they were not his.

There is, however, an amply supply remaining after one has winnowed out the chaff and rejected the spurious. The story about being "within one mile of Hell" (that far from the Capitol) can be contemporaneously traced, and the one about Negro Joe's dilemma between two roads is found in the Welles diary. This story was an example of a Lincoln anecdote which "clicked" perfectly because of its appositeness to the problem in hand. Deliberation in cabinet had turned upon the Dominican problem as of early 1864, in which Lincoln wisely chose to avoid the blundering policy which Grant unsuccessfully attempted a few years later, and which "almost wrecked" the Republican party. In a milieu of local tyranny, civil war, and military action by Spain to recover control over the Dominican republic, the question arose as to whether the United States should intervene and perhaps annex this island domain. To seize control or intervene would have angered Spain; to make a point of refusing to do so would have created resentment among Negroes and their sympathizers.

Having decided to keep clear of this explosive and dangerous entanglement, Lincoln, in cabinet meeting, told of an interview between two Negroes. One of them, a preacher, admonished his friend: "There are two roads for you, Joe. . . . One . . . leads straight to hell, de odder go right to damnation." Joe answered: "I go troo de wood." The Welles diary continues: " 'I am not disposed to take any new trouble,' said the President, 'just at this time, and shall neither go for Spain nor the Negro, but shall take to the woods.' "

Welles is also authority for an uncomplimentary but humorous remark of Lincoln's concerning Greeley, another of those Lincoln sayings that have the reminiscent western flavor. Lincoln recalled that in early Illinois, with few mechanics and small means, it was customary to make a pair of shoes wear as long as possible with much mending, but the time would come when the leather was so rotten that "the stitches would not hold." He thought Greeley was like an old shoe; "the stitches all tear out." It would be a mistake, however, to evolve a broad conclusion from a casual remark of this nature; Lincoln gave repeated expression of a high regard for Greeley.

Sometimes the origin of a Lincoln story is clouded while at the same time the clouding does not indicate that the story was necessarily untrue. So it was with the President's oft-quoted remark that he "hadn't much influence with this administration." This famous quip is supported by reminiscences of contemporaries, yet Noah Brooks doubted that Lincoln ever said it as usually reported—i.e., with special reference to Secretary Stanton and the war department. It was a familiar item of Washington chit-chat, the more so because of its frequent and pointed applicability. It sounds so much like Lincoln that if he did not originate it he probably wished he had.

Yet, as would naturally be true with such a many sided subject, the applicability of this remark was only partial and should not be taken as giving the whole tone of Lincoln's administration. When, for instance, it was suggested that Lincoln should dismiss the postmaster general from his cabinet, he stated clearly that he himself would be "the judge as to when a member of the Cabinet shall be dismissed."

Other Lincolnian items, of varying quality, are substantiated by contemporary record. There was the President's pun at the time when a young captain was arraigned by court martial as a Peeping Tom; Lincoln remarked that he should have been elevated "to the peerage." There was also the devastatingly sarcastic remark apropos of the political principle that you should "be always on the side of your country in a war." The President said: "Butterfield of Illinois was asked at the beginning of the Mexican War if he were not opposed to

it; he said, 'No, I opposed one war. That was enough for me.
I am now perpetually in favor of war, pestilence and famine.'"
To hear such items is like participating in Lincoln's informal
and unpremeditated conversation, listening in, as it were, on
his table talk, and catching his unrehearsed or spontaneous
witticisms, as when he said that troops "dwindled on the march
like a shovelful of fleas pitched from one place to another."
Once in a rather atrocious pun, Lincoln was quoted as saying
that he was "thin as a shad (yea, worse—as thin as a shadder.)"
Pun making was a habit, or disease, of the age, and that remark
was not so bad as some atrocities that appeared, for instance, in
Punch.

Sometimes a story would be associated with Lincoln by
context, his own words being quoted along with those of other
men. There was, for instance, in a string of random jottings on
Lincoln, a recording by Hay of Ben Wade's remark that in
praying for the prolongation of Taney's life (to outlast Buchanan's administration) he was afraid he had "overdone the
matter." Similarly there was a well pointed story—one that
Lincoln probably enjoyed—attributed to General Spinner at
the time when Richmond papers were going so far as to call
Morgan's raid a "success." "Genl Spinner: 'They remind me
of a little fellow whom I saw once badly whipped by a bigger
man, who was on top of him & jamming his head on the floor.
The little cuss, still full of conceit & pluck, kept saying, "*Now,*
damn you, will you behave yourself?"'" Lincoln, his generals,
his intimates, and some at least of his people were going through
the tragic war, certainly with no thought of flippancy, but with
jests on their lips.

Noah Brooks, later to become a friend of Mark Twain and
Bret Harte, was a skilled raconteur, and when he told a Lincoln
anecdote it usually had point and flavor as well as closeness to
the original. Brooks was considerably amused at the President's
brand of diplomacy when dealing with one of the White House
"corps of attaches of Hibernian descent." "One morning the

President happened to meet his Irish coachman at the door, and asked him to go out and get the morning paper. The Jehu departed, but, like the unfilial party of whom we read in Scripture, he said, 'I go,' but went not, and the anxious President went out himself and invested five cents in a *Morning Chronicle*. It afterwards transpired that the coachman did not consider it his business to run errands, which coming to the President's ears he ordered up the carriage the next morning at six o'clock. . . ." This summons at an uncomfortably early hour, presumably for an important presidential purpose, could not be ignored. Instead of using the carriage himself, however, the President "sent a member of his household in the equipage to the Avenue, where he bought a paper and rode back, with the mortified coachee on the box."

Another anecdote via "Castine" (Brooks's pen name) pertained to a gentleman who had "been waiting around Washington for three months" in order to obtain a pass to Richmond. Finally he applied "as a *dernier resort*, to the President for aid." "I would be most happy [said Lincoln] to oblige you if my passes were respected; but the fact is I have within the last two years given passes to more than two hundred and fifty thousand men to go to Richmond, and not one of them has got there yet in any legitimate way."

III

Of all the humorous recordings the best are to be found in Lincoln's own works. This goes far to explain the endless fascination of his writings, even down to the commonest jottings or incidental endorsements. It might be the humor of a sharp dig, homely simile, clownish fun, or play acting. It might be nonsense, to which the best humorists have descended, or rather risen; for if we were to omit delightful nonsense we

should have to discard the gems of Gelett Burgess, of Edward
Lear, and of Lewis Carroll. That Lincoln shared the joyousness
of nonsense was shown in 1848 when he was speaking in Congress on internal improvements. Favoring such improvements
and supporting huge governmental expenditures for the purpose, he was refuting the objection that they should be fi-
nanced, not by the Federal government, but by "tonnage duties,
under state authority, with the consent of the General Government." He continued: "How could we make any entirely new
improvement by means of tonnage duties? How make a road,
a canal, or clear a greatly obstructed river? The idea that we
could, involves the same absurdity as the Irish bull about the
new boots. 'I shall niver git em on,' says Patrick, 'till I wear
em a day or two, and stretch em a little.' We shall never make
a canal by tonnage duties until it shall already have been
made awhile, so the tonnage can get into it." Similarly, applying the idea of absurdity, Lincoln said of Douglas that he was
using the horse-chestnut style or argument. By this Lincoln
meant "a specious and fantastic arrangement of words, by
which a man can prove a horse-chestnut to be a chestnut
horse."

The continual interweaving of good fun in his writings and
speeches shows that humor was no mere technique, but a habit
of his mind. When, as he thought, Polk was mistakenly appealing to a declaration by Thomas Jefferson, Lincoln showed that
Jefferson's true position was against that of Polk. Then he
added: "this opinion of Mr. Jefferson, in one branch at least, is,
in the hands of Mr. Polk, like McFingal's gun: 'Bears wide, and
kicks the owner over.'" Using exaggerated ridicule to destroy
Douglas's position on slavery in the territories (a position which
Lincoln considered a "sort of do-nothing sovereignty . . . that
is exercised by doing nothing at all"), he considered it "as thin
as the homeopathic soup that was made by boiling the shadow
of a pigeon that had starved to death." And when thinking of
courts—how they should be set up—Lincoln dreaded a "Puppy

Court"—i.e., petty local judges, too many of them, and with "salaries so low as to exclude all respectable talent."

Politics aside, one should note Lincoln's whimsical twist in asking a renewal of a railroad pass. "Says Tom to John 'Heres your old rotten wheelbarrow. I've broke it, usin on it I wish you would mend it, case I shall want to borrow it this arter-noon.' Acting on this as a precedent, I say 'Heres your old "chalked hat." I wish you would take it, and send me a new one, case I shall want to use it the first of March.' "

At times a Lincolnian figure of speech would be chosen for its universality and homely appeal: Buchanan after the election of Pierce in 1852, was, said Lincoln, like "a rejected lover making merry at the wedding of his rival." Or the Lincoln phrase would be one that every farmer would understand—e.g., his self-depreciating comment that his speech at Gettysburg would "not scour," or that under John Quincy Adams the post office service "cut its own fodder." He could use current patter (Burnside's "mud march"), or classical mythology ("Procrus-tean bed"), or Shakespearean metaphor ("a shelled peascod," referring to Pierce).

On the question whether Lincoln's jokes were sometimes risqué, reports and reminiscences differ. One finds diametrically opposite statements, but on the whole the answer would be that Lincoln's humor was sometimes as exquisite as the tooled binding of a volume de luxe, while at other times he fell into expressions that were none too choice and anecdotes that were not intended for the parlor. Such robust yarns occurred off duty, on occasions for which they were not, or their hearers thought they were not, unsuited. After meeting informally with Lincoln in Springfield, Donn Piatt reported Lincoln's manner of talking with "those good honest citizens, who fairly wor-shiped their distinguished neighbor." Giving way to his natural bent for fun, Mr. Lincoln, reported Piatt, "told very amusing stories, always in quaint illustration of the subject under dis-cussion, no one of which will bear printing."

Some people like risqué stories; some do not; some like them without admitting it. There are degrees, moods, and tenses of unparlorable humor, and a story may be amusingly risqué without being offensively vulgar. It is known that Lincoln's thoughts and conduct were clean. Most of his humorous chit-chat has evaporated and is impossible to recover. Much of it was off the record. What then? If we had all of it barring none, and if parts here and there would need expurgating, one would still ask, to whom should the task of expurgation be assigned? And after all the purification had been accomplished there would remain for undignified sinners a lively demand for the unexpurgated edition.

IV

Lincoln's humorous diversions were not always appreciated or well received. There were contrasting attitudes in American folkways. American wit was irreverent, and religion itself, if too unbending, "provoked the irreverence of professional jokers." There remained in America something of a holdover from the days, even of Shakespeare, when Puritans made war upon the theater and other forms of amusement. Religion was unimaginative, somber, and rigidly repressive. "The Devil was as real as the Red Indian." To minds under such a killjoy spell, Lincoln's quips seemed almost sinful—or at best profitless frivolity. In his cabinet, when he read some tomfoolery by Artemus Ward, the heavy burden of the occasion—discussion of the emancipation proclamation—was to Lincoln all the more reason for a bit of preliminary playfulness, while to Chase's Puritan mind such levity on a serious occasion was incomprehensible. As a young man Chase had continually chided himself on his unworthiness, had suffered miserably from religious self distrust, had repeated psalms when bathing or dressing, and had considered it a sin to waste time. There was a charming young lady with whom, as he wrote in his diary, he would have fallen in love if she had not been "fond of the gay world" and "disinclined to religion," which he valued "more than any earthly possession."

Much of the contrast between Lincoln and Stanton is revealed by the comment that if Lincoln would be telling a rich story and Stanton would enter, the story and the laughter would die. If the President got along better personally with Seward than with others of his cabinet, it may have been partly because Seward had a sense of humor, as when he said: "Did you ever hear Webster's recipe for cooking cod? 'Denude your cod of his scales, cut him open carefully, put him in a pot of cold water, heat it until your fork can pass easily through the fish, spread good fresh butter over him liberally, sprinkle salt on the butter, pepper on the salt, and—send for George Ashmun and me.'"

Among those who had no ear for Lincoln's humor was Henry Wilson, Republican senator from Massachusetts. When Wilson and Goldwin Smith, with several English friends, were conferring with the President, conversation turned on the subject of battle losses, which the distinguished Englishman illustrated by reciting statistics of killed, wounded, and missing. No one was more emotionally moved by these human tragedies than Lincoln; but, crossing his long legs, he solemnly observed that as to such matters one should apply darky arithmetic. The visitor did not know of two systems of arithmetic, upon which the President offered to illustrate the point by a "little story," much to the embarrassment of the senator; "had he [Wilson] known a thousand stories he would not have told one of them to Prof. Smith and his grave-looking British friends; and he was mortified that the President, who in all things had few superiors in easy dignity of manner [this is the comment of W. D. Kelley], should so inopportunely indulge in such frivolity."

Lincoln went on with the story. Darky Jim wanted to know "what is 'rithmetic?" It's when you add up things, explained the other. " 'When you have one and one, and you put them together, they makes two. And when you subtracts things. When if you have two things, and you takes one away, only one remains.' 'Is dat 'rithmetic?' 'Yes.' 'Well, 'tain't true den; it's no good.' Here a dispute arose, when Jim said: 'Now, you s'pose three pigeons sit on that fence, and somebody shoot one of dem, do t'other two stay dar? I guess not, dey flies away quicker'n odder feller falls.' " The trifling story seemed to the President to illustrate the arithmetic to be used in estimating the actual losses resulting from great battles. "The statements you refer to [he said, turning to the Professor] give the killed, wounded and missing at the first roll-call after the battle, which always exhibits a greatly exaggerated total, especially in the column of missing."

Petroleum V. Nasby wrote: "Grave and reverend Senators who came charged to the brim with important business—business on which the fate of the nation depended—took it ill that the President should postpone the consideration thereof while he read them a letter from 'Saint's Rest, wich is in the state of Noo Jersey,' especially as grave statesmen, as a rule, do not understand humor, or comprehend its meaning or effect."

There were those, such as Adam Gurowski, who simply could not understand Lincoln's language. The ferocious old Count considered Lincoln a "brat" and worse: "he is no fit for be President." Even old-time associates, who comprehended Lincolnian humor readily enough, found occasionally (though not often) that it grated on them. When O. M. Hatch and Jesse K. Dubois asked for a certain appointment, Lincoln wired in 1863: "What nation do you desire Gen. [Robert] Allen to be made quarter-master-general of? This nation already has a Quarter-Master-General." Hatch and Dubois then wrote to Lincoln explaining their request. Allen had notified Governor Yates that there was to be "a new Quarter Master General" and had asked "will you go for me," asking also that he wire the President and get other state officers to do the same. Yates was absent, and, "supposing that General Allen *knew what he said,* . . . and believing him competent," these men (Hatch was secretary of state for Illinois; Dubois was state auditor) had telegraphed Lincoln urging the appointment. They added: "We profess to be your friends and have no desire to embarrass you, . . . We trust the same spirit governs you—though we confess your despatch read harshly to us."

Lincoln's humor had misfired, and he was quick to correct the first impression. On receiving the Hatch-Dubois letter he at once telegraphed: "The particular form of my despatch was jocular, which I supposed you gentlemen knew me well enough to understand. Gen. Allen is considered here as a very faithful and capable officer; and one who would be at least thought of for Quarter-Master-general if that office were vacant."

V

It was a sad thing that Lincoln's fondness for stories and his enjoyment of humor were so inscrutable. His biographer, William H. Herndon, had it all physiologically accounted for. We have a remarkable Herndonian passage in which the humorless partner-biographer mounted his unbridled steed and dashed off on an analytical gallop to clarify the profound subject of Lincoln's laughter. The passage illustrates a curious combination of qualities—a ridiculous approach which has no importance for a serious biographer, combined with a curious readability.

Lincoln, explained Herndon, had a low and feeble circulation. His "whole organism moved slowly to the influences of all kinds of stimuli." His body and mind "needed oiling." He had spells of gloom and melancholy. "This state of Mr. Lincoln made him . . . unconscious of his surroundings and to arouse that somewhat dormant consciousness he needed a stimulant and that was found in a story and tell it he would."

There follows a readable passage in which Herndon vividly pictures Lincoln in a typical story-telling scene with an unappreciative secretary. It comes out as a lifelike portrayal of such a situation (though at second hand, because Herndon knew practically nothing directly about Lincoln as President), but it is all mixed up with one of Herndon's own inventions —a theory of Lincoln's laughter which is something of a howler.

"This story telling [continued Herndon]—this stimulant, sending more blood to the brain, aroused the whole man to an active consciousness. . . . Grave men in grave times, sometimes his ministers, would approach him in order to state the urgency of some matter that needed his immediate attention. Mr. Lincoln would look up to his minister half sleepily— dreamily, saying—'Mr Secretary take a chair': he would, in a moment or two, after the secretary had stated his errand, tell some story much to the disgust of his minister, who would censuringly say—'Mr President, this is no time for story telling —the times are grave and full of war, and the country is fast drifting to ruin.' Mr. Lincoln would good naturedly reply— 'Come Mr Secretary, sit down—sit down—I have a perfect and profound respect for you and were it not for these stories I should die; they are rents through which my sadness—gloom and melancholy escape.' Mr. Lincoln would thus arouse his half dormant consciousness into activity . . . ; and after he had been thus aroused he would listen to what the . . . minister eagerly told him, like a philosopher and in a short moment he would make his answer . . . so wisely and earnestly as to convince the man that that point . . . had been . . . maturely considered before, long, long before this moment of meeting."

In this immediate passage, describing Lincoln's manner

with a humorless cabinet member, Herndon gives something like a reasonable treatment of Lincoln's joking, but what follows indicates the peculiar kind of hash that he was so apt to dish up. "This state of Mr Lincoln [he wrote], particularly so if it was accompanied by a mental & nervous exhaustion, produced by long and intense study, caused him to have delusions —saw apparitions—specters & the like." Lincoln's laughter was thus associated with something supposedly abnormal, as if he was not himself when in good humor. Lincoln, wrote his partner, was usually "a gloomy & melancholy man, but at exceptional times a momentarily happy one." To follow this line of reasoning would be to identify Lincoln's humor with a kind of illusion, as if the laughter-loving Lincoln were seeing things.

Poor Lincoln! He was so beset, or so physiologically sluggish, that he had to whip up these jokes and stories. We ought to understand it and not be too hard on the man. The passage continues: "Let no man blame Mr Lincoln for being sad or seeing apparitions: his sadness and his gloom came naturally out of his organism and his apparitions from the same source somewhat and from nervous & mental exhaustion. Let no man rudely censure Mr Lincoln for his story telling. . . ." And so on.

It is fair to add that we are dealing here with one of Herndon's numerous and voluminous letters to his literary collaborator, Jesse Weik. In these letters, frankly given as something very different from a finished product, Herndon simply poured out his thoughts and ruminations as they rushed through his mind. He didn't try to check them. Sometimes he would admit that they were to be taken only in part, and only for what they might be worth, and that Weik was to be the judge. "Draw on your imagination and fill up [he once wrote]: it will please the people. . . . Pick out what you like and cast away the balance. I have no time to elaborate—amplify &c &c nor correct."

This quality of Lincoln, thought Herndon, was good for

the country. Had Lincoln been ardent, "with swift and strong volumes of blood pouring through his brain," had he been impulsive and rash, the national cause would have failed. "This feeble low circulation—this slow irritability which slowly responded to stimuli—this organism . . . [etc.] saved the nation from disunion and consequent ruin." Herndon knew that his collaborator disliked "such stuff terribly, and yet some persons may like it." He now had Lincoln's humor vivisected. It was explainable. He had cleared up what might have remained a permanent mystery. The great man's story telling actually had its good side! Herndon could reconcile it. It was about like saying that sunshine should not be too much regretted and if a man had his happier moments his friends should do their best to endure it.

Herndon, who was bored by Lincoln's story telling, was explaining Lincoln's humor, as on other occasions, unbeliever that he was, he "explained" Lincoln's religion. This was the biographer who had so much to do in setting Lincoln, and Mary Lincoln, before the world in a manner which the world has too largely accepted. In the whole passage, which has to be read carefully to be believed, the emphasis is on two things: in elucidating his hero's humor Herndon stresses, above all, his utter gloom, sadness, and melancholy; and, physiologically speaking, he puts the stress on the man's sluggish circulation of blood. It did not seem to occur to him that there must have been something other than gloom in a man who could brighten a conversation as Lincoln did, and that the quickening of circulation could just as well have been a cause as a result of mirth.

VI

When one thinks of Lincoln as a man of humor (perhaps a better term than "humorist" which suggests a calling or occupation), one thinks also of Mark Twain. As one develops the comparison—which has already been drawn elsewhere and need not be repeated here—the life and personality of the man Lincoln, set against the man Clemens, becomes a theme of major import. Starting with Pigeon Creek and Holliday (Cardiff) Hill, the subject unfolds till it embraces the human race and touches the mysteries of life. One can show how Lincoln and Clemens were alike and how they differed. Both were of Southern origin, both knew the border between North and South, and both lived their formative years in a pioneer, or near-pioneer society. They shared the same type of native background, folkways, and dialect. Both had a minimum of conventional education and formed their characters and intellects in the school of experience. Both had the advantage— for them—of growing up as poor boys. Both knew the rude horseplay, the side-splitting jest, the practical joke, and the preposterous tall tale of the West. Both were close to nature, with a tenderness for animals, though that was hardly a backwoods characteristic.

The same fascination, spell, and adventurous lure of the river stirred in their hearts. Clemens became a licensed river pilot and produced masterpieces of river literature. Lincoln's love of the river produced no literary results, but his biography would be incomplete without his river experiences. Coming down the Sangamon River in a large canoe was "the manner of A's [Abraham's] first entrance into Sangamon County." His early introduction to the majesty of a local court was related to a boyhood river incident, his specialization in river navigation was of early political importance, and his inventive genius turned to the problem of easing a steamboat over shoals.

Each was to become, in a supreme sense, the very embodiment of that combination of qualities that we call "American." Both were "stamped unforgettably with the American brand." Both had a sympathy for the Negro, and both gave poignant expression (Twain with devastating satire) to a sense of outrage at the mistreatment of the colored race. Both felt a kind of collective guilt on this subject and a long overdue debt which the white race owed to the colored. And of all the traits which they had in common, the most dominant and deeply felt was an overwhelming sense of protest against social abuse and human injustice.

There were, of course, contrasts between them. Lincoln's soul endured the fiery ordeal, and in the heat of war's crisis his leadership was shaped and his character forged. Clemens sat out the war, so to speak, or escaped it in a part of the far West that was, as Lincoln said, "undisturbed by the civil war." They had a similar lack of enthusiasm for military "glory." Both Sam and Abraham recalled their brief army experiences as matters of burlesque and comedy. There was the obvious fact that Clemens was not a political leader and Lincoln not (in the professional sense) a man of literature; but that did not mean that Twain ignored matters of statesmanship in his thinking, or that the President lacked the gift of expression. Mark could have written something like Lincoln's contribution to the Rebecca "Lost Township" letters or some of his less serious speeches, and Lincoln could have done some of the paragraphs of the *Gilded Age*. Mark Twain's comments on political life in Washington, on the party spirit (which he characterized with sharp bitterness), and on the meaning of patriotism, showed how much his mind was occupied with fundamentals of political and social democracy. One of their strongest traits in common was a deep-seated conviction of the need for self criticism in a democracy. For each the intolerable thing was imprisonment of the human mind. One of the faults which they both despised was a smug and unrealistic complacency in the face of crying abuses, North and South.

Lincoln's contrast to Clemens can be extended, both as to environment and as to personality. Clemens's association with men of wealth, his impracticality, his Sellers-like speculative dreams, restless travel, theatrical poses, boyish display, extrava-

gance, craving for applause, and fastidiousness of dress set him
apart from the homely lawyer and unpretentious President.
And, as Dixon Wecter has pointed out, the ultimate philosophical outlook of Twain was, or seemed, the opposite of Lincoln's.

That is to say, Lincoln developed a serenity of optimism
and democratic faith to which he gave classic expression, while
Clemens seemed (or professed) to have a low opinion of the
"damned human race," and, as his writings would indicate,
became in the darkened evening of life bogged and tangled
in a jungle of fatalism and despair. To each, of course, had
come great personal tragedy—to Lincoln in the death of
mother, sister, father, and two boys; to Clemens in a whole
series of family casualties, including the terrible death of his
brother Henry, the loss of children, and the passing of his
beloved Olivia. It was Lincoln whose spirit was better able to
recover from, though never to forget these sorrows; and, though
both had disgust for conventional creeds and dogmas, it was
Lincoln who was better able to grasp for his own personal uplift the eternal assurances of Christianity.

Looking over the whole subject, one realizes that Lincoln
and Clemens would have understood each other if they had
met and conversed, which they never did. It has been remarked
that they would have enjoyed the same jokes, which was true;
but that is a small part of the subject. Each had a spirit sen-
sitized to the tragedies of Adam's breed. The bonds of personality that would have united them were their Americanism,
their humor, and their understanding of the human heart.

VII

There are factors in life which need not so much to be
explained as to be appreciated and accepted. It is those who
have relish for Lincoln's humor who come nearest to under-

standing Lincoln the man.

There is little profit, however, in disquisitions on the cause and purpose of Lincoln's humor. The best place to seek his humor is not in a cheap collection such as *Old Abe's Jokes, Fresh from Abraham's Bosom*. Humor is like caviar or *hors d'oeuvres*. One should not make a meal of it. The passing moment has much to do with the matter. The success of a joke is not always predictable. The mood must be right, also the delivery, timing, and congeniality with the listener. Humor in action or in running discourse is better than humor in bottles with labels, or piled up in joke books. By contemporary accounts Lincoln's humor was successful. It was not of the labored, limping variety which makes the inveterate jokester something of a nuisance.

It was in fact notably successful. People enjoyed Lincoln the better, and had more of a fellow feeling for him, as they repeated tales of how he rode a galloping thunderstruck cow, or how he outwitted a judge in a horse trade by swapping a saw-horse for the judge's sorry-looking nag. His playfulness, in the western tradition, became in his own lifetime at once a mark of popularity and a factor in American folklore.

It was true, of course, that sometimes his humor was turned against him in denunciation or ridicule. For the campaign of 1864 there appeared the following: "Only Authentic Life of Abraham Lincoln, Alias 'Old Abe.' A Son of the West. With an account of his birth and education, his rail-splitting and flat-boating, his joke-cutting and soldiering, with some allusions to his journeys from Springfield to Washington and BACK again. Sold by all Newsdealers in the Country."

The journey *back to Springfield* was to have its unspeakable pathos after April 15, 1865, but in this 1864 leaflet the suggestion was only that Lincoln would be defeated in the coming election. As to making fun of his soldiering, one would need only to quote Lincoln himself. "By the way, Mr. Speaker [said Lincoln in Congress, in his rollicking speech in ridicule

of Cass in the campaign of '48], did you know I am a military
hero? Yes, sir; in the days of the Black Hawk War I fought,
bled, and came away. Speaking of Gen. Cass' career, reminds
me of my own. I was not at Stillman's defeat, but I was about
as near it, as Cass was to Hulls surrender; and, like him, I
saw the place very soon afterwards. It is quite certain that I
did not break my sword, for I had none to break; but I bent
a musket pretty badly on one occasion. . . . If Gen Cass went
in advance of me in picking huckleberries, I guess I surpassed
him in charges upon the wild onions. If he saw any live, fighting
indians, it was more than I did; but I had a good many bloody
struggles with the musquitoes. . . ."

One should not bother too much to settle the questions as
to how Lincoln "used" his mirth and pleasantry. One may think
of it as part of him, indeed as part of his greatness. Tyrants
and dictators do not laugh, nor do they induce genuine
laughter. Popular jokes become associated with them, but the
dictator is the butt or target, not the participant or raconteur,
of the jest. Lincoln's anecdotes were human, close to the soil,
and drawn from life. A famous example was his parable-like
reference in 1858 to Stephen, James, Franklin, and Roger producing timbers which fitted together so perfectly as to convince
the ordinary man that they had worked in collusion. He knew
that this type of illustration would make his point against
Douglas and others memorable. It is always a question how
many statements people will preserve in memory from a speech
which they hear, but it is a rather safe bet they will recall the
homely example or the concrete instance.

Chauncey M. Depew wrote: "His power of managing men,
of deciding and avoiding difficult questions, surpassed that of
any man I ever met. A keen insight of human nature had been
cultivated by the trials and struggles of his early life. He
knew the people and how to reach them better than any man
of his time. I heard him tell a great many stories, many of
which would not do exactly for the drawingroom; but for the

person he wished to reach, and the object he desired to accomplish with the individual, the story did more than any argument could have done.

"He said to me once, in reference to some sharp criticisms which had been made upon his story-telling: 'They say I tell a great many stories; I reckon I do, but I have found in the course of a long experience that common people'—and repeating it—'common people, take them as they run, are more easily influenced and informed through the medium of a broad illustration than in any other way, and as to what the hypercritical few may think I don't care.'

". . . He said that, 'riding the circuit for many years and stopping at country taverns where were gathered lawyers, jurymen, witnesses and clients, they would sit up all night narrating to each other their life adventures; and that the things which happened to an original people, in a new country, surrounded by novel conditions, and told with the descriptive power and exaggeration which characterized such men, supplied him with an exhaustless fund of anecdotes which could be made applicable for enforcing or refuting an argument better than all the invented stories of the world.'"

It was characteristic of Lincoln's joking while President that the very darkest and stormiest of times would set off an explosion of humor. "A frontiersman," he was quoted as saying, "lost his way in an uninhabited region on a dark and tempestuous night. The rain fell in torrents, accompanied by terrible thunder and more terrific lightning. To increase his trouble his horse halted, being exhausted with fatigue and fright. Presently a bolt of lightning struck a neighboring tree, and the crash brought the man to his knees. He was not an expert in prayer, but his appeal was short and to the point: 'Oh, good Lord, if it is all the same with you, give us a little more light, and a little less noise!'"

An appeal was once made to the President on behalf of a lieutenant who was accused of embezzling government money. It was charged that the officer had corruptly received while on duty the sum of forty dollars. "Why, Mr. Lincoln," exclaimed the officer, "it wa'n't but thirty dollars." This reminded Lincoln of an Indianian who got into a quarrel with a neighbor. "One charged that the other's daughter had three illegitimate children. 'Now,' said the man whose family was so outrageously scandalized, 'that's a lie, and I can prove it, for she only has two.' This case is no better [said Lincoln]. Whether the amount was thirty dollars or thirty thousand dollars, the culpability is the same. Then, after reading a little further, he said: 'I believe I will leave this case where it was left by the officers who tried it.'"

A good story that has come down pertained to Lincoln's droll remark about one of his generals. As remembered by Ward Lamon, the President, arousing himself from meditation, remarked: "'Do you know that I think General —— is a philosopher? He has proved himself a really great man. He has grappled with and mastered that ancient and wise admonition, "Know thyself"; he has formed an intimate acquaintance with himself, knows as well for what he is fitted and unfitted as any man living. Without doubt he is a remarkable man. This war has not produced another like him.'

"'Why is it, Mr. President' asked his friend, 'that you are now so highly pleased with General ——? Has your mind not undergone a change?'

"'Because,' replied Mr. Lincoln, with a merry twinkle of his eye, 'greatly to my relief, and to the interests of the country, *he has resigned*. And now I hope some other dress-parade commanders will study the good old admonition, "Know thyself," and follow his example.'"

VIII

By easing into a story Lincoln could change the climate of an interview. He could carry the ball, shape the trend, and control the direction of a conference. Conversation may be partly a matter of holding the floor. Lincoln would do this by bland good nature, his partner or opponent in discussion hardly realizing just how or why the breeze was shifting; then the President would conclude the conference with a smiling face without actually agreeing; or, in a crowd or reception, would slip away behind a barrage of merriment.

Lincoln's joking usually had pertinence to the subject in hand, but to think of every bit of his humor as serving a purpose or carrying a point would be a mistake. His laughter was a kind of release. It was Seward's impression that he "had no notion of recreation as such; enjoyed none; went thro' levees &c purely as a duty—found his only recreation in telling or hearing stories in the ordinary way of business—often stopped a cabinet council at a grave juncture, to jest a half-hour with the members before going to work; joked with every body, on light & on grave occasions. This was what saved him."

Lincoln's humor was not "put on"; it was never artificial. A glimpse of the manner in which his fun making belonged to the daily, or hourly, Lincoln is seen in a newspaper item pertaining to Mrs. Lincoln who was visiting an ocean resort in the summer of '61. When she left for Washington a *Herald* reporter wrote that it was largely because she thought Lincoln was lonely. He needed some one to listen to his fun making. She said that he always joked and jested at the supper table "no matter what the labors and fatigues of the day"; he was always "[l]ively, sociable, and agreeable."

The by-play of laughter was part of Lincoln's knack of

being good company. It was an attribute of his magnetism. He was the man around whom fellow lawyers and courthouse loungers would cluster. Though his published works were usually serious, dignified, and well polished, humor served him as a kind of popular language. More than that, it was an actual resource in thought and deliberation; for the man of humor is superior in mental tools. He does not stop with the obvious stereotype or the conventional stock phrase. He takes another look at a problem, turns it over, gives it a new relevance. He frees himself from uninspired literalness. Characterizing a well known type, Robert Louis Stevenson remarked that "Some people swallow the universe like a pill." These are the folk who take what is ladled out to them, who "fall for" partisan ballyhoo, who accept the politician at face value (which is more than politicians themselves do), and who believe what they see in print. But in a democracy the type of opinion that is vitally needed is of the sort that sees behind the demagogue's façade, or punctures the pompous orator's dignity. Such an attitude, stimulated by Lincolnian humor, is thus actually an element in the formation, or conditioning, of opinion.

To say that playfulness for Lincoln was a life-saver was no exaggeration. It was therapy of the spirit. Turning from dark worry to laughter was not, as Herndon ponderously supposed, a kind of deliberate or laborious setting-up exercise to induce circulation of the blood. Often it was an easing down, a relaxation, a healthy release from mental imprisonment. It is the man who can find such release who has the free intellect. To understand this fully is to attempt to realize, or perceive, pretty much the whole of Lincoln's wartime task, with all of its care, anxiety, immense responsibility, and unending pressure. Remembering this from direct observation of Lincoln, Depew wrote: "He knew the whole situation better than any man in the administration, and virtually carried on in his own mind not only the civic side of the government, but all the campaigns. And I knew when he threw himself (as he did once when I

There is a teasing quality in this picture, though some would consider it a photographic failure. Lincoln was usually photographed in a studio. This was taken in the White House. The legs in the light trousers are those of Nicolay. In one of his detailed descriptions, Herndon wrote: "In sitting down on common chairs he was no taller than ordinary men from the chair to the crown of his head. A marble placed on his knee thus sitting would roll hipward, down an inclined plane. His legs & arms were abnormally— unnaturally long, & hence in undue proportions to the balance of his body. It was only when he stood up that he loomed above other men."

was there) on a lounge, and rattled off story after story, that it was his method of relief, without which he might have gone out of his mind, and certainly would not have been able to have accomplished anything like the amount of work which he did."

For the rest, his lighter moods were a means of disarming (or winning over) an antagonist, of getting a hearing, of assuring popularity, of keeping the common touch, of enriching and enlivening the day's work. Even had there been no more to the subject—and there was vastly more—it would be enough to remember that anecdotes and jests were for Lincoln a source of enjoyment.

Chapter Eleven

COMMANDER IN CHIEF

WAR HAVING BEEN STARTED, A STRATEGIC THEORY OF THE WAR would be imperative. The patriarchal attorney general, Edward Bates, even doubted whether war in fact ought to be waged at all. Bates proposed a plan that "would not necessarily lead to the shedding of a drop of blood," yet would be "very *coersive* [*sic*] and very promising of success." Noting that Southerners were an "anomalous people," being agricultural yet unable to live on home products, he would bring them to terms by stopping the mails, closing Southern ports, guarding the Mississippi River, and enforcing a blockade that would offer the "easiest . . . and most humane method" of restraining them. When a nation blunders into war, its leaders in the first phase are likely to promise painless measures, brief sacrifices and easy victory. But this was not all: what it amounted to was that Bates even after Sumter could not stomach the idea that war was really upon the country.

If this painless theory of the war were not adopted, some military plan would have to be evolved, or rather improvised. Lincoln would have to find a general who, in co-operation with the President, could develop and execute such an plan—or else Lincoln would have to take the full responsibility, himself.

I

To the President the news of Bull Run (July 21, 1861) came with an especially rude shock because it had been preceded by a steady accumulation of convincing assurances. Lincoln spent this eventful Sunday at church, at the White House, and at the war department. While at the war building his interest was in the telegraph office where he "waited with deep anxiety for each succeeding despatch." These despatches were encouraging, and Lincoln was led to believe "that Beauregard was being pushed back." "At supper [wrote Browning] the news was that . . . our army had forced the batteries at Bulls run and driven the enemy back upon Manassas. . . ." Feeling that the news of Union victory had been confirmed, the President went for his usual drive. By the time he returned, the telegraph had announced that the Union general, Irvin McDowell, was in full retreat, that the day was lost, and that it was a matter of saving Washington with the remnants of a broken army. In factual manner Browning recorded the stunned bewilderment at Washington. It was thought that the fight was over with the Unionists "in possession of the field." Then, "in some unaccountable manner, our troops were seized with a panic, and fled. They were not pursued. . . . How it happened no body seems to know."

In all this painful frustration it was a kind of human necessity to put the blame somewhere, the blame of ordering "a battle before our troops were prepared for it." The comment of Winfield Scott, Lincoln's general-in-chief, was given in a remarkable conversation with Lincoln, Cameron, and a group of Illinois men. In mock self-condemnation Scott called himself "the greatest coward in America" because he had fought this battle against his judgment. Lincoln is said to have remarked: "Your conversation seems to imply that I forced you to fight this battle," to which Scott replied that no President had been "kinder" to him than Lincoln.

The problem of responsibility in the premises is more than a question of whether Lincoln "forced" the battle. A congressional opponent, W. A. Richardson of Illinois, though assailing the Republican administration, disclaimed any implication that Lincoln had compelled Scott to fight at this stage. Lincoln's friend Francis P. Blair, Jr., asserted that Lincoln, on learning that Johnston had joined Beauregard, suggested to Scott the propriety of waiting, but that Scott was determined to attack and disregarded the suggestion. Lincoln's secretaries do not so easily relieve the President of at least partial responsibility, for they record that, at a council summoned by the President (June 29), the generals were of opinion that simultaneous victories could be won at Manassas and Winchester, that Scott preferred delay until autumn, and that "the President and the Cabinet, as political experts" intervened on the ground that the public could not brook delay. The secretaries assert flatly that "the Administration was responsible for the forward movement." A good deal of this whole discussion was animated by a purpose to discredit Lincoln's cabinet and advisers. Lincoln was even complimented by some who were damning his administration. Yet the President and his cabinet seem to have been in no serious disagreement on this point.

At least two factors of a torturous nature had acted powerfully against the Union side in this battle: the failure of Patterson and the falling off of three-months volunteers. An essential link in the strategy of Scott and McDowell was General Robert Patterson, in command at Winchester. His task was to keep Johnston busy and prevent him from joining Beauregard at Manassas when McDowell's blow should fall. This he failed to do. Authorities are pretty well agreed that this failure made all the difference; yet Union high command could not be blamed for this unforeseen factor. So also with the aggravating circumstance that the battle came just as the time when the service of three-months militia was expiring. According to McDowell's own words he could neither push on faster nor delay. "A large and the best part . . . of my forces [he said] were three-months' volunteers, whose terms . . . were about expiring, but who were sent forward as having long enough to serve for the purpose of the expedition." "In the next few days [he added], day by day I should have lost ten thousand of the best armed, drilled, officered, and disciplined troops in the Army. In other words, every day which added to the strength of the enemy made us weaker." If the President was responsible for this amazing situation at the time of a major campaign, it was in introducing the three-months limitation in the first place, or in not correcting it before the moment of advance.

It was a case of a war leader suffering when unsuccessful, whatever the cause. Before the battle it seemed reasonable to hope that the Union campaign, not badly planned, might succeed. It was not so much Lincoln, or Scott, or the cabinet, or McDowell, but unforeseeable happenings, together with the unmilitary emphasis of the American democracy, that had produced a failure which to Browning seemed "unaccountable."

More significant than post-mortem recrimination was the forward look which showed an unshaken government backed by a people that could close ranks, re-form lines, and push grimly on. If Lincoln was hurt and stunned, his resilience was equally manifest. The night after Bull Run he "did not go to his bed," but began some pencil jottings which two days later (July 23) had been elaborated into "memoranda of military policy suggested by the Bull Run defeat." In brief his policy was: push the blockade, drill the forces at Fort Monroe and vicinity, hold Baltimore, strengthen "Patterson or Banks" (in the Winchester area), push forward in Missouri (this was Frémont's job), reorganize the main force in and near Washington, discharge those three-months men who declined longer service (a bitter lesson had been learned here), bring up new volunteers as fast as possible, seize and hold suitable points in Virginia, then advance with a co-ordinated movement on western fronts.

For the new program a new commander was needed. Not that McDowell had served so badly; it was rather that this unfortunate commander bore the imprimatur of defeat and that conditions of army morale and popular feeling demanded a change. The name of George B. McClellan was in favor because of a minor but skillfully advertised campaign in western Virginia (June and July, 1861). In an address to his troops ("Soldiers of the Army of the West") he had dramatically acclaimed the achievements of his men; this address, whose publication was not neglected, was dated only five days before McDowell's defeat. More than this, McClellan had real qualities. Training at West Point had been followed by regular army duty, Mexican War service, military surveys, observation in the Crimean War (perfectly reported and published by the United States government), and executive experience with the Illinois Central Railroad.

On July 27, 1861, McClellan formally assumed his duties in command of the Union army with headquarters at Washington.

II

Lincoln's comment that one bad general was better than two good ones was a canny aphorism rather than an effective guiding principle. Certainly in 1862 it could be said that neither in the field nor at the capital was there any co-ordinating and directing mind. In the period while McClellan was still general in chief the attorney general advised Lincoln to "act out the powers of his place, to command the commanders," and become "in fact, what he is in law, the *Chief Commander*." Bates thought this idea entirely feasible, since the President's "aids" could keep "his military . . . books and papers" and do his bidding. If he (Bates) were President he would know what to do with officers who were restive under a superior. As for Lincoln, he thought that a change for the better would occur "if he will only trust his own good judgment more, and defer less, to . . . subordinates."

Whether the advice of "General Bates" was to be taken or not, the turn of the year found the North impatient for action. Summer, autumn, and early winter had passed and McClellan had not moved. End the war in a hurry, or else! This seemed to be the thought of loyal citizens generally as they tired of military parades, noted the mounting expense, watched the enemy grow, heard rumors of a revolution in the Northwest, and witnessed a constant slipping in the administration's hold upon popular confidence. As one of Trumbull's correspondents expressed it: "The people say if we can whip them let it be done at once if we cannot we want to know it now and save ourselves from bankruptcy if we cannot the nation from disunion."

This unrest was evident in the applause given to Greeley on January 3, 1862, when in Washington he declared that national misfortune had been due to reluctance to meet the antagonist. As the elected leader in a democracy the President naturally did not escape the effect of this widespread impatience and disapproval.

A kind of crisis in military affairs (one of many) came in December and January, 1861–62, when McClellan lay ill of typhoid fever for about three weeks. O. H. Browning records that at this time he had a long talk with the President about the war. "He told me [wrote Browning] he was thinking of taking the field himself, and suggested several plans of operation." McClellan's enemies took advantage of the situation, represented that army matters were at a standstill, and intrigued for his downfall. McClellan himself maintained that his intellect was not dulled, that his strong constitution enabled him to continue to transact business daily, and that each of "the chiefs of the staff departments" knew the condition of affairs and could deal, through him, with the President and secretary of war, so that no change in the machinery of army control was needed. Nevertheless there began at this point a series of steps that tended progressively to create those elements of political interference which led at length to McClellan's ruin. Thinking that the sick general ought not to be "disturbed with business," the President, with none of McClellan's confidence, took up the military part of his task with grim intensity. He gave close attention to western operations, advised Halleck to attack Columbus from up-river, concerned himself with affairs in eastern Tennessee where he noted that "our friends" were "being hanged and driven to despair," admonished Buell that "Delay is ruining us," and instructed that general to "name as early a day as you safely can" for a southward thrust. It was at about this time that he took Halleck's *Science of War* out of the Library of Congress, and his secretaries relate that he "read a large number of strategical works," held long military conferences, and "pored over the reports from . . . the field of war." On the tenth of January the President conferred with General Montgomery C. Meigs in the general's office. In "great distress," according to Meigs's account, the President said: "General, what shall I do? The people are impatient; Chase has no money . . . ; the General of the Army has typhoid fever. The bottom is out of the tub. What shall I do?" Meigs suggested a council of military chiefs. Accounts differ at this point. Meigs stated that a council of several generals and cabinet officials met on January 12, and that the President adjourned it till next day so that McClellan could attend. McClellan stated that the conclave was called without his knowledge, that he mustered enough strength to be driven to the White House, and that his unexpected appear-

THE GARDNER FULL FIGURE—1863

One of several photographs taken by Alexander Gardner in his studio
on Sunday, Nov. 15, 1863, a few days before the Gettysburg address.

ance had "the effect of a shell in a powder-magazine." Next day another conference was held, with McClellan present. It was a strained and difficult meeting, at which Chase, according to McClellan's account, showed great anger because the "original and real purpose" was " 'to dispose of the military goods and chattels' of the sick man," and Chase could not bear the "sudden frustration of his schemes." The meeting proceeded with a good deal of desultory whispering; then Chase, with "uncalled-for irritation" of manner, challenged McClellan to present his military program in detail. McClellan declined to reveal his plans in answer to Chase; when the same request came from the President, the general declined to submit his plans to that assembly, some of whom were "incapable of keeping a secret," unless the President would give the order in writing and assume the responsibility. On this note the council was declared adjourned by the President. In the sullenness of McClellan's behavior one can see not only the caution of a field marshal who did not wish his intentions to become the property of everybody including the enemy, but also the resentment of a man who felt that the whole meeting was intended as a plot to destroy him.

In his impatience to get action Lincoln now took a step which almost suggested that he considered himself a general in chief or head of staff. On January 27, 1862, he issued "President's General War Order No. 1," which suggested that there were more to follow, in which he ordered a general forward movement of the land and naval forces to be launched on February 22, with details as to particular armies that were to move on that day. Secretaries, subordinates, the general in chief, and all other commanders were to be held severally to "strict and full responsibilities" for the "prompt execution of this order."

Two things may be said of this presidential paper: (1) It was no mere advice or admonition; it was a peremptory order from the constitutional commander in chief of the army and navy. If it was not an order to be obeyed by all, high and low, its title was a misnomer and its wording a misfit. (2) In terms of actual fact the order got nowhere; nothing happened that bore any resemblance to fulfillment of the President's command.

As a sort of expansion of his "President's General War Order No. 1" Lincoln issued four days later his "President's Special War Order No. 1" directing that on or before February 22 an expedition should move out for the seizure of a railroad point "southwestward of . . . Manassas Junction." The nation's chief was getting down to particulars. One cannot say that military commands in the American army have never been debated; at any rate McClellan was given "permission" to debate this one, and it was never carried out. The President's order got no farther than a proposal. Execution was not required, yet the order was never formally revoked.

In the giving of these orders it was as if Lincoln, though ineffectively, were performing as "Chief Commander" in the manner of Bates's suggestion. The more significant fact was that he was under pressure from all sides, and particularly under political and popular pressure, to send the troops forward. In the sense of military commands his orders were not taken seriously, nor has American army practice proceeded on the theory that the President functions as supreme field marshal. The fundamental meaning of the constitutional provision making the President "Commander in Chief of the Army and Navy" is to be found in the Anglo-Saxon concept that the military power shall be subject to the civil. It is for this reason that the highest civil official is given the power to determine, broadly, the national purpose and occasion for which the troops are used. That he should actually command an army or direct a fleet is not contemplated. Lincoln's giving of these war orders must be considered exceptional, rather than in line with established procedure. Nicolay and Hay state that they were issued when the President was "at the end of his patience."

It is in this sense—i.e., in terms of troubled emergency, perplexing anxiety, and exceptional proposals—that one must read the above-noted remark of Lincoln to Browning as to the possibility of taking the field himself. To do that was not his function, nor is there reason to suppose, as some have superficially done, that such taking of the field would have promoted a better central war direction or strategic success, though it would have thrown the President more fully into the very midst of military controversy than he already was.

Mention should be made of one other occasion on which Lincoln seemingly assumed the function of actual military-naval command. Early in May of 1862, though business was pressing in Washington, Lincoln made a somewhat curious visit to Fort Monroe, taking Secretary of the Treasury Chase and Secretary of War Stanton with him, and there is evidence that on this occasion he not only conferred with naval and military commanders but also took a hand in the actual direction of operations. Chase referred to "a brilliant week's campaign of the Prest." as if the President had been in command, and attributed the Union capture of Norfolk to Lincoln's direction of the movements involved. A Massachusetts gentleman, James D. Green of Cambridge, left an account of this episode on the basis of information which Senator Sumner gave him: "The President [wrote Mr. Green], with his Secretaries, immediately put himself at the head of the troops then under the command of Gen. Macl, & at once proceeded to the capture of Norfolk, which was in no condition to defend itself, & of no importance in a military point of view; but, on the contrary, being surrendered, its garrison forthwith marched up to aid in the defence of Richmond. The President next dispatched three Gun Boats up the James River. . . ."

Historians of this period will recognize at once that Chase and Stanton were the most violently anti-McClellan of the cabinet members, and Mr. Green saw in this episode an effort on the part of the President, by the sending of gunboats up the James, to "anticipate McClellan in the capture of Richmond." He quotes Sumner as saying that Lincoln and his cabinet, just before this, had unanimously decided to remove McClellan from the command of the army (which Mr. Green considered "madness"), but that on receiving news of the evacuation of Yorktown they decided to "let the matter stand for the present." As for the astounding suggestion of removing McClellan just as he had come in front of the enemy, the thought occurred to this Cambridge gentleman, though "it seemed too atrocious to be admitted," that opposition to McClellan was motivated by "a *political object*—the interest of a *political party*"; McClellan was to be sacrificed, and perhaps also his army, because "the politicians in control of the Government had an ulterior object in view, more important in their estimation than the restoration of the Union, viz. that, let what would come, *the war should not cease till slavery was abolished*."

Though Mr. Green in his perplexity (after talking with Sumner) questioned this astonishing theory, he considered it confirmed when he soon heard of Lincoln going with Chase and Stanton to Fort Monroe where the President took charge of operations, as he was led to believe, in the anti-McClellan sense. This whole affair of Lincoln's presence at the front at the time of the capture of Norfolk is a bit hard to unravel in all its aspects, but confirming evidence does sustain the impression of the President serving as actual commander, expressing strong disapproval of what was being done under General Wool's direction, questioning subordinate officers, vehemently throwing his tall hat on the floor, and dictating military orders.

III

After Antietam (September 17, 1862) the credit bestowed upon McClellan was in no proportion to the savage denunciation that would have descended had he failed to drive Lee back. Disparaging the service he had performed, the radical cabal against him was continuing its incessant attack, supported by McClellan's implacable cabinet enemies—Stanton and Chase. Against terrific pressure Lincoln had held an open mind toward McClellan while doubting the main pattern of his strategy, but the case that was being built up against the general was getting even stronger than Lincoln's wavering favor. War weariness was an increasing psychological factor in the North as battle after battle brought frightful casualties with nothing settled. The North had not yet adjusted itself to the concept of a long, serious war with heavy sacrifices. People were impressed by facile assertions that Lee could have been easily crushed once and for all; the failure of McClellan to pursue was made a more prominent thing than his checking of an invasion. There was no adequate appreciation of what was gained by McClellan's caution in face of Lee's formidable power; and just at this juncture it came to Lincoln's ears that a talkative officer, Major John J. Key, had expressed the view that Lee's army was not bagged after Sharpsburg because that "was not the game." Both sides were to be kept in the field till exhausted; fraternal relations were then to be restored with slavery saved; that was the "only way the Union could be preserved." Fearing that this was "staff talk" and that it was indispensable to make a signal example of Key, Lincoln dismissed him from the service, though sending him a personal letter which contained more sympathy than rebuke. On October 1 the President visited the army, viewing the camps, going over the battlefields, and holding "many and long consultations alone" with McClellan. When the general explained his reasons for delay and for preparation before the next round, Lincoln said repeatedly that he was "entirely satisfied." "The President was very kind personally [wrote McClellan]; told me he was convinced I was the best general in the country, etc., etc." "He told me that he regarded me as the only general in the service

capable of organizing and commanding a large army, and that
he would stand by me."

Lincoln's main purpose in visiting the army was to get
McClellan to move. Returning to Washington, he made another
of those efforts at presidential direction of the army which
never quite amounted to positive command of operations.
Through Halleck (October 6) he instructed McClellan to "cross
the Potomac and give battle to the enemy, or drive him south."
Nothing happened. October days passed and McClellan lingered. Then Lincoln sent him a long, earnest letter. "Are you
not over-cautious [he wrote] when you assume that you cannot
do what the enemy is constantly doing? . . . Change positions
with the enemy, and think you not he would break your communication with Richmond within the next twenty-four hours?
. . . If he should . . . move toward Richmond, I would press
closely to him, fight him if a favorable opportunity should
present, and at least try to beat him to Richmond on the inside
track. . . . If we cannot beat the enemy where he now is,
we never can, he again being within the intrenchments of
Richmond."

It is easy to read this well written letter of Lincoln's, a
long epistle whose substance is only briefly suggested here, and
assume that it put McClellan completely in the wrong. To do
so would be to forget that McClellan, in field command, knew
what was needed in reconditioning and concentrating his army,
that he already realized the need for checking the striking Lee,
that the "true approach" via the Peninsula had been barred
by opposition in Washington, and that watchful delay when
Lee was in no position to strike was less dangerous than ill-
planned engagements which were the forte of McClellan's
successors. It was not as if the general needed all this admonition. He had previously written to his wife (September 25)
indicating a purpose to watch the Potomac and to attack Lee
if he remained near Washington, or, if he retired toward Richmond to follow and strike him. With old regiments reduced to

skeletons and new regiments in need of instruction, with a
deficiency of officers and want of horses, McClellan would not
then have maneuvered to bring on a battle unless necessary to
protect Washington yet all the evidence shows that he was
actively building a stronger and larger force and was waiting
to choose his moment for an effective blow when it should fall.
This, of course, was a matter of painful rebuilding. One can
never estimate the full dimensions of the setback to McClellan's
plans and to Union success produced by the incredible removal of his army in August 1862 from its strong position on
the James River near Richmond.

Eager for an immediate knockout victory, Lincoln waited
further, meanwhile reading a despatch in which McClellan, in
an ill-chosen passage, referred to sore-tongued and fatigued
horses. Then Lincoln burst out: "Will you pardon me for asking what the horses of your army have done since the battle
of Antietam that fatigues anything?" A few days later the
President admitted "something of impatience" in his despatch
and assured McClellan of his deep regret if he had done him
any injustice. Self control was becoming difficult. With momentous decisions in the balance nerves were frayed, tempers
were rising, and trivial misunderstandings were in danger of
producing ominous results.

Beginning on October 26 McClellan did cross the Potomac;
a few days later his army was "massed near Warrenton, ready
to act in any required direction, perfectly in hand, and in
admirable condition and spirits." He was now planning and
expecting another battle. He was confident and ready. Then
came the abrupt final blow against him. On November 7 General Buckingham came by special train from Washington and
turned up at Burnside's camp. Suspecting the purpose of this
visit, McClellan kept his own counsel. Late at night sitting
alone in his tent writing to his wife, he heard a rap on his tent
pole. Burnside and Buckingham then entered bearing an order.
"By direction of the President" relieving him of command of

the Army of the Potomac and putting Burnside in his place. There was immense resentment among soldiers and officers, so intense that many were in favor of McClellan's "refusing to obey the order, and of marching upon Washington to take possession of the government." It was to quiet this restless feeling, and in compliance with Burnside's request, that McClellan remained with the army until November 10; then, with feelings beyond description and with "thousands of brave men . . . shedding tears like children," he uncomplainingly turned his command over to Burnside and took his departure not only from the Army of the Potomac, but from active military service. Anger at his removal, felt keenly among raw recruits who had become veterans in his ranks, would have deepened into more bitter anguish of heart if these men had foreseen the sequel.

IV

The army was Lincoln's main anxiety. Morale after Fredericksburg (December 13, 1862) was low and desertions numerous. The men were "disheartened and almost sulky." Having been in a ferment on the subject of cabinet change, the North was now demanding such a shuffle of commanders as would "give more vigor to our armies." Prominent generals—McClellan, Porter, Stone, Buell, McDowell, Frémont, and others— were without commands. In some cases this was fortunate; in others it was a wasted resource and a cause of resentment. With radicals insisting on greater legislative control of army movements, with urgent demands that conservative men should force the administration "to a change of measures and men," with army affairs in a tangle and a conscription act in the making, the civilian mind was deep in the gloom of defeat while the soldier mind was in a state of "savage" dissatisfaction that "tended strongly to mutiny."

This unhealthful state in the army was due to a combination of factors: delay in pay, jealousy among generals, prejudiced proceedings of military courts and of the congressional
war committee, "politicians seeking to influence military movements in favor of their own partisan and selfish schemes,"
legislative patronage in military appointments, and, most of all,
a pervading sense of hopelessness under existing command.
To mention the three men who had the highest military functions at the time, Lincoln had Burnside, he had Stanton, and
he had Halleck, his general in chief. Stanton was as unstable
as he was arrogant and stubborn. Some of his decisions were
reversed by himself, often from "mere caprice"; "there . . .
was none with whom men found it more difficult to deal." "The
extent to which Lincoln interposed his tact and patience between Stanton and generals of the army, . . . preventing injustice and insuring . . . continuity, is a commonplace of history." At times it appeared that the President and his minister
of war were at loggerheads; at other times it seemed that
Lincoln knew Stanton to be "unprincipled" but felt he had to
retain him to get the country's business done. The best of
men found it impossible to get along with the secretary.
Henry W. Bellows, promoting the fine work of the sanitary
commission, sought secretarial co-operation in vain. Welles referred to Stanton as "unreliable" and impatient toward Lincoln;
Bates described him as "brusque—not to say uncivil."

Lincoln would give an order and War Secretary Stanton
would undo it. The secretary had allied himself with radicals,
had withheld co-operation from McClellan, and had been one
of the chief agents in the ruin of that general. Defeats of 1862
were largely of his making.

Halleck's task was no easy berth. Condemnation should
be tempered by a realization of his difficulties, yet it was the
prevailing view of contemporaries that his performance after
taking up his duties in Washington was unsatisfactory. Bates

wrote of his "bad judgment," his "cunning and evasive" manner; he summed it up by referring to "that poor thing—*Halleck*," and again to the "improvidence (not to say imbecility) of . . . Stanton and Halleck." One of the keenest of military observers, General Jacob D. Cox, a man of measured words, referred to the general in chief as "unequal to his responsibility" and as "in no true sense a commander of the armies." In the opinion of Nicolay and Hay, as a nominal general in chief "his genius fell short of the high duties of that great station."

The count against Burnside is simply that of failure. He was a man of courage, of fine military bearing of "single-hearted honesty and unselfishness." As a defeated general, however, he could not have been expected to retain the confidence of his men and officers; this was the less possible in view of his post-Fredericksburg attitude and intentions. Having determined upon a move across the Rappahannock in the face of almost unanimous opposition by his generals, Burnside created a further difficulty for a buffeted President by putting the responsibility for a decision on Lincoln's shoulders; this he did by a letter stating his purpose, with an offer to resign if his plan should not be approved.

The plan of Burnside seemed to smack of reckless blundering, and under these circumstances the President turned for advice to "Old Brains" (Halleck); yet in the very act of doing so he revealed his lack of faith in that general. "If in such a difficulty . . . you do not help," wrote Lincoln, "you fail me precisely in the point for which I sought your assistance." He wanted the general in chief to go over the ground, gather all the elements for forming a judgment, and then come through with an approval or disapproval. "Your military skill," he said, "is useless to me if you do not do this."

This was written on January 1, 1863, the day of Lincoln's definitive proclamation of emancipation and of a protracted public reception. It was a crowded day, one incident of which was a painful conference with Burnside, as a result of which that commander submitted his resignation. On receiving Lincoln's New Year's Day letter through Stanton, Halleck promptly wrote out his resignation. At a time of hazard and anxiety the President was thus presented with the resignations of the general in chief and of the commander of the principal army. The immediate difficulty as to the resignations was patched up. Halleck's was at once withdrawn on the President agreeing to withdraw his January first letter. Burnside also for the time remained.

But Burnside eventually made his own incapacity for command so unmistakable that his removal was no longer open to question. There was nothing to do but relieve the luckless general of his command of the Army of the Potomac. This the President did on January 26, 1863, giving that post to Joseph Hooker.

That the President was uncertain as to Hooker at the moment of appointing him is revealed in an admonishing letter which he wrote to the new chieftain. It is one of the most remarkable of Lincoln's epistles, being of the kind that he sometimes wrote and did not send; this time he sent it. "General," he wrote, "I have placed you at the head of the Army of the Potomac. . . . I have done this upon what appear to me . . . sufficient reasons. And yet. . . ." Then the President explained that he was "not quite satisfied" with the general, that he considered him ambitious, and that in thwarting Burnside he had done "a great wrong to the country." He continued:

I have heard . . . of your . . . saying that both the Army and the Government needed a Dictator. Of course it was not *for* this, but in spite of it, that I have given you the command. . . . What I now ask of you is military success, and I will risk the dictatorship. . . . I much fear that the spirit which you have aided to infuse into the Army, of criticising their Commander, and withholding confidence from him, will now turn upon you. I shall assist you . . . to put it down. Neither you,

nor Napoleon, if he were alive . . . , could get any good out
of an army, while such a spirit prevails in it. And now, beware
of rashness. Beware of rashness, but with energy, and sleepless
vigilance, go forward, and give us victories.

There have been various commentaries on this letter, including the conjecture that Lincoln paced the floor after writing
it before adding his signature.

V

With military and naval fortunes at the focus of his
thought, Lincoln was made to realize the complications of
remote control from Washington and the hazards of interference by civil officials, not to say politicians, in the operations
of his warriors. In general terms, or at times in considerable
detail, he would make known his wish for a particular operation; he would even plead with his generals to bring it about,
only to meet with frustration or to see enacted the very result
he wished to avoid. He strongly desired, almost as a kind of
specialty, that eastern Tennessee, because of its Unionist sympathies, should be occupied and possessed. He urged that
efforts be made against Chattanooga; he wanted to know how
the expedition for that purpose was progressing; he studied
closely the almost unsolvable problem of sending western
troops east, yet launching successful offensives in the West.
"To take and hold the railroad . . . in East Tennessee," he
considered "fully as important as the taking and holding of
Richmond." Noting in mid-October 1862 that Buell's "main
object"—i.e., capture of eastern Tennessee—was unattained,
the President, through Halleck, wanted to know why the Union
army could not do as the Confederate—"live as he lives, and
fight as he fights." This implied that in Lincoln's thought the

people of that mountain region would be as ready to avoid harassment of the Union as of the Confederate army. The activities of guerrilla bands and of bold Confederate raiders in Tennessee and Kentucky were a matter of concern to the President, who advised that vigorous counter measures be taken. The President's hopes for eastern Tennessee, however, were again and again deferred.

Lincoln had constantly to contend with the fog of war, the imperfect state of military intelligence, and the hazardous difficulty of operational direction at a distance. It is seldom indeed that one finds the imperative mood in his communications to generals, but the interrogation point was typical. On September 8, 1862, with Bragg's invasion of Kentucky in full swing, he asked Buell how he could be certain that Bragg, with his command, was not at that time in the Valley of Virginia. Four days later he asked General Boyle at Louisville: "Where is the enemy which you dread in Louisville? How near to you? What is General Gilbert's opinion? With all . . . respect for you, I must think General [Horatio G.] Wright's military opinion is the better. . . . Where do you understand Buell to be, and what is he doing?" In the same letter Lincoln showed his concept of remote control. Referring to the same General Wright, in command in Kentucky, he said: ". . . for us here to control him there . . . would be a babel of confusion which would be utterly ruinous."

No part of Lincoln's military task was more vital than the making of appointments, and at no time was this function more difficult than in the summer and fall of 1862, when also the questions of foreign policy and of emancipation were at their most acute stage. The transfer and elevation of Halleck and Pope, the removal of Buell, and the assigning of important new commands to Rosecrans, Grant, and Schofield—all these western matters had to be studied, argued over, and decided under pressure in the very period when the affairs of the Army of the Potomac and the problem of McClellan were at the stage of greatest anxiety. He even had to write to an aggrieved colonel explaining that he could not "conjecture what junior of yours you suppose I contemplate promoting over you." To another disgruntled officer he wrote that he had "too many family controversies" already on his hands "to voluntarily . . . take up another." The feelings of Rosecrans had to be soothed by the President's assurance that the general had "not a single enemy" in Washington. When Fitz John Porter was convicted in a military trial, it was Lincoln's painful duty to issue the order that he be "cashiered and dismissed from the service . . . and forever disqualified from holding any office of trust or profit under the . . . United States." This matter of military appointment rested heavily upon Lincoln's shoulders. Taking it along with many other military aspects, it shows that the President's task as Commander in Chief was not merely nominal. Every time an appointment, change of rank, or shift of command was made, the President had to study alternatives; he had to deal with military men as persons, as fallible and sensitive human beings; he had to consider not only this or that army or campaign involving perhaps the fate of the nation, but the traditions and attachments of men in the service, the often unknowable capabilities of leaders, the delays of reorientation when a new command was assumed, the numerous pressures and interferences behind his back, and the sometimes difficult questions of senatorial confirmation or congressional attack. Of all the many duties that weighed upon Lincoln in the crowded war years, the function of Commander in Chief of the army and navy was the most serious as well as the most harassing and burdensome.

VI

In September and October 1863 drastic changes occurred in strategic plans, troop concentrations, and high army command, but it is not easy to pin down a statement as to who, in the last analysis, made these decisions. Who decided to put Grant in chief western command, to remove Rosecrans, to advance Thomas, and to move in full force upon Bragg? Who was it that caused the besieged and defeated Union army near Chattanooga to shake off the threat of starvation, seize the initiative, and win the decisive victory of Missionary Ridge? As to these decisions that set the stage of November victory the passive voice appears in much of the writing. We find it stated that "Grant was assigned" to his important command, that he "acquiesced" in the superseding of Rosecrans, and that Thomas "was made commander" of the Army of the Cumberland. Nicolay and Hay state that "the Government" was convinced that Rosecrans must go, that it was "the intention of the Government" to put Grant in supreme command in the West, and so on.

A writer seeking to give Lincoln credit for it all might be tempted to say that the President made these decisions, but evidence is lacking for that conclusion. Piecing together the information gathered by wading through many pages, it would seem that neither Lincoln nor Halleck was the fully controlling mind, and that the shape of things was brought about largely by Stanton among those in authority in Washington and by Grant in the field. Stanton was in touch with the army before Chattanooga through Charles A. Dana, assistant secretary of war, whose reason for being in the West was to advise the secretary. Lincoln did not at this time "find" Grant, though he felt and expressed high regard for him and found his uncomplaining letters, and his lack of a personal ax to grind, refreshing in contrast to other military leaders. Grant had never been a self-promoting general, he had been the target of newspaper abuse, his performance at Shiloh had been severely denounced, and his contacts with Lincoln, even by correspondence, had been slight. Lincoln, as of July 13, 1863, did not remember having ever met Grant, but he congratulated him handsomely on the victory at Vicksburg, and at this time the Illinois warrior, whose career had in 1862 been in serious jeopardy, was advanced to the rank of major general in the regular army. Lincoln referred to him in writing as "a copious worker and fighter," and was quoted as saying: "I can't spare this man; he fights." It cannot be said that Lincoln planned or ordered Grant's November advance against Bragg. The President was thinking principally of "holding" Chattanooga, not of an attack, and was urging Burnside to go to that area, which Burnside did not do.

VII

As the armies renewed their fighting with fierce intensity in the spring of 1864, a new situation presented itself. In three years of indecisive warfare a certain repetitive pattern had become familiar: advance by one or the other side (usually the Federal), concentration on a one- or two-day battle, "victory" by one side or the other (usually the Confederate), Union withdrawal, change of Union commanders, then considerable delay for each side, neither being really defeated, to reorganize for the next concentrated push and sanguinary though indecisive engagement. Seemingly, the war could have gone on indefinitely in such fashion. Now, however, came a kind of struggle that was different as to broad strategy, as to method in the field, and as to pace. These changes coincided with the shifting of Grant from the field of his western triumphs to the main area of operations against Lee in Virginia; moreover, the shift involved the placing of general command of the Union armies in Grant's determined hand. The strategy was now for co-ordinated forward drives, continued assaults though producing no immediate advantage, killing and wounding at a thousand a day, emphasis on fighting and slaughter rather than on this or that battle— in a word, a "war of attrition."

BOSTON DAILY ADVERTISER.

NO. 15,370.   VOL. 102..NO. 186.   BOSTON, FRIDAY MORNING, NOVEMBER 20, 1863.   THREE CENTS.

The Consecration at Gettysburg.

BOSTON.

Dedicatory Address by the President.

GETTYSBURG. Pa., Nov. 19.—The ceremonies attending the dedication of the National Cemetery commenced this afternoon by a grand military and civic display, under command of Major-General Couch.

The line of march was taken up at 10 o'clock, and the procession marched through the principal streets to the Cemetery, where the military formed in line and saluted the President. At a quarter past 11 the head of the procession arrived at the main stand. The President and members of the Cabinet, together with the chief military and civic dignitaries took position on the stand.

The President seated himself between Mr. Seward and Mr. Everett, after a reception with the respect and perfect silence during the solemnity of the occasion, every man in the immense gathering uncovering on his appearance.

The military then formed in line extending around the stand, the area between the stand and the military being occupied by civilians, comprising about 150,000 people, and including men, women and children. The attendance was quite large.

The military escort comprised one squadron of cavalry and two batteries of artillery and a regiment of infantry, which constituted the regular funeral escort of honor for the highest officer in the service.

After the performance of a funeral dirge by the band, an eloquent prayer was delivered by Rev. Mr. Stockton.

Mr. Everett then delivered his oration, which was listened to with marked attention.

The President then delivered the following dedicatory speech:—

"Four score and seven years ago our fathers brought forth upon this continent a new nation, conceived in liberty and dedicated to the proposition that all men are created equal. [Applause.] Now we are engaged in a great civil war, testing whether that nation, or any nation so conceived and so dedicated, can long endure. We are met on a great battle-field of that war; we are met to dedicate a portion of it as a final resting place of those who have given their lives that that nation might live. It is altogether fitting and proper that we should do this, but in a larger sense we cannot dedicate, we cannot consecrate, we cannot hallow, this ground. The brave men living and dead who struggled here have consecrated it far above our power to add or detract. [Applause.] The world will note nor long remember what we say here, but it can never forbid what they did here. [Applause.] It is for us, the living, rather, to be dedicated here to the unfinished work that they have thus so far nobly carried on. [Applause.] It is rather for us to be here dedicated to the great task remaining before us, that from these honored dead we take increased devotion to that cause for which they here gave the last full measure of devotion that we here highly resolve that the dead shall not have died in vain; [applause] that the nation shall, under God, have a new birth of freedom, and that government of people by the people and for the people shall not perish from the earth." [Long continued applause.]

Three cheers were here given for the President and the Governors of the States.

After the delivery of this address, the dirge and the benediction closed the exercises, and the immense assemblage departed about 2 o'clock.

Courtesy of Massachusetts Historical Society

BEST NEWSPAPER REPORT OF LINCOLN'S WORDS AT GETTYSBURG
Charles Hale, of the Boston *Daily Advertiser*, heard the address and made this report.

On February 29, 1864, Lincoln signed an act of Congress reviving the grade of lieutenant general, a rank so high that it had been used only for Washington and (as brevet) for Winfield Scott. It was understood that this high rank was to be conferred upon U. S. Grant, who arrived in unspectacular fashion in Washington to become the sensational center of interest and the cynosure of social eyes at a White House reception remarkable for the presence of the nation's notables (May 8). There was an unusually large attendance in expectation of Grant's presence and a considerable "stir and buzz" (as Welles recorded) when the "short, brown, dark-haired man" appeared. As the general passed into the East Room escorted by Seward, there was clapping and "a cheer or two"; to Welles it "seemed rowdy and unseemly."

Next day, March 9, there occurred a formal ceremony of military investiture at the White House. As Lincoln and Grant had met for the first time on the evening of the reception, the President, with tactful thoughtfulness toward the diffident hero, explained the nature of the coming occasion, giving him a copy of his (the President's) speech and adding a friendly suggestion that a brief response would be in order. In the presence of the cabinet, specially summoned for the purpose, the military notables gathered (Grant and his staff with Stanton and Halleck) and Lincoln presented the unusual commission. It was remarked that the general was "somewhat embarrassed" as he gave his response. On March 10 the President and Mrs. Lincoln invited Grant and Meade to dinner at the White House. Lincoln was omitting nothing that could improve the social and personal as well as the official recognition of the officer who was now regarded as the man of the hour.

For this dinner there was a special courtesy in the inclusion of General Meade; if either Meade or Grant had been of smaller stature, the new situation might have developed into an awkward rivalry of the kind so common among Civil War generals, or at least a sense of hurt feelings. It was not merely that Grant

was elevated to supreme military "rank." He was at the same
time "assigned to the command of the Armies of the United
States." Though in a sense this high general command had been
held by Scott, McClellan, and Halleck, yet it had been exercised
with so little effectiveness that the investiture in the case of
Grant came with all the force of something new and untried.
Lincoln had found Halleck unsatisfactory in the role of general
in chief and his dissatisfaction on that score was well known.
Halleck, with the best of motives, now offered his resignation,
not for the first time, but the President, as previously, made it
clear that "Old Brains" was to remain at his post.

To appreciate the extent of the change now instituted it
must be remembered that general direction of the armies was to
be no longer in the hands of a lofty desk commander in Washington. If Grant had so chosen he might have continued the old
system, but the "new" general from the West, now the main
leader in the East but with authority for all the fronts, promptly
decided that his headquarters would not be in Washington,
but with the Army of the Potomac, with himself as leader of
that army in the field. Yet he never became its appointed commander; that office was retained by Meade. It augured well
for the Union cause, and it revealed much as to the personalities
of these generals, that they could stand in this unusual and
potentially difficult relation to each other—the one the official
commander, the other the effective leader of the main army—
without personal friction and without detriment to efficiency.

The military planning for 1864 soon unfolded itself in terms
of a grand scheme by which the Union armies on all major
fronts would be co-ordinated in a series of encircling or squeezing operations. By simultaneous movements on several fronts
Federal numerical superiority would be brought into play while
the resulting Confederate necessity of manning a number of
distant points would be sure to leave some area exposed to attack.

While at Culpeper in late March and April, Grant planned

the spring and summer offensive of the eastern army, keeping in touch with Lincoln by occasional personal visits to nearby Washington. Lincoln gave Grant a free hand, but it would be a mistake to suppose that the President had nothing to do with strategy or that he was passively inattentive to military matters. Too much should not be made of Lincoln's statement to Grant, as to other generals, disclaiming military expertness while leaving the field commander to act as the effective military leader. It is true that on the eve of the Virginia campaign the President wrote: "The particulars of your plans I neither know nor seek to know." In his *Memoirs* Grant records that Lincoln "told me he did not want to know what I proposed to do." (This was probably a misinterpretation of the Chief's statement that he did not seek to know the "particulars" of the general's plans.) In those same *Memoirs,* written long after the war, the general related that the President "submitted a plan of campaign of his own," illustrating it with a map. The general "listened respectfully," but knew that the President's plan was unworkable. The full truth as to the respective attitudes of Lincoln and Grant is not easy to state. In a careful study T. Harry Williams discounts the validity of some of the general's comments in his *Memoirs.* The general, he said, wrote "under the influence of the postwar Grant and Lincoln myths." "Grant had forgotten much in the years after the war, and his account [of Lincoln's unworkable plan] was wide of the truth."

Lincoln was always generous toward Grant, and when the Army of the Potomac was in the thick of its death grapple with Lee, the President wrote: "My previous high estimate of General Grant has been maintained and heightened by what has occurred in the remarkable campaign he is now conducting. . . . He and his brave soldiers are now in the midst of their great trial. . . ."

The President, with his beloved son Tad, visited Grant's army for several days at City Point in late June, leaving Washington on June 20 and returning to Washington on the 23rd. At this stage in the war the President was "deeply disappointed" that the costly campaign had resolved itself into a siege of Petersburg; he may then have felt "perhaps some doubts of Grant's generalship." The shocking extent of the slaughter was weighing upon the President's mind. Shortly before his visit to the army, he had wired to Grant: "I do hope you may find a way that . . . shall not be desperate in the sense of great loss of life." The war had now reached an unprofitable stage; it would be months before the burdened Chief could see prospects of ending the conflict.

VIII

Besieged as he was in Richmond and Petersburg, General Lee looked for relief, as he informed Jefferson Davis on June 20, 1864, from a stratagem for drawing the attention of the Federals to their own territory. Thereby he might induce Grant to weaken his besieging force by sending part of it northward or, better yet, to bleed his army further by assaulting the strong Confederate defenses. So Lee sent Jubal A. Early with nearly twenty thousand men up the Shenandoah Valley, that convenient approach to the unguarded rear of Washington, a route already well worn by Confederate raiders, who had used it every summer of the war. The Union forces under David Hunter having previously retreated out of the way, over the mountains into West Virginia, Early advanced unopposed through the Valley. During the first days of July his troops crossed the upper Potomac. On July 11, just a week after the adjournment of Congress, his army was on the northern outskirts of Washington, in sight of the Capitol dome.

For a couple of days Washington had a small taste of what was becoming familiar and routine in Richmond—a state of siege—but Washington knew far less than Richmond about the nature and intentions of the besieging force. Communications with the North by rail and telegraph were cut off. No one in the city, not even the President and his cabinet, could do more than guess how large the enemy force was, precisely where it was concentrated or whether it was concentrated at all, and when or whether it was going to attack. In his diary Secretary Welles railed against the "dunderheads" at the War Office, the stupid Stanton and the confused Halleck, and expressed no satisfaction when told that intelligence was poor because fresh cavalry was lacking. Grant himself suffered from defective information, though from his own intelligence and from Washington reports he had a broadly accurate picture of Early's movement. Unaware that Hunter had removed himself from the possibility of effective action, Grant counted upon him to pursue and entrap Early's army.

Fortifications dotted the circumference of Washington, but most of the garrisoning troops had been sent to Grant as replacements for his heavy losses, and the forts were manned by a motley collection of invalids and raw militiamen. At the enemy's approach, civilian employees of the navy and war departments were called into service. When Grant offered to come to the relief of the city, Lincoln suggested but did not order that he do so. On second thought Grant decided to send two corps but not to go himself, and Lincoln calmly accepted this arrangement.

Much alarmed about the President's personal safety, Stanton on July 9 sent Lincoln a note telling him his carriage had been followed by a mysterious horseman and warning him to be "on the *alert.*" Nevertheless Lincoln with his family went out as usual on the next evening to spend the night at the Soldiers' Home, in the northern part of the city, where the enemy was expected to appear. At ten that evening Stanton drafted another warning note, in which he started to tell Lincoln to "come into town at once," then corrected the last two words to read, a little less peremptorily, "tonight." The President, though reluctant, did return with his family that night, in a carriage which Stanton had sent for him, but he was considerably annoyed. He was further annoyed to learn that a gunboat was being readied so that he might flee the city.

The next day he determined to "desert his tormentors" and make a tour of the city's defenses. He went out to Fort Stevens, beyond the Soldiers' Home, near the northern corner of the District of Columbia, on the 7th Street Road. He was on the parapet when the Confederates, advancing through heat and dust from Silver Spring, first opened fire on the fort. A soldier standing beside him—long afterward identified as Oliver Wendell Holmes, Jr.,—"roughly ordered him to get down or he would have his head knocked off." The expected assault did not develop, as Early spent the afternoon in feeling out the strength of the works.

On the following day the President again was under fire at Fort Stevens. Though Early still ordered no attack, he kept up his reconnaissance, and a "continual popping" of gunfire came from pickets and skirmishers on both sides. An officer a few feet from Lincoln on the parapet fell with a mortal wound. A few minutes later Secretary Welles and Senator Wade entered the fort together and found the President sitting in the shade, his back against the parapet towards the enemy. Shells fired from the fort were setting fire to houses in which rebel sharpshooters were hiding. Learning that "the military officers in command thought the shelling of the houses proper and necessary," Lincoln, as he afterwards stated, "certainly gave" his "approbation to its being done."

From the fort, after the shelling had let up, Lincoln had a chance to see at first hand a little of the drama of soldiers in action. There, only a few hundred yards away, in the broad valley below, were men in blue (newly arrived veterans) advancing across open fields, and ahead of them were men in grey running for the wooded cover on the brow of the opposite hills. And here, nearer at hand, were Union stretcher bearers bringing in their wounded comrades. By nightfall the action had ceased, and campfires lighted up the woods around the fort, while the road was clogged with Union stragglers, some weary and worn out, others drunk. In the darkness to the north Early was withdrawing his troops.

All the while Lincoln had worried little if at all about his own safety or that of the city. "With him," as Hay noted on July 11, "the only concern seems to be whether we can bag or destroy this force in our front." And when the force had begun to leave, he became doubly anxious lest it get away. On July 13 Hay recorded again: "The President thinks we should push our column right up the River Road & cut off as many as possible of the retreating raiders." But there was no one to give the necessary orders in time. Grant was too far away. Halleck, never a man to assume responsibility, declined to act without instructions from Grant. And Lincoln, unwilling to interfere with the general in chief, restrained whatever impulses he may have had to take personal command in the emergency. Finally a telegram from Grant started General Wright in pursuit with all available forces. "Wright telegraphs that he thinks the enemy are all across the Potomac but that he has halted & sent out an infantry reconnoissance [*sic*], for fear he might come across the rebels & catch some of them." So, on July 14, Lincoln said to Hay. And Hay observed to himself, "The Chief is evidently disgusted."

Wright, of course, was not really to blame for his delayed and seemingly timid pursuit. As T. Harry Williams has written, "Early got away because the tangled command system in the Washington military area did not make anybody responsible for catching him." Both Lincoln and Grant soon recognized this fact and saw the necessity for reorganizing the command system so as to put the troops in the Capital and the adjacent departments under the control of a single general. Otherwise Early could threaten Washington again and again, Grant would have to keep on detaching troops from the Richmond and Petersburg area, and Lee would never be finally hemmed in and compelled to surrender. This military lesson for the President and his general in chief was one of the important consequences of the Early raid.

IX

With U. S. Grant as general in chief, the army was led by a man whom the President could depend upon. From time to time Lincoln still "interfered" in military affairs, though the myth persists that he allowed Grant to have his own way completely. As late as August, 1864, for example, he insisted that the general come to Washington for consultation about the pursuit of Early's army after the raid on Washington. "In the remaining months of 1864," T. Harry Williams writes, "Lincoln watched intently and sometimes anxiously over the conduct of the vast Union war effort, but he intervened in the management of it only at rare intervals because in general he was satisfied with Grant's direction."

During these months the most spectacular military activity was conceived and initiated by General W. T. Sherman, with the somewhat doubtful approval of Grant and Lincoln. With the capture of Atlanta, Sherman had not won his main objective, which was the capture or destruction of the opposing army under General J. B. Hood. Moreover, Sherman had lost the initiative. To recover it, he proposed to divide his forces and, with about 60,000 men, strike out boldly from Atlanta to some point on the coast, effecting a "devastation more or less relentless" on the way, while he sent General George H. Thomas back with about 30,000 men to hold Tennessee. Grant thought Sherman should dispose of Hood's army before he started off. Lincoln let Grant know that he himself had doubts about the plan. Yet he accepted it when Grant told him that nothing better seemed available.

Executive Mansion,

Washington, *Nov. 20* 1863

Hon. Edward Everett.

My dear Sir:

Your kind note of to-day is received. In our respective parts yesterday, you could not have been excused to make a short address, nor I a long one. I am pleased to know that, in your judgment, the little I did say was not entirely a failure—. Of course I knew Mr. Everett would not fail; and yet, while the whole discourse was eminently satisfactory, and will be of great value, there were passages in it which transcended my expectation. The point made against the theory of the general government being only an agency, whose principals are the States, was new to me, and, as I think, is one of the best arguments for the national supremacy. The tribute to our noble women for their angel-ministering to the suffering soldiers, surpasses, in its way, as do the subjects of it, whatever has gone before—

Our sick boy, for whom you kindly inquire, we hope is past the worst.

Your Obt Servt
A. Lincoln

Original in Massachusetts Historical Society

NOT ENTIRELY A FAILURE

On the day after the Gettysburg address Lincoln wrote his appreciation of Everett's oration, with a happily phrased comment on "our respective parts." It was Everett who wrote "The President of the United States" at the top, with date of receipt.

Early in November Sherman's men moved out of Atlanta and headed southeast, with orders to advance fifteen miles a day by four parallel roads, foraging on the country and laying waste mills, houses, cotton gins, public buildings, and especially railroad tracks and bridges. Sherman did not attempt to maintain lines of communication or supply, and the North had little news of his three-hundred-mile march while it was in progress. The President referred to it cautiously in his annual message on December 6. "It tends to show a great increase in our relative strength that our General-in-Chief should feel able to confront and hold in check every active force of the enemy, and yet to detach a well-appointed large army to move on such an expedition," he said. "The result not yet being known, conjecture in regard to it is not here indulged." He left out of the address one sentence which would have revealed to the people his own very real fear of possible disaster. In this sentence he had written that the general in chief must have concluded that "our cause could, if need be, survive the loss of the whole detached force."

Before Sherman left Atlanta, Hood had moved northward into Tennessee, in the hope of maneuvering Sherman out of Georgia, but Sherman relied on Thomas to deal with Hood. Though defeated at Franklin, Hood pushed stubbornly on to Nashville and besieged Thomas there. Lincoln, as he anxiously watched events from Washington, kept expecting Thomas to come out and fight. Finally he directed Stanton to consult with Grant about Thomas's failure to attack, and he got more of a reaction from Grant than he had bargained for. Grant advised that Thomas be removed from command and, despite Lincoln's unwillingness to approve such a drastic step, sent General John A. Logan to supersede him. Finally Grant went to consult Lincoln, intending to go on from Washington to Nashville to see personally that Thomas was relieved.

On December 15, Lincoln presided at a conference of Grant, Stanton, and Halleck. The President was now in the position, unusual for him, of arguing for the retention of a general who seemed to be afflicted with what, in the case of McClellan three years earlier, he had called the "slows." Lincoln pointed out that Thomas, on the ground, was better able to judge the tactical situation than was Grant, hundreds of miles away. Angrily and stubbornly Grant persisted in demanding Thomas's removal, and at last Lincoln gave in.

That night, before Grant had left Washington, a telegram came to the war department with news of a great victory at Nashville. Stanton immediately drove to the White House, where Lincoln in a nightshirt and with a candle in his hand appeared at the head of the main stairway to hear the news. He smiled and went back to bed.

Next day he telegraphed his congratulations to Thomas on the "good work." Remembering other "victories" which had proved abortive, he also admonished: "You made a magnificent beginning. A grand consummation is within your easy reach. Do not let it slip."

Thomas did not let it slip. He followed up the shock of his first assault with a vigorous pursuit of Hood, who escaped across the Tennessee River with only a sorry remnant of the fine army he had taken out of Atlanta several weeks before. "The victory at Nashville was the only one in the war so complete that the defeated army practically lost its existence," says T. Harry Williams. "It was also a complete vindication of Lincoln's faith in Thomas. Again the President had been more right than Grant."

Grant as well as Lincoln had complete faith in Sherman, who was approaching the end of his march to the sea at the time of the battle of Nashville. He took Savannah in time to give it to Lincoln as a Christmas present. On December 26 the President sent his thanks to Sherman and his whole army. "When you were about leaving Atlanta for the Atlantic coast," Lincoln confessed to him, "I was *anxious*, if not fearful; but feeling that you were the better judge, and remembering that 'nothing risked, nothing gained' I did not interfere. Now, the undertaking being a success, the honor is all yours; for I believe none of us went farther than to acquiesce. And, taking the work of Gen. Thomas into the account, as it should be taken, it is indeed a great success."

X

As Lincoln began his second term, in March of 1865, the war was entering upon its final phase. Sherman's army, having left Savannah, was advancing northward through the Carolinas but had yet to meet the enemy under General Joseph E. Johnston, newly restored to command. Grant's forces were increasing their pressure upon Petersburg and Richmond. If Lee should escape and join with Johnston against Sherman, the end of the war might be delayed for some time. If, on the other hand, Sherman should get past Johnston and combine with Grant against Lee, the Confederate Capital would be isolated from the rest of the Confederacy, and Lee would have to surrender fairly soon.

Lincoln, glad for an opportunity to flee the cares of Washington and observe the fighting from near at hand, eagerly accepted Grant's invitation of March 20 to visit the front. With his wife and his son Tad he left Washington, March 23, on the steamer *River Queen* and arrived the next day at City Point, on the south side of the James River, several miles below Richmond. After a week Mrs. Lincoln went home and brought back a party including Senator Sumner and Senator and Mrs. Harlan and their daughter, the bride-to-be of Robert Todd Lincoln, who was on Grant's staff. But Lincoln himself did not return to Washington for more than two weeks. Making the *River Queen* his home, he conferred with Grant and other officers—most significantly, with Sherman, who made a quick trip from his new base at Goldsboro, North Carolina. He visited the various camps, chatted with soldiers and was cheered by them. All the while he watched with great interest and with intelligent comprehension the progress of the fighting.

Grant kept him informed by frequent telegrams, which Lincoln forwarded to Stanton at the war department, with his own summaries and comments. But Grant, according to his memoirs, did not confide to Lincoln the fullness of his intentions, which were to capture Richmond and Petersburg and dispose of Lee's army without waiting for Sherman's men to join in the final assault. Grant intended to send Sheridan with his cavalry around to the southwest of Petersburg to take Five Forks and thus cut off Lee's lifeline, the railroad leading to Danville and the south. Lee, in an effort to save his communications and protect his flank and rear, could be expected to weaken his defenses before Petersburg and leave them vulnerable to a breakthrough.

Lincoln, from day to day expecting (and fearing) a great and bloody battle, was not sure just when it would come or what form it would take. On March 30 he telegraphed to Stanton from City Point: "Last night at 10:15, when it was dark as a rainy night without a moon could be, a furious cannonade, soon joined in by a heavy musketry-fire, opened near Petersburg and lasted about two hours. The sound was very distinct here, as also were the flashes of the guns upon the clouds. It seemed to me a great battle, but the other hands here scarcely noticed it, and, sure enough, this morning it was found that very little had been done." On April 1 he learned from Grant that, on this day, something had been done indeed: Sheridan had taken Five Forks. The next day the dispatches came to Lincoln thick and fast. "All going finely," he telegraphed to Stanton. The Union troops had broken through the Petersburg intrenchments at several places, and Sheridan's cavalry was busy tearing up the tracks of the Danville railroad.

"This morning Gen. Grant reports Petersburg evacuated;

and he is confident Richmond also is," Lincoln wired again, on the morning of April 3. "He is pushing forward to cut off if possible, the retreating army. I start to him in a few minutes." Lincoln found Grant waiting for him in Petersburg on the piazza of a deserted house. The streets were empty, not a person, not an animal in sight. "I had a sort of sneaking idea all along that you intended to do something like this," Lincoln said, as he shook hands with Grant and thanked him, "but I thought some time ago that you would so maneuver as to have Sherman come up and be near enough to cooperate with you." The tactful general replied: "I had a feeling that it would be better to let Lee's old antagonists give his army the final blow and finish the job." He explained that, if the Western soldiers of Sherman's army should deliver the final blow, Western politicians in after years might taunt the Eastern soldiers of the Army of the Potomac with the charge that the latter had won no important victories in the war, and thus sectional bitterness might arise between the East and the West. Lincoln remarked that, as for himself, he had not cared where aid came from, so long as the work was done.

On his return to City Point he found a telegram from Stanton warning him against visiting Petersburg and exposing his life to rebel assassins. "Thanks for your caution," Lincoln answered; "but I have already been to Petersburg, stayed with Gen. Grant an hour and a half and returned here. I am certain now that Richmond is in our hands, and I think I will go there to-morrow. I will take care of myself."

And to Richmond he went on the following day, by gunboat up the James to where the river was obstructed, then by a boat rowed by twelve sailors to Rockett's wharf. There he landed and, with his son Tad at his side and an escort of army and navy officers around him, proceeded to walk up Main Street a mile or so to the executive mansion of the Confederacy, the house occupied until two days before by Jefferson Davis. On the way the tall President, in his long black overcoat and high silk hat, stood out above those with him. Negroes left the river bank to follow along and crowd around him, many of them singing and shouting their praises. Soldiers white and black cheered as he entered the mansion and took a seat in Davis' chair. His appearance among the people of what had been, until so recently, the enemy capital, deeply moved a Boston newspaper correspondent, who wrote: "He came among them unheralded, without pomp or parade. He walked through the streets as if he were only a private citizen, and not the head of a mighty nation. He came not as a conqueror, not with bitterness in his heart, but with kindness. He came as a friend, to alleviate sorrow and suffering—to rebuild what had been destroyed." In the Davis house he received a number of Union officers and Richmond citizens. He also received and conversed with the only member of the Confederate government who remained in Richmond—John A. Campbell, lately the assistant secretary of war and two months previously one of the Confederate peace emissaries at Hampton Roads. Then he rode about the city in a carriage, to review the troops and to see the sights, especially the extensive ruins left by the great fire which the Confederate authorities accidentally had set at the time of their evacuation.

Back again at City Point, during the next few days he received heartening news of Grant's pursuit of Lee. Grant sent him batches of telegrams, in which the various commanders reported the chase in picturesque detail—"the Road for over 2 miles is strewed with tents baggage cooking utensils some ammunition some material of all kinds"—and in one of which a line of Sheridan's particularly caught the President's eye. "Gen. Sheridan says 'If the things is pressed I think that Lee will surrender,'" he wired to Grant on April 7. "Let the *thing* be pressed." He would gladly have stayed on for news of the surrender itself, but he decided to go back to Washington because of word from Stanton that Seward had been injured badly in a carriage accident.

He arrived in Washington late in the afternoon of April 9, the day that Lee finally surrendered to Grant at Appomattox Court House, ninety miles west of Richmond. Next morning the news was known to everyone in Washington. The people of the Capital, like those of other towns and cities throughout the North, already had indulged themselves in uproarious celebrations at the tidings of the evacuation of Richmond. Now they outdid themselves. In Washington a crowd, swelled by government employees who had been given a holiday, swarmed into the White House grounds and called for the President, while a band played "Hail to the Chief," "Yankee Doodle," and "America." Lincoln, busy with a cabinet meeting, at first declined to appear but finally yielded to the cries of the crowd. He told the people that he supposed arrangements were being made for a formal celebration either that night or the next. "I shall have nothing to say then," he said, "if I dribble it all out before." Then he suggested that the band play "Dixie." The "adversaries over the way" had tried to appropriate that song, but now the Union forces had captured it, and it was a lawful prize. So the band played "Dixie."

Chapter Twelve

THESE HONORED DEAD

ON AN AUTUMN DAY IN '63 LINCOLN REACHED A HIGH MOMENT in his life as he stood at tragic Gettysburg to deliver a simple tribute to the nation's dead. If this formerly peaceful Pennsylvania town brings to mind Reynolds, Pickett, Armistead and Garnett, if it connotes Lee's frustration and Meade's triumph, even more does it suggest Lincoln's timeless words. By these words Gettysburg becomes more than a scene of carnage, for above the waste and slaughter rises the challenge of a society founded and maintained in enduring terms of democracy, order, and sanity. Without Lincoln's ideal, Bloody Angle and Cemetery Hill produce only a shudder of horror. In the bewildering excess of monuments at Gettysburg the one most appealing is the undying flame of aspiration—the perpetual light that points, albeit from a battlefield, to peace.

I

So famous is this dedicatory vignette and so inexhaustible the popular interest in Lincoln's smallest act that writers have probed every corner of the episode. In the voluminous literature covering Lincoln's address one finds less appreciation of its larger world significance than minute inspection of its

most trivial detail. What did the President wear? How did his
white gauntlets look with otherwise black attire? Did he ride
his horse awkwardly or well? What kind of chair was provided
for the nation's Chief on the platform? Not a chair of state,
according to a contemporary report, but "an old, dingy, un-
cushioned settee" which he shared with others. What about his
gestures? None, we are told, except a sweep of the hand at the
words "these honored dead." Did Lincoln smile? Only once,
was one man's memory; that was when telling a story to a
group that included Curtin and Seward. How many times did
he use the word "that" in the address? William E. Barton gives
the answer: thirteen times! How did he adjust his spectacles
and hold his manuscript, how was his "Kentucky idiom" manifest, how did he pronounce his vowels? We have that too. Were
the words "under God" extemporaneously interjected? Competent investigators conclude that they were. When he spoke
of government of, by, and for the people, did he stress the *of*,
by, and *for*, or did he put the accent on the *people?* Barton
would "like to think" that he did the latter. How would the
address read if rewritten in the manner of Theodore Roosevelt,
or of Woodrow Wilson? Barton is "quite certain" that these
men "would have said" so-and-so. Not only the big, solemn
things, but the little things are presented to us. We are given
the picture of Lincoln holding proof-sheets of Everett's address
as he sat to Gardner for what has come to be known as the
Gettysburg portrait. We are told who were in the President's
party, how he was entertained, who were on the platform, who
took notes, how the crowd felt (there are variant accounts
here), what sources he drew from, what the papers said, what
copies were made by Lincoln, and even, in the words of Barton, "what he wished he had said."

There has been much speculation as to where and how
Lincoln prepared the address. Did he jot it down while on
the railway journey to Gettysburg? It is clear to scholars that
this tradition has no foundation, but the story persists. It has

gathered further details: a pencil was borrowed from Andrew Carnegie; the hasty jottings were put down on a yellow or brown envelope (some say a pasteboard), which reposed in the President's tall hat after the manner of his earlier technique as postmaster. To unfounded tradition has been added obvious error; in an article giving "new facts" about the occasion it is stated that while Lincoln was in Gettysburg he received word "that his little son, Willie, who was very ill, had passed the crisis," a statement which overlooks the fact that Willie died in February 1862. One could multiply such samples, but there is no need to go further into the unprofitable realm of Lincoln-at-Gettysburg apocrypha.

The first impulse toward the Gettysburg occasion was the imperative demand of decency and health. Where twenty thousand wounded had shocked Henry W. Bellows of the Sanitary Commission with their "unspeakable" suffering, the battleground presented a "fearful" spectacle. The exposure of horse carcasses and soldiers' bodies, hastily interred and soon uncovered by heavy rains, produced a pressing problem of sanitation, while at the same time the need for a fitting burial of fallen heroes, together with the motive of state pride, led to the acquisition by the state of Pennsylvania of a seventeen-acre plot on Cemetery Hill. Though from the outset the term "national cemetery" was used, the movement was at first a cooperative project of a number of states with Pennsylvania in the lead. It was not until 1872 that the ground was ceded to the United States government, not till many years later that the whole battle area became a great national park.

Arrangements were in the hands of David Wills of Gettysburg, who acted as Governor Curtin's special agent and later as head of a select committee for the purpose. For the ceremony of dedication it was intended that the chief honors should be done by a distinguished orator and a great poet. Edward Everett, orator extraordinary, ex-president of Harvard, "master of elegance," "Apollo in Politics," full of days and public honors at seventy, consented to be the speaker of the day, but a poet was sought in vain. In the absence of a poet laureate, who might have been expected to grow lyrical by official command, unsuccessful approaches were made to Bryant, Longfellow, and other bards of the time. The failure was symbolic. Nobly conceived poetry was and remained lacking during the Civil War; the verse that did appear in enormous reams and bushels was unmitigated drivel. A noteworthy exception, which came just after the war, was Lowell's ode recited at Harvard College on July 21, 1865, in commemoration of the sons of Harvard who had given their lives in the war. The most famous part of the ode, the sixth stanza devoted to Lincoln, "was not recited, but was written immediately afterward." Lowell and Whitman were among the very few of Lincoln's time who could do justice to him in verse. As for a grandly conceived major poem on the theme of the war, that did not come until the appearance of Stephen Vincent Benét's *John Brown's Body* in 1928. In was in the same period that Sandburg's great interpretation of Lincoln, lacking none of the magic of poetry, took the form and substance of biography.

A poet and an orator had been the committee's first thought; the invitation to Lincoln came as a secondary matter. Plans were well advanced in August; Everett was invited on September 23; yet Wills's letter of invitation to the President came on November 2. By that time the date of the dedication, November 19, had been fixed to suit Everett, who asked more time for preparation than was at first allowed. It is not recorded that the President's convenience was consulted in setting the date. Lincoln gave ready acceptance; it was an occasion in which he plainly wanted a part.

II

In ancient Athens appropriate public attention was given to obsequies for those who died in battle. Famed Ceramicus held the remains of men who had fallen. With their appreciation of the fine arts, one of which was oratory, Athenians would not be satisfied unless a master of speech was selected to deliver a panegyric; the elaborate care he would take in its preparation was considered comparable in the Greek mind with that of a sculptor. To have a great thing to say required that it be said well; to achieve great expression was to add to the world's indestructible treasure. The arrangements for the dedication at Gettysburg, especially the choice of Everett, a Webster of his day, gave advance notice of the dignity of the event.

' The President and his party arrived by slow train from Washington on the evening of Wednesday, November 18, 1863, and the President was the overnight guest in the home of Mr. Wills on the central square or "diamond" of the town. That night Lincoln appeared in response to a serenade and made a few undistinguished remarks, mentioning that in his position it was important not to "say any foolish things." "If you can help it," said an impertinent voice in the audience!

This was not the only indication that some among the Gettysburg crowds failed to appreciate their President. Addressing a "large and clamorous" group John W. Forney, newspaper publisher and secretary of the Senate, upbraided his serenaders for inadequate cheers to Lincoln. To that "great man," he said, "you owe your name as American citizens." "He went on," according to the diary of John Hay, "blackguarding the crowd for their apathy" and "went back to the eulogy of the President, that great, wonderful mysterious inexplicable man who holds in his single hands the reins of the

republic; who keeps his own counsels; who does his own purpose in his own way, no matter what temporizing minister in
his Cabinet sets himself up in opposition. . . ."

Throngs filled the town that night; next morning thousands
more poured in, many of them traveling in covered wagons
of the Conestoga variety. The unfinished work of re-interring
the dead by wholesale at $1.59 per body had been temporarily
suspended and coffins were much in evidence, while souvenir
hunters roamed the battlefield to view the scene of death and
pick up a dismal relic—a bullet, button, or fragment of uniform.

Smart young John Hay wrote of the night and the day of
the ceremony with sophisticated sarcasm, recording various
pranks and drinking parties, and indicating withal a restlessness
as to what to do with himself. "[Wayne] MacVeagh," he wrote,
"young Stanton, & I foraged around for awhile—walked out
to the college, got a chafing dish of oysters then some supper
and finally loafing around to the Court House where Lamon
was holding a meeting of marshals, we found Forney and went
around to his place, Mr. Fahnestock's, and drank a little whiskey with him. He had been drinking a good deal during the day
& was getting . . . ugly and dangerous."

Though many of the arrangements had been stupidly
handled, the ceremony itself was elaborate and imposing. A
procession, marshaled by Ward H. Lamon, moved in what Hay
called "an orphanly sort of way" to the cemetery, the homely
President riding horseback. The prepared order of procession
included high military officers, the President and Cabinet secretaries, judges of the Supreme Court, the "orator of the day"
(Everett), governors, commissioners, the Vice President, the
Speaker, "bearers with flags of the States," members of Congress, a Gettysburg local committee, officials of the Sanitary
Commission, religious committees, the telegraph corps, representatives of the Adams Express Company—and so on through
the hospital corps, Knights Templars, and masons, to the press,

loyal leagues, fire companies, and citizens of Pennsylvania, "citizens of other States" and of the territories. During the march minute guns were fired which suggested to a reporter the "roar of battle, reverberating from the hills and mountains."

There was a dirge followed by a prayer, the audience standing uncovered. Old Hundred was played by the band, then the "venerable orator" Everett rose and stood a moment in silence, regarding the battlefield and the distant beauty of the South Mountain range. By the standards of that day Everett delivered a great speech, though for an audience unprovided with seats after a restless night and long travel, it was much too long. "Standing beneath this serene sky," the "Alleghenies dimly towering" before him, the orator raised his "poor voice to break the eloquent silence of God and Nature." He reviewed the funeral customs of ancient Athens, referred to Marathon, paid tribute to the dead, discussed the purpose of the war, and gave a closely documented summary of the three-day battle. Avoiding any flings at the common people of the South, he minced no words in denouncing the "foul revolt" as a crime. The heart of the people, North and South, he said, was for the Union. Some of his best phrases were devoted to "bonds that unite us as one people— . . . community of origin, language, belief, and law, . . . common . . . interests; . . . common pride. . . ." Elements of union, he said, were "of perennial . . . energy, . . . causes of alienation . . . imaginary, fictitious, and transient."

Everett had not spared himself. He had avoided "sentimental or patriotic commonplaces." He had delivered a learned and voluminous address, had piled it high with historical and classical allusions, had omitted no effort to dignify the occasion. In contract to all this stateliness and elaboration the impression of Lincoln's simple speech was that of almost shocking brevity. For the immediate occasion—posterity was a different matter —it was as if the highest official of the republic was playing second fiddle. The President's thought and manner were less conditioned by the immediate occasion than by the timeless aspect of his dedicatory duty, that quality being the greater because achieved in spite of tragic realities and official vexations. Mindful that the war was still raging and that armies were massed for doubtful combat in Tennessee, facing the unsightly work of reburial, immersed in hateful details of politics, surrounded in office by those who distrusted him, pressed, buffeted, roundly assailed, yet remembering that he stood in the presence of the dead, Lincoln looked beyond battles, politicians, and hatred to enduring verities. As revised by himself in the form that has become standard, these were his words:

Four score and seven years ago our fathers brought forth on this continent, a new nation, conceived in Liberty, and dedicated to the proposition that all men are created equal.

Now we are engaged in a great civil war, testing whether that nation, or any nation so conceived and so dedicated, can long endure. We are met on a great battle-field of that war. We have come to dedicate a portion of that field, as a final resting place for those who here gave their lives that that nation might live. It is altogether fitting and proper that we should do this.

But, in a larger sense, we can not dedicate—we can not consecrate—we can not hallow—this ground. The brave men, living and dead, who struggled here, have consecrated it, far above our poor power to add or detract. The world will little note, nor long remember what we say here, but it can never forget what they did here. It is for us the living, rather, to be dedicated here to the unfinished work which they who fought here have thus far so nobly advanced. It is rather for us to be here dedicated to the great task remaining before us —that from these honored dead we take increased devotion to that cause for which they gave the last full measure of devotion—that we here highly resolve that these dead shall not

have died in vain—that this nation, under God, shall have a
new birth of freedom—and that government of the people, by
the people, for the people, shall not perish from the earth.

III

It is not easy to recover the manner of Lincoln's speaking,
nor the reaction of the immediate audience. According to John
Russell Young, reporter for the Philadelphia *Press*, the perfection of Everett was "like a bit of Greek sculpture—beautiful,
but cold as ice." It was "resonant, clear, splendid rhetoric." In
contrast, he said, Lincoln spoke "in his high tenor voice, without the least attempt for effect." "Very few," wrote Young,
"heard what Mr. Lincoln said, and it is a curious thing that
his remarkable words should have made no particular impression at the time." He added that spectators were more interested in the efforts of a photographer to get a picture of the
President while speaking (in which he unfortunately failed)
than in the address. Others, however, reported greater appreciation by Lincoln's auditors. The "right thing in the right place,
and a perfect thing in every respect," was the description by
the Cincinnati *Gazette's* correspondent, who reported long
continued applause as the President concluded. Mr. French,
who was of the President's party, noted that the address was
received with "a tumultuous outpouring of exultation."

Some of the slighting remarks concerning the President's
address were similar to the insulting voice at the President's
serenade; some of the unawareness was traceable to the fact
that humans cannot always be expected to hail a classic at
birth. It is not true, however, as often stated, that the speech
was unappreciated by contemporaries. On the day after the
dedication Everett wrote thanking Lincoln for his kindness to
him at Gettysburg, including thoughtfulness for his daughter's

accommodation on the platform "and much kindness otherwise." "I should be glad," said Everett, "if I could flatter myself that I came as near to the central idea of the occasion in two hours as you did in two minutes." Lincoln replied: "In our respective parts yesterday, you could not have been excused to make a short address, nor I a long one. . . . The point made against the theory of the general government being only an agency, whose principals are the States, . . . is one of the best arguments for the national supremacy."

With equal promptness Longfellow pronounced the speech "admirable." This also was on the day after its delivery, while on the second morning "the *Springfield Republican* declared it 'a perfect gem' and that evening the *Providence Journal* described it as 'beautiful . . . touching . . . inspiring . . . thrilling.'"

Column writers were few in those days, but a near approach to later columnists was George William Curtis, whose little essays on the world in general appeared in *Harper's Weekly* as the comments of "The Lounger." It is of interest to note what Curtis said of Lincoln at Gettysburg. "The few words of the President," he wrote, "were from the heart to the heart. They can not be read . . . without kindling emotion. . . . It was as simple and felicitous and earnest a word as was ever spoken."

In Lincoln's own day the address became famous; this is shown by the demand for its text in Lincoln's hand. It is to this demand that we owe the President's careful attention to the final form of the address, which he rewrote several times and which has therefore come down to posterity as Lincoln wished it. This is not to imply that Lincoln changed his speech substantially, nor that he had failed to give careful thought to the text before delivery. For such an address to have been hastily prepared, or for the President to have trusted to the moment, would have been altogether contrary to Lincoln's habit. There were times when the President appeared in response to crowds and frankly did not try to make a speech. His remarks on such occasions were conversational and intentionally casual, but no public man was more cautious of the public word, written or spoken, than Lincoln. He had more than two weeks in which to prepare for Gettysburg, and the well known correspondent Noah Brooks states that some days before the dedication Lincoln told him in Washington that the speech was short, and that it was "written, 'but not finished.'"

That the President prepared the address carefully may be regarded as certain, and from a study of the evidence, including five autograph copies in Lincoln's hand which have survived to our own day, it is possible to reconstruct the development of the address as it evolved in successive versions. What is known as the "first draft," on official stationery of the Executive Mansion, is accepted as having been written (at least the first page of it) in Washington. The second page, consisting of ten lines, together with a substitution for words deleted on the first page, were written in pencil. In the two drafts that preceded the occasion one can see the turning of the literary lathe, the search for the effective phrase. Instead of the words "It is rather for us, the living, to stand here," the words ". . . to be dedicated here" were substituted. While in the Wills house on the morning of the day of dedication, Nicolay being with him, the President probably worked over his first draft, then made the "second draft" which has survived in his handwriting, and which "is almost certainly that which Lincoln held in his hand when he delivered the Address." It is a slight revision of the first draft.

The third stage in the evolution of the text of the address came a few days after the President's return from Gettysburg when he responded to a request from Mr. Wills, who desired the original manuscript for an official report of the proceedings which he was preparing. The President, as reported by Nicolay, directed his secretaries to make copies of the Associated Press report; using this together with his original draft and his recollection "of the form in which he delivered it," Lincoln made "a careful and deliberate revision." Just what form this revision took is a bit uncertain. Nicolay refers to it as "a new autograph copy," but no such copy has survived and it is more likely that what Wills received was a version made under the President's supervision, with secretarial help, while the President was sick. Though the original of this Wills copy has not survived, it is worth noting that as printed it includes the words "under God" in the passage: "this nation, under God, shall have a new birth of freedom." The speech as prepared had not included these words, but the newspaper reports as well as all of Lincoln's later revisions, contain them; they were added by Lincoln as he spoke.

At the time of the address it was, of course, reprinted in the newspapers. Those papers that used the Associated Press report had an imperfect version; the report that is accepted as perhaps the nearest to an actual recording of the words which Lincoln uttered is that published on Friday morning, November 20, 1863, in the Boston *Daily Advertiser.*

Leaving aside the newspaper reports and returning to the evolution of the oration in successive versions, we may note that a third autograph copy by Lincoln was made at the request of Edward Everett, who "presented it, together with the manuscript of his own address, . . . to Mrs. Hamilton Fish, . . . president of the . . . committee of . . . ladies having charge at the fair in aid of the sanitary commission . . . in New York in March, 1864, to be disposed of for the benefit of our soldiers. . . ." It was bought by an uncle of Senator Henry W. Keyes of New Hampshire and remained for many years a possession of the Keyes family. In 1944 this Everett-Keyes copy, having been purchased from a private owner by hundreds of thousands of small contributions from Illinois school children, was presented to the State of Illinois. Its place of deposit is the Illinois State Historical Library at Springfield.

A fourth autograph version was made by Lincoln at the

request of George Bancroft. It was intended for sale at the Sanitary Fair at Baltimore in 1864, and for reproduction in a volume known as *Autograph Leaves of the Country's Authors.* Since it proved unavailable for this purpose by reason of being written on both sides of the paper, Bancroft was allowed to keep it, and Lincoln made yet another autograph, known as the "Bliss copy." This final version was done by Lincoln "with great care"; it was used both at the Baltimore Fair and in *Autograph Leaves,* edited by Colonel Alexander Bliss. Because it is in all probability the last copy written by Lincoln, and because of the obvious care devoted to it, it has become the standard form of the address.

In recapitulation, it may be noted that Lincoln made five autograph copies of his famous address which have come down to us: (1) the first draft, written probably in Washington, and perhaps partly revised at Gettysburg; (2) the second draft, written probably in the Wills house at Gettysburg and held by the President as he spoke; (3) the Everett-Keyes-Illinois copy, made at Everetts request and sold at the Sanitary Fair in New York in 1864; (4) the Bancroft copy, meant for the Baltimore Fair, but not used for that purpose; (5) the standard and definitive "Bliss copy," written carefully by Lincoln in 1864, sold at the Baltimore Fair, and reproduced in *Autograph Leaves of Our Country's Authors.* In addition, Lincoln directed and supervised the making of the version sent to Wills soon after the occasion, which was prepared with secretarial help and was probably not in the President's handwriting.

IV

In the Declaration of Independence Jefferson's authorship was no less important because he used concepts and phrases which were part of the currency of political thought. Similarly, it takes nothing from Lincoln's fame to find previous utterances which invite comparison with the famous reference to "government of the people, by the people, for the people." In a work published in London in 1794, Thomas Cooper, formerly of Manchester, in advising Englishmen to come to America, wrote: "The [American] government is the government *of* the people, and *for* the people." In 1798 Virginians of Westmoreland County sent an address to President Adams concerning the trouble with France, in which the following sentence occurred: "The Declaration that our People are hostile to a Government made by themselves, for themselves and conducted by themselves is an Insult. . . ." Similar statements were made by Webster * and Marshall,† while Lamartine, paraphrasing Robespierre, wrote of a representative sovereignty "concentrated in an election as extensive as the people themselves, and acting by the people, and for the people. . . ." Bibliographical search has also unearthed expressions of a like character by James Douglas in Edinburgh in 1830 and by Matthew Fontaine Maury in a government report in 1851. The most famous instance, however, and the one most often linked with Lincoln's phrase, is that of Theodore Parker, abolitionist preacher, who in 1850 used these words: "This [American] idea, demands . . . a democracy, that is, a government of all the people, by all the people, for all the people. . . ."

To point out that Lincoln had read Webster and Marshall is superfluous, nor is there much doubt that he was familiar with the saying of Parker, who had been a correspondent of William H. Herndon. That he consciously copied from any of these is less evident. As to the more obscure passages, they belong in the voluminous category of literary coincidence, dealing

---

* It is, Sir, the people's Constitution, the people's government, made for the people, made by the people, and answerable to the people." Webster's second reply to Hayne, Jan. 26, 1830.

† "The government of the Union . . . is . . . a government of the people. . . . Its powers are granted by them, and are to be exercised directly on them, and for their benefit." Chief Justice Marshall, in McCulloch *vs.* Maryland.

as they do with a concept whose universality among demo-cratic minds constituted its main significance. Like Jefferson, Lincoln had the knack of taking an idea that was part of the heritage of the race and immortalizing it by pithy and unforget-table utterance. In the array of quotations here presented, it will be noted that the similarity of Lincoln's words to those of predecessors, while close, is not complete. Whatever his sources, it was Lincoln who gave the phrase its setting, its precise form, and its dominant place in American tradition.

V

More noteworthy than literary parallels is the significance of the Gettysburg address as a tying together of Lincoln's fundamental concepts touching the basic theme of the Ameri-can experiment. If one seeks passages for comparison, they are best to be found in Lincoln's own writings.

In the emotional release that had come with victory after so much delay, the President, on July 7, 1863, responded to a serenade at the Executive Mansion. Already Gettysburg to him meant dominant values: human liberty, democracy, aims of the Fathers, the Declaration, the cause of free government in the world. Frankly the President did not attempt a speech—he was always wary of impromptu utterance—yet in his casual re-marks one can find the germ of the Gettysburg address that was to follow in November. The nation's birth "eighty-odd years since" was the point of departure. At one end of Lincoln's thought was Philadelphia in 1776; at the other, Gettysburg in 1863. From this it was a natural development to note the ele-mental importance of a nation founded on the "self-evident truth" of human equality, "the first time in the history of the world" that a nation had so founded itself by its own represent-atives. Coming to the present year and month, the President noted in victories just achieved "a glorious theme, and the occasion for a speech" which he was "not prepared" to make in a manner "worthy of the occasion." He briefly paid tribute to all who had "fought in the cause of the Union and liberties of their country"; then, mentioning no names lest he might wrong those unmentioned, he made his bow and called for music. It was but a brief appearance before a celebrating crowd, yet the theme, and the clear call for a speech worthy of the theme, were not forgotten.

In his first inaugural Lincoln had expressed his central idea as to what the country was about in maintaining the republic against internal disruption. "A majority held in restraint by constitutional checks . . . and . . . changing easily with deliberate changes of popular opinions," he had said, "is the only true sovereign of a free people. Whoever rejects it does, of necessity, fly to anarchy or to despotism." In the same address he had asked: "Why should there not be a patient confidence in the ultimate justice of the people? Is there any better or equal hope in the world?" In his annual message to Congress of December 1, 1862, he spoke again of America's larger responsibility. Hoping his nation would choose the course which "the world will forever applaud," he warned: "We shall nobly save or meanly lose the last, best hope of earth."

Shortly after the opening of the war Lincoln had said to Hay: "For my part, I consider [that] the central idea pervading this struggle is the necessity that is upon us, of proving that popular government is not an absurdity. We must settle this question now, whether in a free government the minority have the right to break up the government whenever they choose. If we fail it will go far to prove the incapability of the people to govern themselves." When thus thinking aloud to his young secretary the President had been much occupied with composing his message to the special session of Congress of July 4, 1861, in which the following significant words, so like the theme of Gettysburg were used:

And this issue embraces more than the fate of these United States. It presents to the whole family of man the question whether a constitutional republic or democracy—a government of the people by the same people—can or cannot maintain its . . . integrity against its domestic foes. It presents the question whether discontented individuals . . . can . . . break up their government, and thus practically put an end to free government upon the earth. It forces us to ask: "Is there, in all republics, this inherent and fatal weakness?" "Must a government, of necessity, be too strong for the liberties of its . . . people, or too weak to maintain its own existence?"

.   .   .   .

This is essentially a people's contest. On the side of the Union it is a struggle for maintaining in the world that form and substance of government whose leading object is to elevate the condition of men—to lift artificial weights from all shoulders; to clear the paths of laudable pursuit for all; to afford all an unfettered start, and a fair chance in the race of life.

.   .   .   .

Our popular government has often been called an experiment. Two points in it our people have already settled—the successful establishing and the successful administering of it. One still remains—its successful maintenance against a formidable internal attempt to overthrow it. It is now for them to demonstrate to the world that . . . ballots are the rightful and peaceful successors of bullets. . . . Such will be a great lesson of peace: teaching men that what they cannot take by an election, neither can they take it by a war; teaching all the folly of being the beginners of a war.

Where words were so simple it took something of genius to make them so meaningful. As Everett himself generously recognized, Lincoln said more in two minutes than the orator of the day in as many hours. Rarely indeed is Everett quoted for his own sake. Had Lincoln not participated, Everett's stately periods would have gone into oblivion, while Lincoln's phrases are the stuff of literature. Innocent of the cant of the patrioteer, they nevertheless touched the chord of elemental loyalty. It is for such utterance, and for the man he was, that Lincoln has become synonymous with fundamental Americanism.

Both in form and substance the address at Gettysburg was completely Lincolnian. Oratorically it had those elements that made Lincoln at his best a master of words. Fitness to the situation was the first element; the occasion made the speech. This was true, however, not in terms of exigent pressures or superficial demands of the moment, but rather with regard to the occasion as viewed in perspective. The second element, also typically Lincolnian, was a matter of the choice of words: thoughts that touched heights of exalted feeling were conveyed in language at once unpretentious and stirringly effective. Utter simplicity and restraint were somehow suffused with inspired dignity. It is as significant to note what was omitted as what was included in a speech whose brevity made every syllable valuable. There was not a breath of hatred, not a hint of vindictiveness, not a trace of vengeful judgment. Sensing the greater opportunity of the hour, Lincoln used the Gettysburg occasion for two purposes: in unforgettable phrases he paid tribute to those who had fallen; not failing in that, he coupled the deepest and most dominant sentiments of his people with the political idea that was central in his own mind: the wider world significance of democracy's testing, the enduring importance of success in the American democratic experiment as proving that government by the people is no failure. Standing at a cemetery, which men of classical turn were lugubriously calling a "necropolis," he did not confine his thoughts to the dead. Rather he showed that it is only by constructive deeds of living men that the sacrifice of the dead can have value.

Chapter Thirteen

PUBLIC RELATIONS

I

Lincoln's remark that he was "environed with difficulties" (reply to serenade, September 24, 1862) could have related to a variety of vexations. He could have had in mind an uncooperative Congress, bickering among generals, factions in his own party, misguided peace efforts, unsought advice as to his cabinet, innumerable petty demands, patronage seekers, or perchance a muddled condition in Missouri.

Or it might have been newspaper trouble. In journalism it was the heyday of the "special" writer and the ubiquitous reporter. It was at once a time of remarkably active newspaper enterprise and of lax governmental control over the press. "No war," it has been said, "was ever before so waged in the world's eye." Metropolitan dailies spent huge sums on their "war departments," half a million being spent by the *Herald* alone. Correspondents were seemingly on every march and at all fronts. They were accorded special privileges, eating at officers' mess, using army transportation for their baggage, enjoying the confidence of admirals and generals, unrestrained as they overheard camp talk or picked up snatches of military information. Usually they had army passes and sometimes they even carried military messages or orders. Though gestures were made toward governmental censorship, there was little effective curbing of reporters. Steps were taken early in the war to control the issue of telegraph news from Washington, and at the time of the *Trent* affair an effort was made to impose silence as to correspondence between Seward and Lord Lyons, but a committee of the House of Representatives raised charges of undue interference and the idea of a government censor, known as such, was found impracticable. It is true that during the war the telegraph system was under government control by congressional authorization and a special officer was set up with the title of assistant secretary of war and general manager of military telegraphs. This offered some chance for a sifting of news, while at the same time the government had taken over the railroads, so that an offending journal could be denied facilities for transporting papers by train.

Yet the mind of the American people was firmly conditioned against restrictions on the press, and efforts to protect the government proved to be no more than half-way measures. At no time were news channels fully or effectively closed. The mails were open to reporters, messengers could convey material to the home office, "leaks" from a general's headquarters were not uncommon, and confidential communications held up in Washington could be released from other points.

Generals differed in their treatments of journalists. Those ambitious for publicity petted and favored the reporters; if this was not done an offended journalist might vent his spite by misrepresenting a general or sending untrue reports of army conditions. The least effective generals were made to bask in newspaper glory, while abler commanders such as the laconic Grant or the peppery Sherman were basely abused. A Cincinnati editor, questioned as to the dissemination of the newspaper canard that Sherman was "insane," remarked that it was a news item of the day and that he had to keep up with the times. For this and many other reasons Sherman became probably the most severe of Union generals in his attitude toward reporters and editors. He despised the papers, declaring that they had "killed" able generals, incited jealousies, given notice of unexpected military movements, functioned as the "world's gossips," distorted their stories, and injected the names of generals into the political controversies of the day.

Special coloration of certain newspapers in this and other countries is familiar to historians, though perhaps its full effect has not been measured. Francis Lieber, who knew much of European military politics, wrote: "I happen to think of what Joseph Bonaparte once said to me. I had mentioned the saying of Frederic II, that he who has the last shilling remains the master of the field. Joseph Bonaparte replied: Yes, but not because he can pay the last grenadier as Frederic believed, but because he can pay the last newspaper, within and without the country."

In the newspaper world of the time there were great names—Greeley, Bowles, Bennett, Bryant, Raymond, Dana, Forney, and men of like caliber. Lesser men who nevertheless had potent influence included Whitelaw Reid of the Cincinnati *Gazette;* George Wilkes, interested in jockeying and sporting news, whose *Wilkes's Spirit of the Time* combined sports with political comments (seldom pro-Lincoln); George Alfred Townsend, a vigorous correspondent and prolific special writer with a flair for depicting personalities; the picturesque Ben: Perley Poore, notable for wide experience, travel, voluminous compilations, and descriptive column writing; and George William Curtis, influential in his Harper's "Easy Chair."

II

It could hardly be disputed that most of the newspapers were against Lincoln. Among the more partisanly virulent were the Chicago *Times,* the Columbus (Ohio) *Crisis,* the

Baltimore *Exchange,* the New York *World,* and the New York *Daily News,* to mention but a few. The *World* characterized Lincoln's emancipation policy as "miserable balderdash"; the Chicago *Times* described his second inaugural as "slipshod," "loose-jointed," and "puerile." Such journals as the Chicago *Times* and the New York *World* were Democratic sheets, but it was also true that Lincoln had a "bad press" among well known Republican publications such as the *Tribune,* and *Post,* and the *Independent* of New York. Bryant of the *Post,* angered by what he considered the monopoly of patronage by the Seward-Weed faction, wrote: "I am so utterly disgusted with Lincoln's behavior that I cannot muster respectful terms in which to write him." Theodore Tilton was anti-Lincoln though pro-Republican. The Chicago *Tribune* was known as one of the stanch Republican papers, but John Hay wrote as follows of its editor: "I found among my letters here . . . one from Joe Medill, inconceivably impudent, in which he informs me that on the fourth of next March [1865], thanks to Mr. Lincoln's blunders & follies, we will be kicked out of the White House."

If to these few instances there were added a full coverage of newspaper opposition to Lincoln and his administration, one would find provocation for punitive and suppressive measures on the part of the government. Yet in general it was Lincoln's policy to avoid suppression and to endure abuse as the price, often a high price, of press freedom. To understand this statement one must remember that it is a generalization, and that in such a vast arena as the American Civil War, with its hundreds of newspapers and its array of generals and judges advocate, there would be enough exceptions to make a considerable list and yet the generalization would still hold good. In other words, after one has fully listed all the instances of governmental action against journals and editors, even though the list seems impressive in itself, the number untouched and unmolested would still constitute an overwhelming majority of the immense total.

The government was not lacking in potential methods of discipline. Newspaper men who moved with the armies were within military jurisdiction and were subject to the 57th Article of War which prescribed court-martial trial, with death or other punishment, for anyone "giving intelligence" to the enemy. It would, however, be hard to find any application of this part of the military code. Other possible methods of discipline were military arrest of editors, exclusion of offending correspondents from the bounds of a general's command, and the requiring of passes fortified by regulations for their issuance. As an ultimate punishment there remained the severe expedient of dealing with reporters as spies. It was Secretary of War Stanton who was responsible for one of the rare uses of this stern device. On February 10, 1862, he ordered that a Washington representative of the New York *Herald* "calling himself Dr. Ives" (Dr. Malcom Ives) be "arrested and held in close custody . . . as a spy." The offending writer, according to Stanton, had "intruded" himself into a war department conference and Stanton ordered that no news gatherer could thus "spy out official acts." Ives was released after four months, his case not having been prosecuted in any regular manner; his connection with the *Herald* was broken.

On the question of whether newsmen could be considered spies there was one Union general who had no doubts. Sherman so pronounced them, and it was true that Confederate leaders perused Northern papers for the military information which they constantly supplied. Yet aside from the somewhat eccentric action of Stanton this form of punishment does not appear to have been enforced. To have done so properly would have required proof in each case that the offender was in the actual employ of the enemy.

If a newspaper was "suppressed," that usually meant that its publication was suspended for a period. In addition to the famous cases of the Chicago *Times*, the New York *World*, and the New York *Journal of Commerce*, there were less known cases of "suppression," such as those of the Dayton (Ohio) *Empire,* the *South* of Baltimore, the *Maryland News* sheet of Baltimore, the Baltimore *Bulletin,* the Louisville *True Presbyterian.* Sometimes a single edition of a paper would be seized without the paper being suppressed, or the distribution of the paper would be checked.

A controversy arose as to whether offensive newspapers could be denied the use of the mails. Postmaster-General Blair, who had refused postal distribution for certain papers judicially condemned as disloyal, defended his legal right to do so. He disclaimed, however, any intent to strike against legitimate freedom of the press and he sharply denied a charge in the New York *World* that his department conducted a regular espionage against newspapers. The charge, he wrote, was "false in every particular." His department did not open papers to discover their contents, yet where evidence was clear he felt justified in excluding matters designed to stir up insurrection.

There were cases of editors being put under military arrest as "prisoners of state," but where this was done there was a reasonable claim or suspicion of disloyalty against the editors, who were usually released after brief confinement. A notable case of such imprisonment was that of F. Key Howard, editor of the Baltimore *Exchange,* who was confined in Fort Lafayette. Immediately after the Howard arrest the *Exchange,* which continued to appear, burst out with a denunciation of the Lincoln government, whereupon its publisher W. W. Glenn, was also put under military arrest. In like fashion another Baltimore editor, Thomas W. Hall of the *South,* was consigned to Fort McHenry. Baltimore was indeed a kind of hotbed of anti-Lincoln journalism. It has been stated by Robert S. Harper that no newspaper other than the Baltimore *American* "made even a pretense of advocating the Union cause." (Incidentally there is a bit of irony in the fact that this hostile city was the one in which the convention was held which renominated Lincoln for the presidency.) The net result in Baltimore, in view of the widely published denunciations of high handed military action, was unfavorable to the government, and Howard was released after confinement for several months.

Lincoln himself was no suppressor of journalistic freedom. He promptly revoked the Burnside order against the Chicago *Times*, and when General M. S. Hascall attempted a military policy of newspaper suppression in Indiana in 1863, word came from Washington of the President's disapproval of indiscreet assumption of "military powers not essential to the preservation of the public peace." Because of the harm done by an officer "issuing military proclamations and engaging in newspaper controversies upon questions that agitate the public mind" General Hascall was relieved of his provocative Indiana command. Military arrest of editors belongs to the vast problem of arbitrary arrests and political prisoners, but the President's attitude stood out clearly. When the editor of the *Missouri Democrat* was arrested the President regretted the act. He wrote to General J. M. Schofield: "Please spare me the trouble this is likely to bring."

In the matter of a dramatic "scoop" Lincoln stepped in to prevent severe action by Stanton against a news writer. A *Tribune* correspondent, Henry E. Wing, with great difficulty labored his way through to Grant at the time when the country and the government at Washington were without news of what was happening to the Commander and his great army at the time of the fighting in the Wilderness. Having achieved the notable feat of reaching and talking with the general, Wing made his painful way back, partly walking and running and partly by railroad handcar, and managed to send a wire to Charles A. Dana, assistant secretary of war, whom he knew and with whom he negotiated: if permitted to send one hundred words to the *Tribune*, he would tell the war department what he had so laboriously learned. Stanton threatened the writer with arrest, but the President, so goes the account, approved the transmission of Wing's despatch (New York *Trib-*

President Lincoln is a joke incarnated. His election was a very sorry joke. The idea that such a man as he should be the President of such a country as this is a very ridiculous joke. The manner in which he first entered Washington—after having fled from Harrisburg in a Scotch cap, a long military cloak and a special night train—was a practical joke. His debut in Washington society was a joke; for he introduced himself and Mrs. Lincoln as "the long and short of the Presidency." His inaugural address was a joke, since it was full of promises which he has never performed. His Cabinet is and always has been a standing joke. All his State papers are jokes. His letters to our generals, beginning with those to General McClellan, are very cruel jokes. His plan for abolishing slavery in 1900 was a broad joke. His emancipation proclamation was a solemn joke. His recent proclamation of abolition and amnesty is another joke. His conversation is full of jokes, of which those, which we republish this morning are pretty fair specimens. His title of "Honest" is a satirical joke. The style in which he winks at frauds in the War Department, frauds in the Navy Department, frauds in the Treasury Department, and frauds in every department, is a costly joke. His intrigues to secure a renomination and the hopes he appears to entertain of a re-election are, however, the most laughable jokes of all.

As a joker President Lincoln is unique. With the caustic wit of Diogenes he combines the best qualities of all the other celebrated jokers of the world. He is more poetical than Horace, more spicy than Juvenal, more anecdotal than Æsop, more juicy than Boccaccio, more mellow than rollicking Rabelais, and more often quoted than the veteran Joe Miller. Besides this, Mr. Lincoln has a peculiar sort of joke, better than any of those practised by his famous predecessors. An old German joker—a general, if we remember rightly—used to have a somewhat similar style. This general would order out a regiment of soldiers, place them in position upon a mammoth chessboard, and play chess with them for a whole day. The privates he employed as pawns, the captains as knights, the chaplains as bishops, and so on. But where this German joker used regiments President Lincoln uses armies; and the worst of it is that he never wins the game. For instance:—That was a fine joke when he removed General Fremont, on the very eve of victory, and allowed Price's army to escape. That was another fine joke when he held back McDowell and permitted the Peninsula army to be cut to pieces. That was still another brave joke when he removed McClellan, after the triumph of Antietam, and so brought about the massacre at Fredericksburg and the subsequent rebel invasion of the North. The people do not appreciate these stupendous military jokes, however. Perhaps the loss of life and property takes away some of the fun. Nevertheless, we are assured that somebody laughs at them—down below.

"PRESIDENT LINCOLN IS A JOKE . . ."

Portions of a New York *Herald* editorial, Feb. 19, 1864, too long for full reproduction. Later in the article Lincoln is advised "to collect and publish his jokes." "All of the other great jokers have done this. . . . We do not know that any one of them was ever elected to the Presidency in consequence of a joke; but certainly President Lincoln has nothing but his jokes to recommend him, and he ought . . . to make the most of them."

une, May 7, 1864), talked with him on arrival in Washington and (uncharacteristically for Lincoln) rewarded him with a kiss on the forehead.

When a *Herald* writer, Thomas W. Knox, was excluded from Grant's military command, Lincoln intervened in the newsman's favor. Being advised that the offense was "technical, rather than wilfully wrong," the President revoked the court-martial sentence of exclusion, though with the proviso that Knox's reinstatement would depend upon Grant's "express assent." This seems to have been a matter of difficult relations among generals. The correspondent was acceptable to McClernand but unacceptable to Grant. Lincoln's maneuver was designed to placate both generals while undoing a measure of army discipline against a journalist.

III

While Lincoln found that it was best for him to avoid influencing the press by any of the coarser methods such as dictating editorial policy or imposing censorship, he could not ignore the effect of newspaper publicity. It has been remarked that it was "not uncommon" in the period "to place journalists in important military and political positions whence they could write for the papers with a view to directing public opinion." It has been stated that "Lincoln seems to have chosen more newspaper men for official positions than any of his predecessors." A Baltimore paper declared at the outset of the Lincoln administration: "Editors seem to be in very great favor with the party in power—a larger number of the fraternity having received appointments . . . than probably under any previous Administration."

John Bigelow, who had been connected with the New York *Evening Post*, was appointed consul general at Paris, which enabled him to exert influence upon European newspapers. Irish-born Charles G. Halpine, colorful and adventurous author-journalist with a varied record of service with the *Herald* and the *Times,* had military appointment leading up to that of brevet brigadier general. While with the army, on General Hunter's staff, he used his facile and poetic pen to influence sentiment; his pieces under the name of "Miles O'Reilly," fictitious Irish-American private, were popular and influential. John W. Forney, who supported the Lincoln administration with his Philadelphia *Press* and his Washington *Chronicle,* was close to the President. He had been a Pierce Democrat but his support of Douglas in 1860, which involved bitter antagonism to Buchanan, had deepened the split in the Democratic party, thus helping to promote Republican victory in Pennsylvania. Lincoln showed a marked friendliness to Forney and used presidential influence to have him chosen secretary of the Senate. When the editor dedicated his new printing establishment in Washington with a "blow-out" as Hay termed it, the President was in attendance. Having spent an evening at Forney's in December 1863 with "political people," Hay reported that Forney "talked a great deal about the President," emphasizing the "unconditional confidence and the loyalty to his person this is felt throughout this land." It would not be amiss to speak of the *Chronicle* as a pro-Lincoln organ. In one of its issues (December 7, 1864) the paper published an article written in full by the President. (For this purpose Lincoln used the good offices of his friend Noah Brooks who assisted in seeing that the article was printed.) The President's contribution pertained to certain wives' requests that their husbands, held in the North as prisoners of war, be released on the ground that each husband was "a religious man." The President gave his idea of a religion that sets men to fight against their Government in order to benefit by the "sweat of other men's faces."

Among others in the newspaper profession who had governmental appointments were Scripps of the Chicago *Tribune* who became postmaster in Chicago (though Lincoln came to dislike his methods); Charles A. Dana of the New York *Tribune* (later of the *Sun*) who served as assistant secretary of war; and John D. Defrees, an Indianapolis editor who took a keen interest in pro-Lincoln politics and who became government printer by Lincoln's appointment. There were also George Fogg of New Hampshire (minister to Switzerland), James S. Pike of the New York *Tribune* (minister to Holland), Bayard Taylor of the *Tribune* (secretary of legation at St. Petersburg), and James C. Welling of the Washington *National Intelligencer* (assistant clerk of the United States court of claims). But this brief enumeration gives no adequate impression of the great number of appointments given to journalists; the full number of such men is too long to be listed here. Referring to a certain newspaper, Lincoln once wrote of the possible withdrawal of "the patronage it is enjoying at my hand." The power of bestowal or withdrawal was his to be used at discretion; that power was not capriciously applied, but it was natural that one of the firms singled out for printing contracts was that of Forney, whose profits from this source were not inconsiderable.

IV

The case of James Gordon Bennett the elder posed a special problem as to Lincoln's press relations. Though a thorn in the flesh to the President, it was felt that Bennett could possibly be won over. The *Herald* editor, born in 1795, was pre-eminent in Civil War journalism but stood apart in a class by himself. His complex personality and shifting positions cannot be defined in a word. His newspaper, known for its spicy journalism, was outstanding in success as judged by its circulation, estimated at about 77,000. The rising importance of this one journal was a kind of phenomenon, though earnest souls were often angered by its content. During the sectional crisis and the war the *Herald* shifted about, so that a chart of its attitude toward Lincoln and the government at Washington would show sharp peaks and deep troughs. In the crisis before Sumter the paper was pro-Southern (or pro-successionist); then, as a diarist remarked, its "conversion . . . [was] complete" after the April firing started. On May 22, 1863, Lincoln was represented as a strong candidate for the presidency in 1864. On May 28 the word was: "Give us Abraham Lincoln for the next Presidency." There followed suggestions that the President should "at once cut loose from his cabinet (June 6, 1863); on November 3 the verdict was that Lincoln was "master of the situation."

The tone then changed. On December 16, 1863, the *Herald* pronounced that Lincoln's administration had "proved a failure"; on December 18 the country had had "quite enough of a civilian Commander-in-Chief"; on December 21 Old Abe was "hopeless"; and on February 19, 1864, the acme of denunciation was reached in a long and stinging editorial in which the President was contemptuously mocked as this or that kind of joke; a "sorry joke," a "ridiculous joke," a "standing joke," a "broad joke," and a "solemn joke." The Bennett daily then took up for Grant for President in '64, overlooking the patent fact that Grant's indispensable function was that of military commander in the field.

The idea of enlisting Bennett for the Lincoln cause had formed expression at an early date. A curious letter on the subject was written to Lincoln by Joseph Medill of the Chicago *Tribune* on June 19, 1860, who intended to sound out Bennett whom he considered susceptible to a "dicker." "Terms moderate," wrote Medill, "and 'no cure no pay.'" It was suggested that Medill or Ray of the Chicago *Tribune* go to New York taking Norman Judd along. Desiring an interview with his "Satanic Majesty" the Chicago editor reasoned that his "affirmative help" was not important, but he was "powerful for mischief." The journalistic giant did not want money. "Social position is what he wants. He wants to be in a position to be invited with his wife and son to dinner or tea at the White House and to be 'made of' by the big men of the party. . . . He has a vast corps of writers . . . at home and abroad and universal circulation North, South, East, West, Europe, Asia, Africa, and the Isles of the Sea."

This 1860 gesture came to nothing, but the President (who once wrote: "It is important to humor the Herald") persisted in his efforts to enlist the support of the famous editor. As an intermediary he used Weed who is said to have remarked that "Mr. Lincoln deemed it more important to secure the *Herald's* support than to obtain a victory in the field." That Bennett desired favors was shown when he offered the government his fine sailing yacht, the *Henrietta*. The offer was accepted and Bennett's son, at the father's request, was given a lieutenant's commission in the revenue cutter service under the treasury department.

After many shifts the *Herald* support was belatedly given to Lincoln in 1864 and it has been supposed that this result was related to Lincoln's offer to appoint Bennett as United States minister to France. Lincoln's letter extending the offer was dated February 20, 1865. Under date of March 6, 1865 Bennett wrote the President declining the offer but taking special pains to show his "highest consideration" of the President's attitude in "proposing so distinguished an honor." Secretary Welles disapproved of the proffered appointment, referring to Bennett as "an editor . . . whose whims are often wickedly and atrociously leveled against the best men and the best causes. . . ."

Though Lincoln's offer was not written until February of 1865, it was the opinion of A. K. McClure that the President's tender of the French mission to Bennett was one of the "shrewdest of Lincoln's . . . political schemes." This, together with the fact of Bennett's delayed support of the Lincoln ticket, implies that the prospect of the appointment was made known

to the editor during the 1864 political campaign. It is known
that the idea of such a presidential favor was pending in the
pre-election period. Senator Harlan suggested that "it would
pay to offer him a foreign mission." John Hay wrote on September 23, 1864, that Forney "had a man talking to the cannie Scot
[Bennett] who asked plumply, 'Will I be a welcome visitor at
the White House if I support Mr. Lincoln?'" Bennett's biographer, Don C. Seitz, quotes Thurlow Weed as saying that "two
well-meaning friends" were responsible for the affair of the
French offer. Seitz adds: "The surmise left open is that 'the
two well-meaning friends' may have conveyed some word of
the President's intention to honor the editor during the campaign and so brought about the switch in the *Herald's* attitude. . . ."

V

Changing habits of the presidency have brought elaborate
modern processes of "White House publicity," but it was quite
a different matter under Lincoln. There were no "press conferences," no "White House spokesman," no speech writers, and
but few speeches by the President. In 1864 he remarked: "It
is not very becoming for one in my position to make speeches
at great length." His annual messages, though distinguished by
eloquent passages, were not delivered to Congress in person,
and throughout his presidency his principal speeches were his
two inaugurals, his immortal Gettysburg address, and his last
speech (April 11, 1865) pertaining to reconstruction. Showmanship was not congenial to Lincoln's temperament and there
was little fanfare associated with the person or even the public
duties of the Chief Executive.

This, of course, does not signify that the more important
uses of presidential publicity were altogether ignored. Thought

was given to public pronouncements and to their timing. When, after Gettysburg and Vicksburg, the fall of Port Hudson was expected, thus opening the entire Mississippi River, Halleck wrote to Grant: "The Prest will then issue a genl order congratulating the armies of the east & west on their recent victories. This consideration has prevented me from issueing [*sic*] one myself for your army. I prefer that it should come from the Prest."

Such was the Halleck idea, but Lincoln did it in his own way. On July 13, 1863, he wrote a friendly personal letter to Grant expressing "grateful acknowledgment for the almost inestimable service you have done the country." Then on July 15 he issued, not a military "order," but a proclamation to the nation setting aside a special day of thanksgiving for "victories . . . so signal and so effective as to furnish grounds for augmented confidence that the union of these States will be maintained . . . and their peace and prosperity permanently restored." On July 4 he had announced the news from Gettysburg as promising "a great success to the cause of the Union." From time to time he made reluctant but effective use of serenades which were thrust upon him.

The work of the Sanitary Commission—the Civil War counterpart of the Red Cross—made a special appeal to Lincoln's mind and he was called upon to speak at Sanitary Fairs held to raise money. At such a fair in Washington on March 18, 1864, he admitted that he was "not accustomed to the . . . language of eulogy," but added that "if all that has been said . . . in praise of woman were applied to the women of America, it would not do them justice for their conduct during this war." His speech at the Sanitary Fair in Baltimore on April 18, 1864, was somewhat of a major effort. He spoke of slavery, of the meaning of liberty, and of the knotty problem of wartime retaliation which he characterized as a "mistake." At the Sanitary Fair in Philadelphia on June 16, 1864, he made a moderately long speech, praising the Sanitary Commission and the

Christian Commission for their "benevolent labors" and giving a word of encouragement for all voluntary activities to contribute to soldier comfort or relief of sick and wounded. He used the occasion for a morale-building word as to war aims. The conflict had taken three years for "restoring the national authority." So far as he was able to speak, he said "we are going through on this line if it takes three years more." For this he asked a "pouring forth of men and assistance."

One technique of publicity was peculiarly characteristic of Lincoln: he made notable use of the occasional open letter, or the fine art of correspondence with a public purpose. Where an important matter needed to be presented to the people, in lieu of a speech, he would often write a careful letter to the appropriate person or group, intending it for the nation's ear. To Greeley on August 22, 1862, he wrote of his "paramount object . . . to save the Union." To Erastus Corning and others (June 12, 1863) he sent an extended argument concerning wartime executive measures which were being assailed as unconstitutional. To James C. Conkling he sent a public speech to be read at the elaborate Springfield rally of September 3, 1863. For a committee from the Workingmen's Association of New York (March 21, 1864) he wrote an important address on the fundamental relations of capital and labor. Recognizing that "Capital has its rights," he declared that "Labor is the superior of capital." He went on to show that the "strongest bond of human sympathy, outside of the family relation, should be one uniting all working people, of all nations, and tongues, and kindreds." To A. G. Hodges, of Kentucky (April 4, 1864) he wrote of his antislavery views, his official acts concerning slavery, his arming of the Negroes, and his challenge to those who doubted his policy. He did not claim credit for himself, but ended on the note "If God . . . wills." In general, it is in these occasional letters that one finds some of Lincoln's best turned passages of eloquent but unprovocative appeal to public sentiment.

VI

To study Lincoln's letters of consolation is to find a blending of sentiment, uplift, and delicate, unaffected sympathy.
When Colonel Elmer E. Ellsworth of the "Ellsworth Zouaves,"
a personal friend of the Lincolns, was killed at Alexandria in
May 1861, the President's exquisite letter to the young warrior's
parents, though innocent of effusiveness, came from the heart.
Pointing out to the parents that "our affliction here, is scarcely
less than your own," he wrote of the young man's indomitable
yet modest qualities and his promise of usefulness to his country. It was not for him to remove the grief, but he could give
assurance that both the pain and the appreciation of the son's
gallant service were shared by the nation. He concluded: "In
the hope that it may be no intrusion upon the sacredness of
your sorrow, I have ventured to address you this tribute to
the memory of my young friend, and your brave and early
fallen child. May God give you that consolation which is
beyond earthly power." The final touch was in the subscribing
of his name: "Sincerely your friend in a common affliction,
A. Lincoln."

It was characteristic that a Lincoln letter would be fitted
to the case. In his words of sympathy to Fanny, daughter of
Colonel McCullough of Bloomington, Illinois (December 23,
1862), Lincoln's old-time friend, the man in the White House
talked as if face to face with the "young heart" that was suffering "beyond what is common in such cases." Sorrow comes to
all, he wrote, but "to the young, it comes with bitterest agony,
because it takes them unawares." Yet he told the girl, as if
seeking to enter her inmost mind: "You are sure to be happy
again. . . . The memory of your dear Father, instead of an
agony, will yet be a sad sweet feeling in your heart, of a purer,

and holier sort than you have known before."

The most famous of Lincoln's letters of consolation was to Mrs. Bixby of Boston; it has taken a pre-eminent place as a Lincoln gem and a classic in the language. The letter reads as follows:

> Executive Mansion,
> Washington, Nov. 21, 1864.

Dear Madam,—I have been shown in the files of the War Department a statement of the Adjutant General of Massachusetts, that you are the mother of five sons who have died gloriously on the field of battle.

I feel how weak and fruitless must be any words of mine which should attempt to beguile you from the grief of a loss so overwhelming. But I cannot refrain from tendering to you the consolation that may be found in the thanks of the Republic they died to save.

I pray that our Heavenly Father may assuage the anguish of your bereavement, and leave you only the cherished memory of the loved and lost, and the solemn pride that must be yours, to have laid so costly a sacrifice upon the altar of Freedom.

> Yours very sincerely and respectfully,
> A. Lincoln.

It is futile to paint the lily and it is always a question of how far one needs to comment on a literary classic. In the case of the Bixby letter the literature is tremendous. The subject is clouded by controversies, a deal of mythology has been thrown in, and commercialism has invaded the field. As a result the main significance of Lincoln's phrases has been obscured by irrelevant or unhistorical details. If one reads the letter and appreciates its noble meaning and distinguished form, that after all is the prime consideration.

Amid the hundreds of thousands of casualties the Bixby boys were singled out in the following manner. William

Schouler, state adjutant general of Massachusetts, gave a statement concerning the alleged death in battle of the five sons of Mrs. Lydia Bixby of Boston to Governor Andrew; the governor added his endorsement; the record came up to the war department in Washington; and the statement was communicated to Lincoln. It was on this evidence that Lincoln's letter of consolation was based.

The records themselves are confused. The report of five sons killed was erroneous; one of the five received an honorable discharge, and two others are said to have been deserters. Mrs. Bixby was an obscure person who frequently changed her residence; furthermore, there is evidence that her character was not that of respectability. According to one account, she kept a house of ill fame. It must be added that the records clearly show two sons killed, this being truly enough a "costly . . . sacrifice."

Most troublesome of all has been the contention that it was not Lincoln, but John Hay, who composed the letter. If this could be proved to be true it would have to be accepted, but in so famous an instance readers on Lincoln will wish to know how the matter stands. The Hay-authorship theory depends not on clear evidence but on an indirect and delayed transmission of reminiscence. One gets it from Nicholas Murray Butler, who wrote: "John Hay told Morley that he had himself written the Bixby letter. . . ." This was not to be disclosed until after Hay's death. Morley, having talked with Hay in 1904, reported the matter to Butler in 1912, when again there was a pledge of secrecy; nothing was to be said of the matter until after Morley's death.

Some have accepted the Butler-Morley-Hay transmission (reading backward) and have bolstered it with supposed evidence that Hay was an imitator of Lincoln's style, of his handwriting, and of his signature. Butler makes the incredibly erroneous statement: "Abraham Lincoln wrote very few letters that bore his signature. John G. Nicolay wrote almost all of those which were official, while John Hay wrote almost all of those which were personal."

With such flimsy statements as these and with various conjectures that Hay himself would never have approved, the subject has become artificially complex and hard to follow. The notion that Lincoln wrote very few letters is a serious error. He wrote hundreds in his own hand while President. The statement that Nicolay wrote "almost all" the official ones and Hay the personal ones is demonstrably and astonishingly false. As for Hay imitating Lincoln's handwriting as stated by Butler, it has been shown by Bullard that no actual case of such an imitation can be found. "Nobody has brought forward any definite and convincing confirmation" of this claim, to say nothing of the doubtful propriety of such an imitation on the part of a private secretary. Why should he have imitated Lincoln's handwriting and signature?

Hay did not compose Lincoln's personal letters though there may be found a few letters written for Lincoln in Hay's hand—that is, "routine run-of-the-mine documents" which Lincoln signed though they were not holograph letters, and which did not require the special touch of Lincoln's personality. There is a considerable contrast in style between the writing of the young Hay and that of the President. Sometimes a Lincoln letter, if rather long, would be rewritten by a scribe to save labor for the President, but such a letter would be none the less Lincoln's own, probably being based on a draft or working copy in Lincoln's hand.

One of the factors on which careful historians are agreed is that reminiscence is not enough, and it must be repeated that the idea of Hay's authorship rests upon indirectly reported conversations. Memories of honorable men are "fallible," as Bullard shows, and in the case of Hay it is a matter of record that when he talked to Morley in 1904 (eight years before Morley is reported to have talked to Butler), the former secretary of Lincoln was "heavily burdened with grief" from the death of his brother. Hay's own diary account reads: "I talked with him [Morley] hardly knowing what I was saying." It should be added that in this contemporary diary record there is no mention by Hay of having chatted with Morley concerning the Bixby letter; what is more to the point is that one can trace no direct statement by Hay himself that he ever claimed Bixby-letter authorship.

The letter to Lydia Bixby is a genuine Lincoln document printed in the newspapers about the time of its delivery in person to the bereaved mother in Boston and authenticated by inclusion in the *Complete Works of Abraham Lincoln* edited by Nicolay and Hay. On January 19, 1904, the very year of the statement later quoted to Morley, Hay wrote to W. D. Chandler: "The letter of Mr. Lincoln to Mrs. Bixby is genuine. . . ." It must at once be added, however, that the familiar "facsimile" of the letter, or rather several differing facsimiles which have often been used for commercial advertising and for sale, are fakes. Lincoln scholars do not believe that the maker, or fabricator, of any "facsimile" had the actual handwritten letter of Lincoln before him. By comparison with genuine Lincoln letters of the late 1864 period one can see that the "facsimile" lacks the easy flow and the vital quality of letters penned by Lincoln's hand. The writing is a labored and artificial, though superficially plausible, imitation of the President's handwriting. If any one of the facsimile makers had been in possession of the Lincoln original, or of an authentic photographic copy of it, the original would now in all probability be known to collectors, for the process of Lincoln collecting had gone far by the time these "facsimiles" were made. Yet the fact is that the original of this priceless letter has simply been lost, and being a popular topic, it has been a likely subject of forgery. It must be emphasized, however, that it is the *facsimile* purporting to reproduce Lincoln's handwriting which is forged; the Lincoln letter, though long lost, is authentic and its printed form can be trusted as the recognized text.

It is unnecessary to go fully into the mythology of the subject, but it may be briefly remarked that the original manuscript was never at Oxford University (Brasenose College), that it was never in the J. P. Morgan Collection, and that various and sundry "discoveries" of the "original" letter have proved erroneous. Mrs. Bixby did not preserve the letter nor did her family; what happened to it after she received it is unknown.

The vignette-like beauty of the letter, the tender reference to "a loss so overwhelming," the thanks of the Republic to the mother, are given with deep feeling and fitting expression as coming from the spokesman of the whole nation to a parent who stood in a representative capacity for all similarly afflicted parents. Then follows the lofty religious sentiment, the prayer to "our heavenly Father" to assuage the anguish, and the final complimentary mention of "solemn pride" in "so costly a sacrifice." The letter is sincere and heart-to-heart. It is a fine example of Lincoln's personal tact. It stands with the Gettysburg address as a masterpiece in the English language.

Chapter Fourteen

VINDICTIVES AND
VINDICATION

ALL THE WORLD IS FAMILIAR WITH LINCOLN THE EMANCIPATOR, the author of the Gettysburg address, the timeless spokesman of democracy. Few of us are acquainted with Lincoln the baboon, the imbecile, the wet rag, the Kentucky mule. Yet these are typical examples of the names heaped upon him in those cruel days when high office brought him less of glory than of insult and abuse within the ranks of the nation he was struggling to save from dissolution. In the heat of politics, abuse from members of the opposition party was to have been expected, but much of the most bitter denunciation of Lincoln came from his fellow Republicans. The Republican party was divided, and the President himself stood in between the Conservative and Radical factions, though he was nearer to the Conservatives. The Radicals—whom John Hay dubbed "Jacobins"—might better be termed Vindictives. While many of them were high-principled men, they frequently dealt with the President in a vengeful and spiteful way. They dominated Congress and did their best, or worst, to obstruct his policies regarding slavery and the conduct of the war. In 1864 they conspired to sidetrack him as the Republican candidate *after he had been regularly nominated.* He gained a vindication of sorts in his triumphal re-election.

I

How did Lincoln feel about the Congress which the people
—or the politicians—had given him? He once said concerning
a maneuver of Republican senators: "They wish to get rid of
me, and I am sometimes half disposed to gratify them." On
hearing of the proceedings of this group he added: "I have
been more distressed than by any event of my life." "I am to be
bullied by Congress, am I?" he once asked. Again, referring to
appeals for clemency, he said: "Congress has . . . left the
women to howl about me." Ward Lamon recalled that he once
found the President in the private room of the White House
lying on a sofa, "greatly disturbed and . . . excited." Jumping
up, Lincoln said: 'I am President of one part of this divided
country . . . ; but look at me! I wish I had never been born!
. . . With a fire in my front and rear; having to contend with
the jealousies of the military commanders, and not receiving
that cordial co-operation and support from Congress which
could reasonably be expected; with an active and formidable
enemy in the field threatening the very life-blood of the government,—my position is anything but a bed of roses."

There were occasions—just a few—on which Lincoln was
asked to take a hand in intraparty contests for nominating a
representative in Congress. In 1864 a particularly hot campaign
was waged within Republican ranks to prevent the renomination of Isaac N. Arnold of Chicago, who was serving as congressman and desired another term. It was represented to the
President that John L. Scripps, known for his connection with
the Chicago *Tribune* and his authorship of a campaign biography of Lincoln in 1860, was using his position as postmaster
in Chicago "to defeat Mr. Arnold's nomination to Congress."
Lincoln thereupon wrote to Scripps, saying that he was "well

satisfied" with Arnold, and asking Scripps not to constrain any of his subordinates in the exercise of his vote for congressman. The matter developed into a considerable row in the period when Lincoln's prospects for his own re-election were at the lowest ebb. Scripps, himself a candidate for the congressional nomination, denied using postoffice control for his own ends, but went on in a complaining letter to denounce Arnold, accusing him of seeking support among Federal office-holders, boosting Frémont, and taking measures that would lead to the choice of John Wentworth, whom Scripps deemed undesirable. After a considerable flow of denunciatory statements, Scripps asked Lincoln to oppose the selection of Arnold. Meanwhile Arnold was hurt and offended by the episode and freely expressed his feelings in letters to the overworked President. According to Arnold's account he had hoped for a "friendly understanding" by personal interview in Chicago but was met by a "storm of rage and passion" on the part of Scripps.

The upshot of this bickering within the party was that Arnold withdrew, pointing out that both the *Tribune* and the post office were against him. As a result John Wentworth was nominated and elected as a Republican to the Thirty-Ninth Congress. In terms of the purposes of President Lincoln it was no small matter to lose the support of such a man as Arnold.

Commenting on the radical attitude, with emphasis upon Wade, Joshua Giddings wrote of the manner in which senators were denouncing Lincoln; then he generalized: "The truth is that from that day [early in 1861] to the present [January of 1862] Congress has been the theatre for making Presidents and not to carry on the war." One of the milder comments, typical of the radicals, was that of Senator Chandler: "The President is a weak man." Lying "in wait" against the President, these men opposed him on confiscation, on war aims, on methods and pacing as to slavery, on Southern rights, on cabinet composition, on amnesty, on the election of 1864 (in which they would have preferred another man), and on reconstruction.

According to an incident reported in Washington in 1862, a senator once called at the White House and vehemently denounced the President for his "calm and moderate views," ending with the words: "Sir you are within one mile of Hell!" To this Lincoln offered no dissent, but with a gentle nod of his head as if talking to himself, replied: "Yes, yes it is just one mile to the Capitol!"

II

Students of American government will find in the Lincoln administration no such co-operation between President and Congress, and no such presidential leadership in legislation, as existed under Woodrow Wilson or under Franklin D. Roosevelt in the earlier New Deal years. Lincoln's chief effort to promote a specific project of legislation—i.e., to obtain Federal approval and practical financial help to support state emancipation—fell flat despite the President's earnest appeals, conferences with legislators, formal messages, and presidential drafting of a sample bill. In military leadership, in the blockade, in international dealings, and in such matters as the presidential proclamation of emancipation, treatment of disloyal persons, reconstruction, and other important measures, the President either went his way regardless of Senate and House, or was actually checked and angrily challenged by Congress.

As a matter of regular procedure (legitimate, and proper enough if not abused) President Lincoln was questioned by one or the other house of Congress, or requests were sent to him for information. The President usually transmitted the desired documents, almost as a matter of routine, but there were times when requests were refused. He explained the refusal on the ground, traditional in such cases reaching back to the time of Washington, that response to the congressional request would be "incompatible with the public interest." The withholding of information under such circumstances was done with full respect to Congress and no issue was made of it; indeed, members were sometimes careful to point out that questioning the President was not to be construed as a vote of censure.

At times, however (aside from requests for information), the Congress came near to censuring the President, and there were frequent occasions when lack of confidence in the Executive was the dominant sentiment. The fact that censure or want of confidence was not formally voted seems to have been chiefly for the reason that such votes are not a parliamentary custom in the United States. Such lack of formal censure, however, was small comfort to a President having to deal with an unco-operative body whose members gave out frequent censure in their own statements. A few examples of such statements must suffice:

Julian of Indiana, House of Representatives, December 11, 1861: "I . . . infer that the general policy of the Administration . . . renders necessary some action on the part of Congress, looking to a change of that policy."

Thaddeus Stevens of Pennsylvania, House of Representatives, December 16, 1861: "I do not understand where the President gets his facts which he states in this respect [on conditions in Kentucky]. I believe he has been misled. I believe he is laboring under a hallucination of mind upon this subject, as fatal as that of Samson under the manipulation of Delilah."

Hale of New Hampshire, Senate, December 16, 1861: ". . . I venture to predict . . . that if the American people . . . shall find in the future that they have been trifled with . . . there will be such a storm come upon your heads as history has never yet recorded; and it does not want a very great degree of faith to hear the distant rumblings of that thunderstorm that will overwhelm the Administration and the party in power if they do not see the things that belong to the day and the hours before they are hidden from their eyes."

These criticisms, however, were mild when compared to such a document as the "Wade-Davis Manifesto" (August 5, 1864), a scorching denunciation of the President in the midst of the campaign for his re-election, issued by men of importance in congressional leadership.

III

It might have clarified the situation if those who were so vigorously denouncing Lincoln had faced up to the necessity of going on record in an actual vote of censure. The consequences of such a vote would have been serious, but that very fact might have had a sobering effect upon some of those who were hounding the nation's leader. Absence of formal censure should not obscure the fact that, as George W. Julian said concerning one occasion, "the action of the President [as to confiscation] was inexpressibly provoking to a large majority of Congress."

Referring to the attitude of "the leading men of the two Houses," A. G. Riddle wrote: "he [Lincoln] . . . became the theme of criticism . . . [and] reproach on the part of these gentlemen. The New York Tribune was largely the organ of these congressional critics, and . . . Mr. Greeley . . . was diligently searching . . . for a man to succeed him [i.e., to succeed Lincoln]. To such extent did this condemnation reach, that, at the end of the Thirty-seventh Congress [March 1863], there were in the House but two men, capable of being heard, who openly and everywhere defended him—Mr. Arnold of Illinois, and Mr. Riddle of Ohio."

This astounding statement—that the President had only two unwavering defenders (if indeed the two mentioned could be so described)—need not be taken too literally, but Riddle was a keen observer. His statement has significance as indicating the general attitude of the House, which was that of opposition to, or divergence from, the views of Lincoln. If one goes so far as to assume that Riddle and Arnold were the only men in the House of Representatives who were really friendly to Lincoln, it should be remembered that neither of these men was re-elected in 1864. Riddle did not seek re-election, and Arnold, despite his appeal to Lincoln to help him in seeking another term, was stopped in his efforts to remain in Congress. The situation becomes the more remarkable when one remembers Riddle's eulogistic friendliness toward Senator Wade, a bitter and powerfully active opponent of the President.

To document his statement that he was a supporter of the President, Riddle referred to a speech he had made in the House on February 28, 1863, concerning the bill to indemnify the President—i.e., to afford protection for those who had made irregular arrests and seizures in accordance with presidential orders. In that speech Mr. Riddle had declared:

. . . How easy it is to abuse, traduce, and denounce. That it requires neither wit, grace, or truth, is illustrated by the assaults of those gentlemen on the President. . . .

Sir, the Executive is the arm of the people under our Constitution, and with it only can we deal a blow upon the rebellion. . . . Whoever strengthens this arm, strengthens the national cause; whoever weakens it strengthens the enemy. . . . You cannot separate the Executive from the *personale* of the President; and whatever detracts from him personally weakens the Executive force. . . .

The President, without the people, and all of them, can no more conduct this war to a successful issue than can the people without him. . . . with a united people he is irresistible, spite of mistakes and accidents. A united people and President can control fate and compel success. They must stand together; and woe unutterable to the wretches whose words or deeds shall separate them. . . . They [i.e., millions of the people] will discuss the events and management of the war. . . . But I submit if the just limit of criticism and manly debate has not been brutally outraged in the fierce denunciation of the President by gentlemen on this floor, and which have been caught up and re-echoed by their partisan press?

.   .   .   .

. . . If any man here distrusts the President, let him speak forth here, . . . and no longer offend the streets and nauseate places of common resort with their . . . clamor. . . . He [the President] may not have in excess that ecstatic fire that makes poets and prophets and madmen; he may not possess much of what we call heroic blood, that drives men to stake priceless destinies on desperate ventures, and lose them; he may not in an eminent degree possess that indefinable something that schoolboys call genius, that enables its possessor through new and unheard-of combinations to grasp at wonderful results, and that usually ends in failure. . . . He is an unimpassioned, cool, shrewd, sagacious, far-seeing man, with a capacity to form his own judgments, and a will to execute them; and he possesses an integrity pure and simple as the white rays of light that play about the Throne. It is this that has so tied the hearts and love of the people to him, that will not unloose in the breath of all the demagogues in the land. It is idle to compare him with Washington or Jackson. Like all extraordinary men, he is an original, and must stand in his own niche.

. . . contemplate, if you can, . . . the fearful responsibilities imposed upon this man. Is it not a marvel . . . that he sustains them so well?

It is not surprising that Lincoln welcomed the days and months when there was no assembled Congress. When, after a long session, the Senate adjourned in July 1862, the New York *Herald* remarked that this would relieve the President of embarrassment; he could carry on without senatorial annoyance and hindrance. Some of the solons, however, wanted Congress to remain in permanent session. It is significant that many of Lincoln's principal executive measures were taken when Congress was not sitting. This was true of the initial call for troops in April 1861, the blockade, the enlargement of the regular army, the overruling of Frémont, the suspension of the habeas corpus privilege, the preliminary proclamation of emancipation, and the important speech of April 11, 1865, on postwar policy. If Lincoln had had a co-operative Congress, most if not all of these measures ought to have been the combined product of the legislative and executive branches.

At one of those periods when Lincoln was having particular difficulty with an unco-operative Congress, his friend Orville Browning of Illinois called on him at the White House. The day was July 15, 1862. The President was trying to check the course that leaders of Congress were taking on the question of confiscation. At the same time he was shaping up his emancipation policy and was struggling with a military situation that led to the elevation of Halleck and Pope over McClellan. As if this were not enough, the international situation and the coming congressional election were on his mind.

The President, as Browning wrote in his diary, "was in his Library writing, with directions to deny him to every body. I went in a moment. He looked weary, care-worn and troubled. I shook hands with him, and asked how he was. He said 'tolerably well' I remarked that I felt concerned about him—regretted that troubles crowded so heavily upon him, and feared his health was suffering. He held me by the hand, pressed it, and said in a very tender and touching tone—'Browning I must die sometime', I replied 'your fortunes Mr President are bound up with those of the Country, and disaster to one would be disaster to the other, and I hope you will do all you can to preserve your health and life.' He looked very sad, and there was a cadence of deep sadness in his voice. We parted I believe both of us with tears in our eyes."

IV

The anti-Lincoln feeling within the President's own party reached a climax during the summer of 1864, after his renomination for the presidency. Already a group of the extreme Radicals had nominated another candidate, the former general, John C. Frémont. After the Radicals in Congress passed the Wade-Davis bill, providing for a comparatively harsh plan of reconstruction, Lincoln infuriated them with a pocket veto. On August 5 the New York *Tribune* published a statement in which Wade and Davis savagely denounced the President for "this rash and fatal act," this "studied outrage on the legislative authority," which they attributed to "personal ambitions" and "sinister" motives.

Seward read the Wade-Davis manifesto to Lincoln on the night of August 5, and the President commented: "I would like to know whether these men intend openly to oppose my election—the document looks that way." Not long afterward he said to Noah Brooks: "To be wounded in the house of one's friends is perhaps the most grievous affliction that can befall a man." He felt that he had done his best to meet the wishes of Wade and Davis while also keeping in mind his "whole duty to the country." Their bill, however, seemed to him like the bed of Procrustes: "if a man was too short to fill the bed he was stretched; if too long, he was chopped off"; and if any state "did not fit the Wade-Davis bedstead, so much the worse for the State." Grieved though he had been by the passage of the bill, the President was even more distressed by the manifesto, "so needless" and "so well calculated to disturb the harmony of the Union party," as Brooks reported, doubtless expressing Lincoln's attitude as well as his own.

Lincoln had guessed right about the intentions of Davis and Wade when he suspected that these men meant openly to

oppose his re-election. Their "protest" was, in fact, the first
public sign of a move to replace him as the Republican candidate in mid-campaign. Once launched, the movement was
directed (in so far as it had any central direction) by a secret
council of party leaders who met on August 14 and from time
to time thereafter in New York. As the project attracted both
numbers and respectability, it developed into something far
more serious than a mere gesture of Lincoln haters and party
irresponsibles.

What gave it sense, during those dark days of August, was
the seeming hopelessness of Lincoln's chances for re-election
in the fall. Republican politicians gloomily assured one another
that the people would have no more of him. On or about
August 11 the political wizard Thurlow Weed told Lincoln
frankly "that his re-election was an impossibility," and he repeated this conviction in a letter of August 22 to Seward. "Mr.
Swett," he added, in confirmation of his own view, "is well
informed in relation to the public sentiment. He has seen and
heard much." While Weed was writing to Seward, Raymond
wrote to Lincoln a letter detailing the hopelessness of the outlook. Said Raymond:

I feel compelled to drop you a line concerning the political
condition of the country as it strikes me. I am in active correspondence with your staunchest friends in every State and
from them all I hear but one report. The tide is setting strongly
against us. Hon. E. B. Washburne writes that "were an election
to be held now in Illinois we should be beaten." Mr. Cameron
writes that Pennsylvania is against us. Gov. Morton writes that
nothing but the most strenuous efforts can carry Indiana. This
State [New York], according to the best information I can get,
would go 50,000 against us to-morrow. And so of the rest.

Lincoln knew of the movement against him within his own
party, as he also knew of the consensus among political ex-

perts that his chances of re-election were slim, at best. Yet, rather than make concessions to the politicians who beset him on either side, he was willing to accept defeat, if defeat must come. On August 23, the day after Raymond had penned his pessimistic letter on "the political condition of the country," Lincoln wrote the remarkable memorandum which he folded, pasted, and gave to his Cabinet members to endorse, sight unseen. In it he put himself on record thus:

This morning, as for some days past, it seems exceedingly probable that this Administration will not be re-elected. Then it will be my duty to so co-operate with the President elect, as to save the Union between the election and the inauguration; as he will have secured his election on such ground that he can not possibly save it afterwards.

This, as Lincoln was to recall after the election, was at a time "when as yet we had no adversary, and seemed to have no friends." The Democratic convention was six days away. Even when defeat seemed most probable, however, Lincoln had not quite abandoned hope. Earlier he had been reported as saying that the people blamed him for Grant's failure to take Richmond, and that he knew as well as anyone that he was going to be *"badly beaten"*—unless "some great change" occurred in the military situation. Pessimistic though he became, he still counted on that great change. "Lincoln said," according to a letter of August 26, citing a recent White House visitor, "the public did not properly estimate our military prospects, results of which would change the present current," but he himself "relied on this confidently."

V

Lincoln in 1864 protested that he could not see personally to all the details of his campaign for re-election. "Well, I cannot run the political machine; I have enough on my hands without *that*," he wrote. "It is the *people's* business—the election is in their hands."

The election was indeed, as Lincoln said, in the hands of the people, yet he was not content to leave it entirely in their hands. While burdened with his duties as the country's President, he did not evade his obligations as the party's leader. He was himself the master strategist of his own campaign. He did not always leave even the details to workers in the field, many of whom reported directly to him about ordinary tactical questions. Little that went on escaped his eye, and certainly nothing of significance.

He sometimes took a hand in the management of the Republican speakers' bureau, as when he requested General John A. Logan to leave his command in Sherman's army and miss the march to the sea, in order that he might apply his talents as a colorful and persuasive stump speaker in Indiana and Illinois. Apparently Lincoln also suggested to Gustav Koerner that he, as a leading German-American of Illinois, might do much good among the German voters of the Midwest. "My German friends seem to agree with me that I can do a great deal more good by not taking a prominent stand on the stump," Koerner wrote, at Belleville, Illinois, to Lincoln. "The opposition papers have already charged that I had been called home by you to the great detriment of public bussiness [*sic*], to regulate the Dutch, and set them right."

Lincoln did not hesitate to interfere in the operations of the regular party organization when he thought they were being poorly carried on. After the somewhat disappointing results of the October election in Pennsylvania he had reason to believe, from the complaints of Pennsylvanians returning to Washington after having gone home to vote, that Cameron had "botched the canvass badly" in that state. He promptly called Cameron's factional foe Alexander K. McClure from Harrisburg to Washington, discussed the Pennsylvania situation carefully with him, and requested him to devote himself to aiding the state committee. McClure objected that his own participation would antagonize Cameron, but Lincoln promised to take care of that difficulty. Two days later McClure got a letter from Cameron inviting him to join in the committee's work. From that time on, Lincoln kept in close touch with McClure and, through him, with the progress of the Pennsylvania campaign. He even sent Postmaster General Dennison to Philadelphia to talk confidentially with McClure.

Lincoln did not go out and campaign for himself: he could not have done so, of course, because of the taboo which, as late as 1864, still showed no signs of breaking down. He would not even "write a general letter to a political meeting" when requested to do so. And yet, when delegations of soldiers or civilians appeared from time to time in the White House yard, he addressed them with remarks which were intended to influence the voters who heard them and the many more who read them in the newspapers. Indeed, he could scarcely have done or said anything without its having, consciously or unconsciously, some electioneering effect. He, after all, was the President and a candidate for re-election. More than that, he was himself the foremost issue of the campaign.

VI

Even those who saw little difference in issues between the two parties, asserted that there was a vast difference in the personal fitness of the two candidates for the high office of President. Partisans of both sides considered as woefully unfit the candidate they opposed. So a good deal of the campaigning consisted of sheer defamation.

Among Republicans the favorite epithets for the Democratic candidate, George B. McClellan, were "traitor" and "coward," and they ransacked his military record for evidences of his craven ways and his downright villainy. In search of new scandal the zealous editor John W. Forney looked to Lincoln. "Can you tell me whether the arrest of the members of the Maryland Legislature [in 1861] was opposed by General McClellan, or whether it was recommended by him?" Forney inquired. "A single word in reply to this will enable me to complete what I think will be a most damaging article for him for to-morrow's paper." But Lincoln was not the man to abet such a campaign of vilification. "I never heard him speak of McClellan in any other than terms of the highest personal respect and kindness," testified another editor, Alexander K. McClure, who spent a fair amount of time with the President during the electioneering season. "He never doubted McClellan's loyalty to the government or to the cause that called him to high military command."

Lincoln was a target for even more mud than McClellan was. Lincoln was a power-mad dictator, a "scoundrel" and a "tyrant," according to indignant stump speakers, who seemed to think that his opponent would be far less dangerous in the presidency, though that opponent was a military man who once had shown some signs of a Napoleonic complex. The former Whig President, Millard Fillmore, now a McClellan supporter, admitted that he did not favor the election of "military chieftains" as a general rule, but he believed that a "military man of disinterested devotion to his country" (meaning McClellan) could "do more to save it from ruin than any other" (meaning Lincoln). Certainly, in the view of Democrats, Lincoln was not an indispensable man.

The Republicans did not exactly say he was, but they did advise the voters: "It is no time to change leaders when you are confronting a powerful and wily foe—'No time to swap horses in the middle of the stream.'" Lincoln himself had put this "swap horses" expression into currency, when the Baltimore convention was meeting in June. And he did seem to think that, in the circumstances, his continued services were indispensable to the nation. In running for re-election he was motivated not by "personal vanity or ambition," as he told his Wisconsin visitors in the well-publicized August interview, but by "solicitude for his great country."

When not denouncing him for his alleged dictatorial proclivities, the Democrats condemned him for what they considered his loutish ways. The New York *World* characterized the Lincoln-Johnson ticket as made up of "a rail-splitting buffoon and a boorish tailor, both from the backwoods, both growing up in uncouth ignorance." And the New York *Herald*, while editor Bennett was still in an anti-Lincoln phase, had this to say: "Mr. Lincoln is a country lawyer of more than average shrewdness, and of far more than the average indelicacy which marks the Western wit." McClellan on the other hand, was a gentleman with the dignity becoming to the White House, at least according to the Democrats. When installed in the presidential mansion, he would see that callers would "put on their best clothes & make themselves clean," as one of his admirers wrote to Mrs. McClellan. "It is the cultivation of the feeling that the President is no better than any other citizen, that has brought us to the election of such ordinary men as Abraham Lincoln."

Such phrases as "rail-splitting buffoon," the "indelicacy" of his "Western wit," and "Abe, the vulgar joker" were intended to turn against Lincoln one of the traits that most endeared him to the people—his sense of humor. A more elaborate piece of propaganda, adorning the theme of his crudeness and insensitivity, was an old story about the "Antietam song-singing," which the Democrats revived, elaborated, and then repeated, with variations, throughout the campaign.

One version of the canard, published in the New York *World*, was this: "While the President [after the battle of Antietam in September, 1862] was driving over the field in an ambulance, accompanied by Marshal Lamon, General McClellan, and another officer, heavy details of men were engaged in the task of burying the dead. The ambulance had just reached the neighborhood of the old stone bridge, where the dead were piled highest, when Mr. Lincoln, suddenly slapping Marshal Lamon on the knee, exclaimed: 'Come, Lamon, give us that song about Picayune Butler; McClellan has never heard it.' 'Not now, if you please,' said General McClellan, with a shudder; 'I would prefer to hear it some other place and time.'" But Lamon went ahead and sang the funny song, and Lincoln relished it.

Another version, printed in the *Essex Statesman* and (like the *World's* version) reprinted by other Democratic papers, told how, "soon after one of the most desperate and sanguinary battles," Lincoln was being shown over the field by an unnamed commanding general, who was of course McClellan. Finally, Lincoln said, "This makes a fellow feel gloomy." Turning to a companion, he asked, "Jack, can't you give us something to cheer us up. Give us a song, and give us a lively one." Obligingly, Jack "struck up, as loud as he could bawl, a comic negro song," and he kept it up until the general, in deference to the feelings of his soldiers, requested the President to quiet his friend. "We know that the story is incredible," commented the *Essex Statesman* as it proceeded to point the moral of the tale. "The story can't be true of any man fit for any office of trust, or even for decent society; but the story is every whit true of Abraham Lincoln."

Referring to the anecdote as given in the New York *World*, a Democrat wrote to McClellan and asked if it was true. What reply McClellan gave to this inquiry, if any, is not on record, but he issued no public denial to scotch the story.

A Republican appealed to Lamon for a repudiation. Already Lamon had begged Lincoln to refute the slander, but Lincoln had said: "Let the thing alone." Now Lamon took it upon himself to write out a refutation and a protest, which he showed to Lincoln. Lincoln criticized Lamon's remarks as too belligerent and thought it would be better simply to state the facts. The facts were that the incident had occurred sixteen days after the battle and several miles from the battlefield (and, as Lamon recalled in his reminiscences, Lincoln had requested, "a little sad song," not a comic one). "Let me try my hand at it," said Lincoln, and he himself wrote out a statement, then told Lamon to keep it until the proper time to make it public. But Lincoln never found the proper time.

At the close of the campaign he remarked to John Hay: "It is a little singular that I, who am not a vindictive man, should have always been before the people for election in canvasses marked for their bitterness: always but once; when I came to Congress it was a quiet time."

VII

In some parts of the country the Republicans, expecting violence, awaited election day with apprehension. In Illinois, Stanton was informed, more than five thousand armed Confederates were roaming at large. "They intend to vote at the coming election and by terrorism to keep from the polls more than 5,000 *citizens*." In the city of New York, Stanton heard, the rebels intended not only to jam the polls with "enemies" but also to start a general conflagration. From New York and a number of other cities the war department received appeals for troops to protect the polls, and a regiment was sent to New York, but General Halleck exclaimed that if the army were to

LINCOLN AND TAD

"A well-known picture of Tad and his father. . . . Lincoln explained to me that he was afraid this picture was a species of false pretense. Most people would suppose the book a large clasped Bible, whereas it was a big photograph album which the photographer had hit upon as a good device to . . . bring the two sitters together. Lincoln's anxiety lest somebody should think he was 'making believe read the Bible to Tad,' was illustrative of his scrupulous honesty." Noah Brooks.

respond to only half of the requests, "we would not have a single soldier to meet the rebels in the field!"

When November 8 came, however, no serious disturbances interfered with the polling anywhere. In Illinois the qualified voters—white men over twenty-one with a year's residence in the state—patiently waited their turns to vote, standing single file in long lines at many polling places. Saloons were closed, and in Springfield, where it rained steadily most of the day, the *Illinois State Journal* noted that "fewer drunken people were seen upon the streets than usual." From New York, General Butler, in command of the Federal troops, telegraphed laconically to the war department at noon: "The quietest city ever seen."

But Butler had not seen Washington that day. It was even quieter. The day was dark and rainy, and the city was considerably depopulated by the homeward exodus of more than eighteen thousand voters, mostly government employees. "The rush to the cars of those going home to vote was too much for the railroads," a news dispatch reported two days before the election. "Some four hundred were left behind, but by the aid of extra trains, all have been able to get off to-day." The White House was almost deserted, and the President, beginning to look "care-worn and dilapidated," was by himself when Noah Brooks called at noon. Lincoln did not attempt to hide his anxiety about the election. "I am just enough of a politician to know that there was not much doubt about the results of the Baltimore convention," he told Brooks; "but about this thing I am very far from being certain. I wish I was certain."

In the evening, the weather still rainy and "steamy," Lincoln went with a party including Brooks and Hay to the telegraph office, to get the returns as they came in. "We splashed through the grounds to the side door of the War Department where a soaked and smoking sentinel was standing in his own vapor with his huddled-up frame covered with a rubber cloak." Upstairs, the President was handed the reports of the early returns, which were extremely favorable. He sent out the "first fruits" to Mrs. Lincoln. "She is more anxious than I," he explained. Later in the evening the reports began to come in slowly because of the rainstorm, which interfered with the telegraph, and during the lulls he entertained the group around him with anecdotes.

By midnight, though to his great disappointment he had not heard from Illinois (or Iowa), Lincoln could be "tolerably certain" that Maryland, Pennsylvania, most of the Middle West, and all of New England would go for him. A midnight supper was brought in, and Hay observed how "The President went awkwardly and hospitably to work shovelling out the fried oysters." As he received congratulations on what looked like a sure and decisive victory, Lincoln appeared utterly calm, with no trace of elation or excitement. He did say "he would admit that he was glad to be relieved of all suspense, and that he was grateful that the verdict of the people was likely to be so full, clear, and unmistakable that there could be no dispute."

About two o'clock in the morning a messenger brought the information that a crowd of Pennsylvanians were serenading the White House. Lincoln went home and, in response to cries for a speech, he talked for a few minutes, concluding: "If I know my heart, my gratitude is free from any taint of personal triumph. I do not impugn the motives of any one opposed to me. It is no pleasure to me to triumph over any one, but I give thanks to the Almighty for this evidence of the people's resolution to stand by free government and the rights of humanity."

VIII

As of March 4, 1865, the old Congress had met for the last time, and the new one would not meet for several months (until December) unless the President meanwhile should choose to call it into special session. Lincoln now began his second term, which was not expected necessarily to be his last—gamblers soon were betting that he would be re-elected in 1868. After four years as a war President, he could look ahead to nearly four more, at least, as a peace President. More immediately, with no Congress in session to hinder him, he could look ahead to a few months of peacemaking on his own. He could hope, within that time, to complete the preliminaries of the kind of settlement that he desired.

Inauguration day dawned dark and rainy, and rain fell steadily throughout the morning. The streets of Washington, especially Pennsylvania Avenue, were filled with soft mud which oozed up between the bricks even where there was pavement. Before the inaugural ceremonies began, the rain stopped, but most of the spectators, standing in the mud around the east entrance of the Capitol, already were thoroughly bedraggled. The ceremonies themselves were poorly planned, or so they seemed to Secretary Welles, who wrote: "All was confusion and without order,—a jumble." As if the weather and the planning were not bad enough, the new Vice President, Andrew Johnson, made something of a scene when he was inaugurated. Those who heard or read his rambling and maudlin speech wondered whether he was crazy or only drunk. In fact he was unwell. Having been strongly urged by Lincoln to be present, he had fortified himself with whiskey beforehand, and because of his illness and his temperate habits, the effect was only too noticeable.

Lincoln's own inaugural address was short, the shortest any President had ever made. Its opening lines gave the impression that Lincoln had nothing to say. So many public declarations had been made during the war, he remarked, that "little that is new could be presented." He went on to remind his hearers of the circumstances of his first inaugural, then restated the central issue of the ensuing struggle as he saw it: "Both parties deprecated war; but one of them would *make* war rather than let the nation survive; and the other would *accept* war rather than let it perish. And the war came." Then he elaborated upon the basic issue by speaking of the "peculiar and powerful interest" of slavery. "All knew that this interest was, somehow, the cause of the war." He proceeded to describe the sufferings of the people, both North and South, as divine punishment for the sin of slavery, of which both were guilty. He concluded with the paragraph which made the address forever memorable (except to a later President, who in 1945, in characterizing his own war aims, distorted its spirit by omitting the first two phrases): "With malice toward none; with charity for all; with firmness in the right, as God gives us to see the right, let us strive on to finish the work we are in; to bind up the nation's wounds; to care for him who shall have borne the battle, and for his widow, and his orphan—to do all which may achieve and cherish a just, and a lasting peace, among ourselves, and with all nations."

This second inaugural, like the Gettysburg address, was not hailed unanimously as a classic at its birth. Lincoln himself expected it to "wear as well—perhaps better than" anything he had produced, but he believed it was "not immediately popular." Yet (like the Gettysburg address again) it was not entirely unappreciated by contemporaries. The New York *Herald*, misquoting the phrase "the nation's wounds" and making it read "the nation's wound," found aptness and significance in Lincoln's supposed use of the singular noun. On the whole, the *Herald* approved the speech while expressing some puzzlement at the personality of its author, "this remarkable rail-splitter." But the *Herald* was disappointed at its brevity and its generality, its failure to spell out peace terms, a failure which might cause the address to be taken as an "unconditional surrender" manifesto in the South. The Washington *Chronicle*, contrasting the second with the first inaugural, thought the second one much superior, for it was "solemnly affirmative" where the other had been "deprecatory, apologetic, explanatory."

At least one American citizen, however, was ashamed of

the speech as a literary production. "Lincoln's Inaugural, while the sentiments are noble, is one of the most awkwardly expressed documents I ever read—if it be correctly printed. When he knew it would be read by millions all over the world, why under the heavens did he not make it a little more creditable to American scholarship?" So wrote a Pennsylvanian to Simon Cameron. "Jackson was not too proud to get Van Buren to slick up his state papers. Why could not Mr. Seward have prepared the Inaugural so as to save it from the ridicule of a Sophomore in a British University?" But Cameron's correspondent knew nothing of the actual response in England, and if any British sophomore was inclined to ridicule the address, the Duke of Argyll certainly was not. "I . . . congratulate you both on the good progress of the war, and on the *remarkable speech* of your President," the Duke wrote to his friend Charles Sumner. "It was a noble speech, just and true, and solemn. I think it has produced a great effect in England." The *Times* of London, for all its pro-Southern record, commented favorably on the address, and some of the British reviews gave it superlative praise, the *Spectator* declaring: "No statesman ever uttered words stamped at once with the seal of so deep a wisdom and so true a simplicity." If anything, the second inaugural received even greater immediate acclaim in England than in the United States.

After delivering the address, Lincoln took the oath of his office, kissing the Bible which Chief Justice Chase presented to him. At that moment the sun burst forth above the actors and the crowd of spectators. Doubtless many of them, like the Chief Justice himself, looked for a symbol in the sudden change of weather. Later in the day, sending to Mrs. Lincoln the ceremonial Bible, with the kissed page carefully marked, Chase wrote in a note to her: "I hope the Sacred Book will be to you an acceptable souvenir of a memorable day; and I most earnestly pray Him, by whose Inspiration it was given, that the beautiful sunshine which just at the time the oath was taken dispersed the clouds that had previously darkened the sky may prove an auspicious omen of the dispersion of the clouds of war and the restoration of the clear sunlight of prosperous peace under the wise and just administration of him who took it."

Chapter Fifteen

THE GREAT EMANCIPATOR

THE RADICALS OF HIS OWN PARTY INSINUATED THAT LINCOLN WAS willing to see slavery survive the war, and sincere friends of the slave often felt he was too slow and hesitant in striking at the institution. Democrats, on the other hand, portrayed him as a "nigger lover" and fanatical abolitionist. The truth is, he had shared some of the anti-Negro prejudices of the people among whom he lived in Kentucky and southern Indiana and Illinois. But, in the White House, he outgrew his prejudices. He also had possessed antislavery feelings which were rather rare among his early neighbors, and these feelings he did not outgrow during his presidential years. But he doubted whether, as President, he should act upon his personal impulses in disregard of the powers of his office and the demands of state-craft. "I am naturally anti-slavery. If slavery is not wrong, nothing is wrong. I can not remember when I did not so think, and feel." Thus he wrote in April, 1864. "And yet I have never understood that the Presidency conferred upon me an un-restricted right to act officially upon this judgment and feeling." He had moved toward emancipation, he explained, only as it became an "indispensable necessity" for winning the war and saving the Union. "I claim not to have controlled events, but confess plainly that events have controlled me."

I

Congress had taken the lead in emancipation, beginning the work less than four months after the firing on Fort Sumter. The first confiscation act, of August 6, 1861, provided that slaveowners should forfeit those of their slaves whom they used in military service against the United States. The second confiscation act, of July 17, 1862, went much beyond that: it declared "forever free" all slaves of owners who committed treason or supported the rebellion. In other acts of 1862 Congress abolished slavery in the District of Columbia, with compensation to the owners, and in the territories, without such compensation. Also in 1862 Congress provided that enemy-owned slaves serving in the Union armies should be free, and their families as well, and in 1864 Congress also gave freedom to slave-soldiers (with their families) belonging to loyal owners. In 1864 Congress finally repealed the fugitive-slave laws of 1793 and 1850 which, up to that time, had continued to provide an indirect sanction for slavery in the Federal statute books.

Viewing the increasing difficulties that emerged as liberating incidents inevitably arose out of the war, Lincoln seriously weighed the question of colonization—that is, of shipping the freed slaves out of the country. The idea was not new to him. While debating with Douglas he had shown an interest in Negro emigration, and in his first annual message to Congress (December 1861) he advised that slaves presumably freed by the confiscation act of that year be colonized in some genial clime. If any of the states should adopt emancipation measures, Lincoln thought that their ex-slaves might be accepted by the United States in lieu of taxes—a rather curious idea—and that they might be included in a general colonizing scheme. He would also extend the process to those of the free colored who might desire a foreign home.

With such preliminaries colonization came to be treated as an active policy, and Congress appropriated $100,000 for the purpose in the District emancipation act. This was later raised to a total of $600,000, and in the second confiscation act the President was "authorized" to make arrangements for colonizing Negroes freed (on paper) by that enactment, again on a voluntary basis. This action by Congress may have been taken to assist in obtaining Lincoln's signature to a measure which he strongly disliked.

A curious scene in the White House in this period, and one which seems almost to have been forgotten, was a conference between the President and a committee of intelligent colored men who came by Lincoln's special request to confer regarding the departure of members of their race to Central America. To one who thinks of the Emancipator in terms of abolitionist stereotypes the words of his remarkable address to this group, preserved in his published works, will come as something of a surprise. In this address Lincoln's thesis was utterly different from the concepts of those to whom sudden and complete abolition presented no obstacles in terms of post-liberation adjustment. To Lincoln such adjustment, as well as the presence of large numbers of Negroes long free, offered very serious difficulties, and his words could have given little encouragement to his colored auditors.

White and Negroes, he told them, are of different races. Your race, he said, suffer greatly, and we of the white race suffer from your presence. It affords a reason why we should be separated. Even "when you cease to be slaves, you are yet far removed from being . . . on an equality with the white race. . . . [O]n this broad continent not a single man of your race is made the equal of a single man of ours. . . . I cannot alter it if I would. It is a fact. . . ." "But for your race among us [said Lincoln] there could not be war, although many men engaged on either side do not care for you one way or the other. . . . It is better for us both . . . to be separated."

Continuing his unflattering advice, Lincoln told his dark friends that there was an "unwillingness" on the part of whites to allow the free colored to remain. He therefore appealed to intelligent free colored men, as he could not appeal to the systematically oppressed, to make sacrifices and endure hardships, as whites had done, for the sake of a future day. Fearing that Liberia was too remote, he highly recommended an area in Central America, mentioning its natural advantages, its nearness to the United States, its "very rich coal-mines," and its excellent ports on two great oceans. He was referring to Chiriqui on the Panamanian isthmus; already Northern capitalists were inquiring into the profits of a colonization scheme in that area. Referring to the fact that men of the colored race had been "talked to" concerning a speculation by gentlemen who had an "interest" in the project, the President explained that "everybody you trade with makes something," and that he would see to it that they would not be wronged. As to success of the venture he wasn't sure. Having justified the profit interest on the part of capitalists, Lincoln urged the Negro delegation to rally to the support of the project "not . . . for the present time, but . . . for the good of mankind. . . ." On this theme he burst into poetry:

From age to age descends the lay
  To millions yet to be,
Till far its echoes roll away
  Into eternity.

II

In favoring colonization Lincoln was promoting a scheme and a point of view violently opposed by nearly all abolitionists, including notably Senator Sumner. Radical antislavery men were unready to admit that Negroes needed to be separated from whites, nor did they trouble themselves with practical consequences of emancipation. Garrison strongly opposed colonization. On the other hand there were Southerners who favored it, some of them paying from their own pockets to promote private emigration enterprises. This was not the only instance in which Lincoln was nearer to the Southern than to the average abolitionist viewpoint in regard to the Negro race.

Lincoln's efforts toward colonization would make a long story and a dismal one. He asked his cabinet for written advice, sought treaties with foreign nations, and gave detailed attention to the two areas upon which actual efforts of the time were focusing. One of these was the Chiriqui location near Panama, a part of New Grenada (Colombia); the other was a Haitian island known as *Isle a'Vache*. Both ventures were abortive. The Chiriqui project was dropped when samples of the coal deposits failed in scientific tests. This disappointment of promising hopes made it seem the more desirable to proceed with the Haitian experiment, and in an unguarded moment Lincoln became a party to a scheme promoted by one Bernard Kock, an alleged "business man" whom Edward Bates denounced as "an errant humbug" and "a charlatan adventurer." In spite of Bates's denunciation, Lincoln and his secretary of the interior signed a contract with this Kock by which, at fifty dollars a head, five thousand Negroes were to be colonized. With government backing and predictions of colossal profits, Kock enlisted the financial support of certain New York capitalists, and the ill-fated Haitian venture was launched.

Over four hundred hapless Negroes were transported to the island at government expense, but the whole scheme, which, even if successful, could have been no more than "a tub to the whale," collapsed from inadequate planning, want of essentials, poor housing, smallpox, unemployment, cupidity, Haitian opposition, and the strutting unpopularity of Kock. Midway in the venture Lincoln saw to it that the contract with

Kock was canceled. When, on March 20, 1864, the government-chartered *Marcia C. Day* docked near Washington carrying back 368 of these colonists, about a hundred less than were sent, the Washington *Chronicle* reported the great joy of the returning survivors, while remarking upon "the folly of attempting to depopulate the country of its valuable labor."

For Lincoln the idea died hard. This was partly because he considered it an important part of a comprehensive plan of emancipation, and it is interesting to note that Governor John A. Andrew of Massachusetts agreed with him. In February 1861 Andrew wrote: "If our . . . government would establish . . . a colony for the emancipated col'd people, . . . I think it wd. prove a blessing in a thousand ways, . . . would . . . help to . . . create a hereafter for the oppressed race, & would remove the prejudices of many . . . who now refuse to tolerate . . . liberty for the slaves. . . . I wish we might take some pains to prove that we are friends & not enemies to all classes of Southern society. A very strong anti-slavery man myself, I yet am conscious of only kind & fraternal feelings to our Southern people. . . ."

Having made his own rationalization, Lincoln retained in December 1862 his strong interest in colonization, associating gradual emancipation with "deportation" and referring to a temporary adjustment after emancipation while awaiting the time when, for the colored people, "new homes . . . [could] be found . . . in congenial climes and with people of their own blood and race."

III

Where Lincoln gave thought to large-scale national planning in the matter of liberating the slaves, such thought was not embraced within the bounds of the emancipation proclamation. Speaking relatively and with a view to the President's main concept for solving the problem, it is correct to regard the proclamation as of minor importance. The famous edict was to Lincoln a war measure of limited scope, of doubtful legality, and of inadequate effect. In his reaching out for an adequate solution the President developed an elaborate blueprint for freedom in terms of gradual emancipation by voluntary action of the slave states with Federal co-operation in two matters: foreign colonization of emancipated Negroes (already treated), and compensation to slaveowners.

This blueprint was envisaged not merely with reference to the war, though its integration with a broad war policy was a vital factor; beyond the war the President's solution was projected into a peace-minded future with a view to the ultimate, statesmanlike elimination of an institution in which, as Lincoln felt, North and South had a common responsibility and a community of interest. Though the plan failed, a familiarity with it becomes necessary to an understanding of wartime currents and especially of Lincoln's manner of tackling a large problem. As one studies the President's pathetically earnest efforts to promote this "proposition," one is impressed with his conservatism, his sense of fair dealing, his lack of vindictiveness, his attention to legal adjustments, his respect for self-determination in government, his early vision of state-and-federal co-operation, and his co-ordination of a domestic reform with the nation's paramount purpose to restore the Union and then to preserve it. The proposition is also significant as perhaps the major instance in which Lincoln tried manfully to enlist the support of Congress. On no other matter did he so far extend his presidential leadership in attempted legislation. The only other project of the period that compares with it is that of reconstruction, but in that case Lincoln did not rely upon congressional enactment of a presidentially sponsored measure.

Announced in a special message to Congress on March 6, 1862, and fully elaborated in his message of December 1 of that year, Lincoln's plan was unfolded as part of a grand concept of a large and growing people, a nation of untouched resources whose future, he hoped, would not be frustrated "by any political folly or mistake." A long-term policy was envisaged, to be completed "at any time or times" before 1900. Thirty-seven years did not seem too high a maximum for the consummation of such a reform. Though a broad solution was projected, the President was immediately concerned with initiatory steps. Emancipation was to be gradual. Both races were to be spared the "evils of sudden derangement." No Federal claim of the right to impose emancipation upon a state was involved. Abolition was to be voluntary; "absolute control" of the matter by the states was recognized; "perfectly free choice" was to govern their action.

Compensation was to be made to slaveholders, for, as Lincoln said, "the liberation of slaves is the destruction of property." The Federal government was to bear the cost of such compensation but not to administer it. The states would emancipate with compensation; the Federal government would reimburse them "by installments" as abolition proceeded. This it would do by interest-bearing bonds. Freedmen were to be transported at Federal expense to new homes in some foreign land. In this connection the President used the strong word "deportation," though he intended no compulsion; only those freedmen who desired it would be colonized.

Such in brief was Lincoln's emancipation plan. He proposed it first as a congressional resolution expressive of general approval of the whole concept, then as a bill which he himself drafted for applying the plan in Delaware, later in more elaborate form as a constitutional amendment. On no other subject did Lincoln plead more earnestly than on this. But his pleadings and his carefully figured schemes were of no avail.

IV

Meanwhile Lincoln's heart was not in the congressional policy, and he shrank from enforcing the confiscation acts, which in themselves authorized him to give freedom to slaves of disloyal masters. While abolitionists clamored for action, he hesitated.

Lincoln's ending of delay and arrival at a decision are best told in the President's own words. "It had got to be midsummer, 1862," he said. "Things had gone . . . from bad to worse, until I felt that we had reached the end of our rope on the plan . . . we had been pursuing; that we . . . must change our tactics, or lose the game. I now determined upon the adoption of the emancipation policy; and without consultation with, or the knowledge of, the Cabinet, I prepared the original draft of the proclamation, and, after much anxious thought, called a Cabinet meeting upon the subject."

On July 13, on a long carriage ride with Welles and Seward, Lincoln had informally broached the matter of a proclamation, that being "he said, the first occasion when he had mentioned the subject to any one." "He dwelt earnestly [wrote Welles] on the gravity, importance, and delicacy of the movement, said he had given it much thought and had about come to the conclusion that it was a military necessity . . . for the salvation of the Union, ..." Welles emphasized that this "was a new departure for the President, for until this time, . . . whenever . . . emancipation . . . had been . . . alluded to, he had been prompt and emphatic in denouncing any interference by the General Government with the subject."

Gloom rested heavily upon the Union cause. McClellan had failed to take Richmond, the storm raged bitterly for McClellan's removal, a shake-up in military command and in operations was imminent, and, as to slaves, already "thousands

. . . were in attendance upon the [enemy's] armies." It was in this atmosphere of depression and frustration that Lincoln worked out alone the basic problem and the wording of his historic proclamation. His friend Eckert of the military tele- graph service recalled that Lincoln wrote the first draft of the edict in the cipher room of the war department telegraph office. He began it, said Eckert, shortly after the Seven Days (this would put it about the beginning of July 1862). He would write a line or two on long foolscap sheets, study a while, look out of the window, and now and then stop to pass a remark with the operators. This continued for "several weeks," the sheets being locked up at the telegraph office and taken out "nearly every day" by Lincoln for careful composition and revision of every sentence. The President, added Eckert, told him that he had been able thus "to work . . . more quietly and . . . better than at the White House, where he was fre- quently interrupted."

It was on July 22, 1862, that Lincoln broached the subject of his proclamation to the Cabinet. In his undramatic diary Chase gives incidental mention of the President's proposal to proclaim "the emancipation of all slaves within States remaining in insurrection on the first of January, 1863." This proposed proclamation, said Chase, was based on the confiscation bill (which had a clause concerning the freeing of slaves as a penalty for rebellion); yet as a kind of collateral approach to the slave problem it contained a renewed recommendation for compensation to slaveowners within the pattern of Lincoln's proposal for gradual abolition by state action.

It is clear that Lincoln had made up his mind as to the proclamation; of his Cabinet he asked incidental rather than primary advice. His own statement, given in 1864 to F. B. Car- penter, the artist, was: "I said to the cabinet that I had resolved upon this step, and had not called them together to ask their advice, but to lay the subject-matter of a proclamation before them, suggestions as to which would be in order after they had heard it read." Chase gave the proposal "entire support" chiefly because he considered it "much better than inaction on the subject." Cabinet secretaries gave their suggestions, most of which had been anticipated, but Seward came out with a bit of counsel that gave pause to the President. He doubted the expedience of a proclamation issued at a time of depression in the public mind, dreading the effect of such a step following so closely upon recent reverses. The government, he thought, would seem to be "stretching forth its hands to Ethiopia, instead of Ethiopia stretching forth her hands to the government." It "would be considered a last *shriek* on the retreat." The secretary approved the measure, but he said: ". . . I suggest, sir, that you postpone its issue until you can give it to the country supported by military success. . . ." The "wisdom" of this view struck Lincoln "with very great force." "The results was," said Lincoln to the artist, "that I put the draft of the proclamation aside, as you do your sketch for a picture, waiting for a victory."

Lincoln and those near him had a secret to keep the next two months; in keeping it the President was under the embarrassing necessity of seeming to be noncommittal or even hostile toward a policy upon which he was in fact determined. It is amusing to note the manner in which, with the draft proclamation in his desk drawer, Lincoln gave out laborious and unsatisfactory answers on the subject of slavery while enduring severe taunts against his alleged proslavery attitude. It was in this period, for example, that he advocated separation of the races and colonization in a foreign country. His embarrassment was increased in the anxious days of September when a delegation of Christian leaders descended upon him carrying a petition for national emancipation which had been adopted at a public meeting at Bryan Hall in Chicago. The President received these men courteously and listened "with fixed attention" while the memorial was read. Then he gave reply "in an earnest and . . . solemn manner, as one impressed with the weight of the theme, yet at times making a character-istically shrewd remark with a pleasant air" (such was the clumsy report of the delegation).

The main tone of the President's answer was negative and disappointing. "What good would a proclamation of emancipa-tion from me do, . . . ?" he asked. "I do not want to issue a document that the whole world will see must . . . be inopera-tive, like the Pope's bull against the comet." In the "rebel States" such a proclamation could no more be enforced, said Lincoln, than the recent ineffective law offering freedom to slaves coming within Union lines. And suppose they did throw themselves upon us in large numbers, what should we do with them? How could we "feed and care for such a multitude"? Much more the President gave them, impressively piling up doubts concerning the wisdom and feasibility of a liberating edict. Conceding that slavery was the *sine qua non* of the "rebellion," that emancipation would help the cause in Europe, and that it would weaken the enemy by drawing off their laborers, Lincoln would have the visiting committee consider the difficulties of freeing helpless thousands, the danger of their re-enslavement, the impotence of the government to do anything about it if they were re-enslaved, and the danger that arms put into Negro hands would be seized by the enemy. Especially he emphasized the importance of fifty thousand Union bayonets from the border slave states; if in consequence of a proclamation they should go over to the enemy, it would be a very serious matter. He went on thus for "an hour of earnest and frank discussion." Then, with the meeting about to break up, Lincoln remarked, as if giving a broad hint on a matter that could not go into the record: "Do not misunder-stand me, ... I have not decided against a proclamation of liberty to the slaves, but hold the matter under advisement; and I can assure you that the subject is on my mind, by day and night, more than any other." He trusted that in freely can-vassing their views, he had not injured his visitors' feelings.

V

From Greeley's resounding sanctum there came the re-proachful admonition that "attempts to put down the Rebellion and at the same time uphold its . . . cause . . . [were] pre-posterous and futile." In an editorial "Prayer of Twenty Mil-lions" the *Tribune* pundit informed the President that an "immense majority of the Loyal Millions" of his countrymen required of him a frank execution of the laws in the antislavery sense. With bland equanimity for Greeley's fervor and with balanced, noncommittal phrases for his heated rhetoric, Lin-coln replied in the famous "paramount object" letter which showed, among other things, that he was not swayed by abolitionist outcries. Calm down, and get off your dictatorial horse, would be an offhand paraphrase of his opening sentences. "I have just read yours of the 19th," wrote Lincoln to Greeley. ". . . If there be in it any inferences . . . falsely drawn, I do not . . . argue against them. If there be perceptible in it an impatient and dictatorial tone, I waive it in deference to an old friend. . . ." Having thus set the pitch for his even-toned reply, Lincoln wrote:

My paramount object in this struggle is to save the Union, and is not either to save or to destroy slavery. If I could save the Union without freeing any slave, I would do it; and if I could save it by freeing all the slaves, I would do it; and if I could save it by freeing some and leaving others alone, I would also do that. What I do about slavery and the colored race, I do because I believe it helps to save the Union; and what I forbear, I forbear because I do not believe it would help to save the Union. . . .

I have here stated my purpose according to my view of

official duty; and I intend no modification of my oft-expressed personal wish that all men everywhere could be free.

Antislavery folk did not like the calculated restraint of this famous letter. They wanted no such even balance between action and forbearance. They wanted a crusade. One of them sarcastically wrote: "From his policy hitherto, we must infer, that the way he applies it is, to *save the Union with Slavery, if he can do it at whatever sacrifice of life & treasure.* If that is found impossible . . . [his policy is] *to save the Union without slavery,* unless it should be . . . too late. This is like the duel in which the terms . . . as prescribed by the challenged party were, that they should have but one sword between them, & that he should use it five minutes, & afterward the challenger should have it five minutes."

Such complaints, many of them, Lincoln had to endure while all the time he was awaiting the appropriate public opportunity for launching the proclamation on which he had determined. To supply this much-to-be-desired opportunity rested with McClellan and his men. Major Union victories were not so frequent in '62; if McClellan had not checked Lee at Antietam, Lincoln's proclamation, withheld in hope of Federal triumph, would have been indefinitely delayed. From the day (July 22, 1862) when Lincoln put the famous paper aside on Seward's suggestion that it be not a shriek on the retreat, no important triumph for the United States came, except for Antietam, until July 1863. One appreciates the timeliness of this achievement by the much abused McClellan when one tries to speculate just where Lincoln and emancipation would have stood had the story of McClellan in Maryland been of a piece with that of Pope, Burnside, or Hooker.

It was in this very period of waiting for a victory that there came the word of Pope's disaster at Second Bull Run. "Things looked darker than ever." McClellan was grudgingly reinstated. Further anxious days passed. On Wednesday, September 17,

Antietam was fought. Lincoln, according to his own account, was then staying at the Soldiers' Home outside Washington. Here, determining to wait no longer, he finished the "second draft of the preliminary proclamation"; coming in on Saturday, he summoned his Cabinet for Monday.

If contrary to custom there had been an observer at the President's cabinet meeting at the White House beginning at noon of Monday, September 22, 1862, he would have seen all the members in attendance. An important announcement was to come, but it was preceded by a trivial thing, frozen into recorded history as trivial things sometimes are, the better to enable posterity to visualize the human aspects of a significant historic moment. Ready to enter upon the agenda, the Cabinet secretaries, whose formalized visages have been preserved on Carpenter's mammoth canvas, had first to give attention to something that was the antithesis of formal; Lincoln had an Artemus Ward book, sent him by the humorist, and he proposed "to read a chapter which he thought very funny." The "High handed Outrage at Utica" was the selected passage. Lincoln read it "and seemed to enjoy it very much." We are told that the "Heads" also enjoyed it, though Stanton, and (as the context shows) Chase, who recorded the trivial event, were exceptions. One can only picture them sitting with dour faces while the President sought to enliven a serious occasion with the leaven of humor.

Assuming a "graver tone," the President made a statement. He had thought a great deal about the relation of the war to slavery. Ever since the former meeting when he had read an order on the subject, it had occupied his mind; now had arrived "the time for acting." He had determined, as soon as the enemy had been driven out of Maryland, to "issue a Proclamation of Emancipation." He had made the promise to himself and to his Maker; now he proposed to fulfill that promise. On the main matter he was not seeking counsel, his mind was made up; as to the expressions he used, or as to minor matters, he

would be glad to have suggestions. He had one other observation to make. It pertained to himself as leader. He said:

> . . . I know very well that many others might . . . do
> better than I can; and if I were satisfied that the public con-
> fidence was more fully possessed by any one of them than by
> me, and knew of any Constitutional way in which he could be
> put in my place, he should have it. I would gladly yield it to
> him. But though I believe that I have not so much of the con-
> fidence of the people as I had some time since, I do not know
> that . . . any other person has more; and, however this may
> be, there is no way in which I can have any other man put
> where I am. I am here. I must do the best I can, and bear the
> responsibility of taking the course which I feel I ought to take.

Evidence is lacking on which to follow all the implications
of this idea of Lincoln's that he would gladly yield his office
to another if that procedure were possible and were demonstrably in the public interest. It is clear that the whole subject
of his relation to his high office, and the nature of his own personal responsibility to make and enforce a decision, had been
traversed in his deliberations on the emancipation question.
If these deliberations had given him humility, and a sense of
association with Divine purpose (which was more than once
indicated), they had also given executive confidence. In reaching his important decision there is ample reason to believe that
Lincoln had not only endured anxious hours, but had undergone a significant inner experience from which he emerged
with quiet serenity.

The President read the proclamation through with running
comments. In the Cabinet discussion that followed Chase
agreed to take the document as written, though he would have
charted a somewhat different course; Seward wanted it definitely stated that the government would maintain the freedom
proclaimed; only Blair offered a substantial criticism. This was

not an objection to emancipation *per se;* the party-minded secretary, whose position in the postal portfolio was peculiarly associated with "politics," was thinking of the coming elections; he feared the effect of the proclamation in the border area, and stated his apprehensions "at some length."

VI

Of the stereotypes concerning Lincoln one of the most unhistorical is the stock picture of the Emancipator sitting in the White House and suddenly striking the shackles from millions of bondmen at a stroke of the presidential pen. The fact is that Lincoln issued his proclamation and nothing happened in the immediate or prompt freeing of slaves by virtue thereof. The September (1862) proclamation was only a warning and a prediction, while the January (1863) proclamation had the curious feature of making declarations which applied only to areas where Lincoln's arm could not reach. With occupied portions of Louisiana and Virginia, as well as the whole state of Tennessee, excepted, the only regions to which the proclamation extended were those in which the Confederacy was still in control. The measure did not touch slavery in Kentucky, Maryland, Delaware, or Missouri, these being slave states adhering to the Union. Though such a situation was most unlikely, any other slave state could have avoided its emancipatory effect by return to Union allegiance.

President Lincoln, with his proclamations, actually did not go so far as Congress already had gone in the second confiscation act, but he did assert and dramatize the antislavery policy of his own administration. Though in itself even the final proclamation did not free a single slave, it appealed to slaves who heard of it and thus brought thousands within the Union lines, where they were freed according to existing laws. How it operated Lincoln was reminded when, on January 1, 1864, the first anniversary of the proclamation, General R. H. Milroy wrote to him about the use he had made of it in the Shenandoah Valley. First, Milroy announced it to his men, who cheered and sang "We are coming, Father Abraham" and "John Brown's Body" to the accompaniment of the regimental band. Then he posted and distributed over the countryside a handbill, headed in large type "Freedom to Slaves," which contained a summary of the Proclamation and commanded obedience to it. "That hand-bill order," Milroy now told Lincoln, "gave Freedom to the slaves through and around the region where Old John Brown was hung."

Lincoln himself acted in a manner somewhat reminiscent of John Brown when, in August, 1864, he invited the former slave Frederick Douglass to the White House to discuss ways of encouraging slaves to heed the call to freedom. Lincoln suggested to Douglass that he organize a kind of government-sponsored Underground Railroad. Soon afterward Douglass reported back to Lincoln: ". . . I have freely conversed with several trustworthy and Patriotic colored men concerning your suggestion that something should be speedily done to inform the slaves in the Rebel States of the true state of affairs in relation to them." Douglass outlined a plan according to which Lincoln would appoint a number of Negroes as "agents," with a "general agent" over them, to circulate in the South, talk to slaves, and persuade them to cross the line into Union-held territory. But Lincoln soon lost interest in the plan. He had proposed it in the middle of the dark August when his re-election seemed unlikely. After the clouds lifted, he concentrated on other and more effective ways of extending and confirming the work of emancipation.

He still hoped to see it carried on by the slaveholding states themselves. West Virginia had been admitted to the Union in 1863 with a gradual-emancipation clause in its constitution. In those states being "restored" under Lincoln's ten per cent plan, slavery was duly abolished with the adoption of new constitutions—in Arkansas, March 1864; in Louisiana, September, 1864; and in Tennessee, February, 1865. He kept watching the border states and encouraging them to act upon his proposal of 1862 for gradual and compensated emancipation, but he ceased to insist upon either compensation or gradualness. "I am very anxious for emancipation to be effected in Maryland in some substantial form," he wrote to Representative A. J. Creswell on March 7, 1864. "I think it probable that my expressions of a preference for *gradual* over *immediate* emancipation, are misunderstood." He had thought "the *gradual*" would produce less confusion and destruction, but if those who knew best preferred "the *immediate*," he would have no objection to it. The important thing was that all favoring emancipation "*in any form*" should co-operate with one another and not delay or jeopardize the movement by bickering among themselves. After the Republican victory of 1864 Maryland did act, merely repealing the slave code, an ordinary law, on which slavery had been based in that state. On January 11, 1865, Missouri also acted, abolishing slavery by means of a special ordinance passed by a state convention. But Delaware, though within its boundaries in 1865 there were about 20,000 free Negroes and fewer than 2,000 slaves, refused to let these people go. And Kentucky also clung to slavery.

For all that the President, the Congress, and the states had done, the great majority of those who had been slaves in early 1861 remained in bondage at the beginning of 1865. Their future status was uncertain and, indeed, so was the future status of those who were already exercising their freedom. The emancipation proclamation was based avowedly on the President's war powers; once the war was over, its claim to legality would disappear. The various emancipatory acts of Congress were yet to be tested in the courts; though the antislavery champion Salmon P. Chase was now Chief Justice, the constitutional validity of the laws was not absolutely certain. Moreover, these laws conflicted with those of some of the states, and a man claiming freedom under the former might have difficulty in asserting his claim as against the latter. In Kentucky, for example, various state judges held that the Federal law giving freedom to the families of slave-soldiers was unconstitutional, and white employers hiring such person were prosecuted in the state courts for the offense of harboring slaves. If, when the nation was reunited, slavery were to be permanently and unquestionably abolished everywhere in the United States, abolition would have to be written into the Federal Constitution.

VII

Lincoln did all he could to make the antislavery amendment a campaign issue in the election of 1864. From the outset he intended to run on a platform favoring the proposition. In June he called to the Executive Mansion the chairman of the National Republican Committee, Senator E. D. Morgan, and gave him instructions for his speech opening the Baltimore convention. "Senator Morgan," he is reported to have said, "I want you to mention in your speech when you call the convention to order, as its key note, and to put into the platform as the key-stone, the amendment of the Constitution abolishing and prohibiting slavery forever." At Baltimore Senator Morgan did as the President wished him to do, and the delegates responded in adopting the third plank of the party platform, which stated the prevailing Republican view that slavery was the cause of the rebellion and added that the President's proclamations had aimed "a death blow at this gigantic evil" but that a constitutional amendment was necessary to "terminate and forever prohibit" it. In his statements which were used during the ensuing campaign, Lincoln stressed the indispensability of an antislavery policy as a means of winning the war.

On this point, rather than the issue of Union or of peace, he differed most sharply with the rival candidate, McClellan.

When Lincoln was overwhelmingly re-elected, he therefore was justified in feeling that his antislavery program had the sanction of the popular will. When along with him, so many Republican candidates for Congress also were elected that the party would control more than the needed two-thirds majority in the next House of Representatives, he could look forward confidently to the ultimate conversion of the popular will into a constitutional amendment. But the newly elected Congress, the Thirty-Ninth, would not meet in the usual course of events for over a year, that is, not until December, 1865. The President could call a special session of the new Congress to meet at any time after his own re-inauguration on March 4, and he was prepared to do so if the old Congress, the Thirty-Eighth, should fail to act at its last regular session (1864–65). This Congress contained, in the House, the same sizeable minority of Democrats who previously had blocked the passage of the resolution which the Senate had passed. Many of these Democrats now were lame ducks. Lincoln was eager to get the work done, and he counted on enough lame-duck support to get it done before he finished his first term. He stated his views on the subject in his message to the Thirty-Eighth Congress when it met for its final session in December, 1864:

At the last session of Congress a proposed amendment of the Constitution abolishing slavery throughout the United States, passed the Senate, but failed for lack of the requisite two-thirds vote in the House of Representatives. Although the present is the same Congress, and nearly the same members, and without questioning the wisdom or patriotism of those who stood in opposition, I venture to recommend the reconsideration and passage of the measure at the present session. Of course the abstract question is not changed; but an intervening election shows, almost certainly, that the next Congress will pass the measure if this does not. Hence there is only a question of *time* as to when the proposed amendment will go to the States for their action. And as it is to so go, at all events, may we not agree that the sooner the better? It is not claimed that the election has imposed a duty on members to change their views or their votes, any further than, as an additional element to be considered, their judgment may be affected by it. It is the voice of the people now, for the first time, heard upon the question. In a great national crisis, like ours, unanimity of action among those seeking a common end is very desirable—almost indispensable. And yet no approach to such unanimity is attainable, unless some deference shall be paid to the will of the majority, simply because it is the will of the majority. In this case the common end is the maintenance of the Union; and, among the means to secure that end, such will, through the election, is most clearly declared in favor of such constitutional amendment.

Here the President was appealing to the Democratic members of the current Congress, and especially to the numerous lame ducks among them. Other Republicans besides the President were thinking of the possibility of winning over some of the opposition and thus passing the proposal soon, during the winter of 1864–65. "The majority against it in the House was I think *eleven*," a correspondent advised Senator Sumner, "& in view of the feeling of the people, as evidenced by the Presidential vote, I think that a sufficient number of Democrats might be brought over without difficulty to carry it thro at once without waiting for the new Congress." Lincoln did not leave it to his party leaders in Congress to persuade these Democrats to change their votes. He invited a number of them individually to the White House for informal interviews in January, 1865.

One of those he interviewed was James S. Rollins, a representative from the strongest slave district in Missouri and himself one of the largest slaveowners in his county, who had voted against the amendment in the previous session but who had not been re-elected to Congress. Lincoln said to him (as Rollins afterward reported the conversation): "You and I were old whigs, both of us followers of that great statesman, Henry Clay, and I tell you I never had an opinion upon the subject of slavery in my life that I did not get from him. I am very anxious that the war should be brought to a close at the earliest possible date, and I don't believe this can be accomplished as long as those fellows down South can rely upon the border states to help them; but if the members from the border states would unite, at least enough of them to pass the thirteenth amendment to the Constitution, they would soon see that they could not expect much help from that quarter, and be willing to give up their opposition and quit their war upon the government; this is my chief hope and main reliance to bring the war to a speedy close, and I have sent for you as an old whig friend to come and see me, that I might make an appeal to you to vote for this amendment." Rollins replied that he already had made up his mind to vote for it. Lincoln then asked him to see and talk with other members of the Missouri delegation, and Rollins cheerfully agreed to do so.

Possibly, in talking with some of the Democratic holdovers in the House, Lincoln used the more substantial argument of patronage. At least one of the Democrats who changed their votes—Moses F. Odell, of New York—went into a Federal job as navy agent in New York City after leaving Congress at the end of the session in 1865. Representative George W. Julian, Republican from Indiana, may have had patronage deals in mind when he wrote, enigmatically, that the success of the measure "depended upon certain negotiations the result of which was not fully assured, and the particulars of which never reached the public."

VIII

On January 31, 1865, the proposal for the Thirteenth Amendment came to a final vote in the House. As the clerk came to the names of the Democrats who the previous session had voted *nay,* and one after another several of them—Baldwin, Coffroth, McAllister, English, Ganson—now voted *aye,* the crowded galleries burst out with repeated and growing applause, and many of the Republicans on the floor joined in it. All together, thirteen Democrats this day voted in favor of the amendment, besides the four who also had voted for it previously. The resolution carried with more than the necessary two-thirds majority. When Speaker Colfax announced the result, renewed and intensified cheering was heard, and parliamentary order was forgotten. The House quickly adjourned for the day. Outside, cannons boomed.

From Capitol Hill, Representative Arnold with a group of Lincoln's personal friends went at once to the White House to exchange congratulations with the President. "The passage of the resolution filled his heart with joy," Arnold later recalled. "He saw in it the complete consummation of his own work, the emancipation proclamation."

The next day, February 1, 1865, when the resolution was brought to him for his signature, Lincoln signed it, as seemed perfectly natural for him to do. He, along with Speaker Colfax and Vice President Hamlin, had forgotten that the President need not sign a resolution of that kind. On second thought the Senate resolved that "such approval was unnecessary," since the Supreme Court had decided in a case arising in 1798 that the President had "nothing to do" with either the proposal or the adoption of constitutional amendments. Only in a technical sense, however, did Lincoln have nothing to do with this one.

The crowd who, on the evening of the day he signed the resolution, marched to the White House to felicitate him, certainly thought that he had had something to do with it. He had done what he could to eradicate slavery by issuing his proclamation, he told the marchers, but the proclamation "did not meet the evil," or so its critics might maintain. "But this amendment is a King's cure for all the evils. It winds the whole thing up." He could not help congratulating everyone in the crowd, himself, the country, and the whole world upon this "great moral victory."

As the news spread, the old abolitionists were among the most enthusiastic of all who rejoiced throughout the North. To them the President long had seemed timid and ineffectual in dealing with slavery. Now, at last, they could give him unstinted and wholehearted praise. "And to whom is the country more immediately indebted for this vital and saving amendment of the Constitution than, perhaps to any other man?" So William Lloyd Garrison asked in the course of a speech to a meeting of celebrators in Boston. "I believe I may confidently answer," he went on, "—to the humble railsplitter of Illinois— to the Presidential chainbreaker for millions of the oppressed— to Abraham Lincoln!"

"The great job is ended," Lincoln himself declared. That is, the first great obstacle had been overcome. "But," as he told the serenaders on February 1, "there is a task yet before us— to go forward and consummate by the votes of the States that which Congress so nobly began yesterday." He was proud to inform the crowd that his own state of Illinois, this very day, had led off by ratifying the amendment. And Maryland was "about half through."

IX

It would be an oversimplification to say that the Thirteenth Amendment made freemen out of slaves, or even that it was intended to do so. The amendment grew out of a variety of motives, as Henry Wilson said. Some who favored it were motivated by a sense of "religious obligation" or by "humane considerations," but others by "feelings of resentment" against slaveholders, whom they blamed for starting the war. The largest number were moved by "prudential considerations merely," Wilson believed (and, though Wilson did not say so, Lincoln himself was moved by such considerations mainly). "They accepted emancipation not so much from any heart-felt conversion to the doctrine of anti-slavery as from the conviction that the removal of slavery had become a military, if not a political, necessity." The "foul spirit of caste" still "lurked within the hearts of many" who applauded the progress of emancipation. So long as the former slaves suffered from the prejudice of the white community, they would not be free *men* but only free *Negroes*.

The Negroes freed during the war, like those already free when the war began, had to make their way against serious handicaps, whether as soldiers or as civilians and whether as residents of the North or of the South. The plight of the new freedmen was sometimes desperate. Before the end of 1863 fifty thousand of them, mostly women and children, were adrift in the lower Mississippi Valley, with little shelter and practically no food, except occasional army rations of crackers and dried beef. "At present, hundreds of the blacks would gladly return to slavery, to avoid the hardships of freedom," Lincoln was informed. Even the most fortunate of the freedmen faced hardships and dangers to which white men were immune.

1860 and 1865

The 1860 profile by Hesler, taken shortly after Lincoln's first nomination, is shown in contrast to a photograph by Gardner, one of several taken a few days before the assassination. The later face, wrote John Hay, had "a look as of one on whom sorrow and care had done their worst without victory."

Negro soldiers ran an added risk (if captured, they could not count upon the usual protection of the laws of war) and Negro laborers in the army were paid, at first, according to their color and not according to their work. Even Negroes born free and living in the so-called free states lacked many of the privileges ordinarily associated with freedom. They could not enter certain occupations, they could not always travel without restriction, and they could not vote or hold office in most of the states, including Illinois.

Before the end of the war the free Negroes and their white friends began a campaign in the state legislatures and in Congress to free the colored population from discriminatory laws. Most of the anti-Negro legislation of Illinois (but not the restriction of suffrage to the whites) was repealed early in 1865. At about the same time Congress passed and the President signed a bill setting up the Freedmen's Bureau to care for refugees. Senator Sumner, who had got Negroes admitted to practice in the Federal courts, tried to obtain for them the privilege of riding on the Washington street cars. Representative Stevens began to talk of confiscating Southern estates and dividing them among the freedmen—"forty acres and a mule" to each family head. The Fourteenth Amendment, presumably designed to protect Negroes in their civil rights, and the Fifteenth Amendment, to guarantee their right to vote, were to be adopted in the early postwar years. These were only the beginning steps in an undertaking which, nearly a century later, was still to fall short of complete success.

The Negro's advancement was hindered less by laws or the absence of laws than by popular attitudes—the "foul spirit of caste," as Henry Wilson called it. Lincoln himself had yielded to this spirit when, in 1862, he urged the resettlement of freed Negroes in foreign lands, with the argument that the white and black races could not be expected to live together in harmony within the United States. While some Negro leaders approved the idea of colonizing their people outside the country, others denounced it, and one wrote impertinently to the President: "Pray tell us is our right to a home in this country less than your own?" Lincoln not only ceased to press the colonization idea but also proceeded to give repeated demonstrations that, whether or not Negroes and whites could mingle harmoniously in the country at large, they could certainly do so within his own official home.

He opened the White House to colored visitors as no President had done before, and he received them in a spirit which no President has matched since. At his New Year's Day reception in 1864 "four colored men, of genteel exterior and with the manners of gentlemen, joined in the throng that crowded the Executive Mansion, and were presented to the President of the United States," as the Washington *Morning Chronicle* reported the unprecedented news. There was no scene. "We are neither amalgamationists nor advocates of the leveling of all social distinctions," the *Chronicle* commented; "but we rejoice that we have a President who is a democrat by fact as well as by nature." On the Fourth of July that same year Lincoln gave permission to the colored schools of the District of Columbia to hold a celebration on the White House grounds, and on August 6 he allowed Negroes to assemble on the grounds in day-long ceremonies observing the national day of humiliation and prayer which he had ordained. In these and other ways he set an example of tolerance for all his fellow countrymen.

Lincoln invited and welcomed prominent individual Negroes. Frederick Douglass met him several times at the Soldiers' Home and paid at least three calls at the White House. He made his last visit as a guest at the reception on the night of the second inauguration. As he approached the door that night he was seized by two policemen and forbidden to enter, but managed to bolt past them. On the inside two other policemen took hold of him. He thought they were going to lead him to the President; instead, they led him out through a window on a plank. At the door again, he appealed to a guest going in to tell Lincoln he was there. In a moment he was invited into the East Room. There, in the presence of an elegant company of ladies and gentlemen, Lincoln said in a voice heard all round: "Here comes my friend Douglass." He shook hands cordially with him and immediately engaged him in conversation. Afterwards Douglass recalled:

"In all my interviews with Mr. Lincoln I was impressed with his entire freedom from popular prejudice against the colored race. He was the first great man that I talked with in the United States freely, who in no single instance reminded me of the difference between himself and myself, of the difference of color, and I thought that all the more remarkable because he came from a state where there were black laws."

Another former slave, the remarkable Sojourner Truth, had a friendly and unstrained conversation with Lincoln when she dropped in to see him, October 20, 1864. He obliged her by signing his name in her autograph book, for "Aunty Sojourner Truth," as he wrote. When a delegation of Negro Baptist clergymen sought an appointment with him, he had them shown in and nodded his head in assent as they requested permission to preach to colored soldiers. He gave hearty encouragement to another Negro preacher who wished to send missionaries among the escaping slaves, the "contrabands." Numbers of other colored people also came to him, and all went away gratified at their cordial and respectful treatment.

He did more than send his Negro supplicants away with kind words. When a thousand New Orleans Negroes sent a two-man delegation to Washington (in January, 1864) he responded by assigning James A. McKaye, of the American Freedmen's Inquiry Commission, to look into their needs and wants. McKaye went to New Orleans, attended a colored mass meeting, and learned that they desired public schools, recognition as human beings, and the abolition of the black codes. Lincoln, apparently impressed by the behavior of the Louisiana Negroes, was willing to grant them a little more than they demanded. In March he sent a private letter to Michael Hahn, congratulating him on his inauguration as the first free-State governor of Louisiana, and adding: "Now you are about to have a convention, which, among other things, will probably define the elective franchise. I barely suggest to your private consideration, whether some of the colored people may not be let in— as, for instance, the very intelligent, and especially those who fought gallantly in our ranks. They would probably help, in some trying time to come, to keep the jewel of liberty within the family of freedom."

In the presence of his Negro visitors Lincoln was careful not to use expressions or tell stories which might offend them. In the presence of white men approaching him in the Negro's behalf he was not always so careful, but he was equally responsive to their appeals. "Sometime during the year 1864," according to a memoir left by Henry Samuels, several representatives of the Committee for Recruiting Colored Troops were ushered into the President's private room by Secretary Stanton. "The President was seated at his desk with his long legs on the top of it, his hands on his head and looking exactly like a huge katydid or grass-hopper." He quietly listened until his petitioners had finished, then "turned his head and jocularly said, with one of those peculiar smiles of his": "Well, gentlemen, you wish the pay of 'Cuffie' raised." The youthfully brash and earnest Samuels objected: "Excuse me, Mr. Lincoln, the term 'Cuffie' is not in our vernacular. What we want is that the wages of the American Colored Laborer be equalized with those of the American White Laborer." Lincoln replied: "I stand corrected, young man, but you know I am by birth a Southerner and in our section that term is applied without any idea of an offensive nature. I will, however, at the earliest possible moment do all in my power to accede to your request." About a month later the war department issued an order requiring that Negro teamsters and other laborers employed by the army be paid at the same rate as white men doing the same kinds of work.

Though relatively few Negroes ever saw Lincoln, and still fewer talked with him, Negroes everywhere came to think of him as their friend. They were not backward in expressing their regard for him. The colored people of Baltimore, to show their appreciation of the "distinguished services of President Lincoln in the cause of human freedom," contributed $580.75 to have a copy of the Bible bound in purple velvet, mounted in gold, engraved with a representation of Lincoln striking the shackles from a slave, and enclosed in a walnut case lined with white silk. This imposing volume they presented to the President at the White House in September, 1864. "I can only say now, as I have often said before, it has always been a sentiment with me that all mankind should be free," Lincoln remarked, in thanking the colored delegation. "In regard to the great book, I can only say it is the best gift which God has ever given man." The action of the Baltimore colored people, he told Frank B. Carpenter, gave him more real satisfaction than any other public testimonial he ever received.

In the mail that came to Lincoln from colored correspondents, no letter was more touching than the one signed "don carlous Butler," on St. Helena Island, off the coast of South Carolina, who begged the President to see that his plot of ground, with his improvements on it, was not taken away from him. Don Carlos dictated the letter to Laura Towne, a devoted teacher of the freedmen, and she added a postscript. She said that he had formerly been a confidential servant in the famous Alston family (he had been acquainted with Theodosia Burr Alston before her mysterious disappearance at sea in 1812) and explained that he could read and write but was too old to do it with ease. "He, with others of the Freedmen, often expresses a wish to be able to speak to Massa Linkum, feeling that *he* will listen to their plea for land & do what is best for them."

Lincoln, dead, was nearly deified by many Negroes. "There were no truer mourners, when all were sad, than the poor colored people who crowded the streets, joined the procession, and exhibited their woe, bewailing the loss of him whom they regarded as a benefactor and father." So wrote Secretary Welles, after the funeral ceremonies in Washington. And many years later a Negro historian wrote: "The deep, nation-wide grief of the Negroes was an outward sign that their generation would hold the name of the martyred President in everlasting remembrance. The colored people beheld in Lincoln a father image; he was 'the chieftest of ten thousand, and altogether lovely.' His death burdened every black with a personal sense of loss. . . ."

Chapter Sixteen

GOD'S MAN

I

AT FIFTY-SIX LINCOLN HAD NOT YET ARRIVED AT THE FULL DEVEL-
opment and use of his personal powers. Such was Herndon's
firm belief, and while many of Herndon's judgments must be
discounted, there is little reason for doubting this one. Certainly, as the President entered upon his second term, he still
possessed a sturdy and resilient physical constitution, one
capable of withstanding the cares of his office and recovering
from the shocks of ordinary disease.

Not long after returning from Gettysburg to Washington
(November 1863) he became ill. The disease was reported as
varioloid, a mild form of smallpox. The illness came at the
Thanksgiving season, and at a time when the President was
heavily engaged in preparing his important annual message to
Congress with its accompanying proclamation. People wondered about the disease, about which they were not well informed, and whether the President could die of it. There had
been, as Stoddard later explained, slight thought of the President's health. Assassination fears were so familiar as to be
"worn out," but another possible cause of death had hardly
been contemplated. The White House was under a kind of
half-quarantine, resulting not only in an unwonted loneliness,

but in public apprehension. It was feared that Hamlin "could not step into Mr. Lincoln's shoes, and something of inestimable value would be lost to the country, even if Mr. Hamlin were twice as large a man as he is believed to be." It was characteristic of the clamor for office and public favors that "something like engineering" was required to protect the sick President from intruders. One of them, thought Stoddard, may have been thinking that "Lincoln could appoint him to-day and die to-morrow." The President continued to attend to official business in spite of his irritating illness. He even made it a subject of jest, suggesting the advantage of scaring office seekers by the statement that he had the smallpox, and wishing that his office might be in one of the smallpox hospitals, then reflecting on further thought that this would give him no relief. "They'd all go and get vaccinated, and they'd come buzzing back. . . ."

A week or so after his re-inauguration (March 1865) he stayed in bed for a few days, refusing to see visitors, while it was reported on the one hand that he had "no serious illness" but was "only suffering from the exhausting attentions of office hunters" and, on the other hand, that his case had been diagnosed as a "severe attack of influenza." Even after he had improved enough to receive "hosts of visitors," and then to go out with Mrs. Lincoln to a German opera, he remained rather feeble for several days. When he left Washington for his two weeks' stay at City Point, he was seeking to escape the bothersome jobseekers and to rest and convalesce, as well as to oversee the closing of the war. He returned to the White House with renewed vigor and buoyant spirits. At his final cabinet meeting he looked better than ever, at least to Secretary Speed, who remembered vividly his "shaved face well brushed clothing and neatly combed hair and whiskers."

If Lincoln's physical capacity for further accomplishment was great, his mental and spiritual capacities seemed even more so. Mentally, he had grown to a remarkable extent since first becoming President. As the London *Spectator* said (March

25, 1865), comparing his debates against Douglas and the second inaugural, to "apprehend truly the character of Mr. Lincoln" one should notice the tremendous "growth of his mind." Spiritually, as Herndon afterwards observed, Lincoln "grandly rose up" year after year. No doubt the circumstances of his untimely death contributed to his later apotheosis, yet his fame might possibly have had an even more substantial foundation in true greatness if he had lived at least another four years.

II

The heroic image of Lincoln, so familiar to later generations, was not entirely a by-product of his martyrdom. While yet alive he became one of the most admired and best loved Americans of all time—a rival of George Washington for the place of first in the hearts of his countrymen, though there was then no such consensus as was afterwards to give him a clear priority over Washington.

The living Lincoln seemed a hero most of all to the Negroes who hailed him as their deliverer and, among the white people of the North, to women and children. Miss Sarah B. Howell, of Trenton, New Jersey, requesting a lock of his hair "to be woven into a bouquet for the 'Sanitary Fair,'" told him in June, 1864, "no other President has come so near our hearts." Other women sent him even more touching letters. "I only wish to thank you for being so good—and to say how sorry we all are that you must have four years more of this terrible toil," Miss Mary A. Dodge wrote him from Hamilton, Massachusetts, on the day of his second inauguration. "You can't tell anything about it in Washington where they make a noise on the slightest provocation. But if you had been in this little speck of a village this morning and heard the soft, sweet music of unseen bells rippling through the morning silence from every quarter of the far-off horizon, you would have better known what your name is to this nation." Doubtless many children shared the aspiration of Governor Thomas H. Hicks' little son who was "anxious to see" the President and shake hands with him, as Hicks explained in the note he sent along with his servant who, on a May day in 1864, took the boy into the White House.

The living Lincoln seemed a great man also to certain contemporary journalists. Some of these had partisan motives for praising him, no doubt; but others, writing for English publications, viewed him with relative detachment. And, whether English or American, these observers analyzed the elements of greatness in his character as perceptively as any historian or biographer afterwards could do.

An editorial in Henry J. Raymond's New York *Times*, endorsed and reprinted in John W. Forney's Washington *Chronicle*, described Lincoln in the summer of 1863 as resembling Washington in "perfect balance of thoroughly sound faculties," "sure judgment," and "great calmness of temper, great firmness of purpose, supreme moral principle, and intense patriotism." An editorial in the Buffalo *Express*, about a year later, noted Lincoln's "remarkable moderation and freedom from passionate bitterness," then went on to say: "We do not believe Washington himself was less indifferent to the exercise of power for power's sake. Though concentrating in his hands a more despotic authority, in many respects, than had Napoleon, he has never used it for his personal ends, and we believe the verdict of history will be that he has far less frequently abused it than he has failed to use it as terror to evil-doers despite the clamor about arbitrary arrests." The *Spectator* of London, in March, 1865, commented that Lincoln's task was lighter than Washington's but Lincoln had had to meet it without the advantages of Washington's education and experience. Lincoln was great because of his growth to meet his responsibilities. He had outgrown "the rude and illiterate mould of a village lawyer's thought" and had attained "a grasp of principle, a dignity of manner, and a solemnity of purpose, which would have been unworthy neither of Hampden nor of Cromwell," and he had acquired a "gentleness and generosity of feeling toward his foes" which one would hardly have expected from either Cromwell or Hampden. The *Times* of London at about the same time observed that Lincoln, "placed in the most important position to which a statesman can aspire, invested with a power greater than that of most monarchs," fulfilled his duties "with firmness and conscientiousness, but without any feeling of exhiliration."

The Liverpool *Post* (October 1, 1863) believed that, to judge from external appearances, "no leader in a great contest ever stood so little chance of being a subject of hero worship as Abraham Lincoln," with his long legs and long pantaloons, his shambling figure and his general awkwardness, which made him an easy target for caricature and ridicule. "Yet a worshiper of human heroes might possibly travel a great deal farther and fare much worse for an idol than selecting this same lanky American," the Liverpool *Post* continued. His inner traits—his truthfulness, resolution, insight, faithfulness, and courage, together with his equanimity, which was such that none of the bitter personal attacks upon him had ever "drawn from him an explanation of ill humor, or even an impudent rejoinder"— all these qualities would "go a long way to make up a hero," whatever his outward appearance.

III

The concept of Lincoln the hero was inverted in the minds of many of his contemporaries, Northerners as well as Southerners, who thought him no hero but a villain whose death would be a good riddance. A number of them took the trouble to tell him so. One, who signed himself "Joseph," wrote (January 4, 1864): "The same who warned you of a conspiracy, Novr. 18th 1862, is now compelled to inform you, that,—'Your days are numbered,' you have been weighed in the balance & found wanting. You shall be a dead man in six months from date Dec. 31st, 1863." Assassination threats appeared not only in the privacy of crank letters but also in some of the public prints, such as the LaCrosse, Wisconsin, *Democrat*, which avowed during the campaign of 1864: "If Abraham Lincoln should be re-elected for another term of four years of such wretched administration, *we hope that a bold hand will be found to plunge the dagger into the Tyrant's heart for the public welfare.*" To kidnap or kill the President would be easy, the New York *Tribune* cautioned. A band of rebels or rebel sympathizers might fall upon him at home, on the way to church, on one of his visits to the front.

There were incidents when the danger to the President's life was shown to be real enough. In April 1862, on his return from the Navy Yard, there was a minor accident in which horses drawing the President's carriage became unmanageable, creating alarm and compelling a change of carriage. Lincoln was unhurt. One August night, as the record has come down to us, a shot was fired as the President, riding horseback alone, approached the Soldiers' Home. A startled horse, we are told, tore into the grounds bearing a hatless President. A guard, on investigation, found the Chief's tall silk hat with a *"bullet-hole* through the crown."

According to the recollection of Ward Lamon, this incident was told by Lincoln himself, but with an air of playful levity and without any apprehension that it involved danger to himself. He made it an amusing joke as he told how his horse, "Old Abe," his "erratic namesake," made a reckless bound and, as he put it, "separated me from my eight-dollar plug-hat, with which I parted company without . . . assent. . . ." The President seemed unwilling to attach any importance to the

affair. He concluded that the shot "was the result of an accident." Dismissing that aspect of the matter, he went on to compare Old Abe's performance with the "historic ride of John
Gilpin, and [Senator] Henry Wilson's . . . equestrianship on
the stray army mule from the . . . battle of Bull Run." In the
delayed Lamon version we have Lincoln's further comment: "I
can truthfully say that one of the Abes was frightened on this
occasion, but modesty forbids my mentioning which of us is
entitled to that distinguished honor." The President went on to
make it clear that he wanted no publicity given to the event.
It seemed to Lamon that the Chief Executive sometimes "acted
an unnatural part" in order to forget the agonizing loss of his
son Willie.

When in February 1865 certain Union officers were captured by a guerrilla band at Cumberland, Maryland, Thomas
Ewing wrote to Stanton: "I am surprised that it was not the
President and yourself [that were captured] in Washington.
The President could be seized any reception evening, in the
midst of the masses assembled round him, and carried off by
fifty determined men armed with bowie knives and revolvers,
and once out could be put into a market wagon guarded by a
dozen horsemen, and borne off at will,—the conspirators having
first set a dozen or twenty hacks in motion to distract attention
—look out for some such dash soon."

No such dash came, but a story of another kind of assassination plot made news a few weeks later. Raving and cursing in
the Washington jail, Thomas Clements boasted that he and an
accomplice had made the trip from Alexandria to kill the President on inauguration day. Clements said they had arrived just
a half hour too late, and his Savior would never forgive him.
As for his motive, he explained that the President had robbed
him of a large amount of money.

Meanwhile John Wilkes Booth was busy with his secret
plotting and already had set a date for kidnapping the President.

The men around Lincoln, among them Stanton in particular, worried continually about his safety. Seldom was he allowed out of the sight of his personal bodyguard, Ward Hill Lamon, or of other guards, including details of cavalry or infantry and sometimes both. But the President was not inclined to co-operate with the custodians of his welfare, and he frequently disregarded Stanton's advice against exposing his life, as on his visits to Petersburg and Richmond at the end of the war. On April 4, 1865, a correspondent wrote to Lamon from Bloomington, Illinois: "I hope the President will keep out of danger . . . Mr. Lincoln's personal safety is of such vast importance to the country . . . that his friends feel more or less solicitous when they read of his 'going to the front.' But he has made a glorious trip this time."

When the President went about he did not want bodyguards to accompany him, and there was in that day no regular force of secret service men comparable to that of a later day. Once he wrote to Secretary Stanton: "On reflection I think it will not do as a rule for the Adjutant General to attend me wherever I go: not that I have any objection to his presence, but that it would be an uncompensating incumbrance both to him and me. When it shall occur to me to go anywhere, I wish to be free to go at once, and not to have to notify the Adjutant General, and wait till he can get ready." Lincoln added: "It is better too, for the public service, that he shall give his time to the business of his office, and not to personal attendance on me." The correspondence indicates that the suggestion had come from the secretary of war; one wonders, not at the proposal for guarding the President, but at Stanton's impractical suggestion that the adjutant general should be the official assigned to that duty.

Lincoln was not unprotected nor was the problem of his bodily safety ignored. But the guarding of the President was irregular, haphazard, and inefficient, and perhaps he preferred it so. This caused considerable worry, as shown by the advice of an anxious soul who wrote: "You are accustomed in riding out, to be escorted by a Body guard, and you invariably take a distance ahead; and generally any number of persons follow you, either in Vehicles, or Horseback, and your habit is, to frequently ride out to your Summer retreat Soldiers Home. . . . I cannot help, but warn you. If you value your life! *do* I entreat of you discontinue your visits out of the City. Unless, less conspicuously."

If this anonymous writer was concerned about the President's safety, what about his wife? It was a constant and painful worry to Mrs. Lincoln. She would insist that he have some protection—a cavalry guard, for example—as he went back and forth to or from the Soldiers' Home. (It appears that such protection was occasional rather than regular or invariable.) He would brush her off, though far from relieving her fears. "All imagination," he was quoted as saying. "What does any one want to harm me for? Don't worry about me, mother, as if I were a little child. . . ."

Early in the administration General Charles P. Stone, by his own report, took careful, though unostentatious, measures for the guarding of the Executive Mansion and grounds. He placed sentries in the shrubbery, put an armed guard in the basement, and put his guard in touch with Captain Lockwood Todd, cousin of Mrs. Lincoln. In addition to these precautions, service in guarding the President was done by a considerable number of alert volunteers, among whom were Cassius M. Clay and Jim (General James H.) Lane. These men, for a brief time, did nightly guard in the East Room. Part of the earlier arrangements included a cavalry guard at the White House gates, but Lincoln got rid of it. Sometimes he rode to and from the Soldiers' Home with a mounted escort. Frequently, however, he went about, even at night, "unguarded, and often alone, in his open carriage."

His own attitude seemed to vary with his moods. Sometimes he discounted the danger, saying that he did not share his friends' apprehension about his life. On the last day he was alive, when told there had been much uneasiness in the North during his Richmond visit, he cheerfully replied that he would have been alarmed, himself, if someone else had been President and had gone there, but in his own case he had not felt any peril whatsoever. In his more gloomy moments he confessed he did not expect to survive the Presidency. One evening, riding from the White House to the Soldiers' Home, he told an Illinois acquaintance that his cavalry escort had been more or less forced upon him by the military men, but he thought such an attempt at protection rather futile. "He said it seemed to him like putting up the gap in only one place when the fence was down all along." On another occasion a representative of the United States Sanitary Commission, who had walked freely through an unguarded door into the White House, ventured to protest to the President about the latter's lack of protection at a time when assassination was openly threatened. "Well," Lincoln answered, "you know that it is as well to have but one trouble of it. Assassination would be one, but continual dread would make two of it!"

No use in worrying. What is to be, must be. If anyone is really determined to kill me, I shall be killed. So Lincoln generally reacted to the thought of personal danger. His reaction was perfectly in keeping with his profoundly fatalistic outlook.

IV

Though Lincoln's fatalism grew and developed while he was in the White House, it was in itself nothing new with him, not a product of his presidential years. It may have derived from the predestinarian doctrines of his parents and of the Kentucky and Indiana communities in which he was reared.

Anyhow it was firmly fixed in his mind by the time he ran for Congress in 1846. In that election his opponent, the revivalist Peter Cartwright, "was whispering the charge of infidelity" against him, and he replied with a fairly forthright statement of his personal philosophy. Admitting he was no church member, but denying he was a scoffer, Lincoln said that "in early life" he had been "inclined to believe in" what was called the "Doctrine of Necessity"—the doctrine that the human mind was moved by some power over which it had no control. He added that, in the past, he sometimes had tried to maintain this doctrine by argument, though not in public, but for more than five years he had "entirely left off" his "habit of arguing." He did not say he had abandoned the belief itself: he only said he had quit arguing it.

The power that controlled the human mind and the human destiny might be called *God,* and Lincoln as a young man sometimes referred to it that way, though he did so apologetically, as when he wrote (in 1842) to his recently married friend Joshua F. Speed: ". . . I always was superstitious; and as part of my superstition, I believe God made me one of the instruments of bringing your Fanny and you together, which union, I have no doubt He had foreordained. Whatever he designs, he will do for *me* yet." Here was an expression of Lincoln's fatalistic philosophy with religious (or, as he said, "superstitious") overtones. God had designs. He foreordained events. He worked through human agents, and Lincoln on occasion was one of them.

Lincoln as President held to the same belief, but he held to it with a far deeper religious assurance and with an appropriately grander conception of his own role in the divine plan. He came to view the war as God's way of removing slavery and punishing the people, both North and South, for the sin that all shared on account of slavery. And he came to look upon himself, humbly, as God's man, God's human agent in the working out of His mysterious providence.

Lincoln's clearest expression of this religious, predestinarian interpretation of the war is found in his second inaugural. "If we shall suppose that American slavery is one of those offences which, in the providence of God, must needs come, but which, having continued through His appointed time, He now wills to remove, and that He gives to both North and South, this terrible war, as the woe due to those by whom the offence came, shall we discern therein any departure from those divine attributes which the believers in a Living God always ascribe to Him?" If Lincoln had said such things only on public occasions, his sincerity might be questioned, but he expressed similar ideas in private letters and conversations, and he did so with the ring of true conviction. "Men are not flattered by being shown that there has been a difference of purpose between the Almighty and them," he wrote to Thurlow Weed in response to the latter's congratulations upon the second inaugural. "To deny it, however, in this case, is to deny that there is a God governing the world. It is a truth which I thought needed to be told; and as whatever of humiliation there is in it, falls most directly on myself, I thought other might afford for me to tell it." Once he wrote to Eliza P. Gurney: "The purposes of the Almighty are perfect, and must prevail, though we erring mortals may fail to accurately perceive them in advance. We hoped for a happy termination of this terrible war before this; but God knows best, and has ruled otherwise." In conversation at the White House he spoke feelingly of God's will and his own submission to it. Thus, before the end of his life, he had substituted the idea of "God's will" for his earlier concept of a "necessity" abstract and mechanistic.

But Lincoln found room within his predestinarian scheme for human will, human choice. He once told Congressman Arnold how, years earlier, he had declined an offer of the governorship of Oregon Territory. "If you had gone to Oregon," Arnold commented, "you might have come back as senator, but you would never have been President." Lincoln agreed, then said with a musing, dreamy look: "I have all my life been a fatalist. What is to be will be, or rather, I have found all my life as Hamlet says:

> There is a divinity that shapes our ends,
> Rough-hew them how we will."

Or, as Lincoln told Mrs. Gurney, we must acknowledge God's wisdom and our own error. "Meanwhile we must work earnestly in the best light He gives us, trusting that so working still conduces to the great ends He ordains."

V

Since Lincoln's death, more words have been wasted on the question of his religion than on any other aspect of his life. Many preachers in their obituary sermons described him as a true, believing Christian, and one of them obtained from the presumably authoritative Noah Brooks an assurance of "Mr. Lincoln's saving knowledge of Christ; he talked always of Christ, his cross, his atonement." Some of the preachers seemed desperately eager to get Lincoln on the side of Christianity, so eager that the Reverend James A. Reed, one of the staunchest defenders of Lincoln's orthodoxy, was constrained to remind the public that "the faith and future of the Christian religion in no wise depends upon the sentiments of Abraham Lincoln." The earliest biographers—Josiah G. Holland, Isaac N. Arnold— pictured their subject as a paragon in every respect, especially in Christian piety. All this was too much for Herndon, the aggressive freethinker of Springfield, and he set out to prove that his former law partner had been an infidel and very nearly an atheist. Lincoln himself had left off arguing religion some thirty years before he died, but afterward countless volunteers took up the argument for him, and they never left it off.

Sectarians of all kinds, from spiritualists to biosophers, claimed him as one of them.

In fact, however, Lincoln had never signed any creed, never joined any church. After about 1850 he went to Sunday services regularly, at the First Presbyterian Church in Springfield and then at the New York Avenue Presbyterian Church in Washington. In Springfield he was a friend of the Rev. Dr. James Smith, the Presbyterian minister, and he read with interest Dr. Smith's book designed to lead skeptics to the Christian faith by rational argument. In Washington he was again a friend of his minister, the Rev. Dr. Phineas D. Gurley. But neither Smith nor Gurley won him to the fold.

If Lincoln was no professing Christian, neither was he in any sense an atheist. Indeed, even Herndon did not really think he was. Herndon was driven to overstatement by his zeal against the cant of pious moralizers, yet he sometimes qualified his statements and contradicted himself. "I affirm that Mr. Lincoln died an unbeliever—was not an evangelical Christian," he said in rebuttal against the Rev. James A. Reed. On another occasion Herndon declared that Lincoln *"was in short an infidel*—was a Universalist—was a Unitarian—a Theist. He did not believe that Jesus was God nor the son of God etc." Of course, a theist is not an atheist and, except by fundamentalist standards, a Universalist or a Unitarian is hardly an infidel. Nor is a person necessarily an unbeliever simply because he is not an "evangelical" Christian.

Doubtless Lincoln did share some of the basic Universalist and Unitarian attitudes. Like the Universalists he apparently believed in salvation for all and disbelieved in hell, and like the Unitarians he seems to have rejected the supernatural account of the birth of Christ. While, in private letters and state papers, he referred often to God or the Almighty, he very seldom mentioned Jesus as the Savior, very seldom mentioned Jesus at all (despite Brook's unsupported testimony that he "talked always of Christ, his cross, his atonement").

Lincoln also was inclined toward the Quaker point of view, and he acknowledged that his ancestors had been Quakers. Some of the Friends believed, as his correspondence with Mrs. Gurney reveals, that like them he felt a "true concern" laid upon him by the Heavenly Father. There is no need to look for proof of the as yet unproved story that one of Mrs. Gurney's letters, carefully treasured by him, was found in his breast pocket after the assassination. There is ample evidence, in the correspondence itself, to show that he deeply sympathized with the Quakers and did indeed treasure their good wishes.

In common with the Friends he felt a kind of mysticism, a sense of direct communion with the unseen. He did not carry this so far as to become a spiritualist. True, he permitted a few seances in the White House, after the death of little Willie, but these were Mrs. Lincoln's doing, not his. He commented that the seances reminded him of his cabinet meetings: the voices of the spirits, he said, were as contradictory as was the advice of his secretaries. Nevertheless he had a superstitious belief in various kinds of mysterious signs and portents, especially dreams. Once in 1863, when Mrs. Lincoln with Tad was visiting in Philadelphia, Lincoln thought it important enough to telegraph her: "Think you had better put Tad's pistol away. I had an ugly dream about him." On several occasions the President thought his dreams so significant that he brought them to the attention of his cabinet. On the morning of his final cabinet meeting he related the poignant recurring dream in which he was upon the water and, as Welles recorded, "seemed to be in some singular, indescribable vessel" and "was moving with great rapidity towards an indefinite shore."

A believer in dreams, a mystic with some affinity for the Quakers, a rationalist with Universalist and Unitarian views, a regular participant in Presbyterian services—Lincoln cannot easily be categorized as to religion. Yet it is possible to construct a personal creed from his own statements, as William E. Barton has done. Lincoln believed in God. He believed that God was intimately concerned with human affairs, that nations as well as men were dependent upon Him, that men and nations were punished for their sins, in this world as well as the next. He believed in the Bible as the best gift ever given by God to men. And he believed with all humility that he himself was an instrument in the hands of God.

Indeed, Lincoln was a man of more intense religiosity than any other President the United States has ever had. He had not demonstrated this trait very noticeably during his Illinois years. Reacting perhaps against the backwoods religion of his Baptist father, he had turned to skepticism, read such iconoclastic authors as Volney and Paine, and gained a reputation as a scoffer—a reputation which he felt he must deny when running for Congress in 1846. This early Lincoln was the Lincoln that Herndon knew, or thought he knew, and Herndon insisted that the later Lincoln was exactly the same. For this, Herndon got confirmation from Nicolay. "Mr. Lincoln, did not, to my knowledge, change in any way his religious views, beliefs, or opinions from the time he left Springfield to the day of his death," Nicolay replied to Herndon's query. But Nicolay vitiated his testimony as to Lincoln's unchanging religious beliefs when he added that he did "not know just what they were." And in Lincoln's writings and speeches, there is plenty of evidence, whether or not Nicolay could see it and appreciate it, to indicate that Lincoln as President gained a more and more pervasive consciousness of God.

Almost invariably students of Lincoln have noted his spiritual growth, but some have differed in their efforts to account for it. Ruth Painter Randall has explained it as his response to a series of crises both personal and public—the deaths of his sons Eddie and Willie, the awesome responsibilities of his wartime office. Charles W. Ramsdell has suggested that the President's deepening sense of melancholy and charity may have been due in part to a sense of guilt for having contributed to bringing on the war. There may be some truth in Ramsdell's guess—at times Lincoln seemed to make a special point of protesting that not he but God was responsible, as when he wrote: "Surely He intends some great good to follow this mighty convulsion, which no mortal could make, and no mortal could stop." Richard Hofstadter has found a clue to Lincoln's tragic sense of life in an antithesis between Lincoln the ambitious politician and Lincoln the sensitive and humble man of the people. "Lincoln's rage for personal success, his external and worldly ambition, was quieted when he entered the White House, and he was at last left alone to reckon with himself," Hofstadter writes. "To be confronted with the fruits of his victory only to find it meant choosing between life and death for others was immensely sobering."

Whatever the source of Lincoln's religious feeling, it became a vibrant force in his thought and action as President. It transformed him, even in the view of Herndon, who once wrote: "Do you not see Lincoln's Christ like charity—liberality —toleration loom up & blossom above all." It moved Lincoln's friend Jesse W. Fell to say that, though Lincoln subscribed to no sectarian dogma, "his principles and practices, and the spirit of his whole life, were of the kind we universally agree to call Christian." It led John Hay to call him "the greatest character since Christ." Surely, among successful American politicians, Lincoln is unique in the way he breathed the spirit of Christ while disregarding the letter of Christian doctrine. And the letter killeth, but the spirit giveth life.

VI

Lincoln's tastes in literature provide something of a clue to the nature of the inner man. He did not read widely, but he read deeply. He re-read over and over the things he liked, and he liked a rather odd assortment of things. He did not care for philosophical works as such. Though fond of the essays of John Stuart Mill, particularly the famous one on liberty, he considered the tomes of Herbert Spencer and Charles Darwin as "entirely too heavy for an ordinary mind to digest," if Herndon is to be believed. Metaphysical books he considered even worse. "Investigation into first causes, abstruse mental phenomena, the science of being," says Herndon, "he brushed aside as trash—mere scientific absurdities." He liked poetry, including that of Lord Byron and Robert Burns, but his favorite poem was one written by the otherwise undistinguished William Knox, and he often recited it: "Oh! Why should the spirit of mortal be proud?" Among his favorite authors were, at one extreme, the comic writers who went by the names of Petroleum V. Nasby, Orpheus C. Kerr, Artemus Ward, and Joe Miller of the famous jokebook and, at the other extreme, William Shakespeare. Lincoln conformed to the accepted convention of a great man's proper literary tastes in his sincere love of Shakespeare's plays and the Bible.

According to Arnold, he knew the Bible almost by heart. "There was not a clergyman to be found so familiar with it as he." And there is "scarcely a speech or paper prepared by him" from 1834 to 1865 "but contains apt allusions and striking illustrations from the sacred book." According to Brooks, he "would sometimes correct a misquotation of Scripture, giving generally the chapter and verse where it could be found." And according to Brooks, he much preferred the Old Testament to the New.

Actually, Lincoln did not quote the Bible in his state papers quite so often as Arnold believed, nor in his quotations did he indicate such a preference for the Old Testament as Brooks reported. A sampling of Lincoln's works has shown that, in twenty-five speeches from 1839 to 1865, he alluded to the Bible a total of twenty-two times—to the Old Testament eight times and to the New Testament fourteen. A few of the speeches contain several references each, others contain none at all, and there is a good deal of repetition, as for example of the "house divided against itself" passage. From this it does not necessarily follow that Lincoln was less familiar with the Bible than he has been credited with being or that he preferred the New Testament. Apparently there is no close correlation between, on the one hand, his interest in and familiarity with the Bible, either in whole or in part, and, on the other hand, the frequency of his references to it in public addresses.

The same is true also in regard to Shakespeare's plays. In public addresses Lincoln quoted or paraphrased them even less often than the Bible. In private conversations, however, he not only used a great many Shakespearean allusions but he also discussed problems of interpretation, with remarkable insight, and gave effective performances of his own. Doubtless he would have made a powerful tragic actor as well as a discerning drama critic.

"Unlike you gentlemen of the profession," he wrote to the Shakespearean actor James H. Hackett, "I think the soliloquy in 'Hamlet,' commencing 'O, my offense is rank,' surpasses that commencing, 'To be or not to be.'" The first of these soliloquies —spoken by the King after the murder of Polonius—was a favorite with Lincoln. In the presence of Carpenter he once recited the entire passage from memory, and with more feeling and better understanding than Carpenter had ever heard it done on the stage. Lincoln complained that the passage usually was slurred over by professional actors, and so, he said, was another of his favorites, the opening lines of "King Richard the Third," beginning "Now is the winter of our discontent." This soliloquy, too, Lincoln repeated in Carpenter's presence, "rendering it with a degree of force and power that made it seem like a new creation" to Carpenter. While at Fortress Monroe, in 1862, the President read feelingly from "Hamlet" on the theme of ambition. On shipboard returning from City Point, in 1865, he delighted his fellow passengers, including the Marquis de Chambrun, with Shakespearean readings which lasted for several hours. He was especially moved, and moving, with the verses in "Macbeth" in which Macbeth speaks of Duncan's assassination:

> Duncan is in his grave;
> After life's fitful fever he sleeps well;
> Treason has done his worst: nor steel, nor poison,
> Malice domestic, foreign levy, nothing
> Can touch him further.

With Lincoln, the play was the thing, not the acting, and in the play it was the thought that counted. "It matters not to me whether Shakespeare be well or ill acted," he once remarked; "with him the thought suffices." Unless the acting was unusually good, Lincoln preferred his own reading and interpretation of the play. After seeing Edwin Booth (brother of John Wilkes Booth) as Shylock he said to Brooks: "It was a good performance, but I had a thousand times rather read it at home, if it were not for Booth's playing. A farce, or a comedy, is best played; a tragedy is best read at home."

At home, in the White House, there was little rest for Lincoln during those tumultuous days and nights of celebration following the surrender at Appomattox. Now, as always, the theater offered him an escape in a physical as well as a psychological sense. It was a place to go to get away from people and be alone while in their midst. Time and again in the past he had sat with an audience and had remained abstracted and unmoved as scene after scene passed. On the evening of April 14, 1865, he planned to seek that accustomed relaxation, this time at Ford's Theater, where a comedy "Our American Cousin," was playing. At dinner he complained of being worn out from the toils of the day, and he looked forward eagerly to an opportunity to laugh. Mrs. Lincoln, troubled with a headache, suggested that they stay home, but he insisted on their going out; otherwise, he said, he would have to see visitors all evening as usual. And so they went.